AMERICAN INDIAN ACTIVISM

American Indian Activism

ALCATRAZ TO THE LONGEST WALK

EDITED BY

Troy Johnson, Joane Nagel, and Duane Champagne

UNIVERSITY OF ILLINOIS PRESS

URBANA AND CHICAGO

Manufactured in the United States of America
P 7 6 5

This book is printed on acid-free paper.

Library of Congress Cataloging-in-Publication Data
American Indian activism : Alcatraz to the longest walk / edited by Troy
Johnson, Joane Nagel, and Duane Champagne.
p.   cm.
Includes bibliographical references and index.
ISBN 0-252-06653-7 (pbk. : alk. paper)
ISBN 978-0-252-06653-5 (pbk. : alk. paper)
1. Alcatraz Island (Calif.)—History—Indian occupation, 1969–1971.
2. Indians of North America—Government relations—1934– .
I. Johnson, Troy R. II. Nagel, Joane. III. Champagne, Duane.
E78.C15A2   1997
979.4'61—dc21   97-1877   CIP

CONTENTS

INTRODUCTION

Troy Johnson and Joane Nagel

The nineteen-month occupation of Alcatraz Island began on 20 November 1969 and ended on 11 June 1971. During that period, Native Americans from all over the United States and delegations from around the world visited the island and contributed their resources and goodwill to the real and symbolic struggle. The spirit of Alcatraz represented both challenge and resistance: challenge to prevailing images of Native Americans as the fading victims of history; resistance to the policies and treatment of Indian individuals and communities in the past and, most important, in the present.

As the voices we have invited to speak in this book tell us, the spirit of Alcatraz has had an important and powerful legacy. What happened in those nineteen months on that small island influenced and reshaped the lives of many native people; they, in turn, acted on that influence, thus reshaping the lives of many others; and so the circle continues. In this way, the ripples that began on Alcatraz Island spread out, washing on the beaches of many lives and many communities, ultimately contributing to the tidal wave of reform that swept across federal Indian policy and launched the self-determination era.

The sixteen essays in this book speak to several aspects of the Alcatraz occupation: (1) the occupation itself—how it happened and what occured on the island; (2) the U.S. government's response and why the events took the course they did; and (3) the aftermath and consequences of the occupation—the patterns of American Indian protest after 1969, the impact on federal Indian policy, the responses of individual Native Americans, and the effect on both reservation and urban Indian communities. Diverse voices are represented in these pages, offering different assessments of the Alcatraz occupation—its meaning and its consequences. What is shared by all the contributors, native and nonnative, is that they grasp the importance of what was happening on the Rock twenty-eight years ago and that they knew these events would change the way we view ourselves and one another.

The essays divide roughly into two sections: detailed accounts and personal reminiscences of various aspects of the occupation; and longer-term analyses of the meaning and consequences of the occupation. Some of the authors were directly involved in the occupation, others visited the island during the months of occupation, and still others witnessed what happened from a distance. Many of these stories are told here for the first time.

Chapters 1–12 provide background, insight, and reflections on the details of events during the nineteen months that Indians of All Tribes occupied Alcatraz Island. "American Indian Activism and Transformation: Lessons from Alcatraz," by Troy Johnson, Duane Champagne, and Joane Nagel, is a history of the Alcatraz occupation and the decade of activism, called the Alcatraz–Red Power Movement (ARPM). Chapter 1 also provides a preview of the impact of the Alcatraz occupation on the lives of several Native Americans, some of whom are contributors to this book. The authors acknowledge that other Native American protest events of the 1960s and 1970s—for example, the fish-ins in the Pacific Northwest during the mid-1960s or the siege of Wounded Knee, South Dakota, in 1973—may have more prominence in the minds of Americans, but they argue that the symbolic importance of the Alcatraz occupation as the launching pad for a decade of American Indian protest must not be underestimated.

In "Alcatraz, Activism, and Accommodation," veteran leader, scholar, and activist Vine Deloria, Jr., reflects on the place of Alcatraz in our collective memory, as well as its impact on the lives of native people and the federal policies that govern many aspects of their lives. Deloria places the occupation in the historical context of the civil rights movement, in particular the Poor People's March of 1968. He notes the disjuncture between such legal bases of change as the Treaty of Medicine Creek and the actions of activists, but he also affirms the symbolic importance of prominent activist events such as the Alcatraz occupation. Deloria's essay recounts his personal involvement in the occupation and provides an insightful and often critical analysis of the events on the island. In his conclusion, he points out the burden that the occupation imposed on those who embraced its symbolism—that self-determination is a responsibility as well as a right.

Adam (Nordwall) Fortunate Eagle, in "Urban Indians and the Occupation of Alcatraz Island" (which is taken from his book *Alcatraz! Alcatraz!*), provides an insightful look into the Bay Area urban Indian community and the organizations that flourished there. It was from these groups, as Fortunate Eagle points out, that a larger, more political umbrella organization called the United Bay Area Council of American Indian Affairs, Inc., was formed. As time passed, the United Council gradually became more politicized and became one of the major forces leading to the occupation of Alcatraz Island. Fortunate Eagle provides an intriguing look into the planning of the Alcatraz occupation as only someone who was an active participant could do.

In "Alcatraz Recollections," Tim Findley provides a professional journalist's view of the occupation and the events that led up to it. At the time of the occupation, Findley was a writer for the *San Francisco Chronicle* and an acquaintance of Adam Fortunate Eagle. He was instrumental in arranging meetings and opened his home to the Indian people who would plan the occupation and to the non-Indian press, which would be so important in placing the issues of the Alcatraz occupiers before the American public. Findley offers poignant glimpses into the lives and personalities of some key participants he came to know well during the nineteen-month occupation.

LaNada Boyer's "Reflections of Alcatraz" provides a firsthand, behind- (and in front of)-the-scenes account of the occupation—its planning and execution. Boyer was one of the original small group that landed on the island in November 1969; she was involved in the occupation until it ended, and she continued afterward as a native activist and leader. In this telling of the Alcatraz occupation, Boyer shows us the decision-making process, the points of agreement and contention, the powerful unity and disunity that characterize all important historical moments. She tells us about the celebrities and national figures who became involved in the occupation and visited the island. Her analysis reveals the odd juxtaposition of the occupiers and the nationally prominent visitors: On the one hand are the native people who took over and lived on the island; on the other are the rich and famous sweeping in and out. Boyer's essay makes the important point that the media plays a central role—for good and for ill—in all activism, and particularly Indian activism.

In "Indian Students and Reminiscences of Alcatraz," Steve Talbot places the occupation in its contemporary context, listing the contributors who provided the meeting grounds, guidance, and vision that formed the foundation upon which the occupation was built. Talbot describes the establishment of the first courses in Native American studies at the University of California, Berkeley, thus identifying the important intellectual atmosphere in which the protest agenda was created. Talbot takes a stand: He names names, he gives credit and criticism, and he provides the invaluable insights gained from his vantage point as an involved participant.

Luis S. Kemnitzer's vantage point in "Personal Memories of Alcatraz, 1969" is both similar to and dissimilar from that of Talbot. Kemnitzer was an advisor and facilitator for the development of the Native American studies program at San Francisco State University, and he worked with Richard Oakes—the now silent but then central voice of the occupation. Kemnitzer reflects on the role of the university as a setting where those who would lead the Alcatraz occupation could come together, define themselves and their goals, make connections with those who came before, and leave a legacy for those who would follow. Kemnitzer admits that while the occupation was interesting at the time, he did not realize the importance it would come to have. This reminds us all of the impossibility of knowing which events are simply "interesting" and which will leave an enduring legacy.

Edward D. Castillo's "Reminiscence of the Alcatraz Occupation" begins with a lament about the world before Alcatraz, where he spent his college years without native peers or professors and without financial support from federal Indian programs. He also tells about the exciting changes underway in 1969, when he became part of the fledgling American Indian studies program at the University of California, Los Angeles, as an instructor of Indian history. A visit from Richard Oakes, who spoke of the planned occupation of Alcatraz Island, set a new direction for Castillo and many of his students. His essay furnishes the details of the November 1969 landing on the island, the role of the media in shaping the national image of the occupation, and his own struggles with his job, his activism, his responsibilities, and his integrity. Castillo's rendering of the occupation reveals the personal costs and challenges of activism as well as the unpredictable course of events that activism can set in motion.

In "The Native Struggle for Liberation: Alcatraz," Jack D. Forbes relates the important role of Native American studies programs as intellectual homes and meeting places for native people interested in social change. He and several of his students in Native American studies at the University of California, Davis, joined the protesters on Alcatraz immediately following the initial occupation. Forbes provides historical background for the Alcatraz occupation and discusses an important legacy of Alcatraz: the establishment of D-Q University in Davis, California, following the successful occupation of a former military communications facility in 1970. He concludes that the 1969 occupation of Alcatraz Island has another legacy: The occupation transformed the island itself into an enduring symbol of native struggle and resistance.

Lenny Foster's essay, "Alcatraz Is Not an Island," illustrates the power of activism to transform the lives of individuals—both those who participate and those who witness the protest from a distance but are pulled in by its magnetism. Like Castillo, Foster recalls the experience of being an Indian before Alcatraz. He recounts his early athletic career in high school, at Western Arizona College, and at Colorado State University, and the growing tension in his life: He was increasingly torn between the world of preprofessional athletics and his contact with Chicano and Indian activists in the late 1960s. The turning point for Foster was when he hitchhiked across the country in December 1969 to join the protesters on Alcatraz Island. During this and several subsequent visits he underwent a personal transformation, which he discusses here and which follows a path parallel to those taken by many others.

George P. Horse Capture writes of the personal meaning of the Alcatraz occupation and its impact on his life in "From the Reservation to the Smithsonian via Alcatraz." He reminds us of the world before Alcatraz, when Native American history and identity were devalued and demeaned by federal policies, social conventions, and personal disparagement. Horse Capture describes the bleakness and despair felt by many native people during the decades before Alcatraz as they struggled to survive in mainstream America. He also tells of the profound personal meaning of the occupation and his visit to the island. Horse Capture reminds us of the tone of those times and of the power of that moment. He argues that "the Indian world would never be the same after this" and notes the disjuncture between his feelings and experiences as part of the Alcatraz moment and his former life. In the years since then, Horse Capture has been able to blend his two lives into one, which has led him back to the reservation and out again.

John Garvey and Troy Johnson offer the story of the government's response to the occupation in "The Government and the Indians: The American Indian Occupation of Alcatraz Island, 1969–71." Garvey and Johnson present a detailed, day-to-day assessment of the events as they unfolded, including Richard Nixon's 1970 self-determination address and the FBI's role in responding to the occupation. Their accounting gives us an inside view of the cast of characters charged with the official handling of the Alcatraz occupation, many of whom were quite well known: J. Edgar Hoover, Richard M. Nixon, John Ehrlichman, Leonard Garment, Bradley Patterson, Walter Hickel, George Murphy, Luis R. Bruce, Ronald Reagan, Bud Krogh, and Robert Kleindienst.

Chapters 13–16 represent more distant assessments of the meaning and impact of the Alcatraz occupation. Some of them reveal that the legacy of Alcatraz is not without controversy. Robert A. Rundstrom's "American Indian Placemaking on Alcatraz, 1969–71" examines Alcatraz as a physical, social, and symbolic "place." Rundstrom tells us that geographers attribute four elements to a place: a physical site; a tangible, created environment; a social milieu; and a set of personal and shared meanings. He then proceeds to examine the ways in which the Alcatraz occupiers reconstructed the island's physical appearance, environmental character, social structure, and personal and collective meaning. Not much of the physical transformation of the occupation remains today; government bulldozers have erased what little was changed. Rundstrom shows us, however, that the meaning of Alcatraz has survived official cleanup efforts: In February 1994, the American Indian Movement selected the island as the starting point for a nationwide Long Walk for Justice, thus confirming the continuing symbolic importance of Alcatraz.

In "The Eagles I Fed Who Did Not Love Me," Woody Kipp reflects on his service in the U.S. Marine Corps and the twenty months he spent in Vietnam as a support combat engineer working on F4-B Phantom jet aircraft. During his tour in Vietnam, Kipp began to draw parallels between late twentieth-century American foreign policy in Southeast Asia and U.S. domestic policy toward American Indians throughout the centuries of contact. This awareness was heightened in February 1973 when Kipp witnessed those same Phantom jets flying over the Pine Ridge Reservation during the siege of Wounded Knee. Kipp's journey from the teenager who joined the Marine Corps to a professor of journalism in his home state of Montana is one of reconnecting with his native heritage and spiritual traditions. He traces his personal rebirth during the turbulent era marked by the Alcatraz occupation, the conflict at Wounded Knee, and the many other acts of protest that occurred during the 1970s.

Karren Baird-Olson's "Reflections of an AIM Activist: Has It All Been Worth It?" is also a story of personal growth and renewal. Baird-Olson recounts an incident in 1976, when she and her children were arrested during a protest outside the Bureau of Indian Affairs offices in Washington, D.C. She uses this incident to illustrate the federal authorities' repressive response to native activism—in particular to members of the American Indian Movement. Then she tries to answer the question she poses in the subtitle of her essay, arguing that AIM's activism following the Alcatraz occupation was crucial to the progress toward native rights that has occurred in the past quarter century. She also notes, however, that she and other AIM activists have paid dearly for those years of protest—in loss of life, careers, and personal relationships. Despite these costs, her answer to the central question is "yes."

In the final chapter, "The Bloody Wake of Alcatraz: Political Repression of the American Indian Movement during the 1970s," Ward Churchill paints a graphic picture of federal violence against AIM activists in the aftermath of Alcatraz and particularly during and after the siege at Wounded Knee in 1973. He argues that, despite federal repression, AIM and other activist groups have accomplished a great deal: the organization of the Longest Walk in 1978, the efforts to free Leonard Peltier, the formation of the Black Hills Alliance, the establishment of Camp Yellow Thunder, the founding of the International Indian Treaty Council, and the effort to protest and balance coverage of the Columbus Quincentenary. Churchill notes the resurgence of AIM chapters and personal Indian identification around the country. He also refers to some of the tensions and controversies surrounding AIM and its leaders, which are yet another legacy of the decades of protest following the Alcatraz occupation.

The sixteen chapters in this book—written by Indians and non-Indians, observers and participant, critics and supporters—reflect the many faces of the Alcatraz occupation. The authors have taken this opportunity to reminisce about their involvement in the occupation, to set the record straight, and to assess the success or failure of Alcatraz itself and the entire activist period. Many of them speak of the personal meaning and impact of the occupation on their lives; others reflect on the personal and collective meaning and legacy of the occupation for the lives of others. While this is by no means a complete or even balanced look at Alcatraz, it is an effort to commemorate an important moment in American history. We hope that you will find reading it as fascinating as it was for us to put it together.

1

AMERICAN INDIAN ACTIVISM AND TRANSFORMATION: LESSONS FROM ALCATRAZ

Troy Johnson, Duane Champagne,
and Joane Nagel

The occupation of Alcatraz Island in 1969–71 initiated a unique nine-year period of Red Power protest that culminated in the transformation of national consciousness about American Indians and engendered a more open and confident sense of identity among people of Indian descent. Between 20 November 1969 and the Longest Walk in 1978, there were more than seventy property takeovers by Indian activists.[1] This series of collective actions is referred to as the Alcatraz–Red Power Movement (ARPM) because it started with—and was modeled after—the Alcatraz takeover. Certainly, many individual Indian people were politically active before and after this period, but what made the movement so powerful were the large numbers of *organized* demonstrations and the property seizures aimed at airing national and local Indian grievances.

The ARPM was predominantly a struggle to secure redress for overwhelming conditions of political, cultural, and economic disadvantage that mirrored the long history of Indian poverty, not only on reservations, but more recently in urban environments. Current theories of social movements focus on situations of group repression or disadvantage while emphasizing elements of individual and group choice, such as active leaders, effectively organized groups, formation of common group and individual interests, and the development of group ideology.[2] Both repressive and voluntarist elements must be analyzed to understand the rise, development, and decline of social movements. Voluntarist elements within the ARPM include charismatic leaders, the legacy of historical Indian resistance and social movements, the tactic of property seizure, a pan-Indian identity, formation of a national activist organization—in this case, the American Indian Movement

(AIM)—and a common national agenda of self-determination for Indian people and communities. Other structural and voluntarist elements are situational and have to be understood within the specific historical context. Some of these situational events are the civil rights movement, the Vietnam War protests, widespread student activism, the rise of radical ethnic groups, the reluctance of the federal government to overtly repress social movements during the late 1960s and early 1970s, and the mass media attention heaped on many Indian takeovers, including Alcatraz Island.

Despite its influence, the occupation of Alcatraz Island has largely been overlooked by those who write or speak today of American Indian activism. Much has been written about the battles fought by Indian people for their rights to hunting and fishing areas reserved by treaties in the states of Washington, Oregon, Wisconsin, and Minnesota, as well as about Six Nations efforts to secure guaranteed treaty rights in the northeastern United States and Indian actions protesting the demeaning use of Native American mascots by athletic teams. The 1972 takeover of the Bureau of Indian Affairs (BIA) headquarters in Washington, D.C., and the 1973 occupation of Wounded Knee are also well known, as is the killing of the young Coeur d'Alene Indian Joseph Stuntz and also the deaths of two FBI agents on the Pine Ridge Reservation in 1975, which resulted in the imprisonment of Leonard Peltier. Yet it was the occupation of Alcatraz Island that launched the greatest wave of modern-day American Indian activism. In the pages that follow, we will describe and analyze the rise, organization, fall, and legacy of the Alcatraz–Red Power Movement.

The Legacy of Native American Activism

The ARPM protests were not unusual in that they were part of a long line of rebellions and social movements among Native Americans as means to resist colonial and U.S. control over their livelihood, culture, government, and resources. To better understand the ARPM, we will compare it with some of the major types of Indian movements occurring throughout history, pointing out similarities, differences, and important continuities.

Religious revitalization movements, numerous in Native American history, have provided spiritual solutions to the conditions of economic marginalization, political repression, and major losses of territory, as well as the ability to carry on traditional life. The more notable movements of this type include the Delaware Prophet (1760–63), the Shawnee Prophet (1805–11), the Winnebago Prophet (1830), the Ghost Dance of 1870, and the Ghost Dance of 1890, but there are also many local and lesser-known movements. In each of these, a prophet relied on ritual knowledge and power to gather a pan-Indian following either to fight against European invaders or to pray for a cataclysmic event that would restore the Indian nations to the peace, plenty, and life they had known before American or European intrusions.[3] Most of these movements were either militarily repressed or the followers abandoned them when the predicted events did not come to pass. In some cases, small groups continued in the religion, but there were no pan-Indian churches or enduring community change. Similar to the ARPM, the religious revitalization movements formed a multitribal gathering of adherents, and both movements were reactions to severe conditions of economic, political, and cultural deprivation. But the ARPM was secular, relying on physical tactics rather than spiritual solutions; and while the ARPM depended on charismatic leaders, it did not focus on prophets or the formation of new religious beliefs.

Social revitalization movements, most of which led to reformed religions with present-day practicing adherents, also served to establish modified forms of community organization designed to better accommodate American-style agriculture, reservation land, and political restrictions. These movements include Handsome Lake Church (1799–present), the Delaware Big House Religion (1760–1910), the Kickapoo Prophet (1830–51), the Shaker Church (1881–present), and the Native American Church (1800s–present). Multiple tribal groups gathered for the Kickapoo Prophet, Shaker Church, and Native American Church, while the Delaware Big House Religion and Handsome Lake Church were exclusively tribal in nature.[4] Unlike these social revitalization movements, the ARPM was not concerned directly with reconstituting Indian communities as a solution to poverty or with political marginalization. Rather, ARPM protests were aimed at getting the attention of U.S. officials and agencies to gain access to material resources to alleviate poverty and redress cultural and political repression. Building Indian colleges, creating Indian studies programs, and preserving Indian cultures through federally funded cultural centers and museums were goals that could be achieved while working within U.S. institutions. The ARPM did not require major institutional change within Indian or reservation societies but rather sought fairer treatment, the honoring of treaty obligations, and financial assistance from the federal government.

While the eighteenth and nineteenth centuries were studded with the rise of Indian religious movements, secular Indian movements have characterized much of the twentieth century. Early national Indian reform movements, led by organizations such as the Society of American Indians (SAI), were composed of well-educated Indian professionals who favored assimilation of Indian people into mainstream American society as the solution to the poverty and misery of reservation life. They formed national organizations and were involved in the Indian policy issues of the 1920s and 1930s.[5]

Like the ARPM, the SAI worked within the larger U.S. societal framework, but the SAI's assimilationist stance generated much internal debate. The ARPM sought not assimilation but the preservation of Indian identity and culture. The SAI, however, sowed the seed for a national Indian policy and a lobbying force in American politics, which came to fruition with the formation of the National Congress of American Indians (NCAI) in 1944.

In the 1950s, the Six Nations peoples[6] used passive resistance and militant protests to block various New York State projects. For example, Tuscaroras and Mohawks demonstrated in opposition to the building of the Kinzua Dam in upstate New York, which required the displacement of Indians and the flooding of Indian land. Activism began to build in the 1950s, as more than twenty major demonstrations or nonviolent protests were orchestrated by Indian people. These demonstrations were aimed at ending further reductions of the Indian land base, stopping the termination of Indian tribes, and halting brutality and insensitivity toward Indian people. This rise in Indian activism was largely tribal in nature, however; very little, if any, pan-Indian or supratribal activity occurred. The militancy was primarily a phenomenon of traditional people typified by the participation of elders, medicine people, and entire communities, not the forging of alliances outside tribal boundaries, such as would later occur during the Alcatraz occupation and which characterized the Alcatraz–Red Power Movement.

A major example of tribally based activism was the dispute over state taxes in New York in the late 1950s. In 1957, Wallace "Mad Bear" Anderson, a Tuscarora Indian, helped the Mohawk fend off a New York State income tax on the grounds of Indian sovereignty on Indian reservations. Anderson led a protest group of several hundred Indians from the St. Regis Reservation to the Massena, New York, courthouse, where they tore up summonses for nonpayment of state taxes.[7] In April 1958, Anderson led a stand against the tide of land seizures, a move that ultimately brought armed troops onto Indian land. The New York Power Authority, directed by its chairman, Robert Moses, planned to expropriate 1,383 acres of Tuscarora land for the building of a reservoir and the back-flooding of Indian lands. Anderson and others practiced such harassment tactics as standing in the way of surveyors' transits and deflating vehicle tires. When Power Authority workers tapped the Indian leaders' telephones, Tuscaroras switched to speaking their tribal language. When the Tuscaroras refused to accept the state's offer to purchase the land, one hundred armed state troopers and police invaded Tuscarora lands. They were met by a nonviolent front of 150 men, women, and children, led by Anderson, who blocked the road by lying down or standing in front of government trucks. At the same time, Seneca and Mohawk Indian people set up camps on the disputed land, challenging the state to remove them. Anderson and other leaders were arrested, but the media attention forced the Power Authority to back down. The Federal Power Commission ruled that the Indians did not have to sell the land, and the tribe did not sell. The *Buffalo Courier Express* reported that Mad Bear Anderson, more than anyone else, was responsible for the tribe's decision.[8]

Following the Six Nations' success in New York State, the Miccosukee Indian Nation of Florida summoned Anderson to help fight the federal government's attempt to take land from them as part of the Everglades Reclamation Project. In 1959, several hundred Indian people marched on BIA headquarters in Washington, D.C., to protest the government policy of termination of Indian tribes, and they attempted a citizen's arrest of the Indian commissioner. In California, Nevada, and Utah, the Pit River Indians, led by Chief Ray Johnson, refused $29.1 million of claims case money awarded by the government and demanded return of their traditional lands. The Pit River Indian people carried on their battle until 1972, at which time they reached a negotiated settlement for partial restoration of land and a monetary payment.

During the 1950s and 1960s, Indian resistance to U.S. policies was galvanized by the common threat of termination of reservation and tribal status. Termination policy sought to detribalize and liquidate Indian land, directly abrogating federal treaties and agreements. The NCAI was joined by organizations such as the Indian Rights Association and the American Friends Services Committee in their fight against termination. Today, the NCAI, composed of tribal representatives—each with one vote—works within the political system as a national lobbying group for tribal-reservation (but not urban Indian) interests. It presents legislation to Congress, serves as a legislative guardian over Indian issues, and organizes Indian support or opposition to congressional actions. By contrast, the ARPM used social protest rather than established political procedures, and it represented the interests and concerns of urban Indians as well as disfranchised reservation Indians, who often were unfriendly to the established tribal governments and their leaders. These differences in approach created tensions between the more established NCAI and certain ARPM organizations, such as AIM, during the 1960s and 1970s.

The federal government's policy of termination led to interest among Indians in strengthening Indian policy, and numerous Indian rights and protest organizations emerged in the early 1960s, most notably the National Indian Youth Council (NIYC). The NIYC was organized by young college-educated Indians following the American Indian Charter Convention held in Chicago in 1961. They adopted some of the ideas of the civil rights movement and staged numerous fish-ins in the Pacific Northwest, where Washington State was attempting to use state laws to restrict Indian fishing rights guaranteed by federal treaties.[9] The NIYC encouraged greater tribal self-sufficiency and autonomy and was therefore critical of federal and BIA policy. Although the group was active throughout the 1960s, it never got the media attention that the ARPM did in the 1970s, nor did it engage in the same protest tactics.

The rhetoric of Indian self-determination can be traced to the early 1960s, when Melvin Thom, a Paiute Indian from Walker River, Nevada, and the cofounder and president of the NIYC, recognized the need to alleviate the poverty, unemployment, and degrading lifestyles experienced by urban and reservation Indians. Thom realized that it was essential that Indian people, Indian tribes, and Indian sovereign rights not be compromised in the search for solutions to various problems. He said, "Our recognition as Indian people and Indian tribes is very dear to us. We cannot work to destroy our lives as Indian people."[10] He understood that family, tribalism, and sovereignty had sustained Indian people through the many government programs designed to destroy them as a people and to nationalize their traditional lands. The official government policy, dating back to 1953, was termination of the relationship between the federal government and Indian communities, meaning that Indian tribes would eventually lose any special relationships they had under federal law—for example, the tax-exempt status of their lands and federal responsibility for Indian economic and social well-being. In other words, Indian tribes themselves would be effectively destroyed. Thom described the termination policy as a "cold war" that was being fought against Indian people:

> The opposition to Indians is a monstrosity which cannot be beaten by any single action, unless we as Indian people could literally rise up, in unison, and take what is ours by force. . . . We know the odds are against us, but we also realize that we are fighting for the lives of future Indian generations. . . . We are convinced, more than ever, that this is a real war. No people in this world ever has been exterminated without putting up a last resistance. The Indians are gathering.[11]

Indian people wanted self-determination rather than termination. This included the right to assume control of their own lives independent of federal control, the creation of conditions for a new era in which the Indian future would be determined by Indian acts and Indian decisions, and the assurance that Indian people would not be separated involuntarily from their tribal groups.

The 1960s witnessed a continuation of localized Indian protest actions such as the brief Indian occupation of Alcatraz Island in 1964. Preceding this event, however, were the fish-ins along the rivers of Washington State. The fish-in movement began when tribal members and their supporters fished in waters protected by federal treaty rights but were restricted by state and local law enforcement. When Isaac Stevens was appointed governor of the new Washington Territory in 1853, he concluded the Medicine Creek (1854) and Point Elliott (1855) treaties, which guaranteed Indian rights to fish both on and off the reservation and to take fish at usual and accustomed grounds and stations. In the mid-1950s, state authorities tried to control Indian fishing in off-reservation areas on the Puyallup River. The Indians protested, arguing that these were "usual and accustomed grounds and stations" within the meaning of the 1854 and 1855 treaties. In 1963, the U.S. Court of Appeals upheld the rights of Indian people to fish in accordance with these treaties. In 1964, in defiance of the Supreme Court decision in *United States v. Winons* (1905), the state courts in Washington closed the Nisqually River to Indian fishermen in areas off the Nisqually Reservation. In the same year, the Survival of American Indians Association (SAIA) was formed as a protest organization to assert and preserve off-reservation fishing rights. Fish-ins were organized by SAIA and held at Frank's Landing on the Nisqually River. A large number of state and local law enforcement officers raided Frank's Landing in 1965, smashing boats and fishing gear, slashing nets, and attacking Indian people, including women and children. Seven Indians were arrested. Dangerous though they might be, the fish-ins nonetheless provided the Indian youth of Washington with an opportunity to express their disillusionment and dissatisfaction with U.S. society and also to protest actively the social conditions endured by their people. Celebrities such as Marlon Brando lent their names to bring national media coverage of these protest actions. The Indian people who participated in the fish-ins would later provide assistance to the occupiers on Alcatraz Island.

In March 1966, President Lyndon Johnson attempted to quiet the fears of Indian people. In a speech before the Senate, he proposed a "new goal for our Indian programs; a goal that ends the old debate about termination of Indian programs and stresses self-determination; a goal that erases old attitudes of paternalism and promotes partnership and self-help."[12] In October 1966, Senator George McGovern from South Dakota introduced a resolution that highlighted the increased desire of Indian people to be allowed to participate in decisions concerning their development. The frustration resulting from years of BIA paternalism and the new Indian awareness of their powerlessness resulting from years of neglect, poverty, and discrimination had finally attracted the attention of the bureaucracy in Washington, D.C.

In the summer of 1968, United Native Americans (UNA) was founded in the San Francisco Bay Area. Many of the Indian occupiers of Alcatraz Island were, or had been, members of UNA; many more were strongly influenced by the organization. UNA had a pan-Indian focus. It sought to unify all persons of Indian blood throughout the Americas and to develop itself as a democratic, grass-roots organization. Its goal was to promote self-determination through Indian control of Indian affairs at every level. Lehman Brightman, a Sioux Indian, was the first president of UNA.

The year 1968 closed with a confrontation between Canada, the United States, and members of the Iroquois League. Canada had been restricting the free movement of Mohawk Indians (members of the Iroquois League) between the United States and Canada, demanding that the Mohawk pay tolls to use the bridge and pay customs on goods brought back from the United States. Members of the Iroquois League felt that this was an infringement of their treaty rights granted by Great Britain, and members of the Mohawk tribe confronted Canadian officials as a means of forcing the issues of tolls and customs collections on the Cornwall International Bridge (the St. Lawrence Seaway International Bridge) between the two countries. The protest was specifically over Canadian failure to honor the Jay Treaty of 1794 between Canada and the United States.[13]

A number of Mohawk Indians were arrested for blockading the Cornwall Bridge on 18 December 1968, but when they pressed for presentation of their case in the court system, the Canadian government dismissed the charges. This protest action was not without precedent. In 1928, the Indian Defense League, founded in 1926, had argued that unrestricted rights for Indians to trade and travel across the U.S.-Canadian border existed based on the Jay Treaty of 1794 and the Treaty of Ghent in 1814. It was not until the 1969 concession, however, that the Canadian government formally recognized these rights, under article 3 of the treaty, and allowed Indians to exchange goods across the border, duty-free, and permitted unrestricted travel between the countries.[14]

The 1968–69 Cornwall Bridge confrontation also brought about the creation of *Akwesasne Notes*, an Indian newspaper, which began as an effort to bring news to Indian people regarding the crisis by reprinting articles from diverse newspapers. Edited by Jerry Gambill, a non-Indian employed by the Canadian Department of Indian Affairs, *Akwesasne Notes* developed into a national Indian newspaper with a circulation of nearly fifty thousand. As a result of coverage in *Akwesasne Notes*, Cornwall Bridge became a prominent discussion topic for Indians across the nation. Later, the Alcatraz occupation would find an Indian media voice in *Akwesasne Notes*.

In addition to his newspaper work, Jerry Gambill assisted Ernest Benedict, a Mohawk Indian, in establishing the North American Indian Traveling College and the White Roots of Peace. The White Roots of Peace harked back to an earlier Mohawk group, the Akwesasne Counselor Organization, founded by Ray Fadden, a Mohawk Indian, in the mid-1930s. The counselor organization had "traveled far and wide inculcating Indian pride among Mohawk youth . . . hoping to influence a group of young Mohawk

. . . to take up leadership roles in the Mohawk Longhouse."[15] This was largely an attempt by Fadden and other Mohawk to preserve and revive Iroquois lifeways. Seeing the spiritual crisis caused by the death of key elders and noting that many young Indians were moving away from the faith, Benedict and Gambill founded the White Roots of Peace, which was committed to the preservation of tradition by bringing back the Great Binding Law through speaking engagements to Indian and non-Indian communities and school audiences.

As part of this increase in Indian activism in the 1960s, the Taos Pueblo Indians of New Mexico reasserted their claims to ancestral lands. In 1906, the U.S. government had appropriated the Taos Blue Lake area, a sacred site belonging to the Taos Pueblos, and incorporated it into part of the Carson National Forest.[16] In 1926, the tribe, in reply to a compensation offer made by the government, waived the award, seeking return of Blue Lake instead. As a result, they got neither the compensation nor Blue Lake. On 31 May 1933, the Senate Indian Affairs Committee recommended that the Taos Pueblo Indians be issued a permit to use Blue Lake for religious purposes. The permit was finally issued in 1940. On 13 August 1951, the tribe filed a suit before the Indian Claims Commission seeking judicial support for the validity of their title to the lake. On 8 September 1965, the Indian Claims Commission affirmed that the U.S. government had taken the area from its rightful owners. On 15 March 1966, legislation was introduced to return Blue Lake to the Taos Pueblo Indians; however, the bill died without action in the Senate Interior and Insular Affairs Subcommittee. On 10 May 1968, House Bill 3306 was introduced to restore the sacred area to the tribe. Although it was passed unanimously in the House of Representatives, it once again died in the Senate Interior and Insular Affairs Subcommittee.[17]

The return of Taos Blue Lake became the centerpiece of Indian policy for the administration of Richard Nixon, the incoming president. Two other significant events also had a strong effect on Nixon's developing policy of Indian self-determination. First was the receipt of a study of the BIA by Alvin M. Josephy, Jr., entitled *The American Indian and the Bureau of Indian Affairs, 1969.*[18] In his report, completed on 24 February 1969, Josephy chastised the federal government for its ineptitude in the handling of Indian affairs. Specifically, he condemned the failure of various presidents to effect any change in the multilayered, bureaucratically inept BIA, the failure of the government's Indian education policy, and the high rates of unemployment, disease, and death on Indian reservations as a result of neglect of Indian people by the federal government. Second was the publication in 1969 of Edgar S. Cahn's *Our Brother's Keeper: The Indian in White America*, a study of the ineptitude of the BIA and an indictment of the BIA for its failure to carry out its responsibilities to the American Indian people.[19] Cahn highlighted the numerous studies of Indian people, all except one conducted by non-Indians, and stated that "recommendations have come to have a special non-meaning for Indians. They are part of a tradition in which policy and programs are dictated by non-Indians, even when dialogue and consultation have been promised."[20]

Other movements, such as the Alaska Native Claims Movement of 1960–71, raged on. This particular movement consisted of regional coalitions of over two hundred Alaska Native villages joined in a statewide land claims protest. A large land claims settlement was finally negotiated in 1971 whereby the Alaska Natives retained 44 million acres of land and received $962.5 million and other benefits.[21] The Alaska Native Claims Settlement Act (ANCSA) of 1971 became a model for many struggling indigenous movements around the world.

Indian protests for assertion of treaty-based fishing rights continued throughout the 1960s and early 1970s and were often associated with arrests and violence. In a 1970 protest over treaty fishing rights at Frank's Landing in Washington State, sixty Indians were arrested. SAIA members, led by Janet McCloud, a Tulalip Indian, gathered in Seattle and marched in protest at the federal courthouse. In January 1971, Hank Adams, a former member of NIYC and now a member of SAIA who had participated in a decade of fish-ins, was shot in the stomach by two white sport fishermen as he slept in his pick-up truck. Adams had been tending a set of fish nets for a friend on the Puyallup River. He survived the shooting, but the police, who sympathized with the non-Indian sport fishermen, disputed his account of the incident and did not search for his attackers. In February 1974, a federal judge, George Boldt, ruled in *United States v. Washington* to uphold the treaty rights of Indian people to fish at their usual and accustomed grounds and stations off reservation and "in common with" other citizens.[22]

Self-determination formed the logic for much tribally based litigation, lobbying, and protest action. The outlines of the Indian self-determination policy were formed during the late 1960s, when Zuni Pueblo took advantage of a little-known law to contract BIA services. The Zuni wanted to minimize BIA interference in their community, preferring to manage their own affairs. The success of the Zuni contracting of BIA programs came to the attention of Nixon administration officials, and the new self-determination policy announced in 1970 was based on contracting of federal and BIA services directly to tribal governments. However, the contracting mechanisms for enabling tribal governments to take advantage of the self-determination policy were not worked out until passage of the Indian Self-Determination and Education Act of 1975. Nevertheless, the new policy of self-determination was designed to give Indian people greater control over their communities, tribal governments, and reservation institutions, all of which had been managed by BIA officials since late in the nineteenth century. Although ultimately the effects of the self-determination policy were limited, most Indian communities strongly favored the new policy.

By the late 1960s and early 1970s, Native Americans thus had a rich and long legacy of social movements. Most were tribally centered around treaty or land issues. Others were multitribal, led by groups such as the NCAI and composed of loose coalitions of tribal groups or members allied temporarily to struggle against a common external threat, such as termination. Most Indian social movements revolved around issues of injustice, deprivation, or suppression, something they shared with the Alcatraz–Red Power Movement. The fact that the ARPM relied on a history of past incidents to inform and organize its members and leadership also was not unusual. The ARPM drew selectively on many elements of Indian history, especially symbols of resistance. Geronimo, the Apache leader who fought against U.S. control over reservation communities in the 1880s, was one such symbol for the Alcatraz Island occupiers. Custer's defeat in 1876 was used to symbolize Indian victory and defiance, and the Wounded Knee Massacre in 1890 became a major symbol of Indian repression during the Wounded Knee seizure in 1973.

The ARPM was very different from earlier and contemporary Indian social movements. Its members sought change and inclusion in U.S. institutions while preferring to retain Indian cultural identity. This was a form of nonassimilative inclusion that was not well understood at the time but later helped form the contemporary vision of a multicultural society. The defining characteristics of the ARPM were its emphasis on a supratribal identity and the tactic of property seizure, which was used only sparingly by other Indian social movements. Since most Indian people were repressed and marginalized throughout the 1960s, there was much activism, but nothing of the scale or significance of the Alcatraz–Red Power Movement in terms of tactics, new identity formation, visibility in U.S. society, and bringing attention to Indian issues. So we must look to other issues beyond the legacy of Indian social movements for explaining the rise of the ARPM, its goals, pattern of organization, and tactics, as well as its legacy.

Change and Protest in American Society

The occupation of Alcatraz Island occurred at the height of considerable urban unrest in the United States. To understand both the causes of the occupation and its consequences for American Indian activism, individual ethnic consciousness, and Native American community survival, it is important to recall the atmosphere of the 1960s and the changes underway in U.S. social and political life at the time.

The United States was deeply involved in an unpopular war in Vietnam. The new feminism was stirring, and the civil rights movement, Black Power, LaRaza, the Latino movement, the New Left, and Third World strikes were sweeping the nation, particularly its college campuses. While U.S. armed forces were involved in the clandestine invasion and bombing of Cambodia, the 1969 announcement of the massacre of innocent civilians in a hamlet in My Lai, Vietnam, burned across the front pages of American newspapers.[23] Ubiquitous campus demonstrations raised the level of consciousness of college students. People of all ages were becoming sensitized to the unrest among emerging minority and gender groups who were staging demonstrations and proclaiming their points of view, many of which were incorporated by student activists. Sit-ins, sleep-ins, teach-ins, lock-outs, and boycotts became everyday occurrences.

The occupation of Alcatraz Island was part of the much larger movement for social change, which had its roots in the 1950s and 1960s and was now being promoted by people of many colors, genders, and ages. The 1960s witnessed a marked upsurge in political awareness and activity sparked by events in the national arena such as the civil rights movement. The Student Non-Violent Coordinating Committee (SNCC), founded in April 1960, was made up of black-led, nonviolent sit-in activists. It combined with Students for a Democratic Society (SDS), founded in 1962, to form what came to be called the "New Left." Young black Americans were hearing an angrier and more militant voice, a voice coming from former members of SNCC and participants in the civil rights movement. Between 1964 and 1967, more than a hundred major riots and scores of minor disruptions occurred in cities across the country. By the end of 1968, racial upheavals had resulted in more than two hundred deaths and property destruction valued at approximately $800 million. It was during this time that the Black Panther Party (BPP) was born.[24]

The activist movements of the 1960s were marked by a variety of racial, class, and gender groups: young college students were joined by Vietnam veterans, gay rights activists, women's liberation activists, urban American Indian people, Mexican American farm workers, and members of LaRaza, the newly emerging Chicano/Chicana empowerment movement. These disparate groups came together in an era marked by dynamic personal change, cultural awareness, and political confrontation. Meanwhile, many Indian activists observed the civil rights movements and contemplated how this activity could be brought to bear on Indian issues.[25]

The Vietnam War came to be defined in the minds of many Indian men and women as a war fought to defend a freedom that they themselves had never experienced. While Indian people may have been the forgotten Americans in the minds of many politicians and bureaucrats during peacetime,

this was not the case in time of war or national emergency. American Indians were required to serve and did so honorably: 1,000 in World War I;
44,500 in World War II; and 29,700 during the Korean conflict. The Vietnam War proved no exception, with a total of 61,100 Indians serving during that era.[26] Beginning with the commitment of troops to Vietnam in 1963,
Indians either volunteered or were drafted into military service for this un-
declared war against a people some Indian servicemen considered to be as
much of an oppressed minority as American Indians themselves were. Mad
Bear Anderson, the Tuscarora activist, visited Vietnam seven times and stated, "When I walk down the streets of Saigon those people look like my
brothers and sisters."[27] Robert Thomas, a Cherokee anthropologist, commented that Indian people understood the war in Vietnam better than his
university colleagues did: "The conflict in Vietnam was tribal in origin, and
the Vietnamese were tired of the war machine flattening their crops."[28]

American Indians coming back from Vietnam faced difficult choices.
Those who returned, or attempted to return, to life on the reservation found
high unemployment rates, poor health facilities, and substandard housing
conditions—as did Indian veterans coming back from World War II service.
Those who elected to relocate or settle in urban areas encountered what can
best be described as "double discrimination." First, they were faced with the
continuing discrimination against Indian people that resulted in high unemployment, police brutality, and, very often, alcoholism and death. Second, they experienced the discrimination felt by other Vietnam veterans
viewed as participants in an unpopular war; rather than being hailed as heroes or shown some measure of respect for their sacrifices, they were considered third-rate citizens and treated as outcasts. In an attempt to retreat
for a period of time, to adjust to a changing society, or perhaps simply to
acquire skills for future employment, many of the returning Indian veterans utilized their GI bill educational benefits and enrolled in colleges in the
San Francisco Bay Area. Indian students from these colleges, many of them
Vietnam veterans, filled the ranks of the rising Indian activism movement
now emerging as "Red Power."

Organization and Protest in the Urban Environment

In 1990, more than 50 percent of American Indians lived in cities. This trend
toward urbanization began during World War II as a result of wartime indus-
trial job opportunities, federal policies of relocation (in tandem with the termination of tribal rights and the forced assimilation of Indians into non-Indian
society), and the urbanization of the U.S. population as a whole. Many Native Americans migrated to the Bay Area during this time to work in defense

industries; thousands of others were relocated there by the federal government. In the Bay Area, which was one of the largest of more than a dozen relocation sites, the newly urban Indians formed their own organizations to provide the support that the government had promised but had failed to deliver. While some groups were known by tribal names such as the Sioux Club and the Navajo Club, there were also a variety of intertribal organizations, including sports clubs, dance clubs, and the very early urban powwow clubs. Eventually, some thirty Bay Area social clubs were formed to meet the needs of the urban Indians and their children—children who would, in the 1960s, want the opportunity to go to college and better themselves.[29]

Many of these organizationally connected urban Indians were dissatisfied with conditions in the cities and on reservation homelands—specifically, with the lack of self-determination in both communities and with federal policies concerning Indian affairs. They represented a population that was poised on the brink of activism: disillusioned Indian youth from reservations, urban centers, and universities who called for Red Power in their crusade to reform the conditions of their people. Native American scholar Vine Deloria, Jr., in *Behind the Trail of Broken Treaties*, states: "The power movements which had sprung up after 1966 now began to affect Indians, and the center of action was the urban areas on the West Coast, where there was a large Indian population."[30]

These Red Power groups strongly advocated a policy of Indian self-determination, with the NIYC in particular emphasizing the psychological impact of powerlessness on Indian youth. This powerlessness and lack of self-determination was explained by Clyde Warrior, a Ponca Indian and cofounder of NIYC, when he told government officials in Washington, D.C., in 1967: "We are not allowed to make those basic human choices and decisions about our personal life and about the destiny of our communities which is the mark of free mature people. We sit on our front porch or in our yards, and the world and our lives in it pass us by without our desires or aspirations having any effect."[31] An article in *Warpath*, the first militant, pan-Indian newspaper in the United States, established in 1968 by UNA, summed up the attitude of the Bay Area Indian community: "The 'Stoic, Silent Redman' of the past who turned the other cheek to white injustice is dead. (He died of frustration and heartbreak.) And in his place is an angry group of Indians who dare to speak up and voice their dissatisfaction at the world around them. Hate and despair have taken their toll and only action can quiet this smoldering anger that has fused this new Indian movement into being."[32]

On 11 April 1969, the National Council on Indian Opportunity (NCIO), established by President Lyndon Johnson by Executive Order 11399, conducted a public forum in San Francisco before the Committee on Urban Indians. The purpose of the forum was to gain as much information as possible on the condition of Indian people living in the area so as to help find solutions to their problems and ease the tensions that were rising among young urban Indians. The hearings began with a scathing rebuke by the Reverend Tony Calaman, founder of Freedom for Adoptive Children. Reverend Calaman attacked the San Francisco Police Department, the California Department of Social Welfare, and the Indian child placement system, stating that the non-Indian system emasculated Indian people. When asked to explain, he said: "it is a dirty, rotten, stinkin' term [emasculation], and the social workers are doing it and the police officers are doing it when they club you on the head. It is a racist institution, just pure racism—and you all know what racism is, and you all know what racists are. Look in the mirror, and you will see a racist."[33]

Earl Livermore, director of the San Francisco American Indian Center, appeared next and concentrated his testimony on problems Indian people face in adjusting to urban living, particularly Indian students faced with unfavorable conditions in the public school system. Those conditions ranged from lack of understanding by school officials to false or misleading statements in school textbooks. Livermore pointed out that many of the textbooks in use damaged the Indian child's sense of identity and personal worth. His testimony also addressed urban Indian health problems, which often were the result of Indian people not being properly oriented to urban living and the frustration and depression that often followed. Lack of education, according to Livermore, resulted in unemployment, which in turn led to depression, which led Indian people deeper into the depths of despair. Alcoholism, poor nutrition, and inadequate housing were also highlighted as major problems.[34]

A total of thirty-seven Indian people took advantage of the opportunity to appear at the public forum to highlight the problems and frustrations felt by urban American Indians. Twenty-five of them would be among the occupiers of Alcatraz Island seven months later. Dennis Turner, a Luiseño Indian, testified before the committee about his personal frustrations resulting from the relocation program and about the inadequacy of the educational system to meet Indian needs. He also highlighted problems of inadequate housing and lack of counselors for Indian people newly relocated to the urban areas. More directly, Turner addressed the problem of governmental agencies such as the NCIO conducting hearings and making promises, and the frustration of seeing no change as a result of hearings such as the one before which he was presently testifying. Addressing LaDonna Harris, a Comanche Indian and chairperson of the Committee on Urban Indians, Turner stated: "After it's [the hearing] over with, you're going to wonder what is going to happen? Is something going to come off or not? The Indian is still hoping. If he keeps on hoping, he's going to die of frustration."[35]

In response to a press query, "Are you going to have some militant Indians?" Harris replied, "Heavens, I hope we will."[36] Her statement was, in fact, a look into the future, to plans not yet formalized but soon to capture the attention of Americans throughout the nation and to be played out as a nineteen-month drama on Alcatraz Island. But her premonition was not without precedent. In a 1969 meeting at the San Francisco Indian Center, Richard McKenzie, a Sioux Indian who was one of the members of a short-lived 1964 Alcatraz occupation party, recognized the uniqueness of the Indian situation as opposed to the civil rights movement. He said, "Kneel-Ins, Sit-Ins, Sleep-Ins, Eat-Ins, Pray-Ins like the Negroes do, wouldn't help us. We would have to occupy the government buildings before things would change."[37]

The rise of Indian activism was also prophesied by Walter Wetzel, the leader of the Blackfeet of Montana and former president of the National Congress of American Indians: "We Indians have been struggling unsuccessfully with the problems of maintaining home and family and Indian ownership of the land. We must strike."[38] Mad Bear Anderson, who had turned back the bulldozers when a dam was planned on Iroquois land, declared: "Our people were murdered in this country. And they are still being murdered. . . . There is an Indian nationalist movement in the country. I am one of the founders. We are not going to pull any punches from here on in."[39]

President Nixon's self-determination policy would be tested in California, particularly the Bay Area, which had become the hotbed for the newly developing Indian activism. Jack Forbes, a Powhatan/Lenape Indian and professor of Native American studies and anthropology at the University of California, Davis, became an advisor and mentor to many of the new Indian students. In the spring of 1969, Forbes drafted a proposal for a College of Native American Studies on one of the California campuses. American Indian or Native American studies programs were already being formed— for example, at UC Berkeley, UCLA, and San Francisco State College. These programs grew out of the Third World strikes in progress on the various campuses and included Indian students who would soon be intimately involved in the Alcatraz occupation: Richard Oakes, Ross Harden, Joe Bill, Dennis Turner, LaNada Boyer, and Horace Spencer.[40]

On 30 June 1969, the California legislature endorsed Forbes's proposal for the creation of a separate Indian-controlled university. Forbes wrote to John G. Veneman, assistant secretary of Health, Education, and Welfare, and requested that Veneman look into the availability of a 650-acre site between Winter, California, and Davis.[41] Additionally, in 1969, the Native American Student Union (NASU) was formed in California, bringing together a new pan-Indian alliance between the emerging Native American studies programs on the various campuses. In San Francisco, members of

NASU prepared to test President Nixon's commitment to his stated policy of self-determination before a national audience by occupying Alcatraz Island. For Indian people of the Bay Area, the social movements of the 1960s not only had come to full maturity but would now include Indian people. In November 1969, American Indians moved onto the national scene of ethnic unrest as active participants in a war of their own. Alcatraz Island was the battlefield.[41]

The Alcatraz Occupations

In actuality, there were three separate occupations of Alcatraz Island.[42] The first was a brief, four-hour occupation on 9 March 1964 by five Sioux Indians representing the urban Indians of the Bay Area. The event was planned by Belva Cottier, the wife of one of the occupiers. The federal penitentiary on the island had been closed in 1963, and the government was in the process of transferring the island to the city of San Francisco for development purposes. But Belva Cottier and her Sioux cousin had plans of their own. They recalled having heard of a provision in the 1868 Sioux treaty with the federal government that stated that ownership of all abandoned federal lands that once belonged to the Sioux reverted to the Sioux people.[43] Using this interpretation of the treaty, they encouraged five Sioux men to occupy Alcatraz Island and issued press releases claiming the island in accordance with the treaty and demanding better treatment for urban Indians. Richard McKenzie, the most outspoken of the group, pressed the claim for title to the island through the court system, only to have the courts rule against him. More important, however, the Indians of the Bay Area were becoming vocal and united in their efforts to improve their lives.

The 1964 occupation of Alcatraz Island foreshadowed the unrest that was fomenting, quietly but surely, among the urban Indian population. Prior to the occupation, Bay Area newspapers contained a large number of articles about the federal government's abandonment of the urban Indian and the refusal of state and local governments to meet Indian people's needs. The Indian social clubs that had been formed for support became meeting places at which to discuss discrimination in schools, housing, employment, and health care. Indian people also talked about the police, who, like law officers in other areas of the country, would wait outside Indian bars at closing time to harass, beat up, and arrest Indian patrons. Indian centers began to appear in all the urban relocation areas and became nesting grounds for new pan-Indian, and eventually activist, organizations.[44]

The second Alcatraz occupation had its beginning on Bay Area and other California college and university campuses when young, educated Indian students joined with other minority groups during the 1969 Third World Liberation Front Strike and began demanding courses relevant to Indian students. Indian history written and taught by non-Indian instructors was no longer acceptable to these students, awakened as they were to the possibility of social protest to bring attention to the shameful treatment of Indian people. Anthropologist Luis S. Kemnitzer has described the establishment of the country's first Native American Studies Program at San Francisco State College in 1969—the spring before the occupation. The students involved in that program went on to plan the Alcatraz occupation:

> . . . a non-Indian graduate student in social science at San Francisco State who was tutoring young Indian children in the Mission District came to know a group of young Indians who . . . all had some contact with college and had come to San Francisco either on vocational training, relocation, or on their own. . . . Conversation with the student tutor led them to become interested in the strike and in exploring the possibility of working toward a Native American studies department.
>   . . . the university and the Third World Liberation Front had started negotiations, and there was limited room for movement. . . . [LaRaza] agreed to represent the Indians in negotiations, and there was close collaboration between representatives of LaRaza and the future Native American studies students. I was one of the faculty members on strike, and, although I was not involved in the negotiations with the university administration, I was informally recruited by other striking faculty to help plan and negotiate with LaRaza.[45]

Richard Oakes was one of the students in the program. He came from the St. Regis Reservation, had worked on high steel in New York, and had traveled across the United States, visiting various Indian reservations. He eventually wound up in California, where he married a Kashia Pomo woman, Anne Marufo, who had five children from a previous marriage. Oakes worked in an Indian bar in Oakland for a period of time and eventually was admitted to San Francisco State College. In September 1969, he and several other Indian students began discussing the possibility of occupying Alcatraz Island as a symbolic protest, a call for Indian self-determination. Preliminary plans were made for the summer of 1970, but other events led to an earlier takeover. During the fall term, Oakes and his fellow Indian students and friends caught the attention of a nation already engrossed in the escalating protest and conflict of the civil rights movement as they set out across the San Francisco Bay for Alcatraz Island.[46]

The catalyst for the occupation was the destruction of the San Francisco Indian Center by fire in late October 1969. The center had become the meeting place for the Bay Area Indian organizations and the newly formed United Bay Area Indian Council, which had brought the thirty private clubs together into one large council headed by Adam Nordwall (later to be known

as Adam Fortunate Eagle). The destruction of the center united the council and the American Indian student organizations as never before. The
council needed a new meeting place and the students needed a forum for
their new activist voice. The date for the second occupation of Alcatraz Island was thus moved up to 9 November 1969. Oakes and the other students,
along with a group of people from the San Francisco Indian Center, char-
tered a boat and headed for Alcatraz Island. Since many different tribes were
represented, the occupiers called themselves "Indians of All Tribes."[47]

The initial plan was to circle the island and symbolically claim it for all
Indian people. During the circling maneuver, however, Oakes and four others jumped from the boat and swam to the island. They claimed Alcatraz in
the name of Indians of All Tribes and then left the island at the request of
the caretaker. Later that evening, Oakes and fourteen others returned to the
island with sleeping bags and food sufficient for two or three days but left
the next morning, again without incident, when asked to do so.[48]

In meetings following the 9 November occupation, Oakes and his fellow students realized that a prolonged occupation was possible. It was clear
that the federal government had only a token force on the island and that
so far no physical harm had come to anyone involved. A new plan began to
emerge. Oakes traveled to UCLA, where he met with Ray Spang and Edward Castillo and asked for their assistance in recruiting Indian students for
what would become the longest Indian occupation of any federal facility.
Spang, Castillo, and Oakes met in UCLA's Campbell Hall, now the home
of the American Indian Studies Center and the editorial offices of the *American Indian Culture and Research Journal*, in private homes, and in Indian bars
in Los Angeles. When the third takeover of Alcatraz Island began, seventy
of the eighty-nine Indian occupiers were students from UCLA.[49]

In the early morning hours of 20 November 1969, eighty-nine American Indians landed on Alcatraz Island in San Francisco Bay. These Indians
of All Tribes claimed the island by "right of discovery" and by the terms of
the 1868 Treaty of Fort Laramie, which gave Indians the right to unused
federal property that had previously been Indian land. Except for a small
caretaker staff, the island had been abandoned by the federal government
since 1963, when the federal penitentiary was closed. In a press statement,
Indians of All Tribes set the tone of the occupation and the agenda for negotiations during the next nineteen months:

> We, the native Americans, re-claim the land known as Alcatraz Island in the
> name of all American Indians. . . . [W]e plan to develop on this island sev-
> eral Indian institutions: 1. A CENTER FOR NATIVE AMERICAN
> STUDIES . . . 2. AN AMERICAN INDIAN SPIRITUAL CENTER . . . 3.
> AN INDIAN CENTER OF ECOLOGY . . . 4. A GREAT INDIAN
> TRAINING SCHOOL . . . [and] an AMERICAN INDIAN MUSEUM.

. . . In the name of all Indians, therefore, we reclaim this island for our Indian nations. . . . We feel this claim is just and proper, and that this land should rightfully be granted to us for as long as the rivers shall run and the sun shall shine. Signed, INDIANS OF ALL TRIBES.[50]

The occupiers quickly set about organizing themselves. An elected council was put into place, and everyone was assigned a job: security, sanitation, day-care, housing, cooking, laundry. All decisions were made by unanimous consent of the people. Sometimes meetings were held five, six, or seven times per day to discuss the rapidly developing events. It is important to remember that, while the urban Indian population supported the concept of an occupation and provided the logistical support, the Alcatraz occupation force itself was made up initially of young, urban Indian students from UCLA, UC Santa Cruz, San Francisco State College, and UC Berkeley.[51]

The most inspiring person, if not the recognized leader, was Richard Oakes, described as handsome, charismatic, a talented orator, and a natural leader. The casting of Oakes as the person in charge, a title he himself never claimed, quickly created a problem. Not all the students knew Oakes, and, in keeping with the concepts underlying the occupation, many wanted an egalitarian society on the island, with no one as their leader. Although this may have been a workable form of organization on the island, it was not comprehensible to the non-Indian media. Newspapers, magazines, and television and radio stations across the nation sent reporters to the island to interview the people in charge. They wanted to know who the leaders were. Oakes was the most knowledgeable about the landing and the most often sought out, and he was therefore identified as the leader, the "chief," the "mayor of Alcatraz." He was strongly influenced by the White Roots of Peace, which had been revitalized by Ray Fadden, and Mad Bear Anderson. Before the Alcatraz occupation, in the autumn of 1969, Jerry Gambill, a counselor for the White Roots of Peace, had visited the campus of San Francisco State and inspired many of the students, none more than Oakes.[52]

By the end of 1969, the Indian organization on the island began to change, and two Indian groups rose in opposition to Oakes. When many of the Native American students left the island to return to school, they were replaced by Indian people from urban areas and reservations who had not been involved in the initial planning. Where Oakes and the other students claimed title to the island by right of discovery, the new arrivals harked back to the rhetoric of the 1964 occupation and the Sioux treaty, a claim that had been pressed through the court system by Richard McKenzie and had been found invalid. Additionally, some non-Indians took up residence on the island, many of them from the San Francisco hippie and drug culture. Drugs and liquor had been banned from the island by the original occupiers, but they now became commonplace.[53]

The final blow to the nascent student occupation occurred on 5 January 1970 when Oakes's thirteen-year-old stepdaughter, Yvonne, who was apparently playing unsupervised with some other children, slipped and fell three floors to her death down an open stairwell. The Oakes family left the island, and the two groups began maneuvering for leadership roles. Despite these changes, the demands of the occupiers remained consistent: title to Alcatraz Island, the development of an Indian university, and the construction of a museum and cultural center that would display for and teach non-Indian society the valuable contributions of Indian people.[54]

In the months that followed, thousands of protesters and visitors spent time on Alcatraz Island. They came from a large number of Indian tribes, including the Sioux, Navajo, Cherokee, Mohawk, Puyallup, Yakima, Hoopa, and Omaha. The months of occupation were marked by proclamations, news conferences, powwows, celebrations, "assaults" with arrows on passing vessels, and negotiations with federal officials. In the beginning months, workers from the San Francisco Indian Center gathered food and supplies on the mainland and transported them to Alcatraz. However, as time went by, the occupying force, which fluctuated but generally numbered around one hundred, confronted increasing hardships as federal officials interfered with delivery boats and cut off the supply of water and electricity to the island. Tensions on the island grew.[55]

The federal government, for its part, insisted that the Indian people leave, and it placed an ineffective Coast Guard barricade around the island. Eventually, the government agreed to the Indian council's demands for formal negotiations. But, from the Indian people's side, the demands were nonnegotiable. They wanted the deed to the island; they wanted to establish an Indian university, a cultural center, and a museum; and they wanted the necessary federal funding to meet their goals. Negotiations collapsed for good when the government turned down these demands and insisted that the Indians of All Tribes leave the island. Alcatraz Island would never be developed in accordance with the goals of the Indian protesters.[56]

In time, the attention of the federal government shifted from negotiations with the island occupants to restoration of navigational aids that had been discontinued as the result of a fire that shut down the Alcatraz lighthouse. The government's inability to restore these navigational aids brought criticism from the Coast Guard, the Bay Area Pilot's Association, and local newspapers. The federal government became impatient, and on 11 June 1971, the message went out to end the occupation of Alcatraz Island. The dozen or so remaining protesters were removed by federal marshals, more than a year and a half after the island was first occupied.[57] Some members of Indians of All Tribes moved their protest to an abandoned Nike missile base in the Beverly Hills, overlooking San Francisco Bay. While that occupation lasted only three days, it set in motion a pattern of similar occupations over the next several years.

The events that took place on Alcatraz Island represented a watershed moment in Native American protest and caught the attention of the entire country, providing a forum for airing long-standing Indian grievances and for expressing Indian pride. Vine Deloria noted the importance of Alcatraz, referring to the occupation as a "master stroke of Indian activism." He also recognized the impact of Alcatraz and other occupations on Indian ethnic self-awareness and identity: "Indian[n]ess was judged on whether or not one was present at Alcatraz, Fort Lawson, Mt. Rushmore, Detroit, Sheep Mountain, Plymouth Rock, or Pitt River. . . . The activists controlled the language, the issues, and the attention."[58] In 1993, Deloria reflected on the longer-term impact of the Red Power movement: "This era will probably always be dominated by the images and slogans of the AIM people. The real accomplishments in land restoration, however, were made by quiet determined tribal leaders. . . . In reviewing the period we should understand the frenzy of the time and link it to the definite accomplishments made by tribal governments."[59]

The Alcatraz occupation and the activism that followed offer firm evidence to counter commonly held views of Indians as powerless in the face of history, as weakened remnants of disappearing cultures and communities. Countless events fueled American Indian ethnic pride and strengthened Indian people's sense of personal empowerment and community membership. Wilma Mankiller, now principal chief of the Cherokee Nation of Oklahoma, visited Alcatraz many times during the months of occupation. She described it as an awakening that "ultimately changed the course of my life."[60] This was a recurrent theme in our interviews with Native Americans who participated in or observed the protests of that period:

GEORGE HORSE CAPTURE: In World War II, the marines were island-hopping; they'd do the groundwork, and then the army and the civilians would come in and build things. Without the first wave, nothing would happen. Alcatraz and the militants were like that. They put themselves at risk, could be arrested or killed. You have to give them their due. We were in the second wave. In the regular Indian world, we're very complacent; it takes leadership to get things moving. But scratch a real Indian since then, and you're going to find a militant. Alcatraz tapped into something. It was the lance that burst the boil.[61]

JOHN ECHOHAWK: Alcatraz just seemed to be kind of another event—what a lot of people had been thinking, wanting to do. We were studying Indian law for the first time. We had a lot of frustration and anger. People were fed up with the status quo. That's just what we were thinking. Starting in 1967 at the University of New Mexico Law School, we read treaties, Indian legal history. It was just astounding how unfair it was, how wrong it was. It [Alcatraz] was the kind of thing we needed.[62]

LEONARD PELTIER: I was in Seattle when Alcatraz happened. It was the first event that received such publicity. In Seattle, we were in solidarity with the demands of Alcatraz. We were inspired and encouraged by Alcatraz. I realized their goals were mine. The Indian organizations I was working with shared the same needs: an Indian college to keep students from dropping out, a cultural center to keep Indian traditions. We were all really encouraged, not only those who were active, but those who were not active as well.[63]

FRANCES WISE: The Alcatraz takeover had an enormous impact. I was living in Waco, Texas, at the time. I would see little blurbs on TV. I thought, These Indians are really doing something at Alcatraz. . . . And when they called for the land back, I realized that, finally, what Indian people have gone through is finally being recognized. . . . It affected how I think of myself. If someone asks me who I am, I say, well, I have a name, but Waco/Caddo—that's who I am. I have a good feeling about who I am now. And you need this in the presence of all this negative stuff, for example, celebrating the Oklahoma Land Run.[64]

ROSALIE McKAY-WANT: In the final analysis, however, the occupation of this small territory could be considered a victory for the cause of Indian activism and one of the most noteworthy expressions of patriotism and self-determination by Indian people in the twentieth century.[65]

GRACE THORPE: Alcatraz was the catalyst and the most important event in the Indian movement to date. It made me put my furniture into storage and spend my life savings.[66]

These voices speak to the central importance of the Alcatraz occupation as the symbol of long-standing Indian grievances and increasing impatience with a political system slow to respond to native rights. They also express the feelings of empowerment that witnessing and participating in protest can foster. Loretta Flores, an Indian women, did not become an activist herself until several years after the events on Alcatraz, but she has eloquently described the sense of self and community that activism can produce: "The night before the protest, I was talking to a younger person who had never been in a march before. I told her, 'Tomorrow when we get through with this march, you're going to have a feeling like you've never had before. It's going to change your life.' Those kids from Haskell (Indian Nations University) will never forget this. The spirits of our ancestors were looking down on us smiling."[67]

The Alcatraz–Red Power Movement: A Nine-Year Odyssey

The success or failure of the Indian occupation of Alcatraz Island should not be judged by whether the demands for title to the island and the establishment of educational and cultural institutions were realized. If one were to make such a judgment, the only possible conclusion would be that the occupation was a failure. Such is not the case, however. The underlying goals of the Indians on Alcatraz were to awaken the American public to the reality of their situation and to assert the need for Indian self-determination. In this they succeeded. Additionally, the occupation of Alcatraz Island was a springboard for Indian activism, inspiring the large number of takeovers and demonstrations that began shortly after the 20 November 1969 landing and continued into the late 1970s. These included the Trail of Broken Treaties, the BIA headquarters takeover in 1972, and Wounded Knee II in 1973.

Many of the approximately seventy-four occupations that followed Alcatraz were either planned by or included people who had been involved in the Alcatraz occupation or who certainly had gained their strength from the new "Indianness" that grew out of that movement. For example, on 3 November 1970, in Davis, California, "scores of Indians scaled a barbed wire fence and seized an old Army communications center . . . unimpeded by four soldiers whose job it was to guard the facility. Raising a big white tepee on the surplus Government property, 75 Indians occupied it for use in development of an Indian cultural center. Several veterans of the successful Indian invasion of Alcatraz Island a year ago took part in [the] assault."[68] Most occupations were short-lived, lasting only a few days or weeks, such as those that occurred during 1970–71 at Fort Lawton and Fort Lewis in Washington, at Ellis Island in New York, at the Twin Cities Naval Air Station in Minneapolis, at former Nike missile sites on Lake Michigan near Chicago and at Argonne, Illinois, and at an abandoned Coast Guard lifeboat station in Milwaukee.

A number of protest camps were established during the early 1970s, including those at Mount Rushmore and the Badlands National Monument. During the same years, government buildings also became the sites of protests, including regional Bureau of Indian Affairs offices in Cleveland and Denver, as well as the main headquarters in Washington, D.C. Many of these occupations took on a festive air as celebrations of Indian culture and ethnic renewal, while others represented efforts to provide educational or social services to urban Indians. The September 1971 attempted "invasion" of BIA headquarters was described as follows:

> A band of militant young Indians sought to make a citizens' arrest of a Federal official today and wound up in a noisy clash with Government guards

at the Bureau of Indian Affairs. . . . [T]hey sought a conference with bureau officials on their contention that Indians were being denied basic rights. Some of the Indians . . . barricaded themselves in two rooms of the public information office on the first floor and others occupied Mr. Crow's [Deputy Commissioner of Indian Affairs] office on the second floor. . . . The invasion of the bureau was directed by the American Indian Movement and the National Indian Youth Council.[69]

As Indian activism in the 1970s progressed, some events were characterized by a more serious, sometimes violent tone, revealing the depth of grievances and difficulty of solutions to the problems confronting Native Americans after nearly five centuries of Euro-American contact. An example was the November 1972 week-long occupation of BIA headquarters. This unplanned takeover occurred at the end of the Trail of Broken Treaties, a protest event involving caravans that traveled across the United States to convene in Washington, D.C., the purpose being to dramatize and present Indian concerns at a national level. The inability of an advance party to secure accommodations in private homes and churches for several hundred exhausted Indians led to the occupation of BIA offices. Angry participants, many of whom mistakenly thought the federal government had agreed to provide housing and then reneged, literally destroyed the inside of BIA headquarters. They barricaded the doors with furniture and office equipment, soaking each pile with gasoline so it could be quickly ignited in the event of forced removal. They smashed plumbing fixtures and windows, covered the walls with graffiti, and gathered up BIA files and Indian artifacts to take back to their reservations. The protest ended a week later after a series of negotiations with federal officials. Damage to the building was estimated at $2.2 million.

During this period, the ARPM protest strategy began to shift from Alcatraz-style takeovers to different forms and terrains of contention linked to the organizational underpinning of supratribal collective action and its urban population base. Researchers and journalists generally reported that participants in activist events in 1970 and 1971 were Indians of varied tribal backgrounds who mainly lived in urban areas and were associated with the NIYC or some other supratribal organization—or else with AIM, the primary organization of the Red Power movement.[70] Before Alcatraz, AIM was essentially an Indian rights organization concerned with monitoring law enforcement treatment of native people in American cities. However, the occupation of Alcatraz captured the imagination of AIM as well as the rest of the country, and as a result, AIM embarked on a historic journey into Indian protest activism.[71]

The American Indian Movement, founded in Minneapolis in 1968, quickly established chapters in several U.S. cities. AIM's membership was drawn mostly from urban Indian communities, and its leadership and membership both tended to come from the ranks of younger, more progressive, and better educated urban Indians.[72] Although not involved in the initial takeover of Alcatraz Island, AIM played an important role in the spread of supratribal protest action during the 1970s and in shaping the Red Power agenda, tactics, and strategies for drawing attention to Indian people's grievances. Ward Churchill and James Vander Wall have noted that "the 19-month occupation [of Alcatraz] . . . demonstrated beyond all doubt that strong actions by Indians could result not only in broad public exposure of the issues and substantial national/international support for Indian rights, but could potentially force significant concessions from the federal government as well. . . . The lessons of this were not lost on the AIM leadership."[73]

The American Indian Movement was enormously influential, but its role in orchestrating Red Power protest events must not be overstated. While many collective event participants claimed AIM membership, the more common thread was education, urban ties, and Indian ethnic identification. AIM and its visible leadership provided a symbolic as well as an actual organizational point of entry for these potential participants in Red Power. Networks of urban Indian centers, Indian churches, and Indian charitable organizations helped plan and support collective actions by AIM.[74] Protest activities and strategies moved through Indian communities via Indian social and kin networks and by way of the "powwow circuit," which passed information along to Indian families who traveled between the cities and the reservations.[75] However, the most important factor contributing to AIM's influence on Red Power protest was probably its ability to use the news media—newspapers, radio, magazines, and television—to dramatize Indian problems and protests.

After visiting the Indians on Alcatraz Island and realizing the possibilities available through demonstration and seizure of federal facilities, AIM embarked on a national activist role. Its leaders recognized the opportunities when they met with the Indian people on the island during the summer of 1970 and were caught up in the momentum of the occupation. AIM leaders had seen firsthand that the bureaucracy inherent in the federal government had resulted in immobility: No punitive action had been taken thus far on the island. This provided an additional impetus for AIM's kind of national Indian activism and was congruent with the rising tide of national unrest, particularly among young college students.

AIM's first attempt at a national protest action came on Thanksgiving Day 1970 when its members seized the Mayflower II in Plymouth, Massachusetts, to challenge a celebration of colonial expansion into what had mistakenly been considered a "new world." During this action, AIM leaders acknowledged the occupation of Alcatraz Island as the symbol of a newly awakened desire among Indians for unity and authority in a white world. In his 1995 autobiography, *Where White Men Fear to Tread*, former AIM leader Russell Means has stated:

> [A]bout every admirable quality that remains in today's Indian people is the result of the American Indian Movement's flint striking the white man's steel. In the 1970s and 1980s, we lit a fire across Indian country. We fought for changes in school curricula to eliminate racist lies, and we are winning. We fought for community control of police, and on a few reservations it's now a reality. We fought to instill pride in our songs and in our language, in our cultural wisdom, inspiring a small renaissance in the teaching of our languages. . . . Thanks to AIM, for the first time in this century, Indian people stand at the threshold of freedom and responsibility.[76]

It was on Alcatraz, however, that the flint first met the steel; it was on Alcatraz that young Indian college students stood toe to toe with the federal government and did not step back.

After 1972, the involvement of urban Indian individuals and groups, such as AIM, in ARPM protests revealed tensions inside the Indian communities themselves—between urban and reservation Indians, between AIM and tribal governments, and between different age cohorts—often arising out of political divisions on the reservations. The tone of protest became less celebratory, less other-directed, and more harsh, more inward, and sometimes more violent. No single event of the Alcatraz–Red Power Movement more clearly illustrates the combination of Indian grievances and community tensions than the events on the Pine Ridge Reservation in South Dakota in the spring of 1973, a ten-week siege that came to be known as "Wounded Knee II."[77]

The conflict at Wounded Knee, a small town on the reservation, involved a dispute within Pine Ridge's Oglala Lakota (Sioux) tribe over its controversial tribal chairman, Richard Wilson. Wilson was viewed as a corrupt puppet of the BIA by some segments of the tribe, including those associated with AIM. An effort to impeach him resulted in a division of the tribe into opposing camps. The two camps eventually armed themselves and began a two-and-a-half month siege that involved tribal police and government, AIM, reservation residents, federal law enforcement officials, the BIA, local citizens, nationally prominent entertainment figures, national philanthropic, religious, and legal organizations, and the national news media.[78]

The siege began with the arrival of a caravan of approximately 250 AIM supporters, led by Dennis Banks and Russell Means, on the evening of 27 February 1973. Although the armed conflict that followed AIM's arrival is generally characterized as a stand-off between AIM and its supporters and the Wilson government and its supporters, the siege at Wounded Knee was

really only one incident in what had been a long history of political insta-
bility and factional conflict on the Pine Ridge Reservation.[79] The next weeks
were filled with shootouts, roadblocks, negotiations, visiting delegations, and
the movement of refugees out of various fire zones. There were also moments of high drama. For example, on 11 March "the occupiers, together
with a delegation of Sioux traditionals who had entered Wounded Knee
during a truce, proclaimed the new Independent Oglala Nation, . . . announced its intention to send a delegation to the United Nations . . . [and]
on March 16, 349 people were sworn in as citizens."[80]

When the siege ended on 9 May, after protracted negotiations between
Leonard Garment, representing President Nixon, and AIM leaders Dennis
Banks and Carter Camp, two Indians and one FBI agent were dead and an
unknown number on both sides had been wounded. Wilson remained in
office (though he was challenged at the next election), and many of the AIM
members involved in the siege spent the next few years in litigation, in exile, and in prison.[81]

Although the action at Wounded Knee was inconclusive in terms of
upsetting the balance of power in the Oglala Lakota tribal council,[82] the siege
became an important component of the ARPM repertoire of contention. In
the next few years, there ensued a number of both long- and short-term
occupations. Many, but not all, of these occupations were similar to Wounded Knee in that they occurred on reservations and involved tribal factions
associated with AIM or urban tribal members. These events included the
six-month occupation of a former girls' camp on state-owned land at Moss
Lake, New York, in 1974; the five-week armed occupation of a vacant Alexian Brothers novitiate by the Menominee Warrior Society near the Menominee reservation in Wisconsin in 1975; the eight-day takeover of a tribally
owned Fairchild electronics assembly plant on the Navajo reservation in New
Mexico in 1975; a three-day, followed by a one-day (several weeks later),
occupation of the Yankton Sioux Industries plant on the reservation near
Wagner, South Dakota, in 1975; and the week-long occupation of a juve-
nile detention center by members of the Puyallup tribe in Washington State
in 1976.[83]

Red Power protests in the mid- to late 1970s were increasingly enacted
in an atmosphere of heightened confrontation. The following, which took
place in 1976, illustrates the tension of later activism:

> With little pomp, unobtrusive but heavy security and an impromptu Indian
> victory dance, the Federal Government today commemorated the 100th
> anniversary of the battle of Little Bighorn. . . . Today on a wind-buffeted hill
> covered with buffalo grass, yellow clover and sage, in southeastern Montana
> where George Armstrong Custer made his last stand, about 150 Indians from
> various tribes danced joyously around the monument to the Seventh Caval-

ry dead. Meanwhile at an official National Park Service ceremony about 100 yards away, an Army band played. . . . Just as the ceremony got underway a caravan of Sioux, Cheyenne and other Indians led by Russell Means, the American Indian Movement leader, strode to the platform to the pounding of a drum.[84]

The last major event of the Alcatraz–Red Power Movement occurred in July 1978 when several hundred Native Americans marched into Washington, D.C., at the end of the Longest Walk, a protest march that had begun five months earlier in San Francisco. The Longest Walk was intended to symbolize the forced removal of American Indians from their homelands and to draw attention to the continuing problems of Indian people and their communities. The event was also intended to expose and challenge the backlash movement against Indian treaty rights that was gaining strength around the country and in Congress. This backlash could be seen in the growing number of bills before Congress to abrogate Indian treaties and restrict Indian rights.[85] Unlike many of the protest events of the mid-1970s, the Longest Walk was a peaceful event that included tribal spiritual leaders and elders among its participants. It ended without violence. Thus, Red Power protest had come full circle, from the festive Alcatraz days, through a cycle of confrontations between Indian activists and the federal government, to the traditional quest for spiritual unity that marked the end of the Longest Walk.

The decline of the Alcatraz–Red Power Movement is generally attributed to FBI suppression. That is probably only part of the story. AIM leaders were jailed, brought to trial, and many AIM members were found dead.[86] Internal debates in AIM underscored a long-standing split in the movement between those who preferred to work for the benefit of the urban Indian community using conventional methods of federal funding and community service and those who favored the activist national/supratribal agenda. The activist leadership began to withdraw from AIM: some moved on to other issues; some were kept busy fighting legal battles or serving jail time; and others were excommunicated from AIM by those who preferred more conventional tactics. Some leaders, disillusioned with the possibilities of attaining recognition of native rights within the United States, sought recognition of treaty, national, and humanitarian rights within international forums such as UNESCO. After 1978, AIM leaders pursued many of the same goals as ARPM leaders, but the tactic of property seizures—the defining characteristic of the ARPM—fell out of favor, signaling the end of a formative period of Red Power activism.[87]

In some sense, the ARPM was no longer needed. It had laid the foundation of Indian activism and achieved many of its goals, mostly by conventional means. More Indian students were attending college, by the early

1980s there were over a hundred Indian studies programs in the United States, many tribal museums had opened, the National Museum of the American Indian was being planned, and an international indigenous rights movement has been recognized by the United Nations. However, throughout the 1980s and into the 1990s, AIM remained a force in American Indian activism and consciousness, organizing and participating in protests in the Black Hills (Camp Yellow Thunder);[88] continuing the battle over land and grazing rights in Navajo and Hopi territory; protesting athletic team Indian mascots, gestures, logos, and slogans; and working for the repatriation of Indian burial remains, funerary items, and sacred objects.

Social scientists have written extensively on the consequences of activism for the individuals and communities involved in protest movements, which can be life-transforming events.[89] Doug McAdam has found, for example, that the lives of participants in the 1964 Freedom Summer voter registration campaign in the South were altered such that these activists remained ever different from their uninvolved contemporaries, and, furthermore, the effects of these changes extended well into their adulthoods.[90] In his study of labor actions and strikes, Rick Fantasia has found that the participants in such activism redefine themselves and others in terms of their awareness of class distinctions and power relations. He has also pointed out that the community divisions arising out of sustained protest can be long lived and sometimes bitter.[91]

Sometimes, individual communities are strengthened by their members coming together in protest action. For example, Annette Kuhlmann, Richard White, and Carol Ward have all found that many Native American communities have benefited from the involvement of former activists, whether as museum curators, newspaper editors, community or legal service providers, or tribal leaders.[92] Joane Nagel has argued that the activist period of the 1970s contributed to the cultural renaissance currently underway in many Indian communities in the form of tribal museum development, tribal language instruction, cultural preservation and apprenticeship programs, tribal history projects, and the preservation and reinstitution of ceremonial and spiritual practices.[93]

Perhaps the most profound effect of the Alcatraz–Red Power Movement was to educate and change the consciousness of people in the United States and around the world. By the 1980s, more Americans were familiar with Indian issues as a result of the attention brought to bear by ARPM activism. While Americans have generally demanded assimilation from Indians, the ARPM made the point that Indians have cultures, traditions, history, and communities that they want to preserve—but that they also want equal justice, economic opportunity, access to education, and more accurate portrayal of Indians in the media and in history books. Along with other ethnic group movements, the ARPM contributed to debate over multiculturalism within the U.S. national community. In the end, the Alcatraz–Red Power Movement may have strengthened and diversified U.S. society and made it a more tolerant place for all.

NOTES

1. Stephen Cornell, *The Return of the Native* (New York: Oxford University Press, 1988), 180.

2. See R. H. Turner, "Collective Behavior and Resource Mobilization as Approaches to Social Movements," *Research in Social Movements, Conflict and Change* 4 (1981): 1–24; Charles Tilly, *From Mobilization to Revolution* (Reading, Mass.: Addison-Wesley); Doug McAdam, *The Political Process and the Development of Black Insurgency, 1930–1970* (Chicago: University of Chicago Press, 1982).

3. Michael Hittman, *Wovoka and the Ghost Dance* (Carson City, Nev.: Grace Danberg Foundation, 1990), 63–64, 182–94.

4. For a discussion of spiritual and social revitalization movements, see Duane Champagne, "Transocietal Cultural Exchange within the World Economic and Political System," in *The Dynamics of Social Systems*, ed. Paul Colomy (Newbury Park, Calif.: Sage, 1992), 120–53.

5. H. W. Hertzberg, *The Search for an American Indian Identity* (Syracuse, N.Y.: Syracuse University Press, 1971), 6.

6. Six Nations peoples consist of the Mohawk, Oneida, Onondaga, Cayuga, Seneca, and Tuscarora Indian tribes of the northeastern United States.

7. Guy B. Senese, *Self-Determination and the Social Education of Native Americans* (New York: Praeger, 1991), 146.

8. Ibid., 147.

9. Fay G. Cohen, *Treaties on Trial: The Continuing Controversy over Northwest Indian Fishing Rights* (Seattle: University of Washington Press, 1986), 69.

10. Quoted in Senese, *Self-Determination*, 145.

11. Ibid., 148.

12. Ibid., 144.

13. Troy R. Johnson, "Part 3: Native North American History, 1960–94," in *Chronology of Native North American History*, ed. Duane Champagne (Detroit: Gale Research, 1994), 355.

14. Ibid., 361–62.

15. Quoted in Senese, *Self-Determination*, 224.

16. Robert Hecht, "Taos Pueblo and the Struggle for Blue Lake," *American Indian Culture and Research Journal* 13:1 (1989): 55.

17. R. C. Gordon-McCutchan, *The Taos Indians and the Battle for Blue Lake* (Santa Fe, N.Mex.: Red Crane Books, 1991), xvi–xvii. This book recounts the story of the government taking of Blue Lake and the Taos Indians' successful campaign to recover it.

18. Alvin Josephy, "The American Indian and the Bureau of Indian Affairs, 1969: A Study with Recommendations," 24 February 1969. Report commissioned by President Richard M. Nixon.

19. Edgar S. Cahn, "Postscript," in *Our Brother's Keeper: The Indian in White America*, ed. Edgar S. Cahn (New York: New Community Press, 1969), 187–90.

20. Ibid.

21. R. D. Arnold, *Alaska Native Land Claims* (Anchorage: Alaska Native Foundation, 1978).

22. Cohen, *Treaties on Trial*, 82–83.

23. The Nixon presidential archives make no mention of the invasion of Cambodia, since it was largely a secret operation (though poorly kept) at the time. President Nixon and his staff make direct analogies among the Indian people on Alcatraz, the events at My Lai, and the shootings at Kent State. It was agreed that the American people would not stand by and see Indian people massacred and taken off Alcatraz in body bags.

24. Judith Clavir Albert and Stewart Edward Albert, *The Sixties Papers: Documents of a Rebellious Decade* (New York: Praeger, 1984), 18.

25. Wub-e-ke-niew, *We Have a Right to Exist* (New York: Black Thistle Press, 1995), xxxix.

26. Veterans Administration Statistical Brief, "Native American Veterans," SB 70-85-3 (October 1985), Washington, D.C.

27. Quoted in Stan Steiner, *The New Indians* (New York: Harper & Row, 1968), 282.

28. Ibid.

29. Joan Ablon, "Relocated American Indians in the San Francisco Bay Area: Social Interaction and Indian Identity," *Human Organization* 23 (Winter 1964): 297.

30. Vine Deloria, Jr., *Behind the Trail of Broken Treaties: An Indian Declaration of Independence* (Austin: University of Texas Press, 1985), 34.

31. Quoted in Alvin M. Josephy, Jr., *The American Indian Fight for Freedom* (New Haven, Conn.: Yale University Press, 1978), 84. Clyde Warrior is often referred to as the founder of the Red Power movement.

32. Quoted in Jack D. Forbes, *Native Americans and Nixon: Presidential Politics and Minority Self-Determination, 1969–1972* (Los Angeles: American Indian Studies Center, University of California, 1981), 28. Brightman founded and began publication of *Warpath* in 1968, providing a voice for the rising urban Indian youth groups.

33. Quoted in National Council on Indian Opportunity, "Public Forum before the Committee of Urban Indians, San Francisco, Calif.," 11–12 April 1969, 3 (hereafter NCIO, "Public Forum"). In the possession of Adam Fortunate Eagle, Fallon Indian Reservation, Fallon, Nev.

34. Joan Ablon, "Relocated Indians in the San Francisco Bay Area: Social Interaction and Indian Identity," *Human Organization* 23 (1964): 296–304.

35. NCIO, "Public Forum," 39.

36. Ibid., 41.

37. Quoted in Steiner, *New Indians*, 45.

38. Ibid.

39. Ibid.

40. Johnson, "Part 3," 355–57.

41. During this period, the University of California, Davis, was attempting to acquire the same site for its own use. It was the occupation of the intended site by Indian youth, some of which had been involved in the Alcatraz occupation, that ultimately led to success for the Indian-controlled university. In April 1971, the

federal government formally turned this land over to the trustees of Deganawida-Quetzalcoatl (D-Q) University, a joint American Indian and Chicano university. One of the demands of the Alcatraz occupiers, in 1964 and again in 1969, was the establishment of an Indian university on Alcatraz Island. While this never occurred, the establishment of D-Q University was seen by many as the fulfillment of that demand.

42. Troy Johnson, *The Occupation of Alcatraz Island: Indian Self-Determination and the Rise of Indian Activism* (Urbana: University of Illinois Press, 1996). The occupations took place on 9 March 1964, the night of 9–10 November 1969, and 20 November 1969.

43. Belva Cottier interview with John Garvey, San Francisco, Calif., 13 May 1989. Copy in the possession of Troy Johnson.

44. NCIO, "Public Forum."

45. Luis S. Kemnitzer, "Personal Memories of Alcatraz, 1969" (chapter 7 of this volume), 114–15.

46. Johnson, *Occupation of Alcatraz Island*, 119.

47. Earl Livermore (Blackfoot) interview with John D. Sylvester, 8 April 1970, Doris Duke Oral History Project, University of Utah, Salt Lake City.

48. Johnson, *Occupation of Alcatraz Island*, 48.

49. Ibid.

50. "Unsigned Proclamation" reproduced in *Alcatraz Is Not an Island*, ed. Peter Blue Cloud (Berkeley, Calif.: Wingbow Press, 1972), 40–42.

51. Johnson, *Occupation of Alcatraz Island*, 71–72.

52. Ibid., 40–41.

53. Ibid., 154–55.

54. Ibid., 206.

55. Ibid., 152, 169.

56. Ibid., 182–83.

57. Ibid., 226.

58. Vine Deloria, Jr., "The Rise of Indian Activism," in *The Social Reality of Ethnic America*, ed. R. Gomez, C. Collingham, R. Endo, and K. Jackson (Lexington, Mass.: D. C. Heath, 1974), 184–85.

59. Vine Deloria, Jr., correspondence with the authors, 1993.

60. Wilma Mankiller telephone interview with Joane Nagel, Tahlequah, Okla., 27 November 1991. Transcript in the authors' files.

61. George Horse Capture telephone interview with Joane Nagel, Fort Belknap, Mont., 24 May 1994. Transcript in the authors' files. See also George Horse Capture, "An American Indian Perspective," in *Seeds of Change: A Quincentennial Commemoration*, ed. Herman J. Viola and Carolyn Margolis (Washington, D.C.: Smithsonian Institution Press, 1991).

62. John Echohawk telephone interview with Joane Nagel, Boulder, Colo., 9 July 1993. Transcript in the authors' files.

63. Leonard Peltier telephone interview with Joane Nagel, Leavenworth, Kans., 1 June 1993. Transcript in the authors' files.

64. Frances Wise telephone interview with Joane Nagel, Oklahoma City, Okla., 24 August 1993. Transcript in the authors' files.

65. Quoted in Judith Antell, "American Indian Women Activists" (Ph.D. diss., University of California, Berkeley, 1989), 58.

66. Grace Thorpe interview with John Trudell on "Radio Free Alcatraz," 12 December 1969. Transcript available from Pacifica Radio Archive, 3729 Cahvenga Boulevard, North Hollywood, CA 91604.

67. Loretta Flores telephone interview with Joane Nagel, Lawrence, Kans., 12 May 1993. Transcript in the authors' files.

68. "Indians Seize Army Center for Use as Cultural Base," *New York Times*, 4 November 1970, 6. This land later became the site of Deganawida-Quetzalcoatl (D-Q) University. See *Akwesasne Notes* (January–February 1971): 17.

69. William M. Blair, "24 Indians Seized in Capital Clash," *New York Times*, 23 September 1971, 49.

70. Ward Churchill and James Vander Wall, *Agents of Repression: The FBI's Secret War against the Black Panther Party and the American Indian Movement* (Boston: South End Press, 1988), 121; Rex Weyler, *Blood of the Land* (New York: Everett House, 1984), 24, 42–43; Peter Matthiessen, *In the Spirit of Crazy Horse* (New York: Viking, 1991), 37–40, 49–52; Alvin M. Josephy, Jr., *Now That the Buffalo's Gone* (New York: Knopf, 1982), 228–31.

71. Johnson, *Occupation of Alcatraz Island*, 219–20; Wub-e-ke-niew, *We Have the Right to Exist*, xl–xlvii.

72. Churchill and Vander Wall, *Agents of Repression*, 121.

73. Ibid. Ironically, several researchers also cite the role of common prison experiences in the formation of the American Indian Movement organization. See Matthiessen, *In the Spirit of Crazy Horse*, 34; Weyler, *Blood of the Land*, 35; Rachel A. Bonney, "Forms of Supratribal Indian Interaction in the United States" (Ph.D. diss., University of Arizona, 1975), 154–55.

74. Fay G. Cohen, "The Indian Patrol in Minneapolis: Social Control and Social Change in an Urban Context" (Ph.D. diss., University of Minnesota, 1973), 52.

75. Ibid., 49–50; Jeanne Guillemin, *Urban Renegades: The Cultural Strategy of American Indians* (New York: Columbia University Press, 1975); Roy Bongartz, "The New Indians," in *Native Americans Today*, ed. H. M. Bahr, B. A. Chadwick, and R. C. Day (New York: Harper & Row, 1968), 495.

76. Russell Means with Marvin J. Wolf, *Where White Men Fear to Tread: The Autobiography of Russell Means* (New York: St. Martin's Press, 1995), 540.

77. Today, most commentators, participants, and observers refer to the 1973 siege at Wounded Knee, South Dakota, as "Wounded Knee." At the time, the press and commentators often called the siege "Wounded Knee II," to distinguish it from the U.S. 7th Cavalry's massacre of Lakotas which took place there in December 1890. See Robert Utley, *The Last Days of the Sioux Nation* (New Haven, Conn.: Yale University Press, 1963), 110.

78. See Edward Lazarus, *Black Hills, White Justice: The Sioux Nation versus the United States, 1775 to the Present* (New York: HarperCollins, 1991), chap. 12; Matthiessen, *In the Spirit of Crazy Horse*, chap. 3; Churchill and Vander Wall, *Agents of Repression*, chap. 5; Stanley D. Lyman, *Wounded Knee 1973: A Personal Account* (Lincoln: University of Nebraska Press, 1991); Rolland Dewing, *Wounded Knee: The Meaning and Significance of the Second Incident* (New York: Irvington, 1985).

79. For instance, Lazarus reports that, up to that point, the "Pine Ridge Sioux had never reelected a president to a second term" (*Black Hills, White Justice*, 309).

80. Ibid., 307.

81. The most celebrated of the cases involves Leonard Peltier, who was tried

and convicted for the deaths of two FBI agents who were shot on the Pine Ridge Reservation in 1975. See Matthiessen, *In the Spirit of Crazy Horse*, 162.

82. For instance, Wilson remained in office and was reelected after a challenge by AIM leader Russell Means in 1974. Wilson died in 1990. See Churchill and Vander Wall, *Agents of Repression*, 189; Martin Waldron, "President of Oglala Sioux Is Re-elected," *New York Times*, 9 February 1974, 23; Matthiessen, *In the Spirit of Crazy Horse*, 581.

83. While several of these post–Wounded Knee occupations were marked by intratribal conflict, the Puyallup occupation of the detention center appears to have been undertaken by a unified tribe.

84. Grace Lichtenstein, "Custer's Defeat Commemorated by Entreaties on Peace," *New York Times*, 25 June 1976, II-1.

85. For a general description of anti-Indian backlash groups and activities in the late 1970s, see the series of articles in "Nationwide Backlash against the Indian Tribes," the 18 July 1977 supplement of the *Yakima Nation Review:* Richard La Course, "Anti-Indian Backlash Growing; Tribes, Groups Form Defense Tactics"; Carole Wright, "What People Have Formed Backlash Groups?"; June Adams, "Three Major 'Backlash Bills' in Congress"; June Adams and Richard La Course, "Backlash Barrage Erupts across U.S." See also Fay G. Cohen, "Implementing Indian Treaty Fishing Rights: Conflict and Cooperation," in *Critical Issues in Native North America*, vol. 2, ed. W. Churchill (Copenhagen: International Work Group for Indigenous Affairs, 1991), 155–73.

86. Ken Stern, *Loud Hawk: The U.S. versus the American Indian Movement* (Norman: University of Oklahoma Press, 1994), 93–98. The deaths were never investigated, but Indian people suspect the FBI was involved.

87. See, for example, Wub-e-ke-niew, *We Have the Right to Exist*, xlv, 232–33; Josephy, *Now That the Buffalo's Gone*, 254–55.

88. Camp Yellow Thunder was established in the early 1980s to protest federal violations of Sioux treaties and the refusal of the federal government to return the Black Hills. See Lazarus, *Black Hills, White Justice*, 411–12; and Donald Worster, *Under Western Skies: Nature and History in the American West* (New York: Oxford University Press, 1992), chap. 8.

89. See, for example, Leila Rupp and Verta Taylor, *Survival in the Doldrums: The American Women's Rights Movement, 1945 to the 1960s* (New York: Oxford University Press, 1987); Doug McAdam, *Freedom Summer* (New York: Oxford University Press, 1988); Rick Fantasia, *Cultures of Solidarity: Consciousness, Action, and Contemporary American Workers* (Berkeley: University of California Press, 1988); Verta Taylor and Nancy E. Whittier, "Collective Identity in Social Movement Communities: Lesbian Feminist Mobilization," in *Frontiers in Social Movement Theory*, ed. A. D. Morris and C. M. Mueller (New Haven, Conn.: Yale University Press, 1992), 104–20; Joane Nagel, "American Indian Ethnic Renewal: Politics and the Resurgence of Identity," *American Sociological Review* 60 (1995): 947–65.

90. McAdam, *Freedom Summer.*

91. Fantasia, *Cultures of Solidarity.*

92. Annette Kuhlmann, "Collaborative Research on Biculturalism among the Kickapoo Tribe of Oklahoma" (Ph.D. diss., University of Kansas, 1989); Richard H. White, *Tribal Assets: The Rebirth of Native America* (New York: Henry Holt, 1990), 124; Carol Ward, "The Intersection of Ethnic and Gender Identities: The Role of

Northern Cheyenne Women in Cultural Recovery," paper presented at the annual meeting of the Society for the Scientific Study of Religion, Raleigh, N.C., October 1993, p. 86.

93. Joane Nagel, *American Indian Ethnic Renewal: Red Power and the Resurgence of Identity and Culture* (New York: Oxford University Press, 1996), 195–200.

SELECTED BIBLIOGRAPHY: ALCATRAZ AND THE ACTIVIST PERIOD

Cornell, Stephen. *The Return of the Native: American Indian Political Resurgence.* New York: Oxford University Press, 1988.

Churchill, Ward, and James Vander Wall. *Agents of Repression: The FBI's Secret Wars against the Black Panther Party and the American Indian Movement.* Boston: South End Press, 1988.

Crow Dog, Mary, and Richard Erdoes. *Lakota Woman.* New York: Grove Weidenfeld, 1990.

Fortunate Eagle, Adam. *Alcatraz! Alcatraz! The Indian Occupation of 1969–71.* San Francisco: Heyday Books, 1992.

Johnson, Troy. *The Indian Occupation of Alcatraz Island: Indian Self-Determination and the Rise of Indian Activism.* Urbana: University of Illinois Press, 1996.

Matthiessen, Peter. *In the Spirit of Crazy Horse.* New York: Viking, 1991.

Means, Russell, with Marvin J. Wolf. *Where White Men Fear to Tread: The Autobiography of Russell Means.* New York: St. Martin's Press, 1995.

Nagel, Joane. *American Indian Ethnic Renewal: Red Power and the Resurgence of Identity and Culture.* New York: Oxford University Press, 1995.

Smith, Paul Chaat, and Robert Allen Warrior. *Like a Hurricane: The Indian Movement from Alcatraz to Wounded Knee.* New York: The Free Press, 1996.

Stern, Kenneth S. *Loud Hawk: The U.S. versus the American Indian Movement.* Norman: University of Oklahoma Press, 1994.

2

ALCATRAZ, ACTIVISM, AND

ACCOMMODATION

Vine Deloria, Jr.

Alcatraz and Wounded Knee 1973 have come to symbolize the revival of Indian fortunes in the late twentieth century, so we hesitate to discuss the realities of the time or to look critically at their actual place in modern Indian history. We conclude that it is better to wrap these events in romantic notions and broker that feeling in exchange for further concessions from the federal government; consequently, we fail to learn from them the hard lessons that will serve us well in leaner times.

Activism in the 1950s was sporadic but intense. In 1957, Lumbee people surrounded a Ku Klux Klan gathering in North Carolina and escorted the hooded representatives of white supremacy back to their homes sans weapons and costumes. In 1961, a strange mixture of Six Nations people and non-Indian supporters attempted a citizens' arrest of the secretary of the interior, and, sometime during this period, a band of "True Utes" briefly took over the agency offices at Fort Duchesne. The only context for these events was the long suffering of small groups of people bursting forth in an incident that illustrated oppression but suggested no answer to pressing problems. In 1964, the "fish-ins" in the Pacific Northwest produced the first activism with an avowed goal; continual agitation in that region eventually resulted in *U.S. v. Washington*, which affirmed once and for all the property rights of Northwest tribes for both subsistence and commercial fishing.

Indians benefited substantially from the civil rights movement of the 1960s and the ensuing doctrines concerning the poor, which surfaced in the Economic Opportunity Act and more particularly in its administration. The civil rights movement had roots in a hundred small gatherings of concerned attorneys brought together by Jack Greenberg and Thurgood Marshall to determine the legal and philosophical basis for overturning *Plessy v. Ferguson*. Concentrating on the concept of *equality*, a series of test cases involving access to professional education in the border states cut away the unexamined assumption that separate facilities for higher education automatically meant equality of treatment and equality of the substance of education.

In 1954, *Brown v. Topeka Board of Education* stripped away the cloak of indifference and hypocrisy and required the dismantling of segregated schools. By extension, if schools were to be integrated, why not lunch counters and buses, and why not equality under the law in all public places and programs? The *Brown* strategy was created on behalf of the oppressed multitudes of African Americans but did not involve the rank and file people until the movement went into the streets and lunch counters of the South. With the announcement of "Black Power" by Stokely Carmichael and SNCC in 1966—made possible in some measure by the insistence of federal War on Poverty administrators that the "poor" knew better than anyone else what poverty was and how to combat it—the civil rights movement became a people's movement.

A people's movement has many benefits—the mass of minority groups are involved, and political strength increases dramatically—but it also has immense vulnerability in that goals that can be seen, articulated, and achieved are surrendered in favor of symbolic acts that illustrate and demonstrate the suffering and frustrations of the people. Symbolic acts demand attention from an otherwise unaware general public, but they also fail to articulate the necessity of specific actions that can and must be taken by the government at the local, state, and federal levels to alleviate the crisis. Consequently, the choice of remedy is given to the institutional structure that oppresses people and to the good and bad politicians and career bureaucrats who operate the institution.

The Poor People's March of 1968 best exemplifies the problem of a people's movement unable to articulate specific solutions and see them through to completion. Organized partially in memory of the slain Martin Luther King and partially as an effort to secure increases in the funding of social programs, the march floundered when participants spent their time harassing members of the cabinet about problems that had no immediate solution and demanding sympathy and understanding from federal officials who could not translate these concerns into programmatic responses. Smaller protests had maintained a decent level of funding for poverty programs in past years, but, this time, the march faced the bitter reality of the Vietnam War and the impossibility of continuing to expand the federal budget into unrealistic deficits.

It is important to note that, while the Indian fishing rights struggle maintained itself with measurable goals, Alcatraz represented an Indian version of the Poor People's March. The proclamation presented by the first invaders of the island demanded a bewildering set of responses from the federal government, focusing on transfer of the island's title to an Indian organization and the funding of an educational center on the island for the thousands of Indians who had made the Bay Area their home. The popular interpretation of the occupation was that Indians were entitled to own the island because it was federal surplus property and therefore qualified under a provision of the 1868 treaty of Fort Laramie.

Unfortunately, the treaty provision was a myth. Red Cloud had simply remained in the Powder River country until the government withdrew its troops from the Bozeman Trail and then, satisfied that the trail was closed, arrived at Fort Laramie in November 1868 to sign the treaty. During the Alcatraz occupation, when White House staff and Department of Interior lawyers looked at the treaty, they could find no phrase that justified returning the island to the Indian occupants; consequently, they were blocked from using any executive powers to resolve the crisis.

The initial group of Indian occupants was composed of students from Bay Area colleges and universities, but, as the occupation continued, these people were replaced with enthusiastic recruits from across the nation and with unemployed people who had nowhere else to go. The mood of the occupants was that they should use the press as often as possible; thus the goal of the movement quickly became confused, with various spokespeople articulating different philosophies on different occasions.

The difference between Alcatraz and the fishing rights fight, and between the Brown litigation and the Black Power movement, should be made clear: Behind the sit-ins and the fish-ins was the almost certain probability that, should activists be convicted at the trial court level, they would have their convictions overturned by a higher court and/or the object of their protest would be upheld at a higher level of litigation. *Brown* and the Medicine Creek fishing rights treaty were already federal law before people went out to protest; the protests were made on behalf of impartial enforcement of existing law. This foundation of legality did not exist for either the Poor People's March or the occupation of Alcatraz. Therefore, in legal terms, these activities meant nothing.

My role in Alcatraz was sporadic and, in a few instances, not welcomed by some of the activists on the Rock. While I was director of the National Congress of American Indians (NCAI), I had worked for several years with people in the Bay Area as part of the NCAI's concern for relocated Indians. I entered law school in the fall of 1967 and, by the time of the occupation, had already written *Custer Died for Your Sins*, which was released in early October 1969. Some years before, Richard McKenzie and others had briefly landed on Alcatraz, and, in the years since that first invasion, Bay Area activists such as Adam Nordwall had disrupted Columbus Day celebrations and, with some modest successes, generally tried to focus the attention of Bay Area politics on urban Indian problems. Ironically, some of the people who were now shouting "Red Power" into every microphone they could find had called me a communist the year before for doing a Frank McGee NBC news interview that advocated Red Power.

Adam Nordwall saw that the occupation would flounder unless it was tied to some larger philosophical issue that could be seen by the American public as important to their own concerns for justice. During the fall of 1969, I was asked several times to come out to Alcatraz to discuss how the people on the island could transform the occupation into a federal issue that could be resolved by congressional action. I favored announcing that not only did Indians want the island but we wanted a federal policy of land restoration that would provide a decent land base for small reservations, return submarginal lands to tribes that had them, and, in some cases, restore original reservation boundaries.

On Christmas Eve 1969, I flew out to California to discuss the land issue with people on the island, but the meeting never got off the ground. Instead of listening to our presentation on land restoration, the activists began quarreling about who was in charge of the operation. Richard Oakes had many supporters, but he also had many rivals. Adam and I were considered intruders because we had not been in the original invasion. About all we got out of the meeting was the sneer that the activists had the whole world watching them, and they were in control of Indian policy. We pointed out that a sensible program had to be articulated so that the administration could act, but we got no positive response.

In January 1970, hoping to highlight a land and treaty issue, I invited Merv Griffin to come out to Alcatraz and do part of a show from there. Unfortunately, many of the people on the Rock had not moved forward in their thinking; Merv got the old response of how the island belonged to Indians under the 1868 treaty and how they wanted to establish an educational and vocational training facility on the island.

In the spring of 1970, a group of us held a national urban Indian conference on Alcatraz in another effort to provide a context for securing the island. In November 1969, this same urban group had held its conference the weekend before the San Francisco Indian Center burned, but now, under different leadership, we were trying to focus everything on the Bay Area in the hope of defining an issue that the public would embrace. The meeting was not long under way when a man and woman began to scream at each other across the room, viciously and seemingly without any provocation. Every time anyone would propose a course of action, one or the other would jump up and let loose a string of curses designed to infuriate everyone. Most people sat there politely listening to the nonsense, but eventually the meeting just dissolved. Later, we discovered they were a husband and wife who went through this performance at every meeting they attended.

While our meeting was being held, we learned that Richard Oakes and his supporters had been thrown off the island the day before and that they were likely to confront us when we returned to the mainland. We met only one sullen young man who warned us that he was going to remember our names and faces. Later that evening, as we sat around trying to figure out what to do, we hit on a plan. We had someone call Oakes's headquarters and, in his best reservation English, relate that he was supervising two buses of Navajo boys who were traveling to the Hoopa Bear Dance and wanted to be housed for the night. The Oakes contingent immediately tried to enlist these Navajo as a force to help Oakes recapture the island. They gave us directions for finding their headquarters, and we promised to come help them. A few minutes after hanging up the phone, we decided it would be even better to include buses of Navajo girls, so we had a rather prominent Indian woman call the headquarters and pretend that she was matron over two busloads of girls from Navajo Community College who were looking to make contact with the Navajo boys. This phone call created a dilemma for us and for Oakes's people. They wanted to get the two busloads of girls and lose the boys; we wondered how long we could continue to drive four phantom buses around the Bay Area.

Our pretend Navajo man then called Oakes's people back and said he had gotten lost and was in Oakland, and we got new directions for reaching their headquarters. Our woman then got back on the phone and told Oakes's group that the girls' buses were only a few blocks away. Their response was that they would go out and buy food and get ready to welcome the girls, apparently forgetting that the boys' buses would be along shortly also. We hung up and pondered the situation we had created. The consensus was that we should call back and confess the whole thing before everyone was inconvenienced. We were just about to confess when one of our group said, "Wait a minute! Real Indians would just go their own way and not say a word; we are thinking like responsible, educated Indians." So we just went back to our hotel to bed.

The next morning, as we embarked for Alcatraz to finish the meeting, we were greeted by two surly Oakes supporters. They told us to go ahead and visit the island, but they assured us that we would not stay long because they had reinforcements of four hundred Navajo arriving momentarily and we would be thrown off the Rock along with the anti-Oakes people. Needless to say, our meeting went well, and the Navajo never did arrive. I will not mention the names in our little group, but I can confess that they are still prominent, responsible, national Indian leaders.

The occupation of Alcatraz lingered on. A rougher group of people occupied the island, and it became useless to try to make sense of the occupation. Increasingly, it became a hazard to go out there. Eventually, many of the buildings were burned, and feeble, nonsensical ultimatums were issued by the declining population on the Rock. Finally, the government swooped down and took the remaining people away. I visited the island about a decade later and heard a surprisingly mild and pro-Indian explanation of the occupation from a Park Service guide. I walked around the grounds and remembered some of the difficult meetings we had held there and how, several times, we almost had a coalition that could have affected land policy. Unfortunately, most of the people involved in the occupation had no experience in formulating policy and saw their activities as primarily aimed at awakening the American public to the plight of Indians. Thus a great opportunity to change federal programs for Indians was lost.

The Trail of Broken Treaties came along in the fall of 1972. By that time, the activists had devised the Twenty Points, which, in my opinion, is the best summary document of reforms put forth in this century. Written primarily by Hank Adams, who supervised the fishing rights struggle until the Supreme Court ruled in favor of Indians, it is comprehensive and philosophical and has broad policy lines that can still be adopted to create some sense of fairness and symmetry in federal Indian policy.

Then came the Wounded Knee occupation, with its aftermath of trials and further violence. Indians were well represented in the media from the Alcatraz occupation through the Wounded Knee trials, but, unfortunately, each event dealt primarily with the symbols of oppression and did not project possible courses of action that might be taken to solve problems.

The policy posture of Indians at Alcatraz was part of a historical process begun during the War on Poverty when people demanded action from the government but failed to articulate the changes they wanted. With the incoming Nixon administration in 1969, we clamored for an Indian to be appointed as commissioner. Because we failed to support Robert Bennett, who was already occupying the office, the inept Louie Bruce was installed. Bruce's chaotic administration produced an era in which résumés were enhanced and job descriptions were watered down so that the respective administrations could appoint Indian puppets to symbolize the presence of Indians in the policymaking process. Today the government, under Ada Deer, is at work trying to create a new set of categories—"historic" and "non-historic" tribes—so that benefits and services can be radically reduced. When Indians do not clearly articulate what they want, the government feels free to improvise, even if it means creating new policies that have no roots in anything except the fantasies of the creator.

Alcatraz was more than a protest against the oppressive conditions under which Indians lived. In large part, it was a message that we wanted to determine our own destiny and make our own decisions. That burden is still upon us and weighs heavily when contemporary tribal chairpeople are consulted about policy directions. Almost always, immediate concerns or irritating technicalities are regarded as important in the consultative process, and, consequently, it is increasingly difficult to determine exactly where people think we are going. Like the activists at Alcatraz, we often mill around, keenly aware that we have the ears of the public but uncertain what to do next. Until we can sketch out realistic scenarios of human and resource goals, we continue to resemble those occupants of the Rock a quarter of a century ago: We want change, but we do not know what change.

3

URBAN INDIANS AND THE

OCCUPATION OF ALCATRAZ ISLAND

Adam (Nordwall) Fortunate Eagle

It was 1951 when my wife Bobbie and I moved to San Francisco with three hundred dollars in savings and all of our possessions in three suitcases. We rented a tiny apartment and set up housekeeping on the forty-eight dollars per week that I earned after taxes.

I endured the mindless racism of being called "chief" and "blanket-assed Indian" on the job, but a year later, at the age of twenty-one, I had passed the state test to become a licensed termite inspector. A decade later, I was vice president and general manager of a major East Bay termite exterminating firm.

Those early years in the Bay Area were a period of financial struggle and hard work, but I was on my way to becoming financially successful. In fact, by the late 1960s, I owned my own business, the First American Termite Company; employed fifteen people; lived in a comfortable, suburban house with Bobbie and our three children; and even drove a Cadillac. Nothing would have been easier than assimilating into middle-class America.

Not only was assimilation tempting, but it was encouraged in a society that preferred its Indians to be caricatures. There was no easy path "back to the blanket," as it was termed, but, for my young family, there was reason—and need—to explore my heritage and theirs. We took trips to the reservation at Red Lake or to Bobbie's family home on the reservation in Nevada, but these trips were touring excursions among relics of something that was no longer a real and daily part of our lives. Perhaps we would have lost even that much of our past had the times not brought it back to us.

During the Korean War of 1950–53, San Francisco served as a hub for returning veterans, many of them Indians we had known from home or from Haskell Institute. We would see them passing through on their way back to a culture and a way of life that was still trivialized by urban Americans who

This excerpt from *Alcatraz! Alcatraz! The Indian Occupation of 1969–71* has been reprinted with the permission of Adam Fortunate Eagle and Heyday Books.

wanted to treat Indians as souvenirs. In 1958, we began to notice a surge of young reservation Indians brought to the Bay Area under the federal relocation program.

Indians began to find each other, partially out of loneliness and confusion in their new urban surroundings and partially out of an urge to share a cultural identity. First came the picnics in Golden Gate Park that grew into drumming and singing sessions. These grew into a powwow circuit of social gatherings that, often unconsciously, made their own subtle political statement of cultural unity and affirmation.

So great was the hunger for powwows that we would gather even when it meant serving a white man's need for a Hollywood version of Native America: the Indian Days powwow at San Jose's Frontier Village amusement park. It was at that powwow that I first met Cy Williams and my life began to change dramatically. The powwow was open to all Indians, and, even if it served to entertain tourists and sightseers, it also filled our growing need for cultural expression. I outfitted my small son Addie with the head of a fox-fur stole I had found at a Goodwill store and suited myself in a turkey-feather approximation of something Chippewa, complete with little Christmas bells about one-third the size of those worn by traditional dancers.

When a mutual friend pointed me out to Cy as someone from his own tribe, I was doing my best in what I imagined then to be good traditional style. I realize now that my dancing was only a "tinkle, tinkle, tinkle" Hollywood imitation in Cy's eyes. Nevertheless, we became lifelong friends and together stepped out onto a new road for urbanized Indians.

Cy and Aggie Williams were Chippewa people from the Cass Lake Reservation in Minnesota, located just fifty miles southeast of my own reservation at Red Lake. Without intending to do so, Cy had become something of a success story for the relocation program. With BIA help, he worked as a machinist and continued to develop his skills. On the job, he also developed a wiry blue-collar grit, a rough-talking independence that always seemed to contrast with Aggie's frail, quiet humor. He and Aggie lived in a pin-neat cottage filled with Indian trinkets, curios, and knickknacks.

Cy's old blue panel van was decorated the same way. Little buckskin dolls sat on the dashboard and decals of animals or Indian faces covered the back end. In later years, many other Indians like Cy would proudly display bumper stickers proclaiming, "I'm Chippewa and Proud of It" or "Custer Died for Your Sins," but, in those early years of the 1960s, Cy and Aggie were making a statement about themselves with all that was available: touristy trinkets. They were a link with home and a way for Cy to express what he felt like shouting.

"Ah, the hell with it," he would say in frequent frustration, throwing his arms across his chest as if he were tossing off a cur dog. The four of us spoke often about the problems faced by relocated Indians, and gradually Cy began to pass on to me some of his great knowledge of traditional dancing and our own culture. With Cy's and Aggie's help and advice, bit by bit I began to replace my fox fur and Christmas-bell imitations with the vibrant beadwork and stiff quills that are authentic and meaningful to our people.

Our neighbors in San Leandro would peer over the fence at us on evenings when Cy rehearsed me and six-year-old Addie in the finer points of traditional dancing. We worked hard as the heavy sleigh bells tied to our ankles chimed to the rhythm of tape-recorded drums and singing.

All over the Bay Area, picnics were growing into powwows almost every weekend. The government had certainly not intended or wanted such a resurgence of traditional gatherings. The relocation program had purposely scattered all its "clients" in the same rundown neighborhoods and slums, but never too near each other. The powwows in rented halls and public parks gradually expanded under the sponsorship of new Indian clubs. Some of them, such as the Sioux Club and the Navajo Club, formed around tribal identities; others, such as the Four Winds Club, focused on social objectives. Weekend powwows brought us all together; new drumming and singing groups were formed, news of home was exchanged. All of it, I'm sure, caused the BIA great consternation.

Cy showed great patience with me and Addie as we learned his smooth, flowing approach to traditional dancing. But he had little tolerance for the sufferings of the increasing numbers of young people and families brought from the reservations. By 1961, Cy had become actively involved in a number of Indian activities, and he served on the board of directors of the newly established Intertribal Friendship House in Oakland, a project of the American Friends Service Committee. "These guys serving on the board," Cy told me with concern, "are mostly white people. A bunch of good-hearted Quakers who just don't know much about Indians. Shouldn't we be more involved in running our own activities? We have had white people telling us what to do and how to do it for too long now. They should be helping us run Indian programs, not directing us!"

I saw what was happening to the Indians in the Bay Area and compared it to "self-determination" for Indian people. I realized that Cy's words made good sense. "What do you want me to do?" I asked.

"Get involved. Help us. We need Indian leadership. You know how to get things done and that's what we need right now," said Cy, who had begun urging other Indians to get involved in the community. "There are a lot of Indian clubs forming right now, and maybe by working together we could do more good for our people."

We contacted all of the Indian groups that we could find in the East Bay; after several meetings at the Intertribal Friendship House, we decided to form an umbrella organization called the United Bay Area Council of American Indian Affairs, Inc. This was shortened to United Council. The Pomo Club, Navajo Club, Haida-Tlingit Club, Chippewa Club, Ladies Club, United Paiutes, Four Winds Club, Intertribal Dancers, Haskell Alumni, Radio-Electronics Training School (R.E.T.S.), Sports Committee, Intertribal Friendship House, and American Indian Culture Group (San Quentin) were all affiliated with the new council.

The United Council was an Indian mini-version of the United Nations. Each affiliated group sent its own representatives to the council, and small name plates were placed in front of delegates during the meetings to indicate the groups they represented. Millie Barichello of the Creek tribe, representing the Haskell Alumni, was elected secretary-treasurer; Al Hicks, an elementary school teacher representing the Navajo Club, was elected vice chairman; and I was elected chairman.

The affiliated groups of the Bay Area were bound together by shared interests and shared concerns for the welfare of our people. Working together, we were able to help maintain a stable Indian community within the larger urban context. Each affiliated group maintained its own identity and conducted its own programs while, at the same time, exercising its voice in formulating larger community objectives. This collective voice gave the United Council its strength and direction. The wide variety of activities undertaken by the United Council would have seemed unrealistic to many experts in community affairs. Yet the diverse makeup of the council allowed us to undertake a wide-ranging set of projects.

Most of our projects were designed to help the newly arrived relocatees overcome culture shock as they adapted to their new surroundings. The Intertribal Friendship House provided a setting for Thanksgiving dinner, Christmas parties, and a variety of ceremonial events, and most of the affiliated clubs held their meetings and social activities there. It served as the hub of the Indian activities in the East Bay, just as the Indian Center in San Francisco served the needs of that community.

The Bay Area Indian community continued to grow as Indians kept pouring into the area, and the United Council gradually took on a more activist orientation until finally, in 1969, it became the driving force behind the occupation of Alcatraz.

Plans for the Occupation of Alcatraz Island

The United Council met every other Wednesday night at the Friendship House. We sat at folding banquet room tables arranged in a square that allowed equal space for each of the twenty or so delegates from affiliated clubs.

"Indian time" or the demands of a family and a day's work sometimes kept us from starting at 7:30 P.M., but our professional careers and obligations gave our meetings a decorum worthy of any boardroom. Folding partitions that separated the dining room from the recreation hall could be opened to give us more space, which we began to need as our organized meetings became more like community gatherings of all interested Indians in the area. In some ways, the council meetings functioned like network news programs. They gathered information, shared it among the people, and allowed us to see what was going on in the country—specifically, the steady attempt to erase American Indian culture from America.

In 1968, when Alcatraz was declared surplus property to be given to the city of San Francisco, many of the members of the United Council remembered the 1964 Sioux action laying claim to the Rock. The government had supposedly put that matter to rest in 1965 by concluding that the 1868 treaty with the Sioux applied only to federal lands taken from that tribe and then abandoned. The government said that Alcatraz had never belonged to the Sioux. If it had ever belonged to any Indians, it would have been California Indians, most of whom did not legally exist as tribes in the eyes of the U.S. government. Yet the Sioux action conceived by Richard McKenzie had been successful in what it set out to do: point out the government violations of the 1868 treaty and make symbols of them. The useless prison island now symbolized the contempt with which the government regarded native claims.

There it was, a dramatic outcropping right in the middle of the bay. Every time you crossed the Golden Gate Bridge or the Bay Bridge, you saw that little spot in the water and remembered. Even at night, the revolving searchlight on the Coast Guard lighthouse beckoned to you. And you thought, "Those twenty acres and all those buildings, all empty, falling apart from neglect. And we have nothing."

Even so, when Alcatraz came up in United Council discussions, the talk was only tentative. We had a lot of other projects that occupied our time, our limited resources, and the talents of our people. Alcatraz and the future we envisioned for it only slowly came into focus.

Basically, our initial idea was to write a proposal for the use of Alcatraz by Indian people and then file the necessary application. If this would not work under the terms of the Sioux treaty, then we would try some other arrangement. We were not thinking of taking radical action; another surprise invasion and occupation was then still far from our minds. We were thinking of negotiating with the federal authorities to attempt to acquire Alcatraz peacefully. We did not even necessarily want the whole island; some portion of it would have been sufficient for a start. Essentially, the message would be this: There is an abandoned prison out there, sitting idle and falling apart. We have a need for it. Let us have it; let us use it.

Of course, we realized that some of the old prison buildings were clearly unsuitable for our purposes. But Alcatraz was a powerful symbol, and we thought it had enough facilities to give it some real potential. We hoped that we could use that potential to galvanize the urban Indian community and reach out to the Indians on the reservations.

We asked for everyone's input and eventually started drawing up a formal plan to use Alcatraz as a cultural center, with a vocational training program, an Indian museum, and a spiritual facility. We did not submit the plan that first year, but over the next several months we refined it. Together we developed our ideas of the practical, historical, and political reasons why Alcatraz should become Indian and what exactly we would do with it. All of our thoughts were later incorporated into the proclamation made at the takeover, but, for the present, our plan was simply to make a formal application to the federal government and await their answer.

Then, suddenly, two events shoved Alcatraz to the front burner. The first was a vote by the San Francisco board of supervisors in favor of preliminary plans submitted by Lamar Hunt, of the Texas Hunt family, for commercial development of Alcatraz. That came as a bombshell. There must have been stories in the papers about Hunt's plans, but somehow we had missed them. In fact, the first time we heard of his ideas was when the supervisors voted in their favor.

The implications were enormous. If Hunt's plans succeeded, the federal title to Alcatraz Island would be transferred to private developers. Hunt was reputed to be a billionaire, and he certainly had enough money to accomplish his Texas-size plans to build a huge apartment and restaurant complex on the grounds of the former prison. The whole thing was supposed to be some kind of giant monument to the space age. The idea was that, if the East had the Statue of Liberty, the West would have this space-age colossus, complete with an underground space museum. It all sounded very grandiose and unreal, but it was obviously real enough to impress the board of supervisors and start them dreaming of new tax revenues rolling in from what was then a white elephant.

But the board's vote was not yet the final word. Hunt's proposal agitated a lot of non-Indians who wanted to keep the bay free of commercial exploitation. The anti-Hunt forces ran a big ad in the local newspapers, complete with a coupon to be filled out by readers who were opposed to the project. According to the San Francisco papers, the supervisors were inundated with thousands of those coupons protesting the Hunt decision. Yet we had no idea how powerful the commercial forces might be, and we realized that, if Hunt went much further, we could kiss our plans for an Indian cultural center good-bye.

A short time later, the second calamity befell the San Francisco Indian community. On 10 October 1969, the San Francisco Indian Center on Valencia Street burned down. No cause was ever discovered; it could have been accidental, or it could have been arson. Whatever caused it, the fire was an unmitigated disaster for the Indian people. The center had been a popular meeting place; an administrative center for all sorts of programs; and a place for social and educational activities, including powwows. People could socialize with others from their own tribe, find help with their problems, or just get off the streets. There was even a shop that sold Indian arts and crafts.

When the center went up in flames, Indian people throughout the Bay Area mourned it like a close and beloved friend. Everyone asked, "What now? Where do we go?" With outside help, a temporary location was soon established, but it was small and totally inadequate. Something had to be done, and fast. Alcatraz immediately came to mind.

With the loss of the Indian Center, the emphasis of the Alcatraz discussions shifted from leisurely negotiation to a desire for immediate action. For a year or more, we had batted the idea around, gradually moving toward what we considered a reasonable, if idealistic, proposal for federal transfer of Alcatraz to the Indian people. In early September 1969, we were still talking about proposals and applications. When we first heard about Hunt's grandiose plans, we realized that there was no way we could counter his proposal with just another proposal. He had money and political clout, and we had neither. To get anywhere, we would have to develop a different strategy. Then we were confronted with the emergency. There was no way that the people who had relied on the Indian Center would be satisfied with pie-in-the-sky ideas or the slow and unwieldy process of negotiation. They wanted action.

The United Council talked and argued and in the end came down to this: "Take it. Let's do it again, but this time let's do it with sufficient force, and in a way they can't stop. And this time, we'll not only take it, but we'll hold it. They won't be able to push us off."

Like distant smoke from a prairie fire, the idea and its potential attracted attention. Our meetings had grown into general gatherings of Indian people, especially since the federal War on Poverty had begun in 1964. The programs made no provisions for Indians and left many more frustrated than ever. More people flocked to our meetings. As 1969 stomped past midyear with riots in Berkeley and massive, electrifying antiwar protests in San Francisco, council meetings began to find focus and energy from the restless spirit of more and more young people, many of them college students.

In our enthusiasm, we sometimes forgot that Alcatraz was really a cold and desolate place, abandoned even as a prison. We forgot because at last we were daring to take back something of all that had been stolen; we would have one isolated place to renew what had been lost. That enthusiastic energy swirled through our meetings, and some on the council worried that we were being carried away by it and riding a dangerous tide of the times. Yet, when each person spoke around the table, the consensus was there: Alcatraz should be ours.

As chairman of the United Council, I was responsible for conducting the meetings that tentatively determined strategy, a date for the landing, and the wording of the proclamation. When we had made some preliminary plans, I called Don Patterson, a dapper-dressing Oklahoma native who had established his reputation as a southern drum singer while serving as chairman of the San Francisco Indian Center board of directors. On behalf of the United Council, I told him of a plan to replace their burned-out building with something bigger and better.

"What? Where?"

"Alcatraz."

Patterson then invited me to come and lay out our plans for his board and members. They liked what they heard and agreed to support the occupation and the proclamation.

I next called the chairman of the San Francisco board of supervisors to tell him that Indian people did not approve of the plans for commercialization of Alcatraz. I told him we wanted the island to become an Indian cultural resource. I told him that his board should be pleased: We would end all the years of agonizing by white people over the fate of the abandoned federal prison. We would buy them out for twenty-four dollars in beads—exactly the same amount the Dutch paid the Indians for the island of Manhattan. This was clearly a bargain, since Manhattan is several times larger than Alcatraz.

There was an awkward silence on the line. San Francisco politicians pride themselves on knowing the amalgam of ethnic ideals that make up their city and their region. Until then, I had usually been considered among the less threatening of the pressure group leaders.

"Uh, well, yeah, Adam. We could sure think about that," he replied.

Indian students at local colleges, especially San Francisco State, now began to get more involved in the planning. Up to that point, Indian youth had been only sporadically involved in our activities. The Indian students in the United Council had participated when they had time and when there was a discussion of issues that directly affected them or their institutions. But with Alcatraz as the catalyst, student input into the council increased by leaps and bounds, until many became actively involved.

Although many people were gung-ho for an Indian Alcatraz and any radical action necessary to achieve that goal, there were still voices of caution and concern. "Do you really think we ought to do something like that? Isn't it too big for us? Is it too hot to handle? What if it gets out of control?

What if the federal government uses force? What if somebody gets killed?" Some people worried that an occupation would create more problems than it solved and that it might be too complex for our resources. But when each of us spoke around the table, the consensus was still there. Take the island.

We decided that Alcatraz would definitely replace the Indian Center and thus moved the planning sessions from the United Council meeting rooms to the temporary quarters of the San Francisco Indian Center. I was to be the council representative at these meetings, although I acted as the chairman of the crucial meeting when we made final decisions on the date of the invasion and the wording of the proclamation.

The interim quarters of the San Francisco Indian Center certainly met our needs. So different from the former center—a gloomy meeting hall inherited from some forgotten Masonic lodge—the temporary center was a ground-floor storefront in the Mission District. Huge show windows looked into a yawning, empty room the size of a five-and-dime. There were no chairs, but nobody seemed to mind standing. Those long, chilly meetings were warmed with bodies crowded into the unheated display room.

Some of the college students suggested waiting until Christmas to invade, in order to avoid disrupting classes and thus assure greater student participation. I saw their point, but I knew that if we were going to do it at all, we had to move as soon as possible. We had to proceed before plans to exploit the island had gone any further and before the authorities could take steps to prevent any kind of landing. I also knew of some really big anti–Vietnam War rallies being planned for December. If they happened at the same time as our takeover, they would probably overshadow us in the media and thus ruin what we were trying to accomplish.

I proposed 9 November as the day of the invasion. That would not give us much lead time, but it also would not give the government a lot of time to snoop out our plans and throw us a curve. I pointed out that the news was so dull, the papers were reduced to printing boring stuff that would normally have landed in the wastebasket. "You know, it has to be a pretty slow time for news," I said, "for the media to be printing speeches by Spiro Agnew. We have to take advantage of that. We need to strike soon, the sooner the better, to get maximum exposure."

So we agreed that 9 November 1969 was Indian D-Day.[1] The rest of our plans were still vague, because we realized we could only plan so far. We had many fine ideas and ideals, but we knew that many of our actions would be determined by reactions from the federal authorities. We had no way of knowing what those reactions might be, but, throughout all this preparation, the possibilities never left our minds.

We constantly stressed that this invasion would be peaceful, just like the Sioux invasion in 1964. *Nonviolent* was the overriding watchword—no violence, no liquor, and no drugs of any kind. We were going to be a positive example for Indian people and show a positive face to the world.

The question of who, or what group, would represent the Indian people had already been much discussed in our United Council meetings, and it was now an active topic of discussion at the chilly storefront in San Francisco. Everyone agreed that we wanted to promote a movement rather than any one individual or tribe; therefore, we wanted to find some designation that would proclaim our unity. The 1964 invasion had been an exclusively Sioux action because it took place under the terms of the Sioux Treaty of 1868, but this was different. Our protest involved people from many Indian nations. Tlingit, Iroquois, Blackfeet, Chippewa, Navajo, and virtually every other Native American tribe were represented among the thousands of Indians in the Bay Area. Finally, we agreed on a name we could use to structure the occupying force and sign the proclamation: Indians of All Tribes. We then agreed that our proclamation should be a mixture of humor, serious intentions, and hope. But the humor should not be just the laughing kind; it should also have a sting.

Once these decisions were made, our preparations were squeezed into a very narrow timeframe. The center had burned down on 10 October. The landing on Alcatraz was set to take place less than a month later, on 9 November. During those few weeks, there would be a crucial discussion with a young student leader named Richard Oakes and an announcement to the media to prepare for something big in the Indian community.

The Message

As we continued to discuss the proclamation, there was a flood of suggestions about what to include in this historic document. Many of the ideas were good ones, and the final proclamation reflected this involvement. But we had not yet learned that the media and the public have very short attention spans: If you want a message to sink in, it has to be short and to the point. However true or important the words might have been, most of the final proclamation never made it onto the air or into print. For the record, here it is:

> To the Great White Father and All His People:
>
> We, the native Americans, re-claim the land known as Alcatraz Island in the name of all American Indians by right of discovery. We wish to be fair and honorable in our dealing with Caucasian inhabitants of this land, and hereby offer the following treaty: We will purchase said Alcatraz Island for 24 dollars ($24) in glass beads and red cloth, a precedent set by the white man's purchase of a similar island about 300 years ago. We know that $24 in

trade goods for these sixteen acres is more than was paid when Manhattan Island was sold, but we know that land values have risen over the years. Our offer of $1.24 per acre is greater than the 47 cents per acre the white men are now paying the California Indians for their land. We will give to the inhabitants of this land a portion of that land for their own, to be held in trust by the American Indian Government—for as long as the sun shall rise and the rivers go down to the sea—to be administered by the Bureau of Caucasian Affairs (BCA). We will further guide the inhabitants in the proper way of living. We will offer them our religion, our education, our life-ways, in order to help them achieve our level of civilization and thus raise them and all their white brothers up from their savage and unhappy state. We offer this treaty in good faith and wish to be fair and honorable in our dealing with all white men.

The Bureau of Caucasian Affairs was, of course, meant to be a dig at the Bureau of Indian Affairs, although, during the course of the occupation, the BCA became something entirely different from what we had in mind. In the next section of the document, we used gallows humor and a little tongue-in-cheek exaggeration to make some important points we wanted the government and the public to take to heart:

We feel that this so-called Alcatraz Island is more than suitable as an Indian Reservation, as determined by the white man's own standards. By this we mean that this place resembles most Indian reservations, in that:
1. It is isolated from modern facilities, and without adequate means of transportation.
2. It has no fresh running water.
3. The sanitation facilities are inadequate.
4. There are no oil or mineral rights.
5. There is no industry and so unemployment is very great.
6. There are no health care facilities.
7. The soil is rocky and non-productive and the land does not support game.
8. There are no educational facilities.
9. The population has always been held as prisoners and kept dependent upon others.
Further, it would be fitting and symbolic that ships from all over the world, entering the Golden Gate would first see Indian land, and thus be reminded of the true history of this nation. This tiny island would be a symbol of the great lands once ruled by free and noble Indians.

Then we got to the heart of the matter: the way we wanted to use Alcatraz if we could persuade the government to turn it over to us. There was nothing funny about this; it was all very straightforward. If, in retrospect, our idealism surpassed our sense of the possible, I think we can be forgiven. In those days, we really thought almost anything was possible if we just tried hard enough and got enough people on our side. If I felt some gnawing doubts in the back of my mind, I sure did not let them bother me.

The most important thing was to establish the clear cut conflict between what Indians needed and the present plans for the exploitation of the island. We were partially successful; at least Alcatraz did not become some real estate speculator's private domain and source of fat profits. This section of the proclamation was entitled "Use to Be Made of Alcatraz Island":

> What use will we make of this land? Since the San Francisco Indian center burned down, there is no place for Indians to assemble. Therefore, we plan to develop on this island several Indian institutions:
> 1. A Center for Native American Studies will be developed which will train our young people in the best of our native cultural arts and sciences, as well as educate them in the skills and knowledge to improve the lives and spirits of all Indian peoples. Attached to this Center will be traveling universities, managed by Indians, which will go to the Indian Reservations in order to learn from the people the traditional values which are now absent for the Caucasian higher educational system.
> 2. An American Indian Spiritual Center will be developed which will practice our ancient tribal religious ceremonies and medicine. Our cultural arts will be featured and our young people trained in music, dance, and medicine.
> 3. An Indian Center of Ecology will be built which will train and support our young people in scientific research and practice in order to restore our lands and water to their pure and natural state. We will seek to de-pollute the air and the water of the Bay Area. We will seek to restore fish and animal life, and to revitalize sea life which has been threatened by the white man's way. Facilities will be developed to desalt sea water for human use.
> 4. A great Indian Training School will be developed to teach our peoples how to make a living in the world, improve our standards of living, and end hunger and unemployment among all our peoples. This training school will include a Center for Indian Arts and Crafts, and an Indian restaurant serving native foods and training Indians in culinary arts. This Center will display Indian arts and offer the Indian foods of all tribes to the public, so that all may know of the beauty and spirit of the traditional Indian ways.
> 5. Some of the present buildings will be taken over to develop an American Indian Museum, which will depict our native foods and other cultural contributions we have given to all the world. Another part of the Museum will present some of the things the white man has given to the Indians, in return for the land and life he took: disease, alcohol, poverty, and cultural decimation (as symbolized by old tin cans, barbed wire, rubber tires, plastic containers, etc.) Part of the Museum will remain a dungeon, to symbolize both those Indian captives who were incarcerated for challenging white authority, and those

who were imprisoned on reservations. The Museum will show the noble and the tragic events of Indian history, including the broken treaties, the documentary of the Trail of Tears, the Massacre of Wounded Knee, as well as the victory over Yellow-Hair Custer and his Army. In the name of all Indians, therefore, we re-claim this island for our Indian nations, for all these reasons. We feel this claim is just and proper, and that this land should rightfully be granted to us for as long as the rivers shall run and the sun shall shine.

The proclamation was signed with the words "Indians of All Tribes, November 1969, San Francisco, California."

It seems we should have known that none of this would come to pass, no matter how much truth and justice we had on our side. For one thing, where would we get the money for all of these plans? Desalinization plants? Museums? And we were talking about tens of millions of dollars. All for Indians? Even then, in our heart of hearts, maybe we knew that Alcatraz would never be what we planned. Or maybe we felt that, if we expressed extravagant hopes and made extravagant demands, some part of them, however modest, might become a reality. Nothing could make things worse than they already were for Indian people. Besides, compared to what Indians have lost since the coming of white people, no demand for redress can be considered extravagant—unrealistic, perhaps, but not extravagant.

Once we had agreed on the action and the proclamation, we set about involving the media. We already had one good contact. Tim Findley, a young reporter for the *San Francisco Chronicle*, had become a friend of my family. (Later on, Tim even became our adopted son.) He had a strong interest in the urban Indian— Indians were his "beat"—and he eventually covered the Alcatraz story from beginning to end. We told Tim that there was something coming down in the Indian community, something big and newsworthy. Could he suggest a way to announce it to the media? A press conference, perhaps? Would anyone besides him come to a press conference called by a bunch of Indians?

"It so happens I am giving a party for some media people at my house," he said, "and that might be a good opportunity for you. I'm also thinking of inviting Richard Oakes and his wife, Anne, if that's fine with you. But other than that, you and Bobbie will be the only Indian people there."

This was a better opportunity than we had dared hope for. I accepted, of course. I felt that inviting Richard, an activist student leader at San Francisco State, was a great idea. It was also a lucky break for me, because I wanted to sound him out. I hoped to get him involved in something bigger than his Indian student group—something involving a large part of the Bay Area Indian community.

Yet I was really anxious about approaching Richard, a husky, handsome young Mohawk with a shock of thick black hair. Richard was of the younger generation, and Indian people felt some of the same alienation between the young and the old that white society felt in those days. Young Indians felt particularly removed from those of us who had moved into a more privileged economic status. I wanted to find out for myself what kind of leader Richard could be, and the best place to do that was away from other young activists who might expect him to be adversarial. I hoped the party would be the place. We were looking for somebody to lead the charge, but I wanted to feel sure that Richard was the right man.

Richard and I might have had comparable blue-collar backgrounds, but we seemed to be worlds apart. I was over forty at a time when the prevailing slogan was "never trust anyone over thirty." I had been out of Indian school for more than twenty years and had become a well-off, independent businessman, with a nice house and an expensive car. Richard was a much younger man, an activist student leader who came from the dangerous and risky world of high steel. He was certainly much closer than I to the typical hand-to-mouth existence of minority students in California. In any event, we did have something in common to bridge the gulf between us: a deep concern with the Indian cause. We both believed in an Indian Alcatraz, at least then, and we were both family men. Richard and his wife had five children, ranging in age from two to twelve, so we both had a big personal stake in the future.

When we arrived at the party at Tim Findley's house, I told Richard of our plans. He jumped at the idea and quickly responded, "Yeah, let's take it." "You going to lead the charge?" I asked. "Okay," he replied. That clinched it.

The decision to go ahead was now irreversible. We called Tim over and told him first, because he was our host and a reporter involved with the urban Indian story.

"Man," he exclaimed, "that's going to be one hell of a story."

Of course, he was not completely surprised. He knew there was something big in the works, something radical we had up our sleeves. He also knew that it had to do with Alcatraz. He had known all along what was happening at the United Council and the temporary Indian Center; we had talked about Alcatraz and its pros and cons for more than a year. As a reporter on a big city daily, especially a reporter with a strong interest in Indian activities, he wanted a real story as much as we wanted to stop being invisible. And this was one *real* story.

"No danger of that [invisibility]," Tim assured me. He pointed out that he was getting the full story at exactly the same time as his colleagues, some of whom certainly knew that something was bound to happen with Alcatraz sooner or later. He, like everyone else, would also have to observe restrictions on the story's release. Tim nodded to me: "Go ahead and make your speech."

Several reporters from the Bay Area papers and radio and television stations gathered around. I gave them a bit of the history of the Alcatraz action and then outlined our plans. I told them a proclamation of the Indian plans for Alcatraz was in the works. It was self-explanatory and would be handed out to them and read aloud on the day of the big event—9 November 1969—and not before. I warned them that, if any one of them broke the story in advance, there would be no story. Not one of them so much as hinted at the takeover before it happened.

Thus it was that the Bay Area media were tipped off to what we called the "takeover "and what later became known as the "Indian invasion of Alcatraz." This involvement paid off later. Since we supplied the media with some essential background beforehand, we got more complete coverage than many of us expected from the establishment media.

The First Attempt

As D-Day approached, the meetings and telephone calls became increasingly urgent. The first order of business was to secure transportation. We contacted several charter boat outfits and told them only that we were a group of Indians planning an outing to Alcatraz and that we needed several good-sized boats. That was not a lie—we really were planning an "outing." What we did not add was that not everyone who sailed to the island intended to return to the mainland. Five skippers agreed, and we were elated. Five boats were enough to transport the seventy-five Indian people who were eager to be in the first wave of occupants. Pier 39 was our point of embarkation, and we had notified the media accordingly.

The weather on Sunday morning, 9 November 1969, was beautiful and calm, just the kind of day we had hoped for. My family and I set out from our home in San Leandro. We had our tribal outfits packed and the twenty-four dollars in beads and colored cloth already arranged in a wooden bowl for the symbolic purchase of the island from the government. Feeling optimistic, we were soon on the Nimitz Freeway heading for Fisherman's Wharf and Pier 39 in San Francisco. I began thinking that we were doing a pretty strange thing: Twentieth-century urban Indians who had gathered in tribal councils, student organizations, and clubs were now joining with concerned individuals from all over the Bay Area to launch an attack on a bastion of the U.S. government. Instead of riding horses and carrying bows, arrows, and rifles, we were riding in Fords, Chevys, and Plymouths and carrying only our proclamation and our determination to change federal policies that oppressed our people.

We were excited, but there was still room for tension and anxiety. I was worried about the media. Would we get decent coverage? And what if things went wrong? The media could subject us to public ridicule, something Indian people certainly did not need. Finally, I worried about the federal government. We had thought a lot about the government's reaction to an Indian protest of this kind, but we could only speculate about what would be done to us. After all, Indian people had been killed for a lot less in the old days, and we had not seen much change in attitude or policy in recent times.

We were nearing Fisherman's Wharf; smells of the delicious seafood for which the wharf is famous filled the air. As we pulled up to the dock, we could see several Indians and a couple of television crews milling around. We were greeted by shouts of "Where the hell are the boats?" As calmly as possible I replied, "They are supposed to be over by the Harbor Tours dock. There should be about five of them."

"Nope. There ain't a damn thing there next to the wharf except the Harbor Tours boat. The bastards must've chickened out!" They certainly had. Everyone was worried and angry. Another worried voice exclaimed, "Jesus Christ! We've got to find ourselves a boat or we're in big trouble with the press; those guys will tear us up!"

I hurriedly parked the car and ran over to the growing group of Indian students. I asked them to keep everyone occupied any way they could while we went looking for another boat. Richard Oakes asked if they could read the proclamation; it would take a bit of time, and he felt the need for more participation by the students from San Francisco State. I handed him a copy.

Richard and his group set out for the end of the pier, the other Indians and the television crews following. The students settled down in a clearing of benches and planters, with Alcatraz Island as a hazy backdrop—a perfect setting for an outdoor press conference. The reporters took notes while several different Indians read the three main sections of the proclamation aloud. When they finished, we began singing and dancing so the media would have some action to tape.

Tim Findley approached me and asked if there was a problem; it was becoming apparent that we were stalling. I quickly explained our predicament. He felt that if we did not get something started quickly, the whole thing would be treated as a joke, and we would be in big trouble. "You know, 'Indian time' and all that," Tim confided. I assured him we were very much aware of the problem, but we had the skippers' pledge of boats. I asked the whereabouts of the reporter from Reuters who had promised to show up. Tim pointed toward the Rock. "See that boat sitting off to the side of Alcatraz? That's where he's at, along with a photographer and a television crew. They want to catch the actual landing. That's what I mean when I say you'll be in big trouble if this doesn't come off."

I left Tim to check on the boat. It was still tied to the dock, with no skipper in sight. This is no way to launch an attack, I thought, just too damn complicated. How much nicer in the old days! First there was a big powwow. Warriors prepared themselves for battle by taking purifying sweat baths and then gathering their personal medicine to ward off enemy bullets or arrows. They made offerings and prayers to their protector before joining the war dance. Oh, the songs and dances were thrilling to behold; as the dancing went on, the tempo of the drum increased, and its sound grew louder and louder, adding to the fervor. Dancers acted out what they intended to do to the enemy.

I brought myself back to reality and wondered what our next move should be if the skipper did not show up at all—and it was becoming increasingly evident that this might be the case. As I stood on the wharf, I noticed a beautiful, three-masted barque named the *Monte Cristo* that looked as if it had come right out of the pages of maritime history. I watched the crew members go about their tasks under the observant eye of a handsome man with an air of authority. He had to be either the captain or the owner. From a distance, his tight pants, ruffled shirt, and long, blond hair made him look like Errol Flynn in an adventure movie. I later learned that his name was Ronald Craig, and he was the owner of the beautiful vessel.

Still wearing my full tribal dress, I approached him. He called over to me, "Hey, I'm curious. What's going on over there with all those Indians?" I did not hesitate for a minute, because I realized he could be our solution. I explained our predicament and pointed out the sizable media contingent that had now gathered. He gave it all a moment of thought. Then he started asking questions that showed concern and sympathy for Indian people and their problems. Finally I could hold back no longer and asked if he could take us to Alcatraz on his beautiful boat. He stood deliberating. He looked at the whole scene: a growing crowd of Indian men, women and children, all wearing different tribal outfits; the news media with their paraphernalia; the bystanders and tourists who waited out of curiosity for something to happen. He looked at his ship, then again at the Indians. I held my breath. Finally he spoke: "I'll do it on the condition that we get permission from the Coast Guard to put out to sea and that we take no more than fifty people aboard. The boat rides deep in the water because of the keel, so I can't land on the Alcatraz dock. We'll just circle the island a couple of times, if that's all right with you. Just a sort of sightseeing tour to get your message across, okay?"

Was it okay? Man alive! At this point, I was ready to accept a kayak, and he wanted to know if his offer was okay! I ran back to the wharf to share the good news. Worried looks quickly turned into big smiles as word spread among the Indians, and here and there a whoop of joy went up from the crowd.

In a rush, we all converged on the *Monte Cristo*. In no time, her decks were awash with Indians, reporters, photographers, and even some of the curious bystanders who wanted to come along for whatever adventure lay ahead. But we quickly realized that we had far more that fifty people. Captain Craig approached me, shaking his head.

"We can't shove off with this many people aboard," he warned. "The Coast Guard will never let us cast off at this rate. "We took a head count and then started the unpleasant task of asking people to leave the boat. The media people had to stay, because without them much of our plans and efforts would be wasted. If nobody could read about our action or watch it on television, it might as well never happen. As somebody once said, If a tree falls in the forest and there's no one to hear it crash, does it make any sound? Besides, the media had shown exceptional patience and forbearance. So we considered safety and politely asked everyone who could not swim, especially the young children and the older people, to leave the boat.

We immediately felt sorry. The expressions of the elders told all too plainly the deep hurt they felt at being left behind. They had waited a lifetime for Indian people to assert themselves and reclaim their pride. They now stood in somber silence, some with misty eyes: Oh, to be young again and have the vigor and strength of the students!

There was one old Dakota Sioux who had told me earlier why he wanted so much to be part of this action. For him, he said, it would be a small revenge for what had happened to his people back in 1890 at Wounded Knee. During the massacre (the army called it a battle, but the Indians called it what it was, an unprovoked massacre of their men, women, and children), his father, then a small child, had huddled in his family's tepee while dozens of bullets splattered through its thin buffalo-hide walls. His grandfather had gone out to call for peace, but he was shot down by the men of the 7th Cavalry. His grandmother ran out to the side of her mortally wounded husband, and she, too, was killed; another soldier charging on horseback through the center of the camp ran a saber into her body.

I thought about that as I watched him slowly leave the *Monte Cristo* and return to the dock. He stood watching with clear disappointment on his face. Many elders left the boat in silence. But the children were outraged at being left behind, and they loudly let us know their feelings in no uncertain terms. Yet orders were orders, and if we were ever going to push off from the dock, Captain Craig's request had to be honored.

When he had satisfied himself that there were about fifty people left aboard, he ordered the crew to cast off all the lines. The *Monte Cristo* had a small cannon mounted on the bow, and one of the crew set it off with a terrific blast. What a romantic gesture! The crew worked with well-trained precision, and we were soon underway. People on the dock waved and cheered, while amateur and professional photographers caught the symbolic moment.

What a strange turnabout of history, I thought. Here were nearly fifty Indians on an old sailing vessel, heading out to seek a new way of life for their people. I thought of the *Mayflower* and its crew of Pilgrims who had landed on our shores 350 years earlier. The history books say they were seeking new freedom for themselves and their children, freedom denied them in their homeland. It did not matter to them that Plymouth Rock already belonged to somebody else; that was not their concern. What did concern them was their own fate and their own hopes. What a sad commentary on this country that we, the original inhabitants, were forced to make a landing 350 years later on another rock, the rock called Alcatraz, to focus national attention on our struggle to regain that same basic freedom.

Yet we were in a festive mood as the *Monte Cristo* made its way across the bay to Alcatraz. Several Indians had set a large drum on the roof of the captain's quarters, and they were pounding the drum and singing war dance songs. Alcatraz loomed ever larger straight ahead, and the photographers were all over the place, trying to get Alcatraz and the Indians in their colorful dress into the same picture.

It felt wonderful to ride on that beautiful vessel, slicing through the water to the sound of the Indian drum and war songs, listening to the laughter and the excited chatter about what lay ahead. The boats on either side of us were loaded with the camera crews from several television stations and reporters from the local papers and the wire services—Associated Press, United Press International, and Reuters. Pleasure boats filled with curious onlookers joined the group and its celebratory spirit.

The *Monte Cristo* headed for the west side of Alcatraz. There was the prison, with its catwalks and huge walls topped with coiled barbed wire. The old guard towers, now silent and empty, stood as grim sentinels of the island's famous and horrific past. As we drew closer, we could see that the steel ramps and catwalks had rusted from the corrosive salt air; they were buckled and broken into grotesque shapes. The empty machine shops and laundry facilities came into view as we rounded the northwest corner of the island. Abandoned and rusting equipment sat forlornly everywhere we looked. I thought of how beautiful the island must have been before white people came to it and left part of their culture and its ugliness.

My somber thoughts were suddenly interrupted by an unexpected drama on the ship: Richard Oakes had climbed onto the railing, stripped off his shirt, and plunged into the water, still wearing his boots! A cheer went up from the Indians as they jammed against the rail. One of the other students followed Richard into the frigid waters, and then another! Three Indians were swimming toward the island as hard and fast as they could before the captain had a chance to react. But react he did, and in no uncertain terms.

"What the hell are those guys doing, Adam?" he shouted to me.

"They're swimming to Alcatraz," I replied as calmly as possible.

"What the hell for?"

"To take the island for the Indian people."

"Jesus Christ, man," shouted Captain Craig, "don't you realize we are flying the Canadian flag? This could be considered an act of war! You've got to stop them!"

Somebody, probably a crew member, thrust a bullhorn at me. "Tell them that, by order of the captain, everybody has to stay put. No more jumping overboard." I could not argue with that; the captain is the boss on a ship. I pressed the trigger of the horn to make the announcement: "The captain has just instructed me to relay his orders. No more Indians are to jump overboard. It is the captain's orders. I am giving you his words: No more Indians are to jump overboard!"

The immediate response was a loud splash as another Indian took a flying leap over the side. Everyone cheered except an Eskimo named Joe Bill, who was wise to the ways of the sea. He stood shaking his head, saying, "No good, no good." We all began to see what Joe Bill had seen earlier: The tide was flowing in the wrong direction for the swimmers and sweeping them out to the Golden Gate instead of toward Alcatraz. As the ship continued toward the eastern side of Alcatraz the sweep of the tide grew more favorable. Without another word to me, Joe Bill quickly stripped off his shirt and shoes. Just as the captain noticed and rushed toward him, Joe Bill plunged over the side.

The captain issued orders for the helmsman to swing wide of the island to discourage any more leaps into the water. The *Monte Cristo* made its final turn and headed back toward San Francisco. We had escaped a potential fiasco with the press and given hope to our people. But was this enough? I still had the bullhorn, and with it I called to the group, "Have we done enough?"

There was a loud chorus of "NO!"

"Do you want to go back and take Alcatraz? Really take it?"

"Yes! Let's go!" came the ready answer, with war whoops added for emphasis.

"All right," I answered. "When we get back to the wharf, spread the word that we'll meet at the Indian Center." Indian people of all ages and tribes were already jammed into the building when we arrived. Everyone was discussing the events of the day. We found the same consensus we had found on the *Monte Cristo:* Everyone wanted to go back that very night and land in force on the island.

Night Landing

Following the meeting at the Indian Center, I talked to the captain of a deep-sea fishing boat called the *New Vera II* that had just docked at the wharf; her crew were still washing down the deck. The captain agreed to take us out to the island if we guaranteed him a minimum payment of fifty dollars, or three dollars per person. Once again, we headed for Fisherman's Wharf, but the situation was different when we arrived in the growing dusk. There were no press people, no curious bystanders, no tourists, and only a small band of Indians. We walked with an air of secrecy past Castagnola's Restaurant, the boats lying waiting for repairs, and the reeking fish containers until we found the *New Vera II*. She was sitting almost out of sight across from Scoma's Restaurant, her deck still wet and glistening from her recent scrubbing.

The captain opened the throttle of the *New Vera II*, and we slipped out into the bay for the second time that day, but this time we slipped into the gathering darkness. Of the two hundred or so Indians who had been prepared to assault the island that sunny afternoon, there were no more than twenty-five of us on the voyage of the *New Vera II*. It was all so beautiful it was difficult to tear ourselves away and direct our attention to Alcatraz. And what a contrast as we turned to face the island! We were just able to make out its gloomy silhouette against the lights of Richmond and Berkeley before the quick flash of the lighthouse beacon caught our eyes. The underwater cable warning sign glowed with a ghostly bluish light, and the mournful moan of the island's two foghorns were there to drive off evil spirits; or perhaps Alcatraz itself was the spirit—an evil spirit with a circling Cyclops eye and an awful voice sweeping across the waters.

As if to turn us from our goal, stormy weather completed the dismal picture. The tide was going out, thwarting the captain's attempts to sidle up to the large water barge at the Alcatraz dock. The riptide swirled around our boat, swinging us dangerously about; the lone light on the dock cast only useless, eerie shadows. We swung wide to avoid colliding with a barge, circled around, and headed for the boat slip where we had seen the custodian's boat. The captain revved the throttle to help push us into position, but the tide, the darkness, and the unfamiliar dock all kept him from making the landing.

The captain was already getting frustrated when a huge watchdog appeared out of the dark and ran up to our noisy boat, barking furiously. Would the caretaker hear the commotion and start shooting as the caretakers used to do when Alcatraz was still a prison? The captain did not want to stick around long enough to find out. He swung the wheel sharply and headed straight for the barge. Quickly we passed our sleeping bags and blankets to the dock and lined up anxiously to disembark.

"Hey, what's going on here?" demanded the skipper. I explained in an offhanded way, "Well, we are going to take over the island."

"Oh, my God," he exclaimed, "they might take my boat away for this!" The captain had been fighting to keep the nose of his vessel against the barge, but he now became completely agitated. Realizing that he could be charged with aiding and abetting our takeover and concerned with the rushing tides and the possibility of being shot any minute by a panicked caretaker, he suddenly threw the gears into reverse once again. The tie line snapped, knocking one of our men back into the boat.

"Goddamn it," the man hollered, "we aren't even unloaded yet!" But the captain paid no attention as he pushed the throttle wide open to get out of there. We were disappointed at being left behind on the boat, but we could count fourteen Indians, a sizable contingent, on the shore of Alcatraz. One was Richard Oakes; three were women. They all flew up the stairway of the old fort and quickly disappeared into the darkness. The watchdog looked on with tail wagging. We joked that our fourteen friends had only two loaves of bread between them but that, if they got really hungry, they could always cook the dog.

The occupation of Alcatraz Island had become an accomplished fact. What an ironic twist of fate for an old prison island with a grim and sadistic past: In its heyday, desperate men went to any extreme, even certain death, to escape the island; in 1969, Indian people were just as desperate to get onto the island to seek their freedom.

NOTE

1. The events of 9 November 1969 were written up three days later for presentation to my class at California State University at Hayward.

4

ALCATRAZ RECOLLECTIONS

Tim Findley

I have always been reluctant to write anything that might be taken as an "insider" piece on Alcatraz and the Indian occupation. To those who have asked for more than just a journalistic rehash of my reporting for the *San Francisco Chronicle*, I have tried to say, over the years, that the story belongs to the Native Americans who were there and not to a white reporter who came eventually to be resented by at least some of the Indians whom he had once counted as friends on the island.

That's not just liberal guilt or "political correctness" I feel, and I certainly don't regard it as some kind of racism. It's just that I know that a number of Native Americans, whether they were on the island or not, would disagree with my perception of the details, and I have never found it worth damaging the significance of the Alcatraz occupation by haggling over my own credentials and memories connected to it.

As far as I'm concerned, any Native American who was living at the time and claims to have been on Alcatraz was on Alcatraz. In one sense, anyway, they all were.

I remember John Trudell on that cold day in March 1971, when everyone knew it could not last much longer and when the exhilaration of invasion had, in some ways, worn down into the bitterness of exile. "You can be certain we will not leave Alcatraz," Trudell said. "We have come too far and through too much to start giving land back to the white man."

Three months later, Trudell and what looked to be a discouraged handful of others were finally removed from the island by federal authorities. But Trudell was right; they never really left. In fact, the presence of Indians on the bleak, old prison "Rock" might be more significant today than it was even then.

As a story, I prefer to hear about the Alcatraz occupation as it is still told in oral legend, almost like a folk tale. In fact, like a folk tale, it's a story that does not really have a clear beginning or a certain ending. It's still going on, and it seems to me to get better with every telling.

The early part of it is certainly Adam's to tell, although even he has to recall that old McKenzie had the basic idea years before he did. Richard's story is the story of the invasion itself, but it turns out even more sadly than most people realize. And, in the end, it deserves to be Trudell's story, because he was there when it ended and because he carried that off with a certain nobility that wasn't always part of the rest of it.

It is also Stella's story, an angrier version than others, I suppose. And LaNada's story, which, I would only guess, rides high and low over changing emotions. Myself, I'd like to hear Joe Bill tell it from the beginning as only he could, in that devilish, good-natured way of his. Or maybe Anne, Richard's wife, who just seemed to have stopped talking to anybody.

Many more people than were ever there in person have told their own stories. I think that, too, is okay. Alcatraz in 1969 was not a place; it was an idea, an electrifying moment like the March on Washington or the Chicago convention. If you say you were there, I believe you, even if I didn't see you.

For all the many Indian versions, there are also the white guys' stories of Alcatraz. Mine is only one of them, and maybe not even the most significant one. I was, after all, a reporter who not only was paid for most of what I did but was also quite aware of its potential for my professional reputation. Many others gave to the cause without any expectation of payment or recognition and even with some considerable risk to themselves and their property.

That's the big problem I have with Alcatraz. I find my own involvement to be ultimately compromising: something mixed up and locked in place between pride and humility. I keep having this feeling I should apologize for it to some Native Americans and not even mention it to others. Getting "correct" with what happened at Alcatraz is a process I have witnessed evolving over all the twenty-five years since it began.

It leaves a lot out to say it began with that Halloween party at my house in Sausalito, but that is where I remember it first coming into focus. You have to keep in mind what an incredible year 1969 really was for its sense of young people all over the world thrashing out from under the old, cold hand of restraint and bigotry that held the planet forcibly together after World War II. Everywhere in the Western world, at least—France, Germany, and the United States especially—there were eruptions of dissent and self-expression that surged into the streets in overwhelming numbers but still seemed powerless against the grim, gray institutions of wealth and worn-out social policy. In San Francisco alone that fall, more than a quarter of a million people—some still say half a million—marched in just one of many rallies against the war in Vietnam. They flooded into Golden Gate Park and sprawled out across the green to hear and see the very cream of contemporary culture express their opposition for them.

The year had already seen the government's pathetic and outrageous attempt to blame the riots at the Democratic convention in Chicago on a conspiracy of seven young men who became instant folk heroes. In Oakland, the trial of Black Panther founder Huey Newton for the murder of a police officer had become an indictment of the system itself, in which rallying public opinion would acquit Newton and then condemn him to an ultimately more fatal status as social martyr. In May, James Rector, a rootless young adventurer without real connections to any of it, was shot to death and given posthumous fame by police carrying out the orders of Governor Ronald Reagan to stop the Berkeley riots over Peoples' Park, "even if it takes a bloodbath." The "Summer of Love" in San Francisco's Haight-Ashbury was only two years past, and mysteriously aging hippies still wandered about in confusion over the rapidly changing styles that had incorporated them into a camouflage of colors and trends and drugs and had made them almost invisible in the new "Woodstock generation."

Everywhere it was happening in 1969, but possibly nowhere else as much and with as much variety as in San Francisco. The Panthers, Peoples' Park, and the antiwar movement were "mine" at the *San Francisco Chronicle*. My forte was to cover "them" from their point of view, while other reporters took respectable places behind police lines. I partied with the Panthers, got arrested and beaten up at Peoples' Park, and promoted the hell out of antiwar marches whenever I could. That wasn't especially unique or brave either, because the truth in San Francisco in 1969 was that the political establishment of the city itself was evolving with much the same sympathies, even if they weren't always translated down to the street cop level.

The *Chronicle* and its publisher were as hidebound backward conservative as any other major paper—probably more so because of the influence of the paper's city editor, who refused to see any demonstration as more than an act of overfed and undereducated kids. He did not like what I wrote, but the times were just too overpowering for him to do more than try to put it— and me—in a wiggly box of our own labeled *analysis*.

Parties at my house were becoming fairly common events. It was a dream place for a young, pseudo-intellectual reporter like me, with a panoramic view of the bay and San Francisco, looking all the way to South Oakland in the distance. At night, the beam from Alcatraz traced a steady pulse, even through the fog.

Everybody I knew was invited, including Black Panthers, student radicals, professional Marxists, local politicians, a horde of other reporters, and the bartenders from the places where we drank. If you couldn't find some excitement at one of these parties, it was a sign of cortex rot.

Adam and Bobbie Nordwall were unusual in the mix, not because they were Indians, but because they had been my friends longer than anybody else in the whole party except for my wife. Adam and I had worked together in my days as a field representative for VISTA Indian projects. He and Bobbie had been there when I ended my Washington, D.C., career by punching a bureaucrat sent to reduce the federal commitment to Indian recruitment.

You have to know Adam, of course, to really understand how an Indian could make an impression on that crowd without getting at least as drunk as they were. Other Indians will complain about Adam's out-front salesmanship as long as Adam lives, and even Bobbie still cringes at his sometimes shameless good nature. But I'll tell you what, I also knew Browning Pipestem at the time and Lee Brightman and even Russell Means. None of them could have gotten it done the way Adam did, nor would they even have tried.

The truth is, Adam sometimes still embarrasses me with his reckless self-confidence and his certainty that everybody is bound to like him and his ideas. I think he sometimes is unaware that there are people who don't take him seriously.

Adam may have been serving as a mentor to Richard Oakes at that time; I think that's one reason why Richard was with the Nordwalls that night.

It's well known that the federal government put Alcatraz up for grabs after it closed the prison in 1963. The hypocrisy of that is revealed now as the U.S. Park Service rakes in the cash from possibly its biggest money-maker, which it would have given away if the Indians hadn't taken it. The Park Service owes Adam a medal.

But in that early fall of 1969, nobody was sure of what to do with Alcatraz. The only thing certain among the rising breed of new politicians in San Francisco was that they did not want to turn the island over as some gaudy amusement park and casino proposed by Texas magnate H. L. Hunt. It was a near thing, though—so close that designer Alvin Duskin was paying for a public campaign to head off the federal giveaway to Hunt.

Alvin Duskin was out of my league. Alcatraz was just a good spot in the overall view from my house. But I had an interest in the San Francisco Indian Center, which had burned down only two days before. Most Indians blamed it on the Samoans, but I was not about to get into that particular turf war in the Mission District. My interest, dating back again to those federal days, was in trying to help scare up some financial support to rebuild the center.

As I was later prepared not to tell any grand jury that asked, it was Adam's idea to take Alcatraz. "What?" I'm sure I must have said when he called me with the idea. "You mean claim the thing and keep it? Or just take it and trade for it?"

Adam, I think, saw it first the way I did—as a dramatic demonstration, meant to show the numbers and needs of American Indians in the Bay Area, that would eventually bring some return in financing for a new Indian center. A week, maybe, was all I thought the story might run, and then people would get behind building a new place in the city.

But Duskin had made some converts already, whom I underestimated. It seems to me that, in my kitchen, around the old whiskey barrel where people were bobbing for apples, something happened between people the likes of Willie Brown and Dianne Feinstein, Adam Nordwall and Richard Oakes, and a bunch of bleary-eyed reporters and bartenders, and that something seemed to make it all possible.

I'm not saying that Willie Brown or Dianne Feinstein were in on some kind of conspiracy. Maybe they didn't even hear it, but I do know that, before the party was over that night, there was tacit agreement from political forces in San Francisco that the invasion would have no serious local opposition and general agreement among what I thought to be the best reporters in the Bay Area—including representatives of the *New York Times, Newsweek*, and the Reuters News Agency—that they would await word from Adam on when the invasion would begin.

Only in 1969, I think, could such a deal have been struck in my lifetime.

It's also significant to keep in mind that, for all the rising social consciousness of those times, Indians were not well recognized or understood in cities like San Francisco. They were still the "vanishing Americans," all but invisible to most urban dwellers who were distant enough from a reservation to continue to draw their opinions from romanticized old movies.

In some ways at least, it seemed to me that young Indians were choosing to remain invisible; they consistently opted out of participation in civil rights demonstrations and antiwar rallies. A few, like Lee Brightman, made angry appearances to accuse the federal government, but most young Indians I knew did not want a place alongside black civil rights activists or tie-dyed peaceniks. There was not one single cause or overwhelming outrage that seemed capable of bringing them into lasting focus among the "movement" in the late 1960s.

Richard, unlike Adam and Bobbie, had gotten as drunk as the rest of us by the time the party finally dribbled out into dawn. His part in that night's fledgling plan would have to be translated through whatever pieces of memory survived through the next morning.

I was not yet thirty and certainly no model of wisdom for organized behavior, but even with my background in federal Indian affairs, I had only a vague understanding of what was forming as a Native American youth organization at San Francisco State University. My experience with the National Indian Youth Council years before had convinced me that the leadership would be distrustful—almost to the point of wasting better effort—of white people meaning to be helpful. I knew the stories, already almost legendary, of Clyde Warrior; I had a sense of a brewing militancy among

Indians that I could not approach even as easily as I had the leadership of the Black Panthers. As far as I knew, Richard alone would serve as the link between a possible idea and the young people who would carry it out.

Adam, of course, was more unrestrained than ever. Now I was talking to him on the phone at least once a day, and usually more. Immediately he was everywhere, like some messenger running from village to village with a new torch. Whatever Richard was doing at San Francisco State, it could not have kept pace with Adam's rapidly and relentlessly broadening network of phone calls and personal visits to people, many of whom he hardly knew at all.

But I have to say that I do not think Adam could have done it by himself. Even then, there was jealousy and resentment among Indians in the Bay Area about what they saw as Adam's desire for publicity—something to which I suppose I had contributed in earlier stories about the United Bay Area Council. Lee Brightman, a rising star in the media himself, resented Adam, I think, and so did Stella Leach, who felt slighted by Adam in the organization and activities of the council. If it had been a matter of Adam's organizing his own generation, the Alcatraz invasion might not have happened.

But Richard certainly could not have done it or even conceived of it without Adam, either. Some things about Richard seemed just too obvious to accept easily. He had sculptured good looks and a full, muscular stature that kept calling up media comparisons to Victor Mature—an Indian who looked like an Italian who played an Indian. He was a Mohawk; when asked, he would confirm that he, like all cliché Mohawk men, had worked in high steel. He had a beautiful wife and six children, and he was working his way through college toward some uncertain degree. Richard seemed ready-made for the media.

I took my own job rather self-importantly as being beyond such shallow veneers; I felt that my work was directed at the greater insights and issues that would influence the times (and even the *Times*).

Adam was always available and ready for a quote, but I thought he was wearing out his originality and becoming a celebrity without enough depth of standing. If the affair of Alcatraz was to be seen seriously as a means to create support for urban Indians, it needed more raw, unpolished material than Adam himself could provide. Richard would serve that purpose for much of the media, but few of them knew of Richard's difficulty in organizing and maintaining support among the young Indians who would be vital to the effort.

That makes it sound as if I know more than I really do about the organizing efforts that November. All I am sure of is that a young Native American woman, a fellow student at San Francisco State, seemed to me to have done the hard logistics work that would ultimately produce a triumph for

Richard. Her story, I think, deserves to be told more than any other from those days, but she herself never sought recognition and ultimately, in what I regard as a tragic incident, left it all to the fates in unplanned contention. Let me tell you about that incident now, even though it occurred much later in the narrative of the Alcatraz experience.

It was near the time for the most important action, and Richard had asked to meet with me to be certain about the details. As always, the young woman who kept track of the important names and numbers would join us. And, as always, she arrived first at the little bar behind the *Chronicle*.

Richard came in later, alone, but was instantly recognized by the other reporters and local luminaries who frequented the place. The three of us sat at a table and went over the plans, between interruptions from various people who were already in on the loosely kept secret. The young Indian woman was rightfully concerned that Richard was getting carried away by the attention and was not focusing on what could be some very problematic logistics. Richard, though, remained confident, almost boisterous, as beer after beer cluttered the table.

Suddenly, Richard's wife, Anne, came through the door. Richard had not told us that, for all the time he sat talking and drinking with us at the table, he had left Anne and their children outside in the car. Anne was furious to find Richard talking with another woman. She sat down only momentarily before bursting into a tirade against both of them. At last, in a rage, she grabbed a bottle and threw it with full force into the face of the other woman.

Richard comforted neither of them. He and Anne left together. The young woman, who was really more responsible than Richard for organizing the invasion, left alone and, to my knowledge, never had anything more to do with Alcatraz. For what it's worth to anybody, there was nothing sexual or romantic between her and Richard. Nor do I think Richard was intentionally abusive or indifferent to Anne and the children. It was just that he was carried so wildly away with his own image.

From the beginning of my experience with it, there were always those two stories about the Alcatraz occupation: One of them, as represented by Adam, was the showmanship and daring good nature that could capture the public spirit; the other, seen early in Richard, was something brooding and ultimately uncertain about the real purpose. I know how this will be regarded by others, but I came to see these aspects as the contrasting faces of comedy and tragedy, sometimes a farce, sometimes a bitter melodrama, never really understanding each other.

Adam, of course, never doubted himself, not even in the first attempt to reach Alcatraz, when somebody in Oakland convinced the boat owners not to go through with it, and the pack of loyal media were about to record a memorable failure. Adam simply stalled them by having Richard read the statement comparing the island to a neglected and oppressed reservation, while Adam, in full Chippewa dance regalia, went to talk the captain of a three-masted barque into carrying the Indians on a bluffing sail around the island, complete with booming cannon fire.

Without the publicity of that incredibly fortuitous sail of the *Monte Cristo*, there might not have been support for a real invasion later. Yet there was near-tragedy that could have ruined all plans: Richard and three others jumped off the ship and attempted to swim to the island; strong currents very nearly carried them out to the Golden Gate before some of us in circling media boats picked them up. Joe Bill made it, however, and deserves to be remembered as the first Indian to invade Alcatraz in 1969.

Later that same day, Adam arranged for still another boat from Fisherman's Wharf and took fifteen Indians, including Richard, out for a successful landing. Adam came back with the boat and called me, and I called the caretaker on the island to inform him that he had company. Despite his denials, the Indians were found the next day by federal officials accompanied by a pack of media. I should say, actually, that the Indians found us. Richard nearly sent me over a wall when he popped out of a window to say hello.

The federal man in charge, Tom Hannon of the General Service Agency, seemed to take it all in a good spirit, asking the Indians, "You guys want a ride back to town?" "Got any food on board?" was the first response.

From then on, really, the two stories of Alcatraz began to diverge more and more from each other. Adam still held to his busy enthusiasm of rounding up support from anybody who would listen—and from many who would not. He led the older, established community of Bay Area Native Americans, whom he knew from weekend powwows and gatherings of the United Council. Richard, on the other hand, had his group of students who seemed to keep changing their title in search of one that fit. He and the students set about with determined focus to meet an invasion date, keeping the details as secret as if it were D-Day but hardly able to disguise that it would have to conform to some break in the college semester schedule.

I think Adam, even though he saw the possibilities of a prolonged occupation, still thought of Alcatraz as a bargaining chip for something better in recognition of the Indian presence in the Bay Area. But Richard and the younger people wanted no compromise; they now had tasted success and wanted nothing more or less than the island.

The problem was that neither Adam's group nor Richard's had any boats or knew where to get any. That's where the party became important again. Peter Bowen was a scrimshaw artist and the bartender at Sausalito's No Name Bar, where every writer and journalist who could afford to live in or visit Marin County hung out, at least from time to time. It was the sort of well-lighted, well-read, wink-at-a-joint place where the newly prosperous young intelligentsia swapped lies. Peter also owned a neat little motor sailer docked in Sausalito and was the de facto leader of an equally irreverent group of ragtag young yachtsmen who also hung out at the No Name.

Brookes Townes, himself a former *Chronicle* reporter and denizen of the Sausalito yacht harbor, had the sort of practical spirit and gadfly energy that filled in whatever gaps there were between Peter and the other boat owners. Richard asked me to help also, but without Bowen and Townes and the No Name in general, I would have been useless on the waterfront.

Again, it was those times, the convergence of many events. Even if Alcatraz became government surplus again, I don't think an occupation could happen today. Even then, Bowen and the other boat owners knew they were risking the loss of their vessels or worse if they were caught by the Coast Guard, not to mention the considerable risk to life and limb from attempting night landings in a slip where none of them had ever before docked.

But Peter saw it almost immediately as a reckless adventure perfectly suited to his spirit and those of the other boat owners. It was the Adam part of the story. The role I played presented ethical problems as obvious to me as they would have been to my editors had they been called on to make a decision. The truth is, they knew without my having to tell them. It was a good story, and, by helping to arrange for the boats myself, I was ensuring that the *Chronicle* would have an exclusive part of it.

Amazingly, however, the paper remained reluctant to permit the depth of coverage that I had prepared for by spending considerable time on the island with the occupiers. For me, covering the story was always much less of a problem than getting what I wrote past the city editor. To him, this was still just a bunch of college kids creating a "stunt" because they had too much time on their hands.

The night of the invasion has caused me some headaches for the two decades and more since. Adam was in Minneapolis, set to announce the action as soon as it was done. All the other older leaders were involved in setting up the land-based support, which remained in doubt. Richard had to handle the invasion force himself.

Photographer Vince Maggoria and I hung out in downtown Sausalito and in the No Name until the designated closing hour of the bar, by which time Indians were supposed to have filtered into the upscale tourist town unnoticed. They were about as unnoticed as eighty or more Indian men and women milling around with packs and sleeping bags could expect to be. But I think the police just did not make the connection.

Brooks insists he has been unfairly characterized as overreacting when he went out in a small boat to check on the presence of the Coast Guard and mistook a lighted dredge for the island, lit up as if anticipating an invasion. Still, that is how I remember it, and I know there were some uncertain moments about whether to go ahead until we determined for sure it was a dredge and not the island that was flooded with lights.

There were not enough boats to take everybody in one trip, and the boat owners were rightfully concerned about overloading. I wanted Richard with me and Vince on Peter's motor sailer in the first wave of the landing. Say whatever you will, there was a certain high drama and excitement to powering up to the looming shadow of the island with only one small splash of light showing around the small caretaker's shack. Peter nervously bumped his boat into the concrete slip and hissed sharp warnings to wait for the waves before jumping off. I shared his terror at the thought of someone falling between the boat and the dock in the dark. But no one did, and as soon as we felt the solid concrete platform under our feet, we made a commando-like dash for a crane parked nearby, where we crouched and waited to see if there would be some kind of reaction from the guard shack.

Glenn Dobson must not have believed his ears or his eyes when he awoke. The little assistant caretaker, then at least in his fifties, had been left on his own to watch the island while the former guard who ran the place was off on the mainland with his scruffy little dog, fishing, as we later learned.

"Mayday! Mayday! The Indians have landed!" Glenn started shouting for no possibly good purpose. I immediately remembered Jake Gunn in the old *Treasure Island* movie I had seen as a child. I had lost track of Richard, and I don't think I saw him again until we had all scrambled up the long hill from the waterfront to the cellblock that dominates the island. By then, Peter and the other boats had made another trip to pick up the second wave.

In the cabin of his boat, Peter had hung a prized walrus tooth carved with scrimshaw and held on a leather thong. When I found Richard on the hill, I noticed that he was wearing it. That was the Richard part of the story again. Peter confronted Richard about it in the prison exercise yard that night, and Richard just shrugged. A fight almost broke out, but I had the impression that Richard was already feeling secure about calling whatever shots he chose to on the occupied island. Eventually, I talked him into returning Peter's scrimshaw, and Peter remained helpful for days to come, but some real damage had already been done to the good will and support of the white boat owners who would be needed again and again in the occupation.

Just as it had been in that incident with Anne, it wasn't that Richard had intended to do anything wrong. I think he meant to give the scrimshaw back, but that night he also felt the irrepressible need for some sort of talisman, some symbol appropriate to his image. You couldn't blame Richard for feeling a sense of power, that night especially. We all felt it, even Peter. Nothing like this had ever been done before, and no matter what happened in the morning, we were, for that night, totally and gloriously in control of our own island and our own destiny. We sat with Richard on the carpet liner that still remained in the old warden's house and, frankly, enjoyed it.

As those first exhilarating days of the occupation went on with comic encounters between yachtsmen of all descriptions eager to help us, and the Coast Guard clumsily trying and failing to head off their supply runs to the island, Adam and his group of older Indians on the mainland were trying quietly to pull something together that would make permanent sense of the invasion. Adam's people weren't much older than the college students occupying the island—a generation at most, only a family and a full-time job's difference. Most of them had already served in some capacity with other Indian organizations or through their own businesses.

In those days, though, a serious and often uncrossable gulf existed between those who were under thirty and those who were older. The younger people on the island were getting most of the media attention, Richard especially, and the mainland support group was not really necessary to keep the supplies coming: Enthusiastic whites were eager to carry full banquets out to the island from pricey restaurants, just for the chance to look around. Some of it—a lot, maybe—was in support of the Native Americans and their cause, but some—a lot more of it than many admitted—was really just curiosity about the old prison, the same curiosity that today makes the island San Francisco's most successful tourist attraction.

It made good sense, then, that the Indians trying to live on the island and secure it from a counterinvasion by the federal government would establish some form of control over visitors, who crowded onto boats and bartered their way onto the island in exchange for a frozen turkey or a jug of wine. Alcatraz security even included the presence of Joe Bill himself, still as good natured as ever. But security somehow always has a way of taking itself too seriously. Even before Anne and Richard's daughter Yvonne was fatally hurt that December in a fall down a stair shaft in the old barracks, talk on the mainland was that the occupiers were splitting themselves into two groups: security and everybody else.

The analogy to William Golding's *Lord of the Flies* was just too obvious to miss. I knew from the incidents between Richard and Anne and then Richard and Peter that I had become too close to the whole story to write about it with professional objectivity. What I had written had helped to create it, and what I had chosen not to write had helped to perpetrate it. I am not really sorry about that. Given the same set of facts and the same situation again, I don't think I would feel obligated to "expose" Richard or somehow tarnish the fervor of it all.

But by mid-December 1969, I did feel obligated to correct some illusions I had helped to create, not just among white readers, but among Indian occupiers and their supporters as well. Thanks primarily to Adam, I still had entree to the innermost circles of the organizing groups, especially the older mainland supporters. Vine Deloria was someone I had known even longer than I had known Adam; I regarded him as my mentor on Indian issues from the time I was a teenager reporting news on rock-and-roll radio. Vine's presence in the Bay Area that winter as part of an effort to head off a growing political split among Indians over Alcatraz was the most hopeful sign I had seen. But one night I was in the Mission District, within a block or two of where the burned-out hulk of the old Indian Center still sagged, when the younger, more militant Indians from Alcatraz told Adam and Vine that the mainland Bay Area Native American Council would have to take direction from the island from then on. Richard had already left the island and was involved in planning and staging a new occupation on the Pit River that I think he hoped would revive the personal image stilled and muted by Yvonne's death.

With the young occupiers' demand for control, the Adam part of the story, the part that was characterized by brash good humor and marvelous, if lucky, successes in public relations, was over. Richard's story would go on without Alcatraz, but it would always be linked to Alcatraz, and it would be more tragic than ever. The fun was gone.

I wrote a three-part series about the dissension on the island, referring to Golding and even making references to racist ditties about "ten little Indians." I showed it to both Adam and Vine before I put it across the city desk. I hated writing it, and I wished someone else on some other paper had done it so I could criticize them. When some of the article was changed by an editor, I asked to have my byline taken off the story. In the end, though, I felt it was my responsibility to say what had to be said.

I know that some Native Americans on the island whom I had once counted as friends felt betrayed. I know that some of the younger people, and certainly Stella Leach among the older ones, regarded me as taking "Adam's side" in a dispute over the purpose of the invasion and occupation. But I had done it with the same intention—and with some of the same fudging of professional ethics—that had gotten me so involved in the first place. I thought that at least if people could get mad at me, they might be less mad at each other. As it turned out, the city editor was right; I did belong in a wiggly box.

Through all of that, though, the government was still looking for some way to settle the matter of Alcatraz and the Indians without a confrontation. Since that first morning when Tom Hannon of the GSA had offered everybody a ride back to the mainland, I had maintained at least a working relationship with the federal authorities. Although Adam still held a trusted place in policymaking, I felt that perhaps I could serve as a convener and host to some kind of talks about a deal. William Daveron, who had been appointed by the Nixon administration as coordinator for the Department of the Interior on the matter, evidently held the same view. In January, Daveron asked if I could help him convene a meeting of the principals on the issue.

Daveron chose his house in Tiburon as the site for informal talks; I was there only to introduce the Alcatraz leaders and to offer what insights I could about public opinion. It was friendly and cordial, as Daveron intended, but the bottom line was that the government was willing to offer the Indians their own chosen piece of the park-like Fort Mason on the San Francisco waterfront, some of the most valuable public property in the United States, if they would give up Alcatraz.

Richard was gone. Adam was not calling the shots. None of the leaders on the island regarded me as being owed anything but grudging trust. They said, "No," and vowed to stick it out on the island, and I still regard that as a major error.

I went to Pit River with Richard and, with less direct involvement, had much the same exclusive rights to the story of the occupation of power company lands there. I continued to write about Alcatraz also, as the occupation went into its first full year, even though the people there had altered their attitudes in response to shifting pressures from the outside, including from some of my old friends in the New Left movement.

The old Age of Aquarius attitude of 1969 wore away rapidly with the change of the decade, and with it faded a lot of hope for an easy transition into peace, real justice, and goodwill in America. There was a fire on Alcatraz. I noticed it that night crossing the Bay Bridge on my way to some other story, but I didn't write about it, and I don't know how it started.

Richard came back from Pit River and was beaten half to death with a pool cue in a Mission District bar. Indians said a Samoan did it. This time, I did write something about it, attributing this incident to the same cultural conflict that some say set a torch to the Indian Center and touched off the Alcatraz invasion in the first place.

The last thing I did in connection with Alcatraz was, in its own symbolic way, the most curious of all. After the fire, the federal government cut off power on the island. They had always avoided that before, because some power was necessary to keep the old lighthouse running. But now, the government said, new buoys in the water off shore made the lighthouse unnecessary.

That was too much for Scott Newhall, the executive editor of the *Chronicle*, who lived in a high-rise apartment building almost exactly across the bay from my house in Sausalito and enjoyed the opposite end of the pulsing Alcatraz light. He ordered me to find out what the Indians needed to restore the light. Aside from fresh bulbs and lenses, they said, they needed a major gas generator.

I ruined a leather coat from spiraling up inside that sooty lighthouse to help the newspaper's electrician repair the lenses, but the marks on the coat are the only tangible souvenirs I have from the occupation. I remember going out to the island earlier in the day to talk about what would be needed, and, on the way, LaNada Means told me she was so bitter about things I had written that, if she could, she would throw me off the boat.

By the time Trudell and the others were finally forced to leave Alcatraz, I had moved on to another job with *Rolling Stone* magazine. Richard had been killed. He had called only the night before to tell me that he was going to set up a deer ranch that would draw more attention than Alcatraz. Something mystical happened the night he died: I thought I heard and saw a big, dark bird call my name and fly away. Adam adopted me into his Crow family, and they gave me a new name that I try to live up to. The house in Sausalito belongs to someone else now. The No Name is not the same place. All the editors have died. Alcatraz is the money-maker of the National Park Service, which still refuses to erect anything seriously acknowledging the Indian occupation.

In 1994, Adam officially "discovered" Sweden and claimed it, by right of discovery, for Native American people. The Swedes loved it; go figure.

5

REFLECTIONS OF ALCATRAZ

LaNada Boyer

It was 5 January 1965 when I left on the Greyhound bus from my home reservation of the Shoshone and Bannock tribes to go to San Francisco. I was a participant in the Bureau of Indian Affairs Relocation Program, which sent tribal members from their reservations into the major cities of the nation to get work or learn a trade.[1]

There were no jobs on the reservation, and the "No Indians or Dogs Allowed" signs had barely been taken down in my home town of Blackfoot, Idaho.[2] Poverty, hardship, and despair had grown to be the way of life on the reservation. As a result of governmental rule, our reservation and people were suffering.

I was raised from childhood in an environment of tribal politics. My father was the tribal chairman for a number of years. His resistance to the government's attempts to steal our water and lands through the Shoshone Nation Land Claims put our whole family in jeopardy.[3] I would help my father write letters to officials to get assistance for our reservation, and it was in this way that I began to understand about the continuing war against our people.

It was a very hard time for us all; the 1960s did not bring change. When the BIA offered relocation to the city, I took the opportunity, along with many others who left their reservations. We were not aware that the federal government's plan to "drop us off" in the cities was another insidious method of depriving us of our reservation lands and membership in our tribes. Some of us knew that non-Indians were exerting intense political pressures to gain more of our lands for their economic benefit.

We began our new lives in the cities, socializing primarily with our own people. On the reservations, it was easy to divide Indians against Indians; but in a major city, we are so glad to see other Indians, we don't care what tribe they are. They are natives, and that's all that counts.

The San Francisco Indian Center became a focal point of social life for many relocated tribal members in the Bay Area. The center sponsored both powwows and non-Indian dances. It published a newsletter that many Bay Area Indian residents received. Other Indian organizations, such as the Oakland Friendship House and the San Jose Indian Center, grew out of the Bay Area where Indians were living. Our organizations eventually became a part of the city, and we were acknowledged along with other city minority organizations. Whenever Mayor Alioto went to the Mission District where many of us lived, he would meet with the Latino and Spanish groups, the Mission Rebels (blacks), and the Indians. We were recognized as a political unit, and gradually we became politicized.

I cofounded United Native Americans with Lehman Brightman, who actively led our political efforts in the Bay Area. Lee was a former University of Oklahoma football star whose intelligence, wit, and concern led him to become a strong Native American advocate. We networked with other organizations and the California Indian Education Association. One of our first efforts was to seek reform of Bureau of Indian Affairs policies to allow relocated Indians more than a one-way ticket to the city. We wanted to attend the universities in the Bay Area, but since a college education was beyond our means, we requested assistance from the BIA, which had put us there.[4] Instead, the BIA ended the relocation program in 1966.

With the support of the San Francisco Mission District organizations, I was accepted by the University of California, Berkeley. In January 1968, I was the very first Native American student to be accepted through special admissions into the Economic Opportunity Program, on probationary status. I kept up my grades and went off probation. At first, it was lonely being a native on a campus of fifty thousand students; then I met Patty Silvas, who was a Blackfeet from Salinas, California. She was the only other native on campus and had entered through regular admissions. We worked together to develop good university support.

It was not long before other native students were admitted; my program allowed me to recruit for UC Berkeley. After a while, we had enough students to form our own native student organization, which I chaired. The campus was still simmering from the free speech movement, the civil rights and antiwar protests, and it was natural for us to get caught up in the heat of campus unrest with the Third World Strike.[5]

The Third World Strike at Berkeley in 1969 was the most expensive of the Berkeley campus protests, because the university assembled the largest force of Berkeley police and National Guard ever. They marched in with their bayonets unsheathed and fogged the campus with pepper gas. Every class was interrupted and stopped. All of the Third World Strike leaders were arrested on various charges.[6] After the gas cleared away, I became one of the coalition leaders on the four-person negotiation team for our Third World College. We were victorious in establishing our own Department of Ethnic Studies, consisting of black, Chicano, Asian, and Native American studies programs within the university. Ours was the very first such department in the nation.

It was during this time that the issue of Alcatraz Island became a target of interest for us. In 1964, after the prison had been abandoned, a group of Lakota, consisting of Russell Means,[7] Hank Means,[8] Belva Cottier,[9] Richard McKenzie,[10] and others, had tried to reclaim the island as federal surplus property. Their efforts had been treated as a joke[11] by the media.

Now the island was being considered for purchase by a wealthy developer who wanted to build a casino there. We were concerned that the developer would be allowed to build his casino and the earlier claim would be ignored. This would mean that the federal government had no intention of honoring either the federal surplus laws giving lands back to native peoples or the 1868 treaty that was the basis of the Lakota claim in 1964. This failure to uphold another treaty[12] was enough to push our buttons.

The students at UC Berkeley and San Francisco State had already formed a native student alliance, so when Richard Oakes,[13] chairman of the San Francisco State student organization, contacted me at Berkeley about having the students symbolically take Alcatraz Island for the Indians, I said, "Sounds great. Let's do it." He informed me that Adam Nordwall,[14] a local Bay Area Indian businessman, was going to rent a boat to sail around the island to publicize the Indians' claim. We made arrangements to get the students together on a Sunday afternoon to sail around the island. Four of our students jumped off the boat and attempted to swim to the island. We got very little publicity, but it was a nice boat ride on a Sunday afternoon, compliments of Adam Nordwall.

During this time, the San Francisco Indian Center burned to the ground. The community was devastated. The students got together and decided to take over the island as our new center for Indians in the Bay Area. On 14 November 1969, we met on the San Francisco docks and looked for a boat to rent. Finally, we spotted some fishermen just pulling in, and I approached the first man off the boat, asking him to take us to the island one way. Since the island was closed to the public, I had to convince him that we wanted to go for a special purpose. I told him we wanted to go to the island for a ceremony, which might take us a while. He asked where our food was, and I told him we were fasting. He agreed to take us and charged us three dollars per person. Earl Livermore[15] paid for those of us who did not have any money.

As we waited for the rest of our group, it began to grow dark. The fishermen were getting impatient, and I was afraid they would back out, so we pulled away from the dock. As we were leaving, I could see outlines of figures and legs running, so I asked the fisherman to go back and pick up our friends. It was Richard Oakes and a few of the San Francisco State students. This gave us a total of fourteen Indian students. The fisherman took us out to the island and dropped us off.

We were on the island and it was beautiful. The view was a "knockout," with lights all over the Bay Area. Earl Livermore was on the mainland and would contact the press to let them know we were on the island. We split into groups and agreed that, if some of us were found, the others would continue to hide out and hold the island. It felt like a game of hide-and-seek, and we were not afraid. At times, a search party would be very close to us, and it was hard to keep from giggling or laughing. All that night, the Coast Guard looked for us with searchlights in the old buildings, but we eluded them.

In the morning, we got together and decided to splinter off into smaller groups. A few hours later, Rick Evening,[16] Kay Many Horses,[17] and I were hiding out when we heard our names being called. I said to Rick, "I thought we were going to hold out and not give ourselves up." He said he would go see what was going on. A few minutes later, he came back and said Richard Oakes had identified himself when the press arrived and had made a deal with the Coast Guard that none of us would be arrested if we all gave ourselves up. I did not want to say anything to Richard in front of everybody for the sake of unity, so, reluctantly, I got into the boat.

When we got back to the mainland, the rest of the students[18] were upset with us for coming back. They had begun mobilizing a statewide effort to get other native students to join us on the island. They were upset with Richard for making a deal to come back. We decided to continue the mobilization effort and go back to the island.

On 20 November 1969, Native American students from the major California colleges and universities arrived with their families to take the island. My sister, Claudene Boyer,[19] and my son, Deynon Means,[20] arrived with this landing party. My oldest son, Devon,[21] was not with me when we went to Alcatraz. When we arrived on the island and made our way up to the second level, I sensed a wonderful, forbidden excitement among our group. The weather was good and the view spectacular as we set up our lookout points on top of the prison. We camped out in sleeping bags all over the island. It felt great to be there and to direct our energies into a stand for Indian people everywhere.

We took the island because we wanted the federal government to honor our treaties and its own laws.[22] The previous claim had been made back in 1964, so we were the follow-up. We also wanted to focus attention on Indian reservations and communities throughout the nation where our people were living in poverty and suffering great injustice.

The next day, the press and all kinds of people arrived on the island. The international media focus embarrassed the federal government. The United States is always the first to point out human rights violations in other countries, without regard to its own treatment of Native Americans, blacks, Chicanos, Asians, and poor people. We hoped to expose the atrocities that the federal government has perpetrated and continues to perpetrate against our people. Every day, as news of the island takeover traveled throughout the country, our people kept arriving. We were in full view of the entire world, and the government made no move to take us off the island.

Many people, diverse tribal groups and nonnatives alike, came to visit the island. Some were just now re-identifying as Indians and wannabes.[23] We were the tattered remnants of a proud and cultured people—what was left of our once strong and healthy nation. We did not all look or behave like our ancestors, because we were the products of our times. We were finally "civilized Indians," from liars and thieves to genuine Indian chiefs. The government's racist efforts to deny us our heritage and to assimilate us into the American mainstream had backfired with the Alcatraz takeover.[24]

In the weeks to follow, the residents quickly set out to organize the island. Everybody wanted to claim fame and to be included in the formation. I sat back and watched everyone scramble for leadership and for recognition by the media.

We had good leadership. As long as everybody wanted to be involved in the hard work of organization and island logistics, that was great. We had a big job ahead, and everybody was doing what needed to be done. Because I did not intend to drop out of school, I needed to attend to my classes, so I did not want to take on any extra responsibilities unless I had to.

The media identified Richard Oakes as the leader on the island, and he wanted the responsibility, so that was agreeable with us. Richard was smart and aggressive—a handsome Mohawk who always knew what to say. We were proud of Richard. We maintained our student autonomy on the island, recognizing the separate campus organizations and community organizations. The students and their families stayed on the island as long as they could but eventually left to continue their studies.

I continued my residence on the island but kept my apartment on the mainland and commuted to the university to maintain my studies. My sister did not leave the island during most of the occupation. Deynon and I would hitchhike off the docks at Alcatraz and would occasionally catch a sailboat or speedboat to the marina on Sunday afternoon, clean up, and check into my classes.

When the government blocked our water barge and boats from docking on the island, Richard successfully brought in food and provisions on the opposite side of the island, where it was impossible to dock because of the high cliffs. When the government took the water barge away, we brought water over in a boat that Creedence Clearwater Revival bought for us. They bought the boat from "Captain Cliff," whom we hired to take us back and forth from the mainland to the island. We named our boat the *Clearwater*.

Initially, we took up residence in the prison block. It was winter in the Bay Area, and it rained most of the time, but we were able to survive under those conditions because life was not very different from the poverty on the reservations or in the urban ghettos. It was inconvenient to live on the island without water, electricity, or heat, but most of us became conditioned to the elements. People who were not conditioned to the elements got sick when they stayed.

We formed an island organization called Indians of All Tribes. A lot of rivalry and competition always existed on the island. I sensed that the Indian men did not want to recognize the authority of the women, because they had been assimilated into white society and its male chauvinism.

Everyone had a job on the island—to help on the boats, with the school, or anywhere else they were willing to work. Stella Leach,[25] a registered Indian nurse, and Dr. Tepper had moved out to the island right after the invasion. They operated the first aid unit and provided medical support. Dr. Tepper finally went back to his medical practice in Oakland, but Stella stayed on the island.

Grace Thorpe[26] kept up public relations with the mainland. Sometime later, she bumped heads with the island council and left, but not until after she had helped the Pit River Indians to hold their land in Northern California, which was threatened by Pacific Gas and Electric (PG&E) Company. A group of Alcatraz Indians joined the Pit River Indians to protect their sacred site; in a confrontation with the police, it took nearly a dozen officers to carry Grace Thorpe off the property.

Richard Oakes was hurt on the mainland during a fight in a bar; he was hit over the head numerous times with a pool stick. He made a miraculous recovery in the hospital, thanks to Thomas Banyacya[27] and an attending group of medicine men (including Mad Bear Anderson) from the Iroquois Confederation, only to face great sadness later. Richard and his family left the island when his stepdaughter Yvonne died after falling four stories in an apartment building in the guards' quarters.

During the occupation, a number of Alcatraz Indians left for Washington State to support the Nisqually Indians, who were fighting for fishing rights at Frank's Landing. President Nixon signed a bill that returned the sacred Blue Lake to Taos Pueblo. More funding was appropriated by Congress for programs on the reservations. Indians from Alcatraz supported the Pyramid Lake Paiute people in their efforts to keep their sacred lake. Alcatraz provided help to Indian efforts to establish D-Q University in Davis, California. Alcatraz was a "rock" that hit the water and sent out a thousand ripples: Nearly a thousand documented events resulted from the occupation of Alcatraz.

Spiritual Rebirth

I took up residence on the second level of a house. My house, which I had painted red, had a beautiful view of the bay, and my room had enough space for my two double beds, like a hotel room. The other bed was for my guests, such as medicine man Pete Mitten and his wife, from New York, who stayed with me during their visit to the island, and Thomas Banyacya and his wife, Fermina.

Thomas Banyacya told me that he had traveled internationally since being appointed as a translator by the chiefs in 1945. After the bombing of Hiroshima, the Hopi had become alarmed at the destructive direction of the United States. According to their rock writings and prophecies, the bomb marked the beginning of a harmful era and had to be stopped somehow by warning as many people as possible of what was to come.

Thomas told me that he and his wife had come to Alcatraz to see for themselves what was happening. In accordance with the Hopi prophecies, the "tree of Indian life" was cut off at the base, but, through the nourishment of the ancient roots, sprouts were growing out of the base of the tree. It was encircled with a design that matched the Bay Area, and the tree growing new sprouts was located where Alcatraz lay in the bay. He said that the young people are the new sprouts growing out of the Indian tree of life. The takeover of Alcatraz symbolized this rebirth.

Thomas told me about the Hopi prophecy.[28] To my understanding, the world had ended three times before this world. It was always the result of misusing modern inventions for destructive purposes instead of for peace. This time, it was not supposed to happen. All people would have the choice of continuing in the destructive direction or coming back to the sacred circle of life and perpetuating the spiritual ways of our forefathers. We need to clean up the earth and the environment now, before the three purifiers come from the east. If the people do not change their ways, the earth will shake to wake up the people. Our ancestors will help us survive through the purification if we maintain our beliefs, practices, and spiritual ways.

My personal experience happened one night while I was asleep in my room. I woke up to see a fire in the curtains. Because I was still half asleep, I did not think; I followed my first instinct, which was to protect my son. I threw myself at the fire and put it out with my hands. There had been two other fires that same night, and the men had just finished battling another blaze on the island. I lived over the dining hall, and the men were downstairs having coffee when I emerged from my room carrying my son, with smoke following behind me.

I handed Deynon over to someone and then fell over. My hands were badly burned, and I had gone into shock. Shock felt good to me, because I felt no pain and it was good to see everyone working together. Several people ran upstairs to see if the fire was out; others rushed to put my hands into cold milk and to carry me to a bed they had assembled in the kitchen. They put my hands into milk because we had no water. There was no boat scheduled until the next day, so they could not take me to the mainland.

They must have suspected arson, because they put me on a cot in the kitchen and guarded me all night. My eyes were closed, but my spirit could see everything all around me. It was an experience I'll never forget. I saw Stella sitting by me all night, and I knew when she fell asleep. I knew who looked into the window at me during the night while on guard duty. I remember the first rays of dawn coming over the horizon, and I remember our one rooster crowing. Stella covered me with the Pendleton blanket that my parents had given me. I remembered my mother telling me how to receive spiritual strength from saying her prayers at sunrise. I gathered my blanket around me, slipped out of the kitchen into the yard and over to the edge of the island. I lifted my hands to the sun and prayed as it rose over the Bay Bridge in the east. I experienced a deep knowledge inside me that I would be all right.

The boat arrived in a few hours, and Stella took me over to Dr. Tepper's office in Oakland. My hands were charred black, and my fingers were huge and swollen like boiled wieners. I had from first- to third-degree burns on both hands. The doctor said they were burned down to the tendons. His medical diagnosis was that I would never be able to use my fingers again.

I refused Dr. Tepper's advice to go to the hospital. He peeled the charred skin off my hands to reveal raw, pink fingers. Then he applied a burn ointment and covered it with bandage dressing. He said it would take six months to a year before I could use my hands. I went back to the island, and, miraculously, my hands healed within six weeks with hardly any trace of scarring. I recovered full use of all my fingers. This was my very first spiritual experience. I had learned what to say by repeating everything my father taught me; I knew what to do by remembering my mother's words of caution and guidance.[29]

The federal government sent Bob Robertson to negotiate with us on the island.[30] We looked forward to this occasion and were as friendly as possible in order to encourage a good relationship. We did not have much, but we offered him coffee and brownies for this occasion. We did not use sugar, because it attracted insects; instead, we used saccharin in small tablets, which was much more efficient for our living conditions. We asked him if he wanted sugar in his coffee and he said "yes," so we put in saccharin. His report to Washington said that we had put LSD[31] in his coffee and he had refused to drink it. Actually, I never noticed whether he drank his coffee. How paranoid he must have been!

This experience gave me keen insight into how the game of "divide and conquer" is played. Robertson told us he would not work with a "bunch of young militant Indians" who did not have the support of the responsible adult Indian community. We told him we were not militant Indians because we were unarmed.

To further our negotiations to obtain the island for our people, we formed the Bay Area Native American Council (BANAC),[32] composed of all the Bay Area Indian organizations as a support group for Alcatraz. Robertson's first ploy was to fund BANAC, hoping that the Alcatraz residents would resent the government's funding of the off-island organization while the island organization was dependent on contributions. However, this did not cause anyone to blink an eye, because no one knew what it was to be funded[33] in the first place. The money gave BANAC a larger voice in Indian affairs and a more vivid profile.

Next, Allen Miller,[34] a San Francisco State student, and I went to Washington, D.C., to gather more support from the National Congress of American Indians (NCAI). This organization was composed of tribes throughout the country, and we needed their formal support. John Belindo, the NCAI director, was not very receptive. Perhaps Robertson had gotten to him before we did. We were told that it would be up to the delegation. Their national convention was in Alaska, so we had to go to Alaska to seek support.

Bob Robertson was way ahead of us in lobbying against Alcatraz. He knew we had formed BANAC to quash his claim that Alcatraz did not have the support of the responsible adult community. Robertson's propaganda to the tribes was not only that we were young militants but also that we were "urban" Indians. He told the tribes that the urban Indians were after a slice of the "federal economic pie." The reservations were already receiving very little federal funding, and the pie would be sliced even smaller if the tribes supported the militant urban Indians. We could not even get on the agenda, and we were barred from the NCAI convention.

Robertson found adversaries to our cause among various tribal chairmen and established the National Tribal Chairman's Association (NTCA).[35] Thus he created an effective tool to divide Indians against Indians. Tribes fell into the trap. Negotiations on the island disintegrated. The government position was to let us stay, hoping that we eventually would lose support and disappear. To speed the process, they would send out "plants" to observe us and to stir up in-fighting among the island residents.

The island council appointed me as the island's public relations representative. I started by talking with press people about the island, about our people, and about the reservations. Then I was invited to the mainland to appear on news programs to discuss the island situation.

Several times, the local media reported that the Coast Guard had seen weapons being loaded on the island. I knew that the federal government was trying to set us up to get killed. When it began to look dangerous for us, I called a press conference on the island to dispel any rumors that we had guns. I had the children line up with their toy guns and throw them away. I said if the Coast Guard had seen guns, it must have been the children's toys, and now there were none.

I was dead set against guns on the island. My experiences at Berkeley had shown me what happened to the Black Panthers after they were reported to be armed and militant. They were all killed. My mother never allowed guns in our home while I was growing up. She always said that my brothers were too young and hot-headed, so I never had any use for guns. Thomas Banyacya told me that the word *Hopi* meant peace and that our people were the true people of peace. I would not allow the symbolism of Alcatraz to be defiled by violence. Besides, I am a mother, and I would not let anyone endanger my son or the other children on the island.

A San Francisco leftist magazine by the name of *Ramparts* had paid my fine during the Third World Strike at Berkeley. Peter Collier of *Ramparts* asked me if he could take some pictures and do a story about the problems on my reservation. When the story came out, I posed for the cover with a red paintbrush in my hand and the words "Better Red Than Dead." To me, it meant we should be proud of being Native Americans and we should not assimilate and let our culture die. I did not realize I was pushing buttons from the McCarthy era. Since *Ramparts* was not a mainstream magazine, I did not think it would receive wide circulation. I thought speaking out would help create a better understanding, but my words were twisted in the press.[36]

Jane Fonda[37] saw the article and came out to the island. She said she wanted to go to Fort Hall, so I took her to my reservation to meet my parents. After she visited with them and some of my father's friends, she went back to California, inviting me to appear on several local television shows in Los Angeles. My son Deynon and I went to Los Angeles, and then I went to New York for the "Dick Cavett Show." Deynon stayed at Henry Fonda's house in California with Jane's husband, Roger Vadim, who remained with their daughter Vanessa and Deynon while Jane and I were in New York.

I had never been on a television show, and it made me feel extremely uncomfortable. During the first commercial break on the Cavett show, I got up and walked off because I thought I was supposed to leave. I felt awkward, wondering if I was supposed to be witty and funny about the injustices perpetrated against our people.

During this time, after Richard Oakes had left Alcatraz, Stella Leach got fed up with the politics and the constant attacks on her and her family and she left also. As a member of the Alcatraz council, I had to become more involved, since many of the other members had left.

John Trudell,[38] who ran "Radio Free Alcatraz," became the spokesperson for the island. John had strong leadership qualities and a good speaking voice and always had something meaningful to say. John became the new leader for Alcatraz, and we worked well as a team. I welcomed the opportunity to have John in the spotlight, making the presentations to the media, while I, in the background, prepared the press releases.

It was about this time that I wrote the planning grant proposal for Thunderbird University and Cultural Center, named for a group of Indians in the Bay Area called the Thunderbirds.[39] The island chose the architectural firm of McDonald and Associates of San Francisco to develop the design and model. We unveiled our plans on our first anniversary on the island, 20 November 1970.

As the executive secretary of the Bay Area Native American Council (BANAC), I was asked to go to Washington, D.C., with the other officers. Before I left the island, we held a meeting at which John Trudell became very angry with me and made some rude accusations. I did not want to throw more fuel on the fire by having a confrontation; instead, I rushed down to the docks to catch my boat for the mainland. All of the island residents were aware of the rift.

Ethel Kennedy set up an appointment for me to discuss the Alcatraz situation with Edward Bennett Williams.[40] On 21 January 1971, I wrote a letter to the island, with copies to the island attorneys and BANAC, requesting approval to secure Edward Bennett Williams as legal counsel to pursue the litigative end for Alcatraz.

While in D.C., I stayed with Edgar Cahn, author of *My Brother's Keeper*, and his wife, Jean, who were responsible for many of the poverty and advocacy programs for Native Americans and poor people throughout the country. President Nixon had been elected and was now taking office. Edgar's contact in the White House, Bobby Kilberg, was writing Nixon's inauguration address, which was to be titled the "President's White House Address on American Indians." This message set the tone for programs directed to benefit Indians on reservations throughout President Nixon's administration. The very first and last help we ever received was too short-lived.

When I received no response from the island, I went back to see what was going on. John Trudell told me that the island attorneys had advised him and the other residents not to give approval to litigate. I wanted to hear what an Indian attorney would recommend and recruited John Echohawk,[41] director of the Native American Rights Fund. Echohawk went to the island and gave his legal opinion that it would greatly benefit the island and the cause if we initiated litigation.

By this time, Trudell's wife, Lou, had given birth to their son Wovoka on the island. The baby was the only Native American born on liberated territory in five hundred years. John had the respect and awe of both the island residents and the non-Indian public. Under the Alcatraz attorneys' advice, the occupiers voted down the litigation. John Trudell could have changed their minds if he had wanted to, but no one could change John's mind about seeking litigation.

I did not give up the litigation issue and went back to the student organizations to seek their support. Richard Oakes had left San Francisco State by then and was living in northern California with his wife's family and tribe. He was eventually shot to death by white racists. Allen Miller and several of the original Native American students were still attending San Francisco State.

The students at UC Berkeley and San Francisco State were still very concerned about Alcatraz. I told them that the island population was under the influence of the attorneys who had advised against litigation. The island people were down-to-earth, good people who had sacrificed the modern conveniences of the mainland and sometimes went without food in order to "hold the rock." I felt helpless to try to reach them; the divisive gap was just too wide.[42]

The students were very supportive. They decided to take back the island, outnumbering the antilitigation population and putting the movement back on track. I was greatly encouraged by this unselfish gesture. We set the date and met with our groups to arrange for boats to go out to the island. All of the students would take their families to live on the island. It would soon be summer, school would be out, and our academic survival would not be immediately threatened.

The day before we planned to go, the federal government took the remaining people off the island without a confrontation. We were devastated. We suspected that we had had an informer among us.

After the government took Alcatraz back, we all went our separate ways.[43] I guess that is how a tree grows; it splits into many branches. We were always afraid that, if the government had given us Alcatraz, they would have said, "We gave you Alcatraz; you got what you wanted!" They would have expected us to be satisfied with that. No, we want much more.

We want to live as free people in our own country. We want the government to pass laws to respect our Mother Earth, with real enforcement to protect the land, the water, the environment, and the people. We want freedom of religion—the right to be human. We want our ancestors' remains to be returned to our homelands. We want the federal government to stop contributing to the destruction around the world and to set a good example so we can all be proud to be Americans.

The Alcatraz occupation could have gone much more smoothly. People could have cooperated and supported us more. We could have had all the answers and no arguments. We have a long way to go before we can live in a balanced world and be the best people that we can be. We made many mistakes, but this is how we learn and grow.

We can see today that the tree of Indian life is growing stronger, more mature and complex. Our ancient roots continue to give our spirits strength and guidance. We did not get the island, but we aroused the consciousness of all people, including ourselves, to our plight. Every individual and every nation still has a story to be told. Within these stories are our guidelines for the future.

The island is a reminder of our ongoing relationship with the federal government. It is an infamous prison that carries the burden of the wicked deeds of others, the bondage and captivity of our people, the painful stories of human misery and suffering. The federal government has never recognized our claim and has failed to enforce many treaties and federal laws protecting our rights and those of many others.

Under the Department of the Interior, the Bureau of Indian Affairs manages our lives in the same way that Golden Gate Parks and Recreation manages Alcatraz Island. The island is surrounded by the water of the bay, just as we are surrounded by the ignorant and selfish interests of capitalistic industrialized societies. The structures on the island grow old and weather-beaten, treated with dishonor and disrespect, as are our culture and religion, and the sacred laws of Mother Earth.

Today, our people continue to live in poverty—the victims of genocide and injustice. We are political prisoners in our own homelands. We have no individual constitutional protections because we are considered "political entities." If truth and justice were truly practiced by the federal government, our traditional governments, our religious leaders, and our people would be recognized today. Our hardships have made our spirits grow stronger. We give thanks for our many blessings and pray that the sacred circle of life continues forever.

NOTES

1. The Bureau of Indian Affairs' assimilationist policy, which relocated the majority of Native Americans from the reservations to the cities, ended in 1967.

2. The 1964 Civil Rights Act made it illegal to discriminate on the basis of race, creed, or religion.

3. Our family suffered great hardships as the result of my father's stand against the government.

4. Education was promised to us under our treaties and federal laws. The 1921 Snyder Act, 25 USCA, specifically stated that the federal government would provide for our education, our health, and our general welfare.

5. This was the coalition of Asians, blacks, Chicanos, and Native Americans on the University of California, Berkeley, campus. We used the term *Third World* because our people were being exploited by international corporations and the government, the same as in any Third World country.

6. I was arrested and charged with assaulting a police officer. The charge was then reduced to a misdemeanor. I was suspended by the university for one semester because of the charges brought against me; but they were dropped, since there was no evidence, and I was readmitted the following semester.

7. Russell Means, who later became an American Indian Movement activist, is my son Deynon's uncle.

8. Hank Means is the father of Russell Means and the grandfather of my son Deynon. They are Oglala Lakota from South Dakota.

9. Belva Cottier, an Oglala Lakota historian, was actively involved in many Bay Area organizations. She is my son Deynon's relative.

10. Richard McKenzie, a Lakota, was a former president of the American Indian Center in San Francisco and was involved in Bay Area Native American issues.

11. The newspapers read "Sioux's Sue" over Alcatraz.

12. The treaties forced Indians to give up territorial hunting, gathering, and ceremonial areas and live within reservation "concentration camps"; in return, the federal government was supposed to provide food, health care, education, and general welfare. Every single treaty ever made was broken, and tribes still live in poverty as the result of the continuing violation of laws and agreements.

13. Richard Oakes was a Mohawk from the Iroquois Confederation. He and his wife, Anne (Pomo), had eight children. Richard was the chairman of the student organization at San Francisco State College. He was an intelligent young man, with natural leadership abilities and charisma.

14. Adam Nordwall, a Chippewa, owned a pest extermination business in the Bay Area and frequented local powwows, where he participated as a fancy dancer.

15. Earl Livermore, a Blackfeet artist from Montana, was the last person to serve as director of the San Francisco Indian Center before it burned down. One of his paintings portrayed Alcatraz Island, with the fog moving in over the Golden Gate Bridge. The fog took the shapes of spirit buffalo and the "Return of the Buffalo."

16. Rick Evening was a Shoshone Bannock student at San Francisco State College.

17. Kay Many Horses was a young Lakota woman who had been relocated to San Francisco from South Dakota. We called her "Kay Kay."

18. Our group from Berkeley and San Francisco State.

19. Claudene is my youngest sister. She was a student at UC Berkeley and assisted me with planning.

20. Deynon was two and a half years old. He is the son of Theodore Means, Sr., Oglala Lakota, who is a younger brother of Russell Means. Deynon is Theodore Means, Jr., also known on the island as "The Alcatraz Kid."

21. Devon was four years old and stayed with my parents on the reservation in Idaho. His father is John B. Owl of Cherokee, North Carolina.

22. The federal government forced us to give up our lands and live on reservations, where we fell into the depths of poverty and many of us died. The government failed and continues to fail to uphold the laws passed to protect us.

23. Many native people who had lost their identities and culture were inspired by the Alcatraz occupation to identify as Indians again.

24. We recognized that it was time to find out who we were and what it means to be connected with our ancestral roots.

25. Stella was a powerful spokesperson and a leader on the island. Her son David participated in both of the landing parties on 14 November and 20 November. Through her guidance and with the help of other community leaders, we were able to survive the in-fighting that resulted from the insecurities and jealousies of various individuals. She was a strong Indian woman, and I admired her for her courage and wisdom. I wish I could have been more encouraging and supportive to her. She contributed greatly to holding the island together during those hard times.

26. Grace Thorpe was the daughter of the Olympic star and great native athlete Jim Thorpe. Her goal was to get her father's Olympic medals back. The island supported this effort.

27. Thomas Banyacya was appointed by the Hopi elders in 1945 to carry the message of peace. He is an important international traveler and a knowledgeable, gifted traditionalist.

28. Banyacya says that the Hopi originated from the ancient civilizations of the Inca, the Maya, and the Aztec. After the sacred laws were violated, which meant the "coming of the continents," they needed to get themselves situated on both continents, with half of them moving into North America and the other half going into South America. The four colors of red, white, black, and yellow represent the four races of humanity. They all practiced the same ancient laws of the universe, and their people were the last contingent left to maintain the sacred laws. When they left for North America, they had to pick a site to implant the ancient roots of their nation. They selected the desert because it would be the last place that anyone else would want. This is when they became Hopi. From this point, they migrated into the four directions. They are known as different people throughout time, but their tribes are from the same roots. It is only the different plants and animals of the geographic regions that make them appear as different tribes, but the practices and beliefs are the same universal laws that everyone around the world practiced at one time.

29. My mother is Olive Burns Boyer, a strong Bannock woman. She is a master of everything she undertakes, from housecleaning to hide- and beadwork. She is a Bannock, Shoshone, and English speaker.

30. Bob Robertson was an aide to former governor Paul Laxalt and went to Washington, D.C., when Laxalt was elected senator from Nevada. Robertson is from Carson City and is far from the Indian expert he thought himself to be, but he always managed to get appointments in Republican administrations.

31. LSD is a synthetic hallucinogenic drug.

32. I liked this name, because the pronunciation was the same as my tribe, Bannock. Everyone always said that they had never heard of my tribe, and I thought it could use some exposure.

33. Organizationally and financially supported by the government or private funds.

34. Al Miller was a Seminole from Oklahoma. He was the next chief in command of the San Francisco State students and a member of the Alcatraz council for a period of time. Al was noted for his intelligence and easygoing wit.

35. The NTCA was funded initially out of Vice President Spiro Agnew's office to counter militant Indians.

36. Collier wrote an article for *Ramparts* describing me in a typically ignorant, degrading, non-Indian fashion.

37. Many people have bashed Jane Fonda's support of Indians, but she was the only mainstream movie star to come out in support of native people during the occupation of Alcatraz. She was no more ignorant of our people than the rest of non-native society, but she was more misunderstood.

38. John Trudell was a Lakota spokesperson and a leader on Alcatraz Island.

39. The Thunderbirds were a kind of Bay Area "warrior society" composed of people who banded together like a family. They were not an official organization, but they were dedicated to supporting the island. My brother Dwayne was one of their leaders.

40. Williams, an East Coast attorney who was renowned for taking sensational cases, was the owner of the Washington Redskins (professional football team).

41. John Echohawk was the first Native American attorney to graduate from the Indian law program of the University of New Mexico. He is a Pawnee from Oklahoma.

42. While I was in Washington, D.C., Herb Caen wrote an article stating that Ethel Kennedy had set me up for a screen test with a movie producer. I did not know anything about it, but the island residents apparently thought I had gone to Washington for a screen test, which caused more jealousies to flare.

43. I graduated with honors from UC Berkeley in 1971 and went back to my home reservation. In 1972, I left for law school in Washington, D.C. The Trail of Broken Treaties came to Washington that year, resulting in the takeover of the Bureau of Indian Affairs and continuing to the siege at Wounded Knee in 1973.

6

INDIAN STUDENTS AND

REMINISCENCES OF ALCATRAZ

Steve Talbot

I was involved in the 1969 occupation of Alcatraz by American Indian students from San Francisco State University and the University of California, Berkeley, during the first six months of that event. I was a volunteer instructor in the then-developing Native American studies program at UC Berkeley, and many of the original fourteen who secretly landed on Alcatraz Island on 9 November 1969 were members of my class on American Indian liberation. I have taken the occasion of the twenty-fifth anniversary of Alcatraz to add some reminiscences and perhaps little-known facts to the story that others are now documenting.[1]

As far as I can tell, the first academic article in the United States to be published on this experiment in Indian liberation was mine. It was published in *The Journal of Ethnic Studies* in 1978 on the eve of the tenth anniversary of the Alcatraz landing. Its title was "Free Alcatraz: The Culture of Native American Liberation."[2] Earlier, in the spring of 1970, I had read a draft of this article before the Northwest Anthropological Association meeting in Oregon. It is interesting to note that anthropologists, who for so long have billed themselves as experts on things Indian, totally ignored this historic event. Although my graduate work was in anthropology at UC Berkeley, my personal association and ethnic loyalties lay with the Native American community, so I made certain that the Indians of All Tribes (as the occupiers called themselves) reviewed my paper and gave me their feedback before I read it at the anthropology meeting.

The Alcatraz paper was also picked up and published by the Soviet Academy of Sciences in 1977 in their journal of ethnography (anthropology).[3] Its editor at the time was the late Julia Petrova Averkieva, who had been a student of Franz Boas, a major figure in U.S. anthropology, and who had done early research under Boas among Northwest Coast Indians. Averkieva, whom I corresponded with and subsequently met when I lived in Europe following the Alcatraz occupation, was sincerely interested in the liberation struggles of Native Americans. Although a committed communist, she had spent some ten years, with her immediate family, in Stalin's labor camps and knew a little about oppression.

The Student Liberators

In his book on Alcatraz, Adam Fortunate Eagle tells us that "the driving force behind the occupation of Alcatraz" was the Bay Area Indian community's United Council, meeting at the Intertribal Friendship House; I remember it somewhat differently.[4] The Indian students from San Francisco State University and the University of California at Berkeley were key players in the 1969 drama from the beginning. I was present at Pier 39 with the students from UC Berkeley when Richard Oakes (Mohawk) read the Alcatraz Proclamation on 9 November 1969. The students held a more militant perspective than Fortunate Eagle and company, and that is why they boarded the ship to circle the island and then daringly decided to jump overboard to swim to Alcatraz; they were making their own statement. They were removed by U.S. marshals the following day but vowed they would return to build an independent Indian community. This they later did, more than eighty persons strong—men, women, and children—on 20 November 1969.

Background Factors

Several factors or events served to create a militant spirit among the students who contributed to taking Alcatraz Island in 1969: Indian protest books, for example, that the students were reading. These included Vine Deloria's *Custer Died for Your Sins* and Stan Steiner's *The New Indians*, both published in 1969, as well as Edgar Cahn's *Our Brother's Keeper* and Harold Cardinal's *The Unjust Society* (about the Indian struggle in Canada), which came out about the same time.

Some of the students knew that Indian leaders of the past had been imprisoned on Alcatraz. Jack D. Forbes (Powhatan-Lenapi) included this in some of his writings, and I told my students about an elderly Tohono O'Odham (Papago) chief who refused to let his men register for the World War II draft, asserting instead his own Indian nationality and allegiance to Mexico. He was imprisoned on Alcatraz by the federal authorities and died shortly after his release, in part as a result of his imprisonment.

Before the occupation, both campuses were visited by an Iroquois traveling college, The White Roots of Peace, and the students saw the film on

the Cornwall Bridge blockade entitled *You Are on Indian Land*. More important, strikes and demonstrations were taking place on the two campuses as
part of the antiwar movement, and there was a six-week strike by Third
World students at Berkeley to establish an ethnic studies department to offer relevant courses and meaningful programs for Native Americans and
other minority students.[5] These events had an important impact on the mood
and thinking of the Native American students, who were embittered by the
termination and relocation policies of the U.S. government and the institutional racism they encountered at almost every turn, including in higher
education.

United Native Americans (UNA) and its spokesperson, Lehman ("Lee")
Brightman, deserve some credit also. Jack D. Forbes, Lee Brightman (La-
kota-Creek), Horace Spencer (Navajo), and I were the core of this group at
the time of the Alcatraz occupation. Although Lee was not directly involved
in the Alcatraz takeover, under his leadership UNA certainly showed the
Indian people of the San Francisco Bay Area some new methods of protest.
Even before he became the director of the Native American studies program
at Berkeley in the fall of 1969, Brightman incited Indians to picket the San
Francisco federal building and other strategic places for Indian rights. One
tactic he employed well was to get Indian student pickets out with signs, make
a little noise, and then call in the press. This way he would catch the media's attention in order to address an important Indian issue and distribute
a UNA press release. He managed to break through the stereotype that
militant protest "is not the Indian way."

UNA published its newspaper, *Warpath*, before and during the Alcatraz
events, giving excellent publicity and coverage to the "new Indian" movement. Students also read *The Renegade*, put out by Survival of the American
Indians (Washington State fishing tribes). Of course, *Akwesasne Notes*, which
had started publishing in 1968 after the Cornwall Bridge blockade, was an
ever-inspiring source of news on the Indian struggle.

For a time, the National Indian Youth Council (NIYC) was headquar-
tered in the old Claremont Hotel in Berkeley, as was the Far West Laboratory for Research and Educational Development. Many of us referred to the
latter as the "Far Out Lab" because the work of this government laboratory
seemed so irrelevant to the needs of the minority community. The single
noteworthy exception was Jack Forbes's department in minority research
which, under his direction and authorship, produced excellent materials on
African-American, Mexican-American, and Indian history and contributions
to the Far West. It was Forbes who became the "father" of the new ethnic
studies programs at UC Berkeley and, later, the program at UC Davis. In
collaboration with the student activists at Berkeley, he drafted a well-rea-
soned proposal for an ethnic studies department at UC Berkeley embrac-

ing African-Americans, Latinos, Asian-Americans, and Indians. (A similar process took place on the San Francisco State campus under the leadership of Richard Oakes.) This development at Berkeley became a reality in October 1969, on the eve of the Alcatraz takeover. The ethnic studies proposal included a wide complement of course descriptions, as well as detailed budget breakdowns. Thus the Far Out Lab became a common meeting ground for NIYC types such as Mel Thom and Clyde Warrior, along with Forbes and those associated with UNA. The California Indian Education Association, with Dave Risling at its helm, and Indian leaders and elders from the San Francisco Bay Area Indian community were not infrequent visitors. I was Forbes's research assistant for a time, until I entered graduate school at Berkeley, so I either witnessed or participated in many of these activities firsthand.

The Course on Native American Liberation

One of the courses developed by Forbes for the new Native American studies program at UC Berkeley was the class on Indian liberation. During spring term 1969, LaNada Boyer (Bannock-Shoshone—formerly LaNada Means) picketed during the Third World Strike, Forbes developed the proposal for ethnic studies, Lee Brightman (also a Berkeley student) agitated under the UNA banner, and Patty La Plant (formerly Patty Silvas, a California Indian) worked in student government to prepare the proper student paperwork. Boyer was the main Indian student activist on the Berkeley campus working for the establishment of an Indian studies program; she later became a leader in the Indians of All Tribes group on Alcatraz. By the summer session, Forbes had scouted out a basement room in a vacant university cottage at the north entrance to the campus, which the Berkeley Indian students then occupied (shades of things to come). It was there that we held our first Indian class, and it was there, also, that the Berkeley and San Francisco State students met and held a strategy session for taking Alcatraz. I remember especially Richard Oakes and Al Miller (Seminole), although others may have been present from San Francisco State.

The course on Indian liberation was first taught in the summer of 1969, just before the Alcatraz takeover. Since the Native American studies program had not yet been finally approved by the university, anthropology professor Gerald Berreman sponsored our course. It offered anthropology credit then and in the fall term of 1969. I was a graduate teaching associate in the anthropology department at the time, so it was arranged that I would coordinate the class. Nevertheless, we were academically autonomous, and the course consisted mainly of guest lectures by Indian community people and spokespersons. By the fall term, I had accumulated enough material to begin teaching the course, but I still supplemented the syllabus with a couple of guest lectures. By winter term, the ethnic studies department had been tentatively approved, the Native American studies program was off and running, and a new faculty member, Henrietta Mann (Cheyenne-Arapaho), took over the course. Henry, as Indian people affectionately call her, became the director of the Native American studies program the following year (after Lee Brightman's departure) and is, of course, well known today as a university educator and activist for Indian religious freedom.

The course description for the five-unit Native American studies (N.A.S.) 130 (Indian Liberation) reads in part, "An introduction to problems and processes involved in Native American efforts to liberate themselves, economically, sociopolitically, and psychologically, from the effects of European conquest and class domination. Attention will focus upon the contemporary field of Indian affairs *and probable future developments.* Attention will also be given to past Indian resistance and liberation movements" (emphasis added). Halfway through the term, the Indian students, about one-quarter of the class, left to liberate Alcatraz. The class, of course, was not the cause of the Alcatraz occupation, but it did have an impact on the Berkeley students and their role in the occupation. I must say that the class really came alive once the Indian students liberated the island. The non-Indian students, both white and minority, who were enrolled in the class followed the news reports and developments avidly, and the Indian student liberators returned periodically to give firsthand reports and to answer questions. I gave all the Indian students "A" grades, as I recall; after all, they did not just study about Indian liberation but actually went out and did it!

One of the original student occupiers, Russell Waldon (Creek), who was also a member of the class, wrote in his final exam essay, "We considered many plans, many programs [in the class]. We felt the only positive way to create self-determination was to do it. If we failed, then we would continue to be wards of the federal government and would resign ourselves to our fate of incompetence."

Planning and Coordinating the Occupation

Although a planning meeting of the two student groups had taken place on the Berkeley campus earlier, I remember a really big meeting that was held in the Indian Community Action Program (CAP) office in San Francisco after the 9 November landing to plan for the return to Alcatraz. Al Miller directed this CAP program from a rented storefront in the Mission District, not far from the San Francisco Indian Center (which had burned down).

Karen Talbot (my wife) and I were present at this meeting, as were the Indian students from Berkeley; when the question arose of securing legal assistance in case of arrests, we put the group in touch with Aubrey Grossman, a personal friend who was a labor attorney in San Francisco. Grossman later defended the Pit River tribe in its land occupation case.

I was asked to coordinate the mainland activities for the forthcoming occupation, but I declined because of family and graduate school responsibilities. Later, I was glad that I had turned down this assignment because I saw what an exhausting task it was for Dean Chavers (Lumbee) when he took over the responsibility. Chavers, who was usually an agreeable person, became testy and rather unpleasant after working for days on end with little or no sleep. Telephone and other messages, money and donated supplies, technical assistance, and many other coordination tasks for Alcatraz support took place out of this CAP storefront.

Karen Talbot was able to bring Alcatraz and the Indian issue to the forefront of the growing West Coast antiwar movement. Fall 1969 saw the largest anti–Vietnam War demonstrations this country had ever seen, with 500,000 people turning out in New York City and 250,000 in San Francisco. My wife was on the program committee, which lined up speakers for the San Francisco rally in Golden Gate Park; in that capacity, she was able to lobby successfully for an American Indian representative in the speaker list lineup. This was no mean task, since everyone wanted to be represented on the speaker's platform for this mass demonstration composed of so many diverse groups united in a broad antiwar coalition. The Alcatraz planners decided on Iroquois traditional leader Wallace "Mad Bear" Anderson, who was then living in the Los Angeles area. I remember how proud the Indian students were to be able to sponsor and then to escort Mad Bear to the speaker's platform on that momentous day. From him one-quarter of a million people learned something about the Indian condition and Indian concerns. The Alcatraz planners had succeeded in bringing the Indian issue to the attention of the non-Indian activist community of San Francisco, thus contributing indirectly to the outpouring of support that materialized with the 20 November occupation.

The Academic Support Committee

The last bit of history I wish to relate concerns the Academic Support Committee, which the Indians of All Tribes council asked me to set up and coordinate after their 20 November occupation, in order to garner support for the Alcatraz occupation among academic and professional people. In this capacity, I made a trip to the Stanford Research Institute near Palo Alto to contact anthropologists Sol Tax and Edward Dozier (Tewa), who were doing a year's stint at this academic think tank. I was able to bring both to the island for a visit and to counsel with the Indian occupiers.

Tax was well known in the anthropology profession during the 1960s. He was editor of the prestigious international journal *Current Anthropology* and founder of the University of Chicago school of action anthropology. It was Tax who, along with Nancy Lurie, organized the 1960 Chicago Conference, with its important Declaration of Indian Purpose; from this conference, the younger, educated Indians went on to found the National Indian Youth Council.

Ed Dozier, the first Indian anthropologist to come along in decades, was doing very promising research and writing at the University of Arizona. His untimely death a few years later was a real loss to Indian scholarship.

Among others on this committee were Joe Muskrat, a promising Indian attorney, and, of course, Jack Forbes, who had taken an academic position at UC Davis. Forbes, however, and David Risling were shortly to lead the occupation of the old Nike missile base outside of Davis, which became D-Q University.

No sooner had Tax visited the island than he began to take over—sending telegrams, contacting the press, speaking for the island unilaterally; that is, he bypassed the authority of the Indians of All Tribes council and did not consult with other members of the committee. A powerhouse of energy and accustomed to being in command, he just could not let the Indians run their own occupation. Dozier, on the other hand, became thoughtfully silent and simply withdrew. I discussed the problem with the Indians of All Tribes council, and it was decided that the best solution was to simply "kill" the committee.

I do not believe that Tax ever forgave me when I stopped all communication with him and failed to reconvene the committee. Perhaps he thought I was simply incompetent, but he later got his revenge. At the 1975 international meeting of the Society for Applied Anthropology in Amsterdam, he told the gathering of action anthropologists that he had just finished reading Deloria's *Behind the Trail of Broken Treaties* and, noting its subtitle, *An Indian Declaration of Independence*, declared that, since this is what Indians want (he had just discovered this fact), anthropologists should take a leadership role in helping them achieve it.[6] He proposed, therefore, that action anthropologists call for another Chicago Conference like the one he had organized in 1961, draft a declaration of independence, and invite the Indians to adopt it. (He apparently had overlooked the fact that the Twenty Point Program put forth by the Trail of Broken Treaties coalition in 1972 was just such a document.) I found his proposal incredibly patronizing and told him so publicly, after which he denounced me as "an enemy of the Indian people." Although he later apologized to me privately, I found the incident a sad example of the paternalistic view held by the old-guard anthropologists toward American Indians. The anthropology community as a whole was silent about Alcatraz.

On the other hand, there was Mina Caufield, now an associate professor of women's studies at San Francisco State University. Both of us were graduate students in anthropology at UC Berkeley in the 1960s. At the time of the Alcatraz occupation, she was a leader of the Teaching Assistants Union (AFT) at Berkeley, which organized a picket line on campus in support of our Third World Strike to establish the ethnic studies department. She and other union members were arrested for their efforts by the same police who arrested and beat up Indians and other minority students during the strike.

Mina and her husband owned a beautiful sailing vessel, the *Saturna*, which became the chief supply ship for the Alcatraz occupation. I went along on a couple of their many trips when Tom was running the Coast Guard blockade in order to take supplies, people, and barrels and barrels of water to the island. It was dangerous and exciting. Today, the *Saturna* is the flagship of the Bay Area Peace Navy, which demonstrates against munitions ships and war-related activities. Mina and Tom never tried to tell Indians what to do, but they were always there to assist when they were needed.

Retrospective

In my 1978 paper on Alcatraz (cited earlier), I highlighted the Indian student subculture and its ethos or themes of liberation. These eight themes remain valid today: self-determination; all-Indian unity; equal educational opportunity; cultural revitalization; mutual assistance among Indian people; changes to the Bureau of Indian Affairs and the Indians' relationship to the U.S. government; peaceful coexistence among "two-leggeds" and with the natural world (ecology); and the rebuilding of the land base for Indian self-sufficiency. Since then, of course, the desecration and religious freedom issues have become of paramount concern. Nevertheless, we can see that the 1969 Alcatraz occupation served to craft an all-Indian program several years before the 1972 Trail of Broken Treaties issued its important Twenty Point Program.[7]

Most of the credit for this contribution lies with the Indian student liberators of San Francisco State University and the University of California, Berkeley. As I stated in my conclusions to the 1978 article:

> Free Alcatraz was one of the first of the current Native American land occupations. The activist students dared hope that indigenous peoples and

nations of the United States might sever the bonds of their oppression and take control of their own destiny. The tremendous outpouring of sympathy and support by non-Indians for Alcatraz indicate that the general public understood the democratic nature of the demands. . . .

Alcatraz [also] became a testing ground for its [Indian student] participants. Great experimentation took place, and a militant cadre was formed.[8]

It is this student component of the "new Indian" movement of the 1960s and early 1970s—of which the Alcatraz occupation was an important episode—that needs further documentation and analysis.

NOTES

1. See Adam Fortunate Eagle, *Alcatraz! Alcatraz! The Indian Occupation of 1969–1971* (Berkeley, Calif.: Heyday Books, 1992); and Troy Johnson, *The Indian Occupation of Alcatraz Island: Indian Self-Determination and the Rise of Indian Activism* (Urbana: University of Illinois Press, 1996).

2. Steve Talbot, "Free Alcatraz: The Culture of Native American Liberation," *The Journal of Ethnic Studies* 6:3 (Fall 1978): 83–96.

3. Steve Talbot, "Free Alcatraz" (in Russian) *Soviet Ethnography* 5 (1977): 60–70.

4. Fortunate Eagle, *Alcatraz! Alcatraz!* 26.

5. See Steve Talbot, "Why the Native American Heritage Should Be Taught in College," *The Indian Historian* 7:1 (Winter 1974): 42–44.

6. Vine Deloria, Jr., *Behind the Trail of Broken Treaties: An Indian Declaration of Independence* (Austin: University of Texas Press, 1985).

7. Ibid.

8. Talbot, "Free Alcatraz: The Culture of Native American Liberation," 94.

7

PERSONAL MEMORIES OF ALCATRAZ, 1969

Luis S. Kemnitzer

One weakness that I have had as an anthropologist has been a failure to make plans for the possibility that someone might ask me details about my life twenty-five years later. I am in the habit of keeping my research (problem-oriented attention to important people doing important things) separate from my life (my day-to-day activities); so, even when I was in the midst of important historical events, I never thought that my part in them was worth describing for posterity. Thus, on this occasion of remembering and memorializing a watershed in the history of Native American survival and resistance, I have only a few random notes to help me organize my memory of my participation in the events of Alcatraz and before. Much was happening at that time, and I found myself willy-nilly in a position to be a small part of processes that I did not know would be as important as hindsight shows.

Actually, in order to get a good picture of the 1969 occupation of Alcatraz, we have to go back to the first occupation, in 1964, and follow the threads through the Third World Liberation Front Strike at San Francisco State University (then College). When Alcatraz was decommissioned as a federal prison, the property entered into an administrative limbo that threatened to inspire lawyers and frustrate developers. Contemplation of this administrative limbo also inspired some Lakota residents in the Bay Area to examine documents relating to Lakota-U.S. government relations. Convinced that the wording in certain parts of the Great Sioux Treaty of 1868 and the Indian Allotment Act of 1887 supported their claims,[1] five Lakota men went to the island and formally staked their claims; after four hours, they returned to the mainland to pursue their legal cases.

The five men who staked their claims were Al "Chalk" Cottier, a house painter from Pine Ridge who had been in the Bay Area since 1952, Dick McKenzie from Rosebud, who was active in the urban Indian community, Garfield Spotted Elk, a twenty-six-year-old section hand on relocation, Walter Means, a retired traveling high-iron worker who was helped in this endeavor by his son Russell, and Martin Firethunder Martinez, who had come to Oakland in the late 1950s on relocation and was a focal person in the urban Indian community. Cottier's wife, Belva, did most of the legal research. At a meeting the next evening at the American Indian Center on 16th and Julian Streets, the "homesteaders" said that although they were staking the claims as individuals, as the law required, they actually had plans for a community center and a refuge and healing place for Indians, in addition to their private holdings. Although they offered to pay the U.S. government the highest price set for Indian land—forty-seven cents per acre—their case never went to court and ultimately was forgotten by a fickle public, if not by the Lakota and their friends, relatives, and associates.

The five homesteaders and their numerous friends staked their claims on Sunday, 8 March 1964, under the hostile eyes of the federal government representative on the island. On the same day, negotiators reported the end of a long sit-in at the Sheraton Palace that resulted in a nondiscriminatory hiring policy; the week before, Bob Satiacum (Puyallup) was arrested for exercising his treaty fishing rights in Washington State (San Francisco Episcopal Bishop J. A. Pike's aide, John J. Yargan, and actor Marlon Brando were also arrested with him).

Fast-forward now to 1968, during the Third World Liberation Front Strike at San Francisco State. A number of the faculty had been supporting the student strike and, in December of that year, went out on strike themselves. No American Indians were identified as participating in the strike or negotiations at this time, and no plans for a Native American studies department were part of the goals of the strike. However, a non-Indian graduate student in social science at San Francisco State who was tutoring young Indian children in the Mission District came to know a group of young Indians who also congregated at the place where the student was tutoring. These young Indians had all had some contact with college and had come to San Francisco either on vocational training, relocation, or on their own; they had formed a group modeled after motorcycle clubs and wore "colors" that identified them as "Indians and Half Breeds of San Francisco." Conversation with the student tutor led them to become interested in the strike and in exploring the possibility of working toward a Native American studies department.

By the time the young Indians decided to work seriously toward these goals, the university and the Third World Liberation Front had started negotiations, and there was limited room for movement or expansion. The LaRaza section agreed to represent the Indians in negotiations, and there was close collaboration between representatives of LaRaza and the future Native American studies students. I was one of the faculty members on strike, and, although I was not involved in the negotiations with the university administration, I was informally recruited by other striking faculty to help plan and negotiate with LaRaza. There were no identified Indians among the faculty involved in these negotiations, but I, at least, had spent some time researching Indian issues in the San Francisco Bay Area and on Pine Ridge Reservation in South Dakota.

As a result of the strike, Richard Oakes, (Mohawk), Al Miller (Seminole), Gerald Sam (Round Valley), Joe Bill (Inuit), Deanna Francis (Malecite), Mickey Gemmill (Pit River), Robert Kaniatobe (Choctaw), Ronald Lickers (Seneca), Joyce Rice (Winnebago), and others were admitted to San Francisco State as the core student body of the Native American studies department (now called the American Indian studies department). Because of my role in the off-campus negotiations, these Indian students who were building and inventing the Native American studies department chose me to aid in this process and in the transition to Native American faculty. (As far as I know, there was only one Native American professor on the campus, in physiology.)

Richard Oakes was the major thinker and actor in this process. We had set up a community advisory board, including Jeanette Henry (Cherokee) and Rupert Costo (Cahuilla), well-known Indian intellectuals who had founded the American Indian Historical Society, and Belva Cottier, who had done most of the legal and historical research for the earlier Lakota landing on Alcatraz. As a non-Indian, I was spared most of the political maneuvering and conflict that accompanied the planning of the program and the search for Native American faculty. I only faintly perceived the negative reaction from some of the principals, including native scholars who had been approached to participate, who perceived the program as "political," "radical," and "mixed blood."

It was evident from the discussions we had during the formation of the Native American studies department that Oakes had a lot of respect for these people and that he listened to them. I also benefited from these discussions. Once, Oakes returned from a conference with Rupert Costo and Jeanette Henry and said to me, "You anthropologists just think of Indians as bugs, don't you?" Immediately, I had to make explicit to myself as well as to him my perception of the relationship between anthropology and ethnic studies. This was something to the effect that, yes, anthropologists, as they are students of humans and human culture in all times and places and as they try to formulate generalizations about human culture and behavior, do think of Indians as "bugs," just as they think of any and all cultures, societies, and people, including the white middle class and the power elite, as examples of humanity to study. In the process of gaining information for their generalizations, they may well acquire knowledge and insights that can contribute to the aims of the particular ethnic studies discipline, and certainly their research should be guided by the needs and direction of the people they study. But the material is going to be interpreted and evaluated differently by those working in a panhuman context and those who are serving the consciousness and self-determination of a particular group. These ends are not mutually exclusive; in an atmosphere of mutual respect, they can be mutually beneficial. Since that time, I think these ideas have become givens, and the basis for much more sophisticated thinking. In 1969, we were still groping toward systematic statements of this kind and actions based on them.

These discussions around the founding documents went on during the spring and summer of 1969, and that fall semester we instituted the first class, Native American Studies 20, "Native American Heritage," which I taught—nominally, because, again, there was no Native American faculty available at the time (this situation changed rapidly, much to my relief). We set up the class as a forum to talk about directions that the Native American studies department could possibly take and as a place where Native American students could examine the various traditional academic disciplines to discover what in their content and methodology could be useful in the development of Native American studies as a discipline. On the first day of class, over one hundred students appeared. I passed around a sign-up sheet and told the students to write their names, tribal affiliations, and class levels on the list. Somebody asked what to write if they had no tribal affiliation; I answered that, in that case, they could not take the class, since it was for Indians only. The non-Indians left and we set to work, all of us possessing vague ideas about what would constitute a curriculum and course content, and all of us wanting to use this course time to work on these questions. (A list of the members of the class is appended.)

A few weeks into the semester, Richard Oakes got word that the White Roots of Peace, an Iroquois Confederation group, was going to be in the area. Acting on his advice, I arranged for them to appear in my class, and I also arranged for appearances at Mills College, at UC Santa Cruz, where I had taught Native American studies courses, at UC Berkeley, I think, and also a public appearance at San Francisco State. White Roots of Peace had been traveling all over the country, appearing in Indian communities primarily, and their message was for Indian communities, not necessarily for non-Indians. Their influence on the American Indian students at UC Santa Cruz and San Francisco State was electrifying, to say the least. After their appearances at San Francisco State, Richard Oakes especially, but other Indian students as well, voiced a dissatisfaction with the structure of college education, with the enclosure in glass and concrete, and with the separation from the land and water and air of natural Indian environments. They said that the structure and content of white people's education was irrelevant to Indian experience and needs (I would like to think it was not just my class they were upset with, that they were taking other unsatisfying classes, too).

Richard Oakes and the cadre from San Francisco State were the main organizing influences. On an evening shortly after the first (9 November) occupation, I was at a meeting of friends of the Native American studies department at the home of John Connelly, professor of education. Belva Cottier was there, and she said that, as in the previous Sioux occupation, she was sworn to secrecy and could not talk about it before it happened. She had advised Richard Oakes and friends about how the Sioux had done it in 1964, and about the legal and historical research she had done and also the dreams and plans that the Sioux and their friends had developed to go with the claims. (In those days, people rarely used the word *Lakota* when speaking English, generally referring to themselves as Sioux; *Lakota* was used when speaking Lakota.) She also said that she and the other elders who had helped the students in their plans were prevented from accompanying them on the landing and that she was disappointed and sad about that, although she understood why the young people wanted it that way. According to her, the young people said that the action was too dangerous to include the elderly people, and, besides, it was the job of the young people to do these actions and the job of old people to advise and support.

Native American students from other campuses also were involved in the planning and occupation of the island. Literally within hours after the first occupation, people from all over California and North America were responding to the action; more than eighty young people landed on Alcatraz early in the morning of 20 November 1969. But it is important that the crucial role of Native American students at San Francisco State be recognized in the Alcatraz affair, and I want to honor Belva Cottier and the other Lakota pioneers in this movement. My role was minor and peripheral. At the time, I thought the action was quixotic—a lot of energy expended for ephemeral and will-of-the-wisp goals. I had no idea that it would have the historical importance it did. (The week before, more than one hundred thousand people had marched in San Francisco to end the war in Vietnam.) Fortunately and naturally, I did not tell anybody this, since it was not my business to evaluate goals and strategy. I was, in some way, a faculty supporter for the Native American studies department, so I continued to support the students in an action that they understood better than I. Alcatraz was a very complex experience, and it touched and transformed many people. This is only one of many views.

APPENDIX

Class List, Fall 1969
Native American Studies 20, "Native American Heritage"

Barron, Gregory Mark
Bill, Joseph [Inuit]
Bright, Constance
Charley, Dorothy Ann
Francis, Deanna May [Malecite]
Gates, Richard Russell
Gemmill, Mickey L. [Pit River]
George, Priscilla
Greensfelder, Sara El
Harden Ross
Hodge, Gary Ray
Jones, Kenneth Grover
Justice, Mary A.
Kaniatobe, Robert [Choctaw]
Lee, Edith Teresa
Lickers, Ronald N. [Seneca]
Lind, Alessandra
McKay, Peter Cameron
Miller, Alan D. [Seminole]
Oakes, Richard [Mohawk]
Ow, Gale
Rice, Joyce [Winnebago]
Sam, Gerald [Round Valley]
Shelton, Ferdinand
Taylor, David
Williams, Carol Ann
Williams, Frank David [Costanoan]

NOTE

1. Under the 1868 treaty, any male Sioux over the age of eighteen not living on a reservation can claim federal land "not used for special purposes." This right was also granted to other Indians in the 1887 Indian Allotment Act. When the right was revoked in 1934, Sioux were specifically exempted. Claimants must make improvements worth two hundred dollars within three years.

8

A REMINISCENCE OF THE

ALCATRAZ OCCUPATION

Edward D. Castillo

With bittersweet fondness, I recall my grandmother's gift of a white shirt and a tie she thought I would need to attend college in the late 1960s. How could she have known? No one in my family had ever graduated from high school, let alone attempted college. I still clearly remember my only visit to a high school counselor who was perplexed by this skinny, dark-skinned youth who kept enrolling in college prep courses. "Don't you understand that you will never get into a fraternity? Why not take auto shop?" At that time, I did not even know what a fraternity was.

Being stubborn and determined to become an architect, I persisted and finally enrolled in the huge, somewhat intimidating University of California at Riverside (about three thousand students). I felt uncomfortable and isolated in the classroom, as most Indian students still feel today. As a result, I withdrew into the last row and cocooned myself in a blanket of uncommunicative silence.

I spent my entire undergraduate career without Native American peers or role models. There were no staff, counselors, or faculty with whom I could share my self-doubts or my anxious dreams for the future. Because the Bureau of Indian Affairs (BIA) had admininistratively decided not to make higher education scholarships available to California Indians, I was denied support. Consequently, I worked two and sometimes three jobs, year-round, to earn money to pay for my education.

Because my grandfather and my father were passionately interested in the past and the old days, I gradually was drawn to the field of history, particularly the history of my own people. Unfortunately, such courses were not available in the curriculum at that time. As a compromise, I majored in American frontier history, but I was always more interested in the various Indians on the largely ignored "other side" of the frontier.

I took a minor in Latin American studies that I hoped would provide me with an understanding of borderlands Indian-Spanish encounters in California and elsewhere. Because I was one of three minority students in the undergraduate population, my Latin American studies professors occasionally would turn to me after describing some Hispanic custom or belief and ask, "Is that not correct, Mr. Castillo?" I usually just embarrassingly nodded my head or ignored the question altogether. Finally, when I wrote my senior thesis on the Kumeyaay Indian destruction of Mission San Diego in 1775, my advisor asked me if I was, in fact, an American Indian. After I confirmed his insightful suspicion, he demanded to know why I had not raised the issue before. My response was that I did not think anybody cared, and, besides, no one had ever asked!

Following my graduation in 1969, I accepted a minority counseling position at the University of California, Santa Barbara. Largely because competing pressures to hire blacks or Hispanics could not be resolved, I was hired as a compromise. One of my duties was to develop a resource guide to higher education programs for minority students. Seeking information, I called UCLA and was connected with a faculty member of the brand new American Indian High Potential Program in Campbell Hall. After speaking to me for a while, she asked if I thought I could teach American Indian history to a select group of about sixty American Indian students who had been provisionally admitted to the university. I was young and ignorant of the great responsibility this job entailed, so I declared quickly that I could do it.

I will never forget ascending the steps of Campbell Hall and being stunned by the ominous sight of a large patch of dried blood. During my interview, I inquired about that disturbing vision and was informed that a murder had been committed on that site as the result of a rivalry between black factions on the campus prior to my arrival. This disturbing news, however, did not deter me from deciding to accept an on-the-spot offer to join the all–American Indian faculty that was being formed to work with native students from all over the country. This was what I had quietly dreamed of throughout my undergraduate career.

I was shocked when I met the students for the first time. About half of them were, in fact, older than my tender twenty years. Nevertheless, it was an electrifying experience to actually meet Indian college students. They were, in large part, eager to learn and had high expectations for themselves. There were, however, some more surprises in store for me. As we were introduced by name and tribe, many of the students from tribes outside of California were amazed that any California Indians still survived. I was further chagrined to learn from some of the older students that many had, in fact, come to California under the BIA's relocation program years earlier and

had had their transportation, their vocational and sometimes academic training, their housing, and even their furniture bought for them by the program.
I was dismayed to think that I had struggled through my undergraduate years
without so much as a cent from the bureau. This was the beginning of my
practical learning about how the BIA pitted one group of Indians against
another by offering tempting rewards for cooperation. Countless other examples followed this one and ultimately led to enlightenment.

I had always wanted to take a course in American Indian history, and now,
ironically, I was assigned to teach the class I had so desperately sought as an
undergraduate. I worked fifteen hours a day preparing my lectures and discussion groups. In retrospect, I realize that the entire faculty of our program
was seeking to forge a Native American perspective in our various specialties of history, literature, art, and other fields. It was a challenging and powerful reorientation for our students, many of whom were exposed for the first
time to a systematic grounding in the national American Indian experience.
Student reactions varied from stunned disbelief to growing impatience for
change. All around us, other minority groups were making great strides in
their political, social, and employment pursuits. Inevitably, many of us began itching to demonstrate publicly our frustration about the many grievances our people held.

I was especially outraged about the systematic disinterment of Indian burials and the routine archaeological digs that the universities continued to mount
despite a diminishing return of meaningful data from these activities that were
so offensive to us. I gathered a number of student and faculty followers and
suggested that we dig up some nineteenth-century Indian fighter buried nearby. We were in the middle of planning activities for that action when, at a faculty meeting in mid-November 1969, our director, Ponca historian Roger
Buffalohead, announced that a Mohawk student from San Francisco State
University wanted to address our students concerning a proposal for a demonstration in San Francisco. His name was Richard Oakes.

I clearly recall Oakes's speech to our students. He made a positive impression: He was a handsome adult, solidly built. Although he obviously was
not a polished public speaker, he delivered his message with simplicity and
power. I was delighted to hear that he proposed to lead a coalition of American Indian students from San Francisco State, UC Berkeley, and UC Riverside to occupy the abandoned federal prison on Alcatraz Island. The action would be carried out under the pan-Indian group called Indians of All
Tribes. He then read the declaration that explained the reasons for seizing
the island. Cleverly, it made truthful comparisons between Alcatraz and
Indian reservations (i.e., isolation, lack of running water, lack of employment)
and, better still, offered to pay the government twenty-four dollars in trinkets for the land!

Oakes's proposal was the catalyst that caused the ethnic ferment among our students to reach a boiling point. One of them was a multisyllable-word-spouting leader of a national youth group for Indians who fancied himself at the forefront of the Indian movement. His sense of self-importance caused him to oppose any students joining a demonstration that was not led by him. This was the first of my many lessons in Indian leadership, where egotism could prevent one from supporting another's ideas or actions.

The rest of the students struggled with a decision involving the real possibility of being arrested and, of course, having their education disrupted. My own reaction evolved from enthusiastic support to more serious reflection: "Oh, no. Here we go again." At that time, all of California's professional Indian leadership positions were held by Indians from out of state. This grated on those of us who were from California tribes, but the non-California Indians could not comprehend our concern. More troubling still, these leaders would be claiming California Indian land based on a treaty the government had made with the Lakota Indians! After some serious thought, though, I decided the positive potential would outweigh the negative. I would take part in the proposed demonstration with hopes that other California Indians would participate as well. I reasoned that we would go to the island, make our stand, be arrested, and then attempt to get the message to the nation that the native peoples of America were being seriously neglected in the civil rights struggle. I notified my boss, who was both understanding and supportive. No one considered for a moment that the occupation might last for nearly two years!

About half of our students decided to participate. We packed our things, and a number of the students checked out university cars to drive to San Francisco. It was arranged that we would all meet at the San Francisco Indian Center. Being a professional and a high roller, I decided to fly up to the city. I recall that the ticket cost twenty-one dollars. I was picked up at the airport by some of my students, and we proceeded to the San Francisco Indian Center prior to our embarkation. It was the evening of 19 November 1969, a night I will never forget.

When our group arrived at the Indian Center, a rancorous debate was under way in a meeting of perhaps two hundred people. A tall, long-haired, non-Indian biker-type (with what appeared to be an Indian wife) was expressing his apprehension about the wisdom of the proposed Alcatraz enterprise. Abruptly, someone jumped up from the audience and punched the biker's lights out. Apparently, the time for debate had passed. Thereafter, the discussion turned to logistical questions about our transportation to the island.

As the meeting broke up, Richard Oakes invited me to accompany him to the boats located at the Berkeley Marina. We made at least one stop for a drink "to keep our courage up," as someone later explained. When we arrived at the Berkeley Marina, Oakes located the designated boat, but the skipper suddenly erupted into an agitated harangue. After a short while, Oakes walked back to the caravan of cars to tell us that the "chicken-shit coward" now refused to transport us to the island. Oakes later explained that the captain feared the Coast Guard had been alerted to this new attempt to take over the island, and he believed his boat would be confiscated. Fortunately, we had a back-up boat and captain at the Sausalito Marina across the bay.

There followed yet another trip across the Bay Bridge, through San Francisco, and over the Golden Gate Bridge. It was my first sight of that famous landmark, and I studied it with a degree of awe. The night was clear and cold, with just a hint of fog coming through the channel. We soon arrived at the Sausalito Marina and, although we did not realize it at the time, abandoned our vehicles. We proceeded quickly aboard our boat, and the captain, apparently more courageous or perhaps more foolish than the other, immediately got under way. The ride was smooth despite the extraordinary overloading of the boat.

Just before we approached a barge that was tied to the island's dock, Oakes urged us all to take different routes up to the warden's house located at the top of the island, across from the main cellblock. We were apprehensive that the authorities had been notified and were waiting to arrest us en masse. As soon as we docked, the seventy-eight college students (including at least two government informants) scrambled across the barge and headed up the road. I ran around the exercise yard behind the main cellblock and, after a tortuous maze of detours, emerged in the plaza in front of the main cellblock. Across the way, I could see a number of our group gathered in a mission-style, two-story house with smoke just beginning to waft from its stately chimney. This was the warden's house.

I joined my fellow tribesmen and women in breaking up some old wooden folding chairs to feed the fire that we needed to fend off the damp chill permeating the island. I was especially chilled; being ignorant about the climate of northern California, I had worn only a denim workshirt, a corduroy sport jacket, and a cotton blanket. My feet were covered with high-top moccasins. I was miserably cold and often damp for the next fifteen weeks.

Soon someone produced a small drum, and we began to sing Plains Indian 49er songs. In this manner, we amused ourselves for the rest of the night. Sometime just before dawn, one of the women produced our food supplies, consisting of two loaves of white bread, fifty slices of baloney, an equal number of slices of American cheese, a six-pack of Coke, and a pound of coffee. Just then, the caretaker of the island, a GSA employee, approached the house to inquire about our presence there. It was a good thing he was calm and had a sense of humor, because, if he had begun to act hostile, we might have torn him apart. We were very pumped up. As things turned out, he was courteous and friendly. No doubt he had already experienced the previous takeover attempts made by much smaller groups of Indians. After informing him of our purpose, we allowed him to return to his quarters and notify the authorities of our actions. Oakes then asked us to round up the other participants, who were scattered throughout the abandoned structures, to discuss our next moves.

We gathered under gray clouds in the plaza in front of the main cellblock. It was clear from the discussion that followed that we fully expected to be arrested that day by federal marshals. The idea of resistance was debated; some boasted that they would not be taken off the island on their feet, while others declared their intention of going limp when arrested and surrendering under protest. I suspect that many, like myself, were willing to be arrested but would offer physical resistance if we saw any of our fellow participants being abused by the authorities. Lookouts were placed at strategic observation points to alert us to the arrival of police authorities.

Following the breakup of our meeting, the caretaker returned to the warden's house, where many of us were huddled around an anemic fire. We were surprised to discover that he had brought coffee for us. He explained also that his wife would be happy to offer shower and toilet facilities to the females from our group. Our conversation was interrupted by the ominous sound of a hovering helicopter, which we immediately assumed belonged to the federal marshals. However, it turned out to be newspaper reporters. The media circus was beginning.

Over the next five days, the expected confrontation and arrests failed to materialize. The Coast Guard did, however, place a blockade around the island to prevent reinforcements and food from reaching us. In keeping with the highest standards of political theater, some of us fashioned bows and arrows from materials at hand and carried out our historic role of showering arrows upon any Coast Guard cutter foolish enough to come too close to the docking barge at the island's landing. Both the "white-eyes" and the Indians rocked with laughter during such "Indian attacks."

During those early days of the blockade, much excitement was created by well-wishers attempting to deliver food, water, and supplies to us. I recall one dramatic episode when, in the early afternoon, a motor-powered Chinese junk rammed one of the patrol vessels. This incident naturally drew the other Coast Guard cutter to the collision site. Apparently, there had been a plan to cause a diversion on the south side of the landing so that supplies could be unloaded from a small fleet of pleasure boats to the north. After witnessing the collision, we ran up to the courtyard in front of the main cellblock and were directed to a series of ladders that descended to a small pebble beach on the north side of the island. There we saw boats coming in close, the inhabitants tossing canned hams, bottles of water, and other food supplies ashore. At that point, we formed a chain of hands stretching from the beach up the steep cliff side, where some of us were clinging to the ladders and handing the supplies upward. It was an exhilarating experience that provoked many laughs and much bragging by all. This was our first substantial resupply, and we consumed it with enthusiasm.

A few days later, one of the island's strangest characters, a ubiquitous Eskimo named Joe Bill, jumped off the landing barge to compel the Coast Guard to rescue him. This tactic would allow several blockade runners to make a quick pass at the dock and toss out food and water to us. Our hilarity quickly turned to fear at the realization that the water was about forty-two degrees and hypothermia and death threatened our brother. Worse still, the treacherous tide was going out, dragging Joe Bill toward the Golden Gate at a frightening pace. Fortunately, he was rescued, and we got even more supplies.

During the first few days of the occupation, we held a formal meeting to institute a governing body for the island's population. That meeting revealed some not-so-flattering character flaws and giant egos among the politically inclined. I was surprised to find myself nominated and elected to the office of chief of security. At first, I was honored. Among my responsibilities was that of enforcing a drug- and alcohol-free populous. The first attempt by this 155-pound individual to confiscate a joint from a group of young adults (each weighing at least 180 pounds) quickly convinced me of my lack of qualifications for the job. Others soon assumed the job, although without any appreciable improvement in efficiency.

I'm not sure Oakes or any of the other plbners had been conscious of the proximity of our demonstration to the Thanksgiving holiday, but it proved to be exactly the kind of tie-in that unimaginative reporters sought to make with this "new" minority group's unique political action. As the Thanksgiving holiday approached, mainland supporters organized a huge turkey dinner, with live music for the island's Indian population. Just prior to that date, the Coast Guard blockade was called off.

Thanksgiving morning, I awoke to the sound of a thunderously loud rock band that had been towed on a barge to our dock. They used car batteries to power their electric music. It was a nice gesture from a sincere group of musicians. By now, network and international reporters were regularly helicoptered to the island to report on the unexpected survival of American Indians and their clever demonstration. An especially large contingent turned up on Thanksgiving morning. Hundreds of Native American supporters also began to arrive with the Thanksgiving turkeys supplied by the Rathskeller Restaurant of San Francisco and others.

The Thanksgiving dinner was served in the exercise court off the main cellblock. A Chumash elder gave a blessing, and we lined up for one of the best turkey dinners I can recall—perhaps because a well-prepared, warm meal was something few of us had enjoyed for a week.

We now were deluged with numerous supporters and supplies and a growing river of funds. Within a few weeks, John Fogerty, of the popular rock group Creedence Clearwater Revival, donated a fishing boat to the island's growing population. The press and media reports were becoming more analytical and were beginning to explore the conditions of Indian peoples nationwide. We were delighted that our demonstration had triggered some significant national reflection on the status of American Indians within American society. Unfortunately, our successful efforts bore within them the seeds of our dream's demise.

The open forum meeting styles of the island's governing body became a focus of discontent for a growing number of island residents. Most of these individuals had arrived more recently, some with serious addiction problems. Many were older, frustrated, unemployed semiprofessionals. Eventually, a power struggle erupted between Richard Oakes and this other faction. Media attention and control of the tens of thousands of dollars being donated to the Alcatraz cause were at the root of most of the problems. Intimidation and violence became the all-too-frequent responses from the small but destructive faction that challenged the college students who had successfully inaugurated our occupation.

Soon after the power struggle began, Oakes's stepdaughter Yvonne fell several stories in a stairwell of the staff apartment building where she and her family lived. She died a few days later. Immediately, there was speculation that her tragic death was a result of the growing violence and intimidation against Oakes and other original participants.

I recognized clearly that power and money were at the heart of our problems. This was about a month into the occupation. Christmas was approaching, and I was both cold and filthy. I had not bathed since 19 November, and I decided to ask the island's leadership for twenty-two dollars and passage to the mainland to get a hotel room and clean up. I invited a recently arrived young female to accompany me to "see the city." The bath we shared was one of the most memorable I have ever experienced. Clean bodies, clean sheets, and a warm room—what a change! The next day I bought new, warm clothes and shoes, and, after a couple of restaurant meals and phone calls to my parents and grandparents, I returned to the island.

I still recall feeling uncomfortable about asking for the hotel room money. By then, I was convinced that major financial ripoffs had been perpetrated by those who controlled the island's finances. I was a relatively well-paid professional compared to others on the island, and I could afford to be critical. Nevertheless, I felt I had now participated in taking money.

More troubling still was the inner conflict I was experiencing over my responsibilities at UCLA that I had abandoned so abruptly. I could see which way the leadership was drifting, and I did not like what I was witnessing. Richard Oakes left the island after his daughter was killed. Rumors abounded concerning her death. Some speculated she was shoved. It was clear to many of us that our original idealism was being replaced by cynical and frankly embarrassing self-declared "leaders" whose interests were more financial and political in nature.

I finally made the fateful decision to leave the island and return to UCLA to fulfill my teaching contract. I was proud of my participation in the occupation, but my personal disillusionment with the unexpected developments of our demonstration left me uneasy. Within a year, I had entered graduate school in UC Berkeley's Department of History and had begun a serious academic career—punctuated by participation in several more attempted land takeovers modeled after the Alcatraz example. Some of those, like the effort of the Pit River Indians in Shasta County, ended in brutal law enforcement attacks on demonstrators. These experiences, for me, drove home the difference between occupation-type encounters in liberal urban areas and those outside of such locales: Rural land takeovers were met with bitter opposition and frequent violence. I soon came to understand that what we had accomplished at Alcatraz was more political theater than substance. I realized that the future of Indian self-determination and economic self-sufficiency lay not in more government entitlement programs that fostered dependency but in the establishment of adequate land bases that can provide Indian residents the opportunity to make a decent living.

I was bitterly disappointed by the self-destructive nature of the leadership following Richard Oakes's departure from Alcatraz. This does not mean I was a blindly loyal supporter of Oakes; I understood his shortcomings. In retrospect, however, I believe I made the correct decision to stand by him. Events following his departure seem to have validated that perception.

Many of the original seventy-eight college students who participated in the 20 November takeover have gone on to responsible, productive, and successful careers. Fellow Luiseño Indian Dennis Turner became an effective tribal chairman of the Rincon Indian Reservation in Southern California and today runs a successful business on his reservation. Creek Indian Linda Arrenado is a physician in Sonoma County. Luwana Quitiquit, a Robinson Creek Pomo, is a former tribal administrator and current director of Ya-Ka Ama (a land takeover effort that has become an educational and native plant business on twenty-three acres of prime Sonoma County agricultural land along the Russian River). Pomo Indian Rosalie Willie completed a library degree at UC Berkeley and administers the Native American studies library on that campus. Sac and Fox Indian Dennis Jennings is a prominent community activist with the International Treaty Council in San Francisco.

I was surprised when I returned home to find my parents and grand-parents in support of my participation in the Alcatraz occupation. I recalled their opposition to street demonstrations by other minorities during the early turbulence of the civil rights movement and did not expect the approval they expressed. Over the intervening years, I grew more cynical about what our efforts at Alcatraz had accomplished. After all, our loss of the island was attributable as much to the abuses of incompetent leadership and the anar-chy and hypocrisy of urban Indian politics as to the government's efforts against us. Yet, more and more frequently, I encounter Indian people of my generation and younger who, on learning of my participation in that effort, describe the profound effect it had on their lives and their perceptions of what was possible for Indian people. Even some of the founding members of the American Indian Movement have publicly credited Alcatraz as a cat-alyst for their own political coming-of-age.

A fairly widely distributed poster for the Alcatraz occupation featured a photo, taken by a *San Francisco Chronicle* reporter, of me—very emaciated, unwashed, cold—and a young woman huddled under a blanket, with the bold declaration, "Alcatraz Is Not an Island." I keep a framed copy of that poster in my home to amuse my friends and guests. Imagine my surprise when, recently, one of my undergraduate students returned from a Grateful Dead concert with a T-shirt she had purchased with that same image on it!

The occupation of Alcatraz Island was a seminal event in the modern American Indian civil rights movement. For that reason, I set aside my re-sponsibilities and research commitments to reflect on the nearly three months I participated in the occupation.

9

THE NATIVE STRUGGLE

FOR LIBERATION: ALCATRAZ

Jack D. Forbes

The liberation of Alcatraz Island by Native Americans in November 1969 occurred when I had just started teaching newly developed courses in our brand-new Native American studies program at the University of California, Davis. I was engaged in the political work of securing additional teaching positions, writing up a major, setting up a student community center (Tecumseh Center), securing adequate space, and all of the other things needed to bring our dreams to reality. I had just moved to Davis from Berkeley in July, and my energy was focused on prying resources loose from administrators and crossing swords with faculty committees.

Several of our Davis students went down to Alcatraz immediately, and some of my fellow members of United Native Americans were among the leaders of the Alcatraz community. I began to realize the unique importance of Alcatraz, even though I personally was only a supporter and visitor, never an occupier. Alcatraz was perhaps the first Indian-controlled "free" piece of real estate within the United States since the whites had conquered southwestern Colorado and southwestern Utah in 1910–15 and assumed control over interior Alaska during the same general period. One thing that made Alcatraz so significant was the fact that, when you left the pier, you left the United States and soon arrived on a native-ruled island, temporarily beyond the jurisdiction of any white authorities. Another significant aspect of Alcatraz was that it liberated the psyche of native peoples, making it "all right to be Indian, headbands and all." Finally, it was an experiment in native self-determination in a communal and political sense.

But Alcatraz developed at a peculiar point in time, a time when many Indians still believed that alcohol and drugs were essential parts of modern native culture and that it was necessary to tolerate drunken behavior. At the same time, however, a return to spiritual values was also occurring. On Alcatraz a great cultural clash took place between booze and the sacred pipe, between drugs and spiritual ceremonies, between hustling and traditional tribal ethics.

The native world learned a great deal from this struggle of values, and, slowly but surely, alcohol and commercial drugs have been barred from ceremonies, gatherings, powwows, and other important functions of contemporary native life. This has made a major change in the quality of Indian communal life in many parts of North America. The Alcatraz experience was a pivotal one in terms of forcing Indian activists to consider spiritual values and the necessity of confronting alcohol head-on if the movement was to avoid self-destruction.

My comments are going to be based primarily on my memory of the Alcatraz period, supplemented by a chronology of Native American history, which we put together at Tecumseh Center in 1971.

The Rise of Native Activism

The return of veterans from World War II has sometimes been regarded as important in the development of modern native activism, to which I would add the return of Korean War vets and, later, Vietnam-era vets. The movement of tens of thousands of Indians to cities such as San Francisco, Oakland, Los Angeles, Denver, and Chicago is also important, as is the growing number of college and university graduates from the 1950s onward, with a much larger number of college students during the 1960s and 1970s.

Activism takes many forms. I believe that it really began with the more traditional native people who were determined to protect their land and way of life and practice their religion. Thus I would trace Alcatraz back to the revival of the Sun Dance by the Arapaho and the Sioux in the 1946–50 period, to the beginnings of modern Hopi and Six Nations resistance to outside interference in 1948–49, and to the struggles of the 1957–68 period involving mostly Six Nations groups and "traditionalists" from the Hopi, Miccosukee, Pit River, Western Shoshone, and other nations.

In the 1950s, the various reservations of the Six Nations Confederacy began to come under increasing assault. In 1954, the New York Port Authority seized some land belonging to the Akwesasne (St. Regis) Mohawk Reservation; from 1956, a federal project, the Kinzua Dam, threatened to flood the Allegheny Seneca Reservation.

The Six Nations people began to react to these threats with new techniques and a revived sense of native nationalism. In 1957, for example, Standing Arrow of the Mohawk led a group of Indians onto lands claimed by non-Indians on Schoharie Creek. The Mohawk claimed the land under the Treaty of 1784. Thus, we find the use of "occupation" and a reference to "treaty rights," both essential to the Alcatraz movement twelve years later.

Alliances of "traditionals" began to develop across the country, with groups such as LONAI (League of North American Indians) and the Indian Defense League providing some leadership. LONAI published a newsletter *(Indian Views)*, which was widely distributed among traditionals.

Around 1958, things began to heat up. The state of New York threatened to levy state income taxes from the Akwesasne Mohawk, the New York Power Authority invaded the Tuscarora Reservation to confiscate land for a power facility, and a reclamation project and non-Indian land grabbers endangered the Miccosukee of Florida. Mad Bear Anderson and Chief Clinton Rickard organized resistance efforts around the country. Fidel Castro of Cuba invited Six Nations and Miccosukee delegates to visit Cuba, which they did in July 1958.

During 1959, the activism continued, with Six Nations delegates being joined by Chief Julius Twohy and Ella McCurely from Utah in a meeting with the Miccosukee in the Florida Everglades. A "United Indian Nation" was to be organized. One messenger (Craig was his name, as I recall) visited us in Los Angeles at a first meeting of the Southwestern Branch of the American Indian Ethnohistoric Conference. He and his wife were carrying the message of native reawakening around the country; he also wrote articles for *Indian Views*. In that same year, Chief Ray Johnson of the Pit River Nation died in Washington, D.C., while picketing for recognition of his people's land rights, and a Hopi delegation visited the United Nations in New York, explaining their prophecies and beliefs.

Thus, in 1958–59, we saw a great awakening among traditional First Nations people, from New York to California, and from Ontario to Florida. The movement broadened in the early 1960s to include some tribal officials, the children of "progressives," and other kinds of indigenous people. In June 1961, the Chicago American Indian Conference brought together 460 persons from ninety tribes. Out of this came a "Declaration of Indian Purpose." In August, the National Indian Youth Council (NIYC) was organized by Clyde Warrior, Melvin Thom, Herbert Blatchford, and others who had been in Chicago. The NIYC became a leading voice for younger Indian people during the 1961–67 period. Slightly later, the Native American Movement (NAM) was organized in the Los Angeles–Ventura area of California, bringing together Chicano-Mexicanos, Chumash, and urban tribal people. NAM developed a series of militant position papers, while NIYC published *American Aborigine* and *Americans before Columbus*.

In 1963, the fishing rights treaty struggle commenced in Washington State. From 1960 to 1961, the American Indian College Committee, led by Carl and Mary Gorman and me, began working for the creation of native-controlled colleges, a university, and a native studies program.

In 1964, Survival of the American Indians was organized in Washington State. It became the cutting edge for indigenous resistance in the Pacific

Northwest, soon to be followed by a Red Power movement in British Co-lumbia. In the East, Six Nations people continued to struggle, and in 1968 the Akwesasne Mohawk staged their famous blockade of traffic across an international bridge in order to stand up for treaty rights.

During this period, Rarihokwats and others established a newspaper called *Akwesasne Notes*, which became a major voice of indigenous resistance around the world. The American Indian Movement was born as a local or-ganization in Minneapolis, later spreading into the upper Midwest and northern Plains areas. In 1969, traditionalist-nationalist First Nations peo-ple gathered on the Tonawanda and Onondaga reservations, and then, on 26 August, some one thousand native people from fifty different nations of the United States, Canada, and Central America met as a part of the North American Unity Convention. On the West Coast, more than one thousand indigenous people gathered at an old Haida village to ceremonially erect the first totem pole since Christian missionaries had tried to suppress native culture there.

In California, 1967–69 was also a very active period, with indigenous peo-ple becoming increasingly confident and militant. In 1967, California Indian people, led by David Risling, Jr., organized the first grassroots native-con-trolled education organization in the country, the California Indian Educa-tion Association (CIEA). The CIEA became a major force in West Coast af-fairs and a model for the National Indian Education Association. California Indian Legal Services was also organized (1968) by CIEA leaders and others. A more militant group was United Native Americans (UNA, 1968), organized by me, Lehman Brightman, LaNada (Means) Boyer, Horace Spencer, Belva Cottier, Muriel Waukazoo, Stella Leach, Carmen Christy, and many others. For about four years, UNA published *Warpath*, a uniquely militant and tradi-tionalist newspaper. UNA picketed OEO offices in San Francisco, forcing the release of money for the Neighborhood Friendship House. Many UNA mem-bers went on to become leaders during the Alcatraz struggle.

An important series of events at this time was the U.S. Senate Indian Education Subcommittee hearings held at the San Francisco American In-dian Center and chaired by Senator Robert Kennedy. Organized by Senate aide Adrian Parmeter and me, the hearings provided an opportunity for California native people to testify. I also helped organize a visit by helicop-ter to the Stewart's Point Reservation School, an all-Indian school north of the Russian River. Senator Kennedy met with the teacher-superintendent, the children and their families, as well as with me and other First Nations people. The Kennedy visit was one among many events that served to alert Bay Area indigenous people to their potential as activists.

In 1969, native students, including Richard Oakes, joined the Third World Strike at San Francisco State University. In the spring of 1969, the

UC Berkeley chapter of UNA joined the Third World Strike on that campus and pushed for the creation of a Native American studies program. UNA located a vacant facility on the campus and occupied it, securing it as a student center and office. Leaders in this effort were LaNada (Means) Boyer, Patty Silvas, Carmen Christy, Steve Talbot, Horace Spencer, and me. The strikes at both UC Berkeley and San Francisco State helped to train indigenous students in militant strategy and gave them a great deal of self-confidence. The occupation of an office at Berkeley also set a direct precedent for Alcatraz. Richard Oakes and several other San Francisco State students met with UNA people in the "liberated" office during the period prior to the landings on Alcatraz.

The San Francisco Bay Area had many very active organizations during this period, including the Bay Area Native American Council (BANAC), the Intertribal Friendship House of Oakland, the San Francisco American Indian Center, the San Jose American Indian Council, Bay Area Indian Health, the Indian Well-Baby Clinic, California Indian Legal Services (CILS), UNA, the American Indian Historical Society, and others. Native Californians were active in CIEA, CILS, and, to some extent, UNA. First Nations people from other states were often divided along tribal lines. Many Sioux people, for example, did not always support the Bay Area Native American Council because it was led by Adam Nordwall (Fortunate Eagle), an Ojibway. Nordwall, who ran his own pest extermination business, was a leading organizer of powwows in the area.

The year 1969 was one of awakened militancy and vigor in the Bay Area indigenous community. A new native studies program commenced in the fall at the University of California, Berkeley, led by Lehman Brightman of UNA. (I had turned down the job in order to start a similar program at UC Davis, because CIEA members preferred a rural campus.) All kinds of marches, sit-ins, protests, planning sessions, and negotiations had taken place at San Francisco State and UC Berkeley, and a cadre of students and supporters were available on the two campuses and at the San Francisco American Indian Center.

It was in this atmosphere that, on 9–10 November, a small group of Native Americans landed on Alcatraz. They stayed only a short time, but on 20 November, a group of fourteen First Nations people went back to the island, followed the next day by eighty to one hundred Native Americans belonging to at least twenty tribes. By 28 November, it is said that there were at least four hundred people on the Rock. Prominent among the Alcatraz leaders were many veterans of the San Francisco State strike and of UNA, including Richard Oakes, Stella Leach, and LaNada (Means) Boyer. A great deal of initial credit must go to BANAC leader Adam Nordwall, but any occupation, if it is to endure, must involve large numbers of people.

Soon after the occupation took a solid hold, I wrote an article entitled "Alcatraz: What Its Seizure Means to Indian People." This article, which appeared in newspapers in California, began by noting:

> In the 1870's Natchez Winnemucca, respected Chief of the Pyramid Lake Paiutes, was arrested and sent as a prisoner to Alcatraz. His crime: attempting to resist and expose the corruption of the government's agents on his reservation. Natchez did not stay on "The Rock" very long, but other Indians, guilty of the "crime" of resisting white conquest, were frequent visitors to the prison. Now, in 1969, modern-day Native Americans are attempting to claim Alcatraz Island in order to both obtain facilities for educational programs and to publicize the desperate circumstances under which the Indian people are living.

I went on to argue that indigenous people had a right to occupy Alcatraz on the basis of the aboriginal rights of native California people. I wanted to provide a firm legal basis for their right to be on the island, which I found in the original title of the Muwekma and other California native people. My article concluded: "The Native Americans on Alcatraz are saying that *they* want to have a place where *they* can control programs which will benefit both Indians and non-Indians. Those who can see into the future will agree, I think, that an Indian museum, memorial and educational center on Alcatraz will be of great benefit and value to all Californians, regardless of race!"

Not long before the Alcatraz occupation, I had become aware that a 640-acre facility near Davis, California, was to become surplus. This communications facility had several usable buildings and good agricultural land and was located in a rural area within sight of sacred Pupunia (Mount Diablo) to the south, the sacred Maidu Buttes (Three Peaks) to the north, Berryessa Peak to the west, and the Sierra Nevadas to the east. We organized a board of trustees for D-Q University and applied for the 640 acres under surplus property procedures. In the end, we had the only complete application, but the federal government decided to award the land to the University of California, Davis, whose application was unsigned and legally incomplete.

In any event, on the night of 3 November 1970, native students from UC Davis climbed over the fence and began the peaceful occupation of D-Q University, logistically supported by Chicano students. People from Alcatraz came to help, but it remained primarily a student occupation during the first crucial weeks. Finally, in April 1971, we secured a deed to the site, and D-Q University got under way. It has been operating ever since.

There are many relationships between D-Q University and Alcatraz. For one thing, I had developed proposals for an indigenous university in the early 1960s and had refined them over the years, with input from grassroots native people from all over. I am sure that my ideas must have influenced La-Nada (Means) Boyer and others who called for the creation of an Indian university on Alcatraz. But Alcatraz was not the best place for a college because of its lack of agricultural land and suitable buildings and its damp climate and inaccessibility. Those of us who were trying to create the university saw the communications facility as offering a much superior location.

In a very real sense, D-Q University represents both a predecessor to and a continuation of Alcatraz. Recognition of the need for a native-controlled center for education and rebirth, foreseen by the founders of the American Indian College Committee in 1961 and before that by stalwart fighters such as Sarah Winnemucca and Luther Standing Bear and asserted by United Native Americans in the newspaper *Warpath* (as well as in speeches and conferences), contributed to what happened on Alcatraz Island.

Alcatraz turned out to be much more than a media event. We owe a great deal to the occupiers, especially to those who hung on and who tried to build a community for Indians of all tribes. Alcatraz has become a special place for all indigenous people, because it still lives, not only at D-Q University, not only in the San Francisco Bay Area, but on every reservation and in every urban center in North America—in fact, I would venture to say, all around the world, wherever indigenous people have decided to dig in their heels and struggle for self-determination.

Thanks go to Adam, to Richard, to LaNada, and to all of the others who helped to make Alcatraz a symbol of hope for native peoples!

10

ALCATRAZ IS NOT AN ISLAND

Lenny Foster

The occupation of Alcatraz Island in the San Francisco Bay on 19 November 1969 was one of the most significant events for American Indians in contemporary history. It spawned a movement that has touched the lives of many in the indigenous community and has resulted in many dramatic changes. The occupation has been called a defining moment in American Indian protest, heralding the beginning of the Red Power movement, but I personally believe it was more than that. It set the stage for the spiritual rebirth of the original peoples of this land, and it was the beginning of the reclaiming of pride and dignity for all Indian nations in the Western Hemisphere. Twenty-five years later, this movement has proven to be the catalyst that released the voices of indigenous people.

My spiritual journey to Alcatraz began three years before the occupation, when I was a student athlete at Window Rock High School in Fort Defiance, Arizona, on the Navajo Reservation. One of the high points of my youth was an invitation to participate in a major league baseball tryout camp conducted by the Los Angeles Dodgers in July 1966 in Albuquerque, New Mexico. I was given very good ratings as a prospect to play professional baseball. For the next two years, 1967–69, I was a member of the Arizona Western College baseball team in Yuma and played in one of the toughest junior college baseball conferences in the country.

In those early years, there were many protests about the conditions and treatment of disfranchised people. The Vietnam War was at its height, as were the Black Panthers, the Poor People's Campaign, and general social unrest. I began to think about the position of Indian people in the United States. I had seen and been a victim of racism in Gallup, New Mexico; Flagstaff, Arizona; and Farmington, New Mexico, and it made me very angry and resentful. The rage our people felt was justified, and we had to stand up and challenge that type of treatment. I began to sense a spiritual vacuum deep inside myself; I did not know this feeling would lead to more than political awareness.

During the summers of 1968 and 1969, I served with the VISTA program, working with indigenous migrant workers in western Colorado and central Utah. I met many Chicano activists, such as Tomas Atencio, Len Avila, Luis Valerio, Cesar Chavez, and Corky Gonzalez, who were heavily involved with their people's struggle, and I wondered where Indian people stood on human rights issues. I attended a conference called United Front against Fascism in mid-July 1969, in Oakland, California, which was sponsored by the Black Panther Party. I was very impressed with their movement and their community involvement.

It was also during this time that I heard about the American Indian Movement (AIM) Patrol in Minneapolis, Minnesota, and read about Clyde Bellecourt and Dennis Banks, cofounders of AIM. I wanted to meet these people; they seemed to possess qualities I had been searching for in myself. I met Clyde Bellecourt in November 1969 in Littleton, Colorado, at a protest against the Bureau of Indian Affairs. It was not until July 1970 that I met D.J. (Dennis Banks) and Leonard Crow Dog, who were dancing at the Sun Dance in Pine Ridge, South Dakota. I was very impressed with them and was immediately drawn into AIM.

I transferred from Arizona Western College to Colorado State University in Fort Collins, where I tried out for the fall baseball team in 1969. One of my teammates was Felix "Tippy" Martinez, who later joined the Baltimore Orioles and became one of the premiere relief pitchers in major league baseball. I was living in one world—a world in which some of my friends came to excel—but I was already beginning to move into another world that would become much more meaningful to me.

I met LaNada Means at a student conference in Fort Collins. She spoke of the Indian students at the University of California at Berkeley and San Francisco State University, whose growing activism included demands not only for recruitment of more Indian students but also for Indian studies programs and courses. She also told me they were planning to occupy Alcatraz Island very soon and asked if I would be interested in supporting and participating in the occupation. Later, when I read in the *Rocky Mountain News* out of Denver, Colorado, that American Indians had taken over Alcatraz, I knew that was the place where I wanted to be, among Indian people who felt the same as I did.

In December 1969, I hitchhiked out to San Francisco through snowstorms in Laramie, Wyoming; Salt Lake City, Utah; and Donner Pass. After several days, I finally arrived in San Francisco and boarded the boat that the occupiers were running between the island and Fisherman's Wharf. The trip to the island was cold and windy. Under other circumstances, it might have been depressing, but our spirits were high. When I finally reached Alcatraz Island, I encountered an old friend, Patrick Geneeha of Holbrook,

Arizona, and he introduced me to Joe Bill, Al Miller, and Richard Oakes. I met other very interesting people as well, such as John Cutnose, Lance Yellowhand, Jim Vaughn, Frank Chase, John Trudell, Ray Spang, and Ed Castillo. Of course, LaNada Means was there also. In addition, two young Navajo men from my hometown, Glen McLemore and Howard Nez, had left high school to come and support the occupation.

I stayed for three weeks in December and then returned in May 1970 to attend an American Indian studies program conference at the University of California, Berkeley. At this time, the United States had just invaded Cambodia, and there was much unrest in the Bay Area. In the fall of 1970, I joined the Denver chapter of the American Indian Movement, under the leadership of Vernon Bellecourt and Rod Skinadore. I went out to Alcatraz again in December, but that was my last time; in June 1971, federal marshals landed on the island and arrested the small group of people who remained after everyone else had left to go to the Pit River protest or to the Sun Dances in South Dakota.

One thing that impressed me about Alcatraz was that the people were all searching for something: a spiritual identity as Indian people. John Trudell named this group Indians of All Tribes because, although the people were from all parts of the country, a sense of unity and brotherhood was evolving. Alcatraz was a place where urban and reservation Indians were coming together and examining the U.S. government's failure to honor its treaties and its obligation to Indian people. We were becoming Indian activists, and it was time to reclaim our Indian dignity. The Indian Nation had awakened.

The Indian rights movement was accelerating: Alcatraz; Pit River; AIM Patrol; the Northwest fishing rights struggle; Sun Dances; the Trail of Broken Treaties; protests and demonstrations in Gallup and Farmington, New Mexico, and Flagstaff, Arizona; Wounded Knee II; the incident at Oglala; and the Longest Walk. Indian people began to emerge as active participants in the struggle for human rights and environmental protection.

My participation in the American Indian Movement solidified my spirituality: I believe it was my fate to be part of this movement, and it was our destiny to go to Alcatraz in 1969. Wovoka did not choose to lead a movement, just as Crow Dog and Black Elk, Vernon and Clyde Bellecourt, Dennis Banks, Leonard Peltier, John Trudell, Wilma Mankiller, Janet McCloud, and Russell and Bill Means did not choose to be leaders but were chosen by the Great Spirit. The movement returned dignity and spirituality to Indian people. Beginning with Alcatraz on 19 November 1969, we got back our worth, our pride, our humanity; the prophecy was fulfilled that the Red Nation would occupy its rightful place as the caretaker of Mother Earth.

I have been Sun Dancing since July 1973 as the result of a vow I made during the seventy-three-day occupation of Wounded Knee. Since 1980, I have been working with native prisoners' rights groups to protect inmates' freedom of worship. Many people have had personal success because of the movement that began with Alcatraz. I testified in March 1994, in Washington, D.C., before the Senate Select Committee on Indian Affairs, about native prisoners' religious rights and practices. On 15 January 1993, in Phoenix, Arizona, I received a Dr. Martin Luther King, Jr., Civil Rights Award, but I think of it as a "human" rights award. I attribute all of this to the vision "Alcatraz is not an island."

11

FROM THE RESERVATION TO THE

SMITHSONIAN VIA ALCATRAZ

George P. Horse Capture

I found myself once again leaving my beloved Indian reservation that blustery March morning, but an unspoken realization that my circle would soon be complete carried me forward. After saying the proper and sometimes emotional farewells to my family and the mountains, I climbed into the van and headed eastward across the rolling prairie to New York City.

Seeking a positive way in which to occupy the many traveling hours ahead, the historian in me began to record my perceptions and thoughts and to describe the beauty of our spectacular country. After a few hundred miles and many hours of constructing this journal, a theme began to emerge.

As various sites and geological features passed the van's windows, I noted and commented on them and fitted them into the grand scheme of things. For example, down the road are two rocks that have been moved to their present site from what is called the Cree (Indian) Crossing of the Milk River. They are shaped like kneeling buffalo and are part of a larger distant group. The sign by the road says "Sleeping Buffalo Rock." They are now considered sacred, and Indian people stop there and pray.

Further on are the two Porcupine Creek names that figured in determining the boundaries of the Fort Peck Indian Reservation long ago. Later, I passed the Garrison Dam, which flooded Indian land on the Fort Berthold Indian Reservation. Later still, I passed the Red River of the north, as well as the Sauk Centre, the Missouri River, Illinois, and so on; these names and places are filled with past and present Indian history. It became obvious that Indian people have been here a long time and that we have left our proud imprint upon the face of this continent. As I considered these things, it occurred to me that the eyes and mind that were observing these things now were not always so filled with Indian history and the pride such things evoke. Long ago, I was a markedly different person.

I have told this story before, but it is worth remembering, because it "grounds" me and keeps me stable in this chaotic world. My brothers and I were born here long ago when it was not popular to be Indian. In fact, it was quite painful. We were born on the Fort Belknap Reservation in northern Montana. For many reasons, both traditional and contemporary, my earliest thoughts are of my grandmother, Clementine, whose Indian name is Singing Rock and who was our parent in the early days. We lived on the northern edge of the reservation, right at the turn of the Milk River—where the thickets and mosquitoes were almost overpowering—in a place called Little Chicago because of the high death rate that occurred there.

It was a chaotic time for our people. Governmental and religious forces had been at work on our traditions for almost seventy-five years and had damaged them very badly, many critically. Our grandparents, who had experienced bitter discrimination by whites all of their lives, took steps to protect us from such pain by not teaching us our tribal traditions. We existed from day to day in our little world, with our grandmother keeping us away from town and white people as long as she could; in reality, they were only four miles away.

After all these years, I look back at those times with warmth and humor. Although a large interstate highway passed not too far from our place, it did not exist to us; it occupied another dimension. But whenever an automobile came down the gravel road at our cutoff, we stopped our play to stare. It always seemed like an outside threat of some sort. If the car slowed down and turned into our dirt road, a hundred yards down the gravel road from the highway, we kids scattered and hid in the high weeds, peering out like little frightened deer. Although the days were filled with hunger, they are but gentle memories now, and the great sadness caused by the outsiders has almost faded away. These early days with my brothers, cousins, and other relatives, shepherded by my grandmother, are very precious to me. As we played in the bright sunshine, we all thought we were equal and free. We ran around barefoot, little knowing that we were setting the fashion trends of the future: We wore big, faded overalls, sometimes torn but never dirty; our hair was long and shaggy, but a quick swim in the nearby river would fix that.

One fall morning, our world changed. This was the first day of school. Slicked up as best we could, we marched onto the yellow school bus and headed to the nearby off-reservation school a few miles away. Although there were a lot of other Indian students there, we soon learned that we were in a totally different world. It was no longer ours, and we were no longer equal. We were in the white world, where we were viewed as subhuman. Our eagerness, our anticipation, our curiosity, and our naïveté quickly vanished. Our clothes revealed that we were poor; on Christmas we had no money with which to exchange gifts. We could not bring handkerchiefs every day, as some classes required. The school curriculum was barren of Indian people except as part of some distant history: Squanto (whoever he was) and Pocahontas (some fancy Indian woman to the east who married a white man). The non-Indian students and their parents taunted us constantly. Soon we began to withdraw into ourselves, drying up inside, enduring each day by waiting for that final bell when we could go home again. It was a painful, souring experience.

After a few years of such treatment in school, our future course seemed set. There was little at home and nothing in school. As we grew older, each of us developed ways of coping with this stifling situation. Some withdrew into themselves, some opted for geographical isolation and seldom left the reservation, others became belligerent toward the forces that had inflicted this damage on us, and still others tried to assimilate into the outside world. Our parents chose the latter course. My father, Joseph, was always a bright man, seeing further than many others could. So when World War II happened, he joined as a volunteer, along with thousands of other Indian people, to protect our country as Indian warriors have done since the beginning.

While honorably serving in faraway countries, my father's generation of Indian people saw a whole new world. In many places, there was no discrimination, and everybody had plenty; most even had inside toilets. When my father was honorably discharged, he came home and took us off the reservation to live in the town, where he could work and make money for our future. We had a good life for many years; a few photographs have survived the years, attesting to this fact. But slowly my father became depressed, perhaps because he was in the city, away from home. Eventually, alcohol controlled his life and our family disintegrated. We children were rescued by our grandmother, who, in a brave, desperate action, ventured forth from the protected reservation, across Montana, to bring us home to sanctuary. Over the years, we went back and forth: from city to reservation, grandmother to parent or parents, always on the edge.

As we got older, we stayed with our mother and stepfather in the city and tried to fit in there, but it never did work. Again, racism followed us; we were teased about our long hair and our shyness. Although we had one or two close friends, we never really fit in. The situation only became more aggravated in high school. I was living in the white world, but I was never accepted when everybody else took part in school activities or chased girls. A barrier always kept me out and made me feel bad and ashamed.

Soon after high school, I fled Montana and joined the U.S. Navy, where personal accomplishments were more important than race. For the next four years, in the closed fraternity of the military, I began to achieve some success. Rising through the ranks, I achieved the highest level an enlisted man could attain during that four-year time span. Upon my honorable discharge,

I settled in the San Francisco Bay Area. My string of good luck continued. I landed a good job at the San Francisco naval shipyard, advancing from welder's helper to metals inspector and then to state steel inspector for California. My second wife and I were flying pretty high by then. We had our two boys, and we lived in a nice apartment (with an indoor toilet), owned a used but reliable automobile, a clear and sharp television, decent clothes, and a fourteen-foot motorboat. Together we enjoyed movies and picnics, went to zoos and an occasional powwow, and visited my parents.

Every summer, I would try to return to my reservation to see my grandma. She was getting old now, and her blindness caused her much pain. I especially remember one visit. She was sitting in a darkened room on the edge of her bed, among all her bundles and things. As soon as I said, "Hello, Gram," she greeted me, and I sat down beside her. We hugged and sat in silence for a while, as Indians often do. Then she leaned over, reached under the bed, and pulled out a big package, which enclosed a beautiful star quilt, saying, "I've been saving this for you." I guess she gave it to me because I was her oldest grandchild. Later I wondered, How long was that package there? She was quite a lady.

Our lives seemed to level out. I wasn't really happy, nor was I sad. We lived on a long, even plateau of "success," but it was all empty and lifeless. There was no joy of victory. I had climbed the white mountain, looked over its summit, and found nothing. We might have stayed there forever and eventually bought a house, but something came up that changed my life and the Indian world.

On the morning of 20 November 1969, fourteen Indian students, braving the choppy waters of San Francisco Bay in their rickety craft, landed on the rocky shores of the island prison called Alcatraz. "The takeover," as the action was later identified, made national headlines. It caught us all unawares; previous to this time, we had struggled quietly to survive as the government and state forces continued to take over Indian land or attempt to negate and abrogate our treaties. We had only just fended off termination, and suddenly the headlines screamed "Takeover." Wow! I remember reading about it at the breakfast table as I prepared to depart for work. I sat there stunned, unable to believe that we could get together and do such a thing—but here it was. The newspapers provided daily accounts of activities and statements by Indian people concerning the need for this action, and I remember one that said, "It's cold and bitter out here, there's no fresh water, no electricity, no sanitary facilities and everybody is unemployed, but we're not lonesome. This island reminds us of our reservations." So, on a daily basis, we kept a close account of what was happening, but at a distance.

It suddenly occurred to me that this was a key point in Indian history. No matter what happened, the Indian world would never be the same after this. Indian people were declaring their independence, challenging the status quo, taking chances, being committed, being warriors; none of these things is new to our race, but they have been absent of late, or forgotten. As each day passed, I became closer and closer to the situation, and I began to feel the superficiality of my present life. I knew it would be better for my children in the long run if I at least explored this "Indian" alternative. So, one weekend, I went down to the bay, where the boats from the island landed, parked my car, and walked over to the wharf. Because of my dark hair and skin, I was immediately welcomed and accepted. I jumped down onto the wharf and began to help the others move boxes of supplies and load the small island-bound boat. Riding to the island, the refreshing spray of the bay splashing in my face, I felt, for the first time in decades, as if I belonged, as if I were home. There was no ridicule among us tribal people, only laughter. I knew I would never be the same again.

After landing, we unloaded the boat and hauled the boxes across a wooden wharf, up some stone steps, and into the guard house, or whatever it was called, near the entrance. When I took time to look around, I saw a sign on the big sterile wall that read, "This land is my land." My heart soared.

I will always remember my first night on the island. I arrived with my damp bedroll and no pillow. I did not know anyone, but everybody else seemed to be on their own, too, milling here, laughing there, going out to the fire in the exercise yard, or just walking around. I glanced up at the giant guard tower and wondered what it had witnessed over the years. Inside, my footsteps echoed around the main cellblock of the prison, attesting to its emptiness. I made my way through the labyrinth to a smaller section of enclosed cells that looked secure and secluded; there I made my bed. Listening to the clamor of voices and laughter in the night, I finally fell asleep. Later, I realized I had slept on death row.

Sunday night, I took the last boat back to the mainland, returning, at least physically, to my other life. But the next weekend, I took my sons and went back to Alcatraz. Although they were small, they helped as best they could with the boxes of supplies. They fit in well, running hither and yon, like all the other Indian children. Although they did not understand the full impact of the occupation, they enjoyed themselves. We brought along a small, cheap camera and two penlights, and, when the work was done, we began to explore the prison proper. The stairs descending into the dark dungeon were quite scary, because we knew that the basement had been the scene of evil and painful events. My sons stood at a designated spot, holding the light between them in the total darkness. Carrying the camera, I paced a distance away and took their picture. The resulting photo shows them with wide, apprehensive eyes, but unafraid. Later that day, we volunteered to cut wood—just as we did back on the reservation—bringing it into the yard and stacking it up where a communal fire was kept burning for cooking and other purposes.

One evening, after the chores were done, I stood looking at San Francisco. Nothing grandiose was happening; the stars were making their appearance gently alongside the flickering lights of the distant city. While I was enjoying the view, a young Indian came up from the wharf. He had a bedroll on his back and was peering in all directions, filled with bewilderment and wonder. Knowing how disorienting the first visit was, I welcomed him and asked him how he liked his island. He replied that he couldn't believe it. He was a Navajo and had heard that Indian people had taken over this island for all the tribes, but he just could not believe it. He explained that he had taken a long weekend off his job to hitchhike across the Southwest, halfway up California and across this bay, just to see if it was true. He looked around and said proudly, "It is true." He had to leave early the next morning in order to go back to work on Monday, but he had had to come out and see for himself. I'll always remember him.

On subsequent days, while helping with the boat, I saw a new manifestation that would eventually grow to gigantic and menacing proportions. As the dark-skinned, identifiably Indian people moved supplies for the island, white people would come up and ask if they could help, and we would gently reply, "No, thank you. This is an Indian thing, and we really couldn't have non-Indians participate at this level." But then they would suddenly declare their Indianness, stating that they were Cherokee or Lumbee or something else, even tribes we had never heard of before. We would all sneak glances at each other, silently thinking, "Oh, sure." Often they would furnish documents to us to prove that they were enrolled somewhere in Indian Country as tribal members. They seemed to be waiting eagerly for an opportunity to become affiliated with some Indian action. Today, this category has grown to a point where pretenders don't even have documents; they say they prefer not to be involved in the enrollment system, but they still claim Indianness. Of course, we all know about "wannabes." They have no identity of their own, so they conjure up a fantasy that they are Indian. Eventually, they believe it themselves. Some even move to Indian Country and marry Indian men or women. I pity them, for they are lost, but I also resent them, because they replace real Indian people who desperately need the jobs and benefits these impostors may take. I wonder, too, where they were twenty or thirty years ago, when we were in deep trouble and needed help. I'm sure that, when the interest in Indians swings the other way, when being Indian is viewed unfavorably again, they will desert us and go back to being French, Armenian, or Turkish—anything but Indian.

For historic reasons, media interest focused on Alcatraz during the first Thanksgiving after the Indian takeover. When we went to the wharf that day, we noticed much activity: Boats laden with photography equipment were heading for the island; the camera crews came from around the world—Italy, England, and elsewhere. The Indian leaders apparently thought this exposure was good, and they welcomed everyone. A major restaurant in San Francisco— I believe it was Giovanni's—donated forty or fifty cooked turkeys; they were still warm when we off-loaded them, with all the trimmings. Apparently, Robert Vaughn, a popular TV hero of the time, rented a barge, filled it with fresh water, and had it towed to the island for our use. I have always appreciated what these people did, because they made that day special.

We had our "first Thanksgiving" dinner in the exercise yard. Because of the media, we saw Indians there whom we had not seen before. There were "chiefs" bedecked in their finery who went back to the Mark Hopkins Hotel to sleep at night, but that's okay. It was a good time, and word got out to the world that the Indians were alive and well. The media attention had an effect on all of us; I know it affected me. I began to understand that I was not a white man, and then, with deeper understanding, I realized that I did not want to be one; I only wanted a fair shake. As an Indian person, I was visibly different from white people, but, in the Indian world, I was fully accepted and welcomed. And I learned that Indian people cannot operate individually; we have to come together as a group, because only then, through unity and cooperation, can we attain political and social strength. I learned all of this and more on the island.

The movement called for 110 percent from everyone, and that was impossible to give over a long period of time. After a year, the spokesmen moved on, having turned down several offers from the government to build an educational osdcultural institution on the island. With the quality of leadership diminished, the movement fizzled out. But, like a nova, its force and brilliance had exploded and reshaped the psyche of the Indian world, and the force generated is still being felt today. Our real strength now lies not in the San Francisco Bay Area but in the hundreds of reservations that dot our country from coast to coast.

As for me, my leave expired eventually and I had to return to work. Sadness filled me when I saw the movement diminish on the island, but I knew what had taken place and what that meant for me. My non-Indian wife and I discussed my feelings and our future, and we agreed on a bold, new direction. I quit my job and enrolled in junior college full time to learn skills that would be helpful to Indian communities.

Going from the youngest steel inspector to the oldest student in one fell swoop was a bit of a shock for me, but I found that I could think and write along with the best of them. With assistance in the form of grants, I was able to transfer to the University of California at Berkeley, one of the most respected academic institutions in the country.

UC Berkeley was a whole new world, filled with mental riches I had never known before. It opened a thousand intriguing doors. The Indian students gathered daily at the Indian studies department, part of ethnic studies, and all of us took on this institution. We developed our own classes on Indian singing and art, and we volunteered at the local friendship house as tutors and summer camp counselors. It was a dynamic, enriching life.

On campus, all the classes we took were Indian-oriented in some way. For example, if we took an anthropology course, it would have to focus on Indians in North America; or if we took archaeology, it would have to have something to do with North America. We took linguistics to learn about the languages of American Indians. One of the most interesting courses I took was bibliography. In order to make it meaningful to me, I focused on my tribe, commonly called the Gros Ventres of Montana, even though our own tribal name is A'Ani, which means "White Clay People." I spent the next quarter researching all of the newly located works in the prescribed manner. In the process, I learned all sorts of things unknown to me before. I had grown up in a historic and cultural vacuum because my reservation had no libraries, no lecture halls, one Catholic school, and no cultural studies of any sort. Here on campus, I found "mind food" beyond my wildest dreams. In my research about my tribe, I found relevant monographs, printed long ago and forgotten in an archive. Photographs, secured in their wooden drawers, came to light at last. Together, all this information gave me a view and a knowledge previously impossible to obtain.

My research attested to the fact that, beyond doubt, we were a great tribe. We even burned three forts; few Indian tribes can claim that fame. Our area extended from mid-Saskatchewan down to New Mexico. We were well known and very much feared by other tribes and non-Indians alike. Among the photographic works of Edward S. Curtis, I found my great-grandfather, Horse Capture, whom I had never heard of before. He was a great leader and a member of the Frozen Clan, the clan of chiefs. He conducted the last A'Ani Sun Dance in the late 1800s and was the last Keeper of the Sacred Flat Pipe, the holiest item in our world. There were many other great leaders among our tribe—our George Washingtons and our Thomas Jeffersons. With each discovery, I made a photocopy of the printed material for myself and sent one to the reservation.

My search soon extended beyond the written word to photographs, then to audio, then to ethnographic art. In Indiana, I found songs recorded long ago to preserve the sounds of our early people. I located art pieces as far away as Germany. Piece by piece, our history took form for me. And what started as a simple college course began to take over my life. I eventually received a small tribal research grant from the Rockefeller Foundation that allowed me to visit the sites of our history in Wyoming, Montana, and Saskatchewan. So, for the first time in at least 150 years, a tribal member visited Pierre's Hole in Wyoming, where we had early encounters with white fur trappers. In Canada, at the South Branch House, Pine Island, and Chesterfield House, I found the locations of the forts we burned.

The search was thrilling. Each new success added to my confidence and abilities, making the next step easier. Eventually, I developed enough confidence that I stopped caring what people thought of me. I knew that I had accomplished respectable work and that my activities were helpful to American Indian people—to my tribe in particular—and perhaps allowed others to understand us better. As for the few ignorant non-Indians, I really did not care about them. As I grow older, this view becomes more firm.

After I finished my B.A. degree, my wife and I decided to move back to Montana, hoping to work on the reservation. We packed a U-haul and headed for Indian Country. In Dillon, the first Montana town we entered, we stopped at the local A&W drive-in for something to eat. A little white girl immediately began staring at me and my wife, making me uneasy because I know Montana contains many racists. Being somewhat bold, she eventually came up to us and, with a sneer, asked my wife, "Are you married to him?" Inwardly I groaned, "Oh, no. It's not happening already." After my wife answered affirmatively, the little girl looked at me and then at my wife and, with disbelief, said, "But, he's so . . . so . . . short!" I burst out laughing, because my wife was at least two inches taller than I. That incident taught me a very good lesson: Don't prejudge.

My life was truly changing, and I no longer wanted much. What other people thought of me had ceased to matter. I just wanted to learn more, produce more, and write more. I hoped that my work might make life easier somehow for those Indian children who would follow the direction I took. This became my goal in life.

Although a relevant job on our reservation never materialized, I eventually found employment as a curriculum researcher at the College of Great Falls. We produced, among other things, a television program about the culture and traditions of Montana Indians, utilizing people from all the tribes of Montana. We knew it was a success when the local churches began to change their mass schedule on Sundays to avoid competing with our program.

It was quite an exciting life back in old Montana. I was lobbying for programs to make teachers more sensitive toward their Indian students; writing to congressmen about Indian affairs; creating Indian curricula; and producing Indian-related workshops. I located a tribal dictionary compiled by a Jesuit long ago, and, with the assistance of the Montana Committee for the Humanities, my colleagues and I assembled a group of linguists who had been studying the A'Ani language and asked them to meet with all of our living speakers on the reservation, in the town of Hays. Only a dozen native speakers were left, all over sixty years old. After seeing these elders so happy, sharing the language once again, I knew we had to do more to keep our language from dying. As a result of that gathering—with my encouragement and assistance—one of the linguists, Dr. Allen Taylor from Colorado, produced a massive two-volume dictionary. Although our native language may never be spoken in the household as it was at one time, at least now it will not be totally lost.

Periodically, my anger still flares when I realize that many bad situations of the earlier days really have not changed. We are still being exploited. First, our lands were taken, then most of our religion, most of our culture; now some non-Indians are trying to take whatever remains, whatever has survived. For example, a growing number of non-Indians make money from publishing previously recorded Indian materials, and the tribes do not benefit in any way. Worse still are the wannabes who find that Indian-related writings sell, so they become "scholars." Since many white people trust other whites more than they do Indian people, white scholars easily become authorities on the subject of Indians. No one thinks to consult the living tribes. These pretenders could really help Indian people, but money leads them astray.

A growing awareness convinced me that I should try to publish some of our tribal materials; it seems to me that it is usually the larger tribes that have books published about them. My first move was to arrange for publication of some WPA materials entitled *The Seven Visions of Bull Lodge*. The story of one of the great warriors of our tribe, this book is still used in some schools today. Developing a concept into something I could hold in my hands, seeing the book actually used in the schools, was a very satifsying accomplishment.

Over the years, my reputation grew and my luck continued. I became well read in the Indian world and was able to accomplish more. My list of publications expanded. I taught Indian studies here and there, began to lecture around the country. In 1979, I was asked to be on the advisory board of the Buffalo Bill Historical Center (BBHC), which was putting together a new Plains Indian Museum. Several Indians from various reservations came together there to offer advice and counsel. One of the suggestions we made that we deemed extremely important was to hire an Indian curator. The BBHC made a great national effort to find one, but these animals were extremely rare. We were never really satisfied, so one day the museum administrators offered me the position, and I accepted. I was the first Indian museum curator in the country on hard money.

We tried to make the Plains Indian Museum the best in the world. It soon had its own publishing fund, its own advisory board, its own powwow ground, its own annual seminar, its own sacred room, its own open storage, and just about everything that was unknown elsewhere at that time. I met some great people and cranked out a lot of Indian exhibitions and publications on many subjects.

In 1990, after recovering from a heart attack, I began to think that I was not immortal. I wanted to devote whatever time I had left to something very special. We decided, my new wife and I, that I should resign and we should move back to the reservation, where we could live among my tribe, acquaint our children with my people and their ways, and, if we were lucky, perhaps establish a tribal museum.

We moved in January. Arriving at the house we had rented, we found that every drop of water in the place was frozen solid. We survived by hauling water in buckets for the basic necessities. My oldest son laughingly observed, "Dad is really making great advancements in this world. Before he left forty-five years ago, he was hauling water to the house for the basic necessities, and today he is still hauling water to his house for basic necessities." Eventually, spring came; around July, the pipes thawed, and life was good. For the first time, I did not have to "punch a clock." I could fairly well do what I wanted, but we still had to make a living. Reservation life was both an exhilarating and a disappointing experience. My children got reacquainted with their relatives and made new friends; now they will always be anchored there.

With my wife's private conservation work and my lecturing and writing, we made a fair living, or at least we survived from check to check. But it was good: big, clean. About two years later, I had another heart attack that required surgery; that gave me a total of eight bypasses. Heart attacks are not unexpected for me. My grandfather died at fifty-one from heart problems and my father at forty-nine. So, at fifty-six, I am in the gravy part of my life. Such episodes cause one to be more appreciative of sunsets and spring flowers and the prairie wind and time, but I don't worry about it constantly; there are new pills, new regimens, and I'm not the only Indian to have experienced heart problems aggravated by diabetes and who knows what else.

For several years, I have been associated with the National Museum of the American Indian, having always believed in the benefits such a museum could provide to our people and others. Because there are no relevant, Indian-based curricula in the schools, we have to rely on museums and other alternative educational institutions to teach others about us. Education is the key to our survival. The Smithsonian Institution asked me to be the first member of the search committee for the new director of the museum. Later I was a cofacilitator for the consultation meetings that were held around the country. It was exciting to see a life-long dream begin to come true.

Occasionally, a trip to Washington was necessary to meet with the administration, and I took it upon myself to give them counsel wherever I could. My hair was gray and I had a place to live, so I was free to say anything I wanted to. Remarkably, they often listened. It was very important to me that this new museum be established by Indians. When traveling around the country, I urged Indian people to become involved in the new museum. If we do not provide input and express our opinions, we cannot expect the museum administrators to know anything in great detail. We have to help if this is going to be our museum.

One day, I read a notice about a job opening for a deputy assistant director for cultural resources; the duty station was the Bronx, New York. I remember thinking, "Who would ever want to live there, working in an office all day?" But in talking with my wife and family and others later, I slowly came to realize that my dream for a tribal museum had never really developed. I was urging others to become involved in the National Museum of the American Indian, but I had not participated myself. So I submitted an application for the job, and, lo and behold, I made number one on the list. My mind had not really changed; I did not want to go back East and work in a big city. I would miss the meadowlarks. Then I figured, What the heck, I spent four years on a destroyer in the U.S. Navy; surely I could do two years in the Bronx. I believed that my experience, knowledge, and reputation could contribute significantly to the new museum, perhaps helping Indian people across the country also. It was a big decision, and we talked about it for some time.

One night, while sitting under the stars and thinking about my life, I remembered a day back in the sixties, just after the takeover of Alcatraz, when I realized the historical impact of the event and how dramatically it had altered my life. Now I recognized that another historical event was taking place: the building of a national museum dedicated to teaching the true story of the American Indian people. The opportunity to be a part of this action was real. Time was passing, but I was still capable of making more contributions. Alcatraz was the beginning of my awareness and involvement; a position with the National Museum of the American Indian could be the formal culmination of my cycle, the completion of my hoop, the renewal of the sacred circle. I accepted the job.

Looking back, I see our tattered, rugged beginnings on the reservation grow into a strong dedication over the years, one that has shaped our family and others as well. Many Indians have followed this way. My oldest son is now Keeper of the Sacred Pipe of our tribe; my second son is attending Montana State University on a presidential scholarship and working in their Museum of the Rockies, majoring in history and Plains Indian art. My daughter is planning to do the first of her four Sun Dances beginning next year, just as her father and two brothers have done before her. My youngest son is learning from all of us, and he will continue the traditions as well.

So the darkened world that I was born into is now a bright one. There is sunshine everywhere, and the pride, perseverance, and reawakening of our ancient Indian culture all started on that rocky little island in the middle of San Francisco Bay. Indian people should build their lives with this advantage; they should be dedicated and always relate to each other. They must do these things, or Indian people will once again fade away. They must keep the faith and find their own Alcatraz.

12

THE GOVERNMENT AND THE INDIANS:

THE AMERICAN INDIAN OCCUPATION

OF ALCATRAZ ISLAND, 1969–71

John Garvey and Troy Johnson

Alcatraz, a twenty-two-and-one-half-acre island situated in the bay between San Francisco and Sausalito, California, became an issue to American Indians in November 1969 when a group of Indians landed at the vacant federal penitentiary and claimed title to the island under the doctrine of "right of discovery."

On Sunday afternoon, 9 November 1969, fifty American Indians circled Alcatraz twice on a borrowed Canadian clipper ship, the *Monte Cristo*. Five men dove off and swam to Alcatraz Island to claim it. Originally, seventy-five Indians had planned to land on the island from five pleasure boats, but the plan failed when the armada did not show up. Richard Oakes got the urge to dive into the water from the *Monte Cristo*, and the other four followed. Walter Hatch was unable to finish the difficult swim, but the others made it to shore.[1] When they emerged from the water, they were greeted by island employee Glen Dodson, who asked them to leave; they left ten minutes later.

That same evening, the same four Indians, plus ten more, returned to Alcatraz on the *Butchie Bee* and landed around 6:00 P.M.[2] The fourteen Indians were students from UC Berkeley, UC Santa Cruz, and San Francisco State College.[3]

Tom Hannon, regional administrator of the federal government's General Services Administration (GSA), region 9, in San Francisco, did not receive word of the landing until 10:00 A.M. the next day. Hannon had complete federal authority over the island. He notified the U.S. marshal, who referred the matter to the U.S. attorney. Hannon contacted Acting U.S. Attorney Richard Urdan, who recommended that Hannon try to meet with the American Indians on Alcatraz and convince them to leave. In addition,

Urdan suggested that Hannon advise them that they had made an illegal entry, were trespassing, and therefore were subject to misdemeanor charges. If they remained, Urdan stated, he would have the U.S. marshal take the trespassers into custody.[4]

There was "a cursory inspection" of Alcatraz Island, and, after a thirty-minute period, the Indians appeared from their hiding places.[5] They "came out of hiding behind shrubs" and gave Tom Hannon the proclamation claiming the island for the Indians by "right of discovery." The nineteen-hour Indian occupation appeared to be over. Hannon informed them that Alcatraz was federal property and that, if they had a claim to the island, they should pursue the matter in court; otherwise, they should seek legislation to convey the property to them. Knowing that a 1964 Sioux claim to the island had proved unsuccessful in the U.S. courts, the fourteen Indians subsequently left Alcatraz.

A larger group of Indian people landed a third time that month at 2:00 A.M. on 20 November 1969. At 1:53 that afternoon, the FBI in San Francisco sent a message to its Washington, D.C., office. The enciphered message reported that the "demonstration [was] peaceful," and "it [was] expected that all Indians [would] leave Alcatraz within twenty-four hours."[6] By midday, however, signs began to sprout up around Alcatraz Island. One read, "You Are Now on Indian Land." On the big water tower on the north end of the island, the occupiers painted the slogan "Peace and Freedom Welcome Home of the Free Indian Land."

While the Indians were beginning to organize on Alcatraz, the government started mobilizing on the mainland to handle the occupation. At 4:00 P.M., Hannon arrived on Alcatraz with two attorneys for the Indians, Aubrey Grossman and R. Corbin Houchins, and a representative from the Department of the Interior. Hannon had informed the Indians the night before that they would be arrested unless they agreed to leave and that the expected supply boat from San Francisco would be impounded by the Coast Guard if it attempted to land.[7]

Initially, Hannon had been given an order over the telephone from Robert Kunzig, GSA administrator, to get the Indians off Alcatraz Island by noon on Friday. Hannon had gone to the U.S. attorney and submitted the formal request to the U.S. marshal for removal of the Indians. At the meeting, the head of the U.S. marshals, Frank Klein, "began to describe how he would do this—using such and such weapons, guns, ammunition, etc." Hannon saw a potential bloodbath and suggested less violent tactics. Klein lashed back at Hannon, telling him "not to try to dictate to him what tactics he would use—that was putting his nose into business where it didn't belong." Upset with the U.S. Marshal Service, Hannon withdrew the request for their assistance and returned to his office.[8]

It was now 11:00 A.M. on Friday. Hannon was sitting in his office, agonizing about what he should do, when the phone rang. It was Kunzig. Of course, Hannon "had visions of Kunzig's giving him hell about not having completed the plans for removal." Kunzig instead told Hannon that he, Kunzig, had been "relieved of responsibility for Alcatraz and that in the future Hannon was to deal with some people at the White House named Garment and Patterson." Kunzig was extremely "vexed" at this, although this official instruction had come from the White House.[9] Soon after the second Kunzig phone call, Patterson called Hannon and established communication that was the essential link thereafter.

The Indian people on the island had thus made their presence felt in the White House. President Richard Nixon (1969–73) had given his aides the authority to handle this crisis for the federal government earlier, when a teletype had informed him of the seizure. Aides Leonard Garment, special advisor to the president for minority affairs, and Brad Patterson, an executive assistant to Garment, handled the crucial situation.

Garment and Patterson told GSA commissioner Robert Kunzig that he was not to do anything; they were going to send a negotiating team instead of armed law enforcement. Patterson said force was never used because the White House did not want a massacre on its hands.[10]

Meanwhile, the occupational force of seventy-nine American Indians were making themselves at home on the Rock, and, sensing government intervention, they started to make plans. The Indians and the government agencies began sensitive meetings.[11] Richard Oakes and R. Corbin Houchins, one of the legal advisors for the Indians, phoned Interior Department regional coordinator William T. Davorenon at 1:15 P.M. on a mobile phone and read a prepared proclamation.

This "proclamation demanded that Interior Secretary Walter Hickel meet with them on Alcatraz and turn the island over to the Indians within two weeks." In addition, the five-point proclamation demanded that the island be governed by an elected "Indian entity without participation in its management by any agency of government" and that the U.S. government supply enough money to develop and maintain "a major university and research and development center for all Indian people." The proclamation from "Indian Territory—Alcatraz" also demanded that supply boats for the occupation force be allowed to land with food and other necessities without harassment. "The choice now lies with the leaders of the American government," the proclamation said, "either to use violence upon us as before to remove us from the Great Spirit's land or to institute a real change in its dealings with the American Indian."[12]

On 21 November 1969, GSA personnel and a representative of the secretary of the interior met with two Indian representatives on Alcatraz. They agreed to inform the secretary of the interior of the Indians' desire for Alcatraz Island. At the time, the FBI was advised that the secretary of the interior expressed his desire that "no arrests be made" on Alcatraz.[13]

The *San Francisco Examiner* reported that a "Coast Guard blockade was established in an attempt . . . to keep Bay Area sympathizers from aiding the invaders, and the patrol warned any sightseeing sailors that they would be violating federal law if they attempted to land on the island."[14] Later in the day, the government eased restrictions and allowed supplies to land with donated food. While government officials were considering all the implications, the American Indian Center in San Francisco "issued a public appeal for money, food, blankets or other articles for the occupation force."[15]

That afternoon, the FBI office in Washington, D.C., received a phone call from San Francisco's assistant special agent in charge, James Moreland. He advised the bureau that he had been contacted by the acting United States attorney at San Francisco, Richard Urdan, who sought FBI assistance. Urdan requested bureau agents to accompany him to Alcatraz Island to confront the Indian group and to ask them to leave. If they refused to vacate the island, Urdan "wanted them forcibly removed." The GSA's noon deadline to vacate the island was approaching on the West Coast. Urdan planned to go over to Alcatraz if the Indians did not leave by noon. In Washington, D.C., the FBI had to make a quick policy decision, and A. Rosen concluded that Urdan's request appeared "to be a function of the United States Marshal's office rather than the FBI." Rosen instructed Moreland that Urdan would have to visit Alcatraz without FBI assistance, because the bureau "should not get involved either in the demands or the forcible ejection of the Indians from Alcatraz." At 9:25 P.M., the San Francisco FBI office advised the bureau that there were about 130 Indians on Alcatraz and that a United States Coast Guard cutter in San Francisco Bay, with U.S. marshals aboard, was preventing landings on Alcatraz.

On 22 November, the Coast Guard maintained a tight blockade of the island, patrolling the bay through the thick fog and preventing the Indians from entering or leaving. That same day, Robert Robertson, the government's middleman and executive director of the National Council of Indian Opportunity (NCIO), phoned Norm Rambeau of the American Indian Association. Robertson would become the government's chief negotiator, while Hannon was a West Coast liaison bureaucrat for the GSA and Garment the key White House figure directing this drama.

Robertson asked Rambeau how he would approach the island occupation, if he were in the government's shoes in Washington, D.C. Rambeau's "own personal feeling" was that a "confrontation wouldn't do the Indian people any good at all."[16]

The government now had a crisis on its hands. What had been planned as a symbolic action to draw attention to the problems of Indians had expanded to a demand for title to the island for exclusive Indian use and money to operate numerous facilities: a university, a cultural center, and a museum. Richard Oakes upset federal officials when he declared, on 25 November, "Alaska is next, yes Alaska."[17] Grossman later stated that there was no court for them to go to. Whether land was taken from the Indians by the United States illegally or improperly is a political question—and no court will consider a political question. The Supreme Court called the issue political or nonjustifiable.[18]

On 24 November 1969, Secretary of the Interior Hickel issued a news release saying that he was available to meet with Indian representatives regarding the future of Alcatraz, without any preconditions—but not on Alcatraz. He also mentioned that he was "glad to pursue such discussions, even though it [was] not in [his] power to transfer ownership of the island or to alter it in any manner."[19] Hickel refused to meet with the Indians while they were on Alcatraz and noted that he would have to consider all possible uses of Alcatraz. At this time, the FBI notified Washington that the Indians on Alcatraz were running out of water and had requested replenishment of the supply.[20]

The same day, after the Indians had refused to leave the island, the San Francisco regional office of GSA asked federal law enforcement officials "to take steps" to bring the Indians back to the mainland, because the deteriorated property was extremely hazardous and the facilities were insufficient to accommodate the large throng on the island. The water supply, intended only for the caretaker, was exhausted and had caused a power failure from an overload on the electrical circuits. The GSA was concerned about the well-being of the Indians and issued a news release saying that there were "hazards on the island besides health; the buildings have broken stairs, crumbling walls, rusty nails, and inadequate lighting." But the Indians ignored the warnings and remained in the ghostly, crumbling buildings.[21]

On 26 November, the Indians issued a press release on Alcatraz that detailed their support. Meanwhile, GSA in San Francisco released a statement that requested the Indians "to come ashore and talk about the Alcatraz situation." The message reported that "it [was] being realized that urban American Indians have real problems." It stressed that "there has been no violence and no deadlines or ultimatums have been given to the Indians" and that the "GSA locally has been instructed by Washington not to force any confrontation with Indians."[22]

The GSA press release had been drafted in the White House.[23] Besides warning the Indians of the dangers on the island, it characterized the occupation as a peaceful demonstration and stated that "the use of force to remove the Indians from the island has been avoided." It further asserted that the government was interested in meeting with the group to discuss local educational and cultural needs, with good faith on both sides.[24]

On 27 November 1969, Thanksgiving Day, islanders invited newsmen to be pilgrims at their feast but warned that they wanted no militants, hippies, or tourists to visit. One Indian remarked, "[E]very day that we stay here, it looks more like we'll be able to remain indefinitely."[25] The president of the United Bay Area Council of Indians, Adam Nordwall, said, "[W]e are attacking the whole system of the white man by attacking Alcatraz" and declared that the island had become a symbol for his people.[26]

On 1 December, the San Francisco FBI informed its Washington, D.C., office that GSA had issued a press release stating that the Indians "must get off voluntarily and no consideration of their problem [would] be given until they have vacated the island and ceased to violate the law."

On 2 December, the Interagency Regional Council held a meeting in San Francisco intended "to determine what interim assistance [could] be properly provided by the federal government to the Indians in establishing a cultural center and to meet their other needs." The regional council was composed of representatives from the Departments of Labor, Health, Education and Welfare, Housing and Urban Development, and the Office of Economic Opportunity. Also included were representatives of the Department of Justice Community Relations Service, Commerce's Economic Development Administration, the Small Business Administration, the Department of the Interior, and GSA.[27] This regional council meeting was called at the request of Leonard Garment at the White House, so that the Interior Department and the BIA could "be convened to review Indian problems to see what inter-agency action could be taken to alleviate them."[28] The meeting resulted in a discussion of a possible planning grant that could be given to an appropriate group of Indians on Alcatraz who would represent all of the occupiers.

Early on, the government dealt with three distinct groups involved in the Alcatraz "drama." The first, led by Richard Oakes, was composed of Indian college students who were more "single-minded" than the others about obtaining title to Alcatraz. The other groups were the United Bay Area Council on Indian Affairs, spearheaded by chairman Adam Nordwall, and the American Indian Center, run by its director, Earl Livermore.

Meetings were tense; not only was the government negotiating with a diverse group of people, but one of the leaders, Richard Oakes, sported a button saying, "We won't move." Hannon stated, "[W]e believe we can induce them to go."[29] The regional administrator said, "[T]hey would just come back here with the same problems. We're trying to learn what their problems are so another Alcatraz won't happen."[30]

In early December 1969, Robert Robertson phoned Brad Patterson and told him that he "thought we could go around [the Indians'] flank by quietly taking care of whatever immediate problems they had in the San Francisco Bay Area." Patterson then quipped that "the strategy is that nothing will really happen until they got off the island." Patterson then stressed that Garment was calling the shots; the government in San Francisco was not to make any promises; and since the press had been involved in the meetings to date "not much can be said."

On 12 December, Browning Pipestem, an attorney representing the Indian occupiers, had an off-the-record conversation with Robertson. Pipestem said that the Indians on Alcatraz wanted a number of significant things, and he believed the difficulty the "government was facing was finding some sort of hook to hang their hat on." He contended that the occupation "points up the desperate nature of the situation." Pipestem was correct in seeing that the island was "the only negotiating instrument they [had]" and that meaningful dialogue could be accomplished only when they were on the island. If they left Alcatraz, they would be in the same negotiating position as they had been before.[31]

On 18 December 1969, California Senator George Murphy informed the press that he had proposed to the White House that Alcatraz become an Indian National Park. Senator Murphy did not get a warm response from the Indians on Alcatraz. Dean Chavers quipped, "A national park, that means it would be federally run, doesn't it? We want it run by Indians and I speak for all two hundred on the island."

On 23 December, Leonard Garment realized the need for an ad hoc group "to give the needed policy direction to Regional offices in San Francisco" and to handle the daily "new account of demands or proposals." The new group was composed of C. D. Ward of the vice president's office, Bob Robertson, Snead, and Wing from the NCIO, Alan Kirk of Interior, Joseph Maldonado of OEO (assisted by James Wilson), Daniel Kingsley of GSA, Kenneth Kugel of the Bureau of the Budget (assisted by Stanley Doremus), designees from the Departments of Labor, HEW, HUD, and Garment and Patterson.[32]

Garment also suggested negotiation. First, forcible removal would not be considered as long as the Indians were peaceful; and second, the administration welcomed all suggestions from Indians on the fate of Alcatraz for initial consideration. Garment mentioned two sine qua nons in reference to the negotiations: (1) The press would not be allowed unless both sides agreed, and the negotiating group for the Indians must be representative of the entire Bay Area; (2) the government did not want to deal with different factions that might repudiate an agreement at a future date.[33]

As the new year began, the Alcatraz Indians were beginning to plan phase two of their occupation. The occupation was phase one, and phase two involved "plans for development of facilities and curriculum for a Native American cultural and education center." With the government seemingly perplexed, the Indians announced that they planned to tear down the historic cellblock built in 1909 by army prisoners and place a large, symbolic, circular building on the island's highest ground.[34]

On Saturday evening, 3 January 1970, tragedy struck for the Indians on Alcatraz. Thirteen-year-old Yvonne Sherd Oakes, the stepdaughter of Richard Oakes, fell to her death in a stairwell of an apartment building.[35] Because of Yvonne's accident, the government began to learn more about conditions on the island. Richard's wife, Anne, told Hannon that they were going to leave because "there was much rivalry among the Indians on the island for leadership" and because of "drinking, use of drugs, fighting and disorder." Mrs. Oakes had "serious reservations on whether the fall was an accident"; she said her other children had been getting a lot of verbal abuse, and their oldest child had been "seriously beaten" two weeks earlier.[36] The Oakeses were also given conflicting reports of the accident by other Indians, which led Richard Oakes to say later, "[M]y daughter was murdered." Hannon did not call an investigation at this time, because he believed there was more "apparent emotion" than evidence. Initially, Richard did not tell Hannon that he thought Yvonne had been murdered, because he believed an investigation would precipitate forcible removal of the Indians.

The FBI did investigate Yvonne's death as a possible crime on government property. Agents interviewed Yvonne's fourteen-year-old cousin, and the facts were presented to former Acting U.S. Attorney Jerrold M. Ladar, who contended "that based on interviews by bureau agents, there was no basis for any further investigation."[37]

On 7 January 1970, an interagency meeting occurred in Washington, D.C. Present at the meeting were the Indians' Washington legal counsel, Montgomery and Pipestem. Those present for the government said they were "anxious" to work out proposals as to what might be done for the Indians in the San Francisco Bay Area. They were quick to point out, however, that "Bay Area negotiations [were] not the place to solve nationwide problems," and they recognized they had "a nationwide audience of urban Indians and Reservation Indians" watching. They sought the establishment of a representative group of Indians in the Bay Area so the government could "minimize the risk of making some agreements and then being whipsawed by dissident factions." It was suggested that the interagency San Francisco Regional Council put together a negotiating team and that Robertson, the executive director of the National Council on Indian Opportunity, become the principal negotiator and handle the press; GSA would remain in charge of logistics and security concerning Alcatraz. A planning grant from OED, HUD, Labor, and HEW was in the works for approximately forty thousand dollars. The government planned to give the funds to the all-Indian group so they could formulate workable proposals based on the needs of the Bay Area urban Indians. They also talked about a GSA arrangement where women and children would leave Alcatraz "for safety's sake" and the adult male Indians on the island would be given permits to remain on the Rock.[38]

The following day, an important step occurred when Robertson met with the council and the group was told that the NCIO was a "coordinating instrument" in the Alcatraz situation. The morning meeting was not a negotiating session but an opportunity to talk to the Washington attorneys. Montgomery and Pipestem agreed with the group that, initially, they must have "negotiations about negotiations" and the composition of both negotiating groups must be discussed.[39] The Indians on Alcatraz did have a seven-member council that met weekly to decide the affairs of their community. Indians over eighteen years old who had lived on Alcatraz for more than a week elected the council.

The next day, Robertson wrote a memo to the vice president and Garment. He mentioned that one of the government officials on the West Coast had said, "[I]f we do nothing for two months the Alcatraz situation would die away but of course we can't do this." He also mentioned that Hannon believed "he should pull back now and not be out front, that he should be concerned only with the physical Alcatraz situation" and that it was agreed upon that Hannon should assume this new role. In a private meeting with Hannon, Robertson observed that the government should determine the tactics in handling the press, that Hickel should absorb the island into the federal park system, and that the local government's feeling was that Alcatraz "was a Federal problem: let them solve it."[40]

On 9 January 1970, the *San Francisco Chronicle* reported that the government planned "to begin serious negotiations," now that the authority to deal with the Indians was shifted from GSA to the NCIO. The paper quoted Robertson as saying that "our major aim now is to begin a meaningful dialogue, we're keeping our minds open on all possibilities," and that he was "willing to talk with the Indians anywhere—including on Alcatraz itself."[41]

On 11 January, Robertson met not only with the council but with all the Indians, including visitors. The council explained to Robertson that decisions were made by everyone, that there were no secret meetings, and that the council could take action only in emergency cases. When the government negotiators asked for the Indians' chairman, they were informed that, since the Indians were practicing "pure democracy," there was no such person. Robertson opened the meeting, noting that they had come to Alcatraz "to discuss the health and safety hazards on the island."[42] After a short presentation by Hannon on the federal law for disposal of property, Grossman said that "the government could do whatever it wanted in spite of the law." The Indians were unimpressed.[43]

In his report to the vice president and Garment, Robertson noted that "there [was] no real leadership" on Alcatraz because of the "pure democracy" of the island group. He stressed that the government should remain patient because, "as the focus of attention [was] shifting to the planning activity on the mainland, the esprit de corps of the demonstrators will weaken even further."[44]

On 17 January 1970, the *San Francisco Examiner* reported a "water barge crisis on Alcatraz." The big steel barge was missing.[45] Hannon reported that the barge, which would hold 160,000 to 200,000 gallons, was merely "being filled," and thus the scare was off for the moment.[46] Eventually, the government would remove and secrete the barge.

At this time, a number of people in the government expressed their support for the Indians on Alcatraz Island. Louis R. Bruce, commissioner of the Bureau of Indian Affairs and an Indian himself, wrote, "I heartily support this determination as vital in the development of the leadership that can help the Indian people effectively chart their own course to lives of dignity, self-respect and independence in modern American society."[47] Others also sympathized with the overall plight of the Indians.

Patterson observed that the Alcatraz episode is symbolic to Indians. To non-Indians, it represents the lack of services for Indians in the San Francisco Bay Area. He also correctly noted that the White House "response to the Alcatraz situation has been one of restraint and willingness to remedy this lack of attention and to look at these unmet needs." Patterson expressed concern for the Indians' safety—he did not "want any more child injuries"—but was "disappointed at the lack of leadership" and their "pure democracy" that had made Robertson's three meetings as the principal negotiator at Alcatraz extremely difficult.[48]

On 30 January 1970, the ad hoc interagency group met in the vice president's conference room to discuss Alcatraz and the Bay Area urban Indians. The group concluded that the lighthouse must be secured; children would be urged to leave the island; the Alcatraz group should be represented on the new Bay Area Indian committee; Robertson could "hold out the possibility of a planning grant up to $40,000"; services should be improved to assist not only Indians but all people in the Bay Area; GSA and the Justice Department should challenge the papers of incorporation by the Alcatraz group; and Interior should prepare the cost estimated "for transforming the island into an Indian managed urban sanctuary, National Historic Site."[49]

After the meeting, Robertson considered the alternatives open to him as the principal government negotiator. The first was to let the situation continue as it was, but it was untenable. He could not "negotiate with a 'pure democracy' group"; they would probably not "accept anything less than all their demands," and they were unwilling to recognize any other Indian group except their own on the island. Further, the government was liable for their actions, and, even with a responsible island council, a maritime disaster could occur any day.[50]

Robertson noted that the current federal position was to do "something positive" with the Indian people regarding Alcatraz. He also realized that, "unless some move is made now all Indian effort expended regarding the island could be lost—that this effort is being undertaken nationally because all Indian people should be involved." Robertson believed that Secretary Hickel should create a park with Indian involvement; that an organization of national Indians should be formed; that the name of Alcatraz should be changed, perhaps to "Indian Island"; that an omnibus Indian cultural center should be constructed; that Indian training programs should be instituted on the island; and that the programs should be such that tourists would be involved. Robertson's argument for this plan was that a "'piece of pie' was better than none at all" and that, when the island was made a park and the buildings were razed, no person would be able to "stay on the island." In concluding his notes, he observed that, "even though it is true that ignoring the island situation [would] eventually cause its demise, [he] knew there [was] a chance to do something positive, imagewise, for Indian people."[51]

On 9 February 1970, the Indians on Alcatraz issued a press release about a newly formed group that would soon meet with government negotiators. Approximately thirteen Indian organizations in the Bay Area had formed the Bay Area Native American Council (BANAC) to represent "40,000 Indians from over seventy-eight different tribes throughout Alaska, Canada, and the United States."[52]

On the night of 1 March 1970, the Indians of Alcatraz held a meeting on the mainland. Vern Conway "lost a round in the continuous battle" with Stella Leach for leadership of the island group, which meant that the government negotiators would now have to bargain with a less intelligent, militant group that condoned the use of alcohol and dope and did not control visitors and sanitary conditions.[53] On 16 March 1970, Robertson wrote an informative memo to the vice president and Garment, noting that the island's current leader, Stella Leach, had said their position was "negotiable." Robertson suggested that the objective of the government's counterproposal was to form a partnership between the "unstable" and "badly fractionated" Indians on Alcatraz and the Interior Department so that a park could be developed. Anticipating the Indians' "non-acceptance" of the offer, Robertson hoped to get "the highest possible visibility," so the reasoning of the action would be understood by all concerned.

Robertson also mentioned that the executive director of BANAC, Norman Rambeau, had informed him that, if the government met the "islanders' demands head-on" and if they were still "unreceptive," BANAC would probably move away from the Indians on Alcatraz and accept the planning grant. He believed the government's "symbolic transfer-of-title act," to be included in the counterproposal, was vital because it was "a face-saver for the island Indians."

Robertson maintained that, if the counterproposal was considered "unacceptable" to an uncooperative island group, the government could "just proceed and leave them" alone as long as the occupation was acceptable. This response, he believed, would "effectively destroy the group." Robertson recommended that the government offer a counterproposal and give the Interior Department the green light to proceed with its park plan.[54]

On 25 March, Robertson began to formulate a serious counterproposal to offer to the Indians. He believed that the government would have "to face the issue squarely." The counterproposal would be considered "final," since the Department of the Interior would then go ahead with its plans for conversion of Alcatraz into a park. Robertson stressed that the "central thrust" of the counterproposal would be that Alcatraz would "become a showcase for Indian heritage and culture and that this would be achieved by involving Indians in the park planning process."

The government's "very best offer possible" included maximizing Indian involvement in the park's planning stages and changing the name of the island, if the Indians so desired. The government would not veto the idea of a university, ecological center, cultural center, and museum but would promise to study the requests. The island could be run by Indian Park Service personnel, but ownership of Alcatraz should remain in Interior's hands "in the best interests of Indians and all other citizens." Finally, the government would deny the Indian group's request for $300,000, because the park plan "would eliminate" the need to acquire support services and materials.

Robertson expected that the more militant Indians on Alcatraz would reject this counterproposal, since they would not settle for anything less than ownership. He believed that, if the government proceeded with its plans, most Indians would leave Alcatraz, but the more militant people would remain and be reinforced by additional militants. Robertson was "against a physical confrontation if there is any way at all to avoid one." The NCIO director stated, "If we are faced with such a situation in the future," sympathy, both Indian and non-Indian alike, would be with the government if it "executed" its "plan properly." Robertson also believed that the current island group was more receptive to the government's proposal, because Richard Oakes had recently returned to Alcatraz and had removed Stella Leach from the council; Oakes was perturbed about the "dope and alcohol problems" on the island, which he thought were destroying "the Indian cause."

Robertson hoped that he could meet with the press before the counter-proposal delivery date of 31 March 1970 to give the media an "off-the-record" account as to what really was happening on Alcatraz. Robertson knew "that the leading press people in San Francisco would give us good treatment." He hoped that the counterproposal would serve "as a high visibility vehicle to restate in solid terms this Administration's Indian policy."[55] On Tuesday, 31 March, the first five months of the occupation ended as the government offered its park plan for Alcatraz with maximum Indian quality, which meant, for example, Indian monuments, Indian park rangers, and a possible name change of the island.[56]

The Indian occupation of Alcatraz had now consumed five months, and high-ranking officials of the U.S. government had yet to find a solution to this vexing problem. They felt impatient but remained cautious in policy. The government decided to continue this cautious response and the constant negotiations in hopes that the Indians would leave on their own.

On Tuesday, 31 March 1970, Robert Robertson met with thirty to forty Indians on Alcatraz, offered them the government's counterproposal, and released Hickel's Interior study, "A New Look at Alcatraz," which had been completed on 25 November 1969. The proposal sought to turn Alcatraz into a federal park with an emphasis on Indian culture. Robertson shied away from making a commitment for a university on the island, noting that such problems as accessibility, water, sewage, heating, and lighting had led to the island's abandonment by the Department of Justice. Robertson told the press that "no deadline was set for a reply and there would be no effort to remove them if they refused the suggestion."[57]

On 3 April 1970, the Indians on Alcatraz turned down the government's proposal, contending that it "was a study that was taken before the Alcatraz invasion, thereby putting the lie to the statement that they had even considered [the Indians'] proposal." To them, it was a slap in the face. The Indians demanded another proposal with a deadline of 31 May 1970. The island group also indicated that the only negotiable items were "money and the time and the day that they will turn over the deed" to Alcatraz.

On 9 April 1970, H. Clyde Mathews, Jr., deputy regional civil rights director, HEW, San Francisco region, wrote Robert Coop, regional director, HEW, San Francisco region, correctly noting that the islanders would "attempt to keep the 'whip hand.'" He observed that the Indians "have conquered Alcatraz and are treating the government as peons." He believed that the government had made progress and that more negotiations might bring about a possible resolution. Mathews contended that the Indians on Alcatraz were basically "trying to get all of the cards on the table and see who has the winning hand."[58]

As the occupation entered the month of May, the situation on the bleak island remained guarded. On 26 May 1970, the government issued a press release stating that it would remove the three caretakers because of "increasing concern" for their safety; the administration feared that the men would be kidnapped and held hostage. The press release also noted that the government would allow the Indians to remain on Alcatraz "because their demonstration has been peaceful and has not disrupted normal government operations." Still, the government would hold to its present course. On 27 May 1970, Hannon announced that, at the request of the secretary of the interior, the island would come under Interior's control. The news release stated that the park idea was deemed "the most appropriate future for this unique island." It would have an Indian theme, and Hannon mentioned that the offer still stood to establish an Indian joint planning committee to confer with Hickel in developing the island park. He then called on the Indians to accept the government's plan and assistance, so "plans for the Golden Gate National Recreation area" could "move ahead."[59]

The Indians were not interested in the park, and it was now apparent that the government had started to flex its muscle with the islanders. In removing the caretakers and replacing the automatic lighthouse with buoys, the government had made it unnecessary to continue supplying the island with water.[60]

On Friday, 28 May 1970, the government cut off telephone service, electricity, and all water supplies. The Indians had a few generators, so the electricity shutoff was not a vital concern, but the water situation would present immediate problems, because hundreds of Indians had been invited to a weekend powwow for Indian Liberation Day on Alcatraz. Hannon said, "[W]e will just have to wait and see what the Indians will do."[61] It was apparent now that the federal government was not going to surrender to the islanders' demands.

On 30 May 1970, hundreds of Indians came to Alcatraz to challenge Hickel's intention to turn Alcatraz into a national park. They wrote a declaration on sheepskin stating that "we announce on behalf of all Indian people, or tribes that from this day forward we shall exercise dominion, and all rights of use and possession over Alcatraz Island in San Francisco Bay." The declaration also asserted that the occupation had been "done for Indians— but to those whites who desire their government to be a government of law, justice and morality, we say we have done it also for you."[62]

That evening, while a thick fog covered the bay, fire destroyed several buildings on the island. The fires had been set in defiance of a country that had turned its back on the Indians' proposal.[63] While the embers were still hot on 1 June 1970, the government announced that Alcatraz would be made into a park as part of the Golden Gate National Recreation Area. The government was low key about the fire; Tom Hannon even told one reporter that a blockade was out of the question since "there [were] some wonderful people on the island."[64] He stated that removal of the Indians was "not worth the risk" and that "it [was] idiotic to fight for an island that's inactive."

On 8 June 1970, the *San Francisco Chronicle* announced that the Coast Guard had plans to restore the island's navigational light as soon as it was "practical." USCG Capt. Charles Scharfenstein, 12th District commandant, reported that "the White House told us to deny electricity to the Indians" to pressure the occupying force to end its island stay.[65] The Indians actually restored the light with the help of Scott Newhall, a yachtsman and the editor of the *San Francisco Chronicle*, who provided a generator to restore the light as a makeshift beacon, but it was extinguished under White House orders.

The government's action against the Indians was a prelude to the ultimate act of removal. On 9 June 1970, GSA in San Francisco called a meeting to discuss plans for removal of the Indians. Realty officer Thomas Scott wrote, "[W]e feel we are prepared to initiate our [removal] plan if asked to do so by the Regional Administrator."[66] On 11 June 1970, the FBI office in San Francisco notified J. Edgar Hoover that the bureau's agents in San Francisco still would not go to the island to conduct any further investigations or assume a policing function. The *San Francisco Examiner* noted that, although "this might be called the battle of the redskins vs. the red faces, the palefaces are becoming red with embarrassment."[67]

The plight of the American Indian received national prominence when Richard Nixon addressed Congress on 9 July 1970. Although the president did not mention Alcatraz, he denounced the "centuries of injustice" to American Indians and proposed a comprehensive program to give them dignity and control over their destiny. He endorsed a "pending House Resolution that would return 48,000 acres of sacred land in New Mexico to the Taos Pueblo tribe." He also deplored a history of white "aggression, broken agreements, intermittent remorse and prolonged failure" in treatment of the Indians.[68]

Shortly after Nixon's message, Robertson wrote, "[I]f it were decided that a decisive move were to be made to remove the Indians from the island there will probably never be a better time than right now." Still, Robertson recommended that the White House avoid confrontation, as Nixon's message "created a fount of good will nationally for him."[69]

Since the Indians on Alcatraz believed their position was "tenable," Robertson thought that "getting them to take the final step actually deciding that they will give up the island—[would] be most difficult." If all other efforts failed, the government's response, according to Robertson, would be to set another deadline so that Interior could begin its park construction. The government would then wage an unofficial media war against the Indians by issuing press releases with substance from Nixon's message to Congress. If the Indians were still on the island, the government would remove them. Since public support for the Indians was "waning," the government had one final choice and that was to isolate the Indians and leave them alone on Alcatraz "to make their lives there more difficult" and thus persuade more to leave.[70]

From the onset, the government had avoided a confrontation with the Indians on Alcatraz, although it seemed only a matter of time before such an encounter would occur. On 28 July, Leonard Garment wrote a memo to director Shultz and John Ehrlichman. He stressed that the entire situation was "well suited to confrontation politics," which the government had recognized from the beginning, but it had "not reacted in any way which would play into their hands." Garment noted the government's "key strategy" of "restraint"; the government did "not want a Kent State on Alcatraz"—a situation, said Garment, that could be repeated on Alcatraz with "little effort." He further noted that BANAC had privately told the government, "[T]he Alcatraz situation will die on the vine if they are given some more time."[71]

Garment's memo was prompted by a letter he received from John Ehrlichman after the latter had visited the GSA regional office in San Francisco. Ehrlichman had concluded that the entire situation "makes the Federal government look pretty bad" and that the morale of the government personnel in San Francisco concerning Alcatraz was "very poor." Ehrlichman recommended to Garment that the White House appoint an Indian as a White House representative to "solve it in a way that saves face for the Indians."

Other White House aides were also making suggestions. Unaware of Garment's memo of 28 July, Don Murdoch and Bobbie Greene, two such aides, commented that "there has been only slight communication between the right Federal hand and the left Federal hand." They recommended that BANAC's planning grant be expedited and that the Interior's Department plan for Alcatraz be postponed indefinitely. Both believed that the Regional Council could insist that BANAC limit its operations to the mainland, which could be accomplished "through the proper use of the big money carrot." The two White House aides wrote that "negotiations between the White House and the Alcatraz group should be allowed to fade out," and "the group should not be honored with anymore visits from White House representatives." Both contended that the government's strategy would be to let the "controversy go out with a whimper, if that."[72]

On 17 August, the government formulated its removal plans, codenamed Operation Parks. The "top super secret" operation would have the Coast Guard make another attempt to reactivate the aids to navigation. If they were repulsed, the marshals would take over and evict the Indians. After the operation, GSA Public Building Service guards would secure the island. The operation was the brainchild of GSA's Hannon and Phil Roach, Marshal Tobin, and USCG Admiral Weyland.[73]

Through Governor Ronald Reagan, the federal government then announced its approval of the fifty-thousand-dollar planning grant on 21 August 1970 to the consortium of Bay Area Indian groups, the BANAC. Reagan also mentioned that the funds were made possible by a grant from the Office of Economic Opportunity.[74]

The Indians, in the ninth month of their occupation, suspected that an attack by the government was imminent. Steps were taken to fortify the island. The prison's recreation yard was dotted with more than thirty garbage cans stuffed with gasoline-soaked rags, to be lit in the event of a helicopter invasion.[75] When a Coast Guard helicopter hovered over Alcatraz on 28 August, taking numerous tactical photographs for the planned eviction, some of the Indians welcomed it with a barrage of rocks.[76]

On the morning of 2 September, the *San Francisco Chronicle* ran Herb Caen's column entitled "Pull Cord to Stop Press." Caen had managed to get his hands on a confidential dispatch from the commander of the 12th Naval District to the commander of the Western Sea Frontier on Treasure Island. Caen told his readers that the government planned to evict the Indians from Alcatraz and that the action was code-named Operation Parks. The removal would be staged from nearby Treasure Island, and it would "be a Coast Guard show with Navy participation." Landing barges were to be employed but not helicopters. Caen queried, "How does the Coast Guard feel about being cast in the role of villain by the Navy?"[77]

That same day, Tom Hannon of GSA issued a press release stating that the government was acting with restraint, that discussions were still open, and that it was still possible to arrive at "an amicable solution." Hannon contended that, if the navigational aids on Alcatraz were reactivated and not interfered with, there was "no present intention to remove the Indians from the island by force." Referring to Caen's column, the regional administrator stated that he had "no knowledge of internal classified Navy messages."[78] The *Stockton Record* quoted Hannon as stating that "there has always been a plan to remove the Indians if and when such drastic action is necessary."[79] The next day, Caen revealed that, when the Indians were to be evicted from Alcatraz, "the actual dirty work [would] be done by U.S. Marshals—thereby providing an authentic Wild West touch."[80]

In the meantime, the government was considering its long-range plans for the island or, at least, some ideas that might persuade the Indians to leave. On 14 September, Garment wrote Ehrlichman, outlining seven steps the government would need to take to change the Indians' status from trespassers to government contractors; return approved navigational aids to the island; and get "the island into the hands of the Cabinet Officer who has the best use for the island in the long run."[81]

First, GSA would relinquish control of Alcatraz and transfer it to the Department of the Interior, as Secretary Hickel had requested. Garment noted that GSA could not give the Indians a lease or permit, because this would come under the terms of the Federal Property Act, which required fair market value. The island's $2 million price tag would mean a monthly lease fee of $17,000, which would be prohibitive. Second, Secretary Hickel should designate the island as a national historic site under 16 USC 461. Third, the National Park Service would contract with "responsible" Indians for maintenance and custodial services. Fourth, the USCG would contract with "responsible" Indians to operate the foghorns and lighthouse on Alcatraz. The hiring of these "lamplighters" was discouraged by the USCG, since they already were able to provide an in-house capacity. Fifth, the National Park Service should allow the Indians to set up and run the concessionaire services on Alcatraz. Sixth, the National Park Service would issue special use permits to the Indians. Seventh, Interior should provide the Indian contractors with power, water, and portable toilets, for a monthly fee. Garment contended that these seven steps would take the "heat" off, because the public would certainly "be outraged by forcible removal."[82]

Garment was quick to point out that the steps did not provide a symbolic ending to the takeover, nor did they guarantee a long-range solution. He noted that there might be a problem with getting the Indians to vacate the island, since they believed that Alcatraz was their "only trump card." The White House aide believed the steps were "just a holding operation; it doesn't really get us anywhere, except out of the box we are in now—which would itself be an accomplishment of some size." Garment stressed that the government's "simple solution" of forcible removal probably would end in bloodshed and create "negative consequences" as the election of 1972 loomed. Nevertheless, a case would have to be made for forcible removal if that road was chosen, and Garment wrote that it "may be the next order of business if the above plan fails."[83] Garment's plan was eventually carried out, and Alcatraz became a national park. There has been very little Indian involvement in running the island, which perhaps suggests what was thought about their motivations at the time.

On 14 October, Robert Robertson informed Brad Patterson that he had gotten word from a third party in Washington, D.C., who was in close contact with the Indians on Alcatraz, that the islanders would never accept any type of settlement. The islanders wanted to remain on the windblown island because "at any time they [could] generate a situation which [would] create publicity, allowing them to speak out on national issues."[84]

Others were concerned with the lack of progress made by the government. On 9 November, Bud Krogh sent a memo to Brad Patterson, asking about the status of the Alcatraz situation and stating that he had "not heard of it since [their] decision not to mount a land-air-sea operation to extract the renegades."[85] Krogh also complained to GSA administrator Robert Kunzig "that those Indians would have been taken off the island long ago if it had not been for 'that asshole' [Tom Hannon] who was the GSA Regional Administrator in San Francisco."[86] News reporter Mary Crawford correctly observed that the occupation was "a thorn in the side of the Administration."[87]

The situation soon turned potentially deadly for the federal government. On 19 November, the Coast Guard cutter *Red Birch* was servicing a buoy almost 160 yards from Alcatraz when eight rounds were fired in the direction of the ship from a handgun on the island. This action prompted the commander of the 12th USCG District, Mark A. Whalen, to inform the commandant that Coast Guard personnel had been harassed since 1 June 1970. Whalen contended that these incidents were "degrading to the Coast Guard personnel." Whalen reasoned that the USCG could not take any action to reactivate the navigational aids until the White House resolved the dispute with the occupying Indians. This "intolerable situation" was unsafe for personnel and equipment, and the commandant should "pursue the subject to this end."[88]

Ironically, the same day, the *San Jose News* quoted Hannon as saying that "the Indians are out on the island, and since they aren't bothering anyone, we aren't bothering them, there is no reason for the government to move against them at this time." The government's policy had to change because of the latest incident. Yet, as reporter Joan Jackson concluded, "Alcatraz today [was] being passed around like a political football."[89]

Others in the government were also becoming impatient. On 27 November, White House aide Geoff Shepard declared to Bud Krogh, "*I recommend we remove the Indians, forcibly if necessary, and prevent their return.*" He urged that the White House request the FBI to "gather intelligence concerning population and activities" by infiltration and surveillance.[90] Shepard observed that Alcatraz had turned into a "public symbol for Indians everywhere." The White House aide stressed that the government had continued to tolerate an "armed trespass on federal property, destruction of federal buildings and property, larceny, drug abuse, and assaults on Coast Guard ships; and [they] have ignored the education and welfare of the children on the island."[91]

Shepard then discussed six alternatives that the government had at its disposal. The first was to remove the Indians forcibly, and the last was to maintain the status quo. Shepard reasoned that Nixon's "current goodwill" toward the Indians would be "jeopardized by movement in this area." The proposal to return Blue Lake to the Taos Indians was coming up soon in Congress. Shepard ended his memo somewhat philosophically: "Having tolerated this problem for a full year, we might conclude that this is a condition rather than a problem that demands an immediate solution."[92]

After reading Shepard's memo, Brad Patterson wrote to Bud Krogh, outlining four options for the government. Initially, Patterson's option A was to "let things continue as they are" and continue to play a "waiting game." However, he crossed out that option and changed it to forcible removal. This option would leave President Nixon "to defend himself alone." Under option B, the government would continue to play a delaying game until Congress approved plans to include Alcatraz in the proposed Golden Gate National Recreation Area. This option would defer confrontation, pass "the buck to Congress," and create a situation where the Indians might disperse because of weather and boredom. Option C was known as the "Garment Plan." This would have the secretary of the interior declare the island a national historic site, whereby GSA would relinquish control to the National Park Service. The final alternative, option D, was Shepard's idea to allow the islanders to set up a daytime center that would assist urban Indians.[93]

Patterson concluded that "if point four, above, is what will really happen, then we are back to options A or B, but this time with the posture of having made a genuine and very reasonable compromise offer, including literally giving the Indians some of the island." Patterson suggested that the White House "gear up a public relations campaign" to point out the "reasonable offer to the public and Congress, especially in the Bay Area," so that "the unhappy consequences of taking the A option may be slightly mitigated."[94]

On 11 December, Bud Krogh informed John Ehrlichman of current developments. The latest intelligence report from the mainland recluse who had been observing the island on a daily basis stated that the island's population was down to twenty Indians. Krogh recommended that the FBI gather intelligence on the island group, that the USCG and GSA "confidentially prepare" to move on Alcatraz at twenty-four hours' notice, and that, if intelligence showed a "diminished number" of islanders, the above agencies should be prepared to move on the island and restore the aids to navigation. If forced eviction should occur, Krogh recommended, the government should not prosecute the Indians on trespass alone, because the government had "tolerated the trespass for too long to prosecute on that basis alone." But the government should "at least" arrest the Indians for trespass and then "ask as a condition of bail" that the court instruct the defendants "not to return to the island."[95]

The situation for the Indians was bleak indeed. On 21 January 1971, after returning from a trip to Washington, D.C., LaNada Means observed, "[T]he government will not budge on the issue and are just watching us struggle" and "momentum of the Alcatraz issue has dwindled considerably." Since the Indian people did not have title and since the state of California would not recognize the legal incorporation of Indians of All Tribes, Inc., or give them federal tax-exempt status, large donors and the average American would not continue to give money to finance the occupation, because they could not "write it off their taxes."[96]

While the Indians' momentum was slowing down, the FBI was stepping up its investigations of the island group. J. Edgar Hoover's agents were now actively investigating the Indians to turn up anything that could be used against their cause and could serve as a reason for eviction. On two occasions early in February 1971, the FBI's San Francisco office determined that the islanders had transported copper, brass, and lead from Alcatraz and sold them to a local scrap dealer. U.S. Attorney James L. Browning, Jr., decided that the government should not take action, because a witness would be needed. The FBI continued to keep a tight surveillance on the Indians.[97]

While the investigative branch of the Department of Justice watched the Indians like a hawk, the enforcement branch of the Department of Justice, the U.S. Marshal Service, sent a deputy to Alcatraz with the Indians' attorney on 11 February. The FBI report stated that, "when the Deputy Marshal landed on the island, he was met by approximately twenty young Indians, half of which were armed with .45 caliber automatics." A verbal confrontation ensued, and the U.S. marshal, outnumbered and outgunned, departed the island in disgust after failing to carry out his inspection.[98]

On 12 March, a meeting was held in San Francisco with U.S. Attorney James Browning, Harlington Wood, and Wayne Colburn, chief U.S. marshal, Washington, D.C. These officials considered many plans to retake Alcatraz, but the one that stood out was an "assault by force of U.S. Marshals to forcefully remove Indians." The FBI observer at the meeting told the group that the FBI would "furnish intelligence data" but "no agent would physically go to Alcatraz."[99]

On 4 April 1971, the San Francisco FBI notified its Washington, D.C., office that U.S. Attorney James Browning had advised them that a secret meeting would occur on 13 April between the government and the Indians. Government participants included Browning, Harlington Wood (assistant attorney general, Department of Justice), Bob Ireland (acting regional director of the GSA), and Larry Anderson (GSA special agent, Office of Audits and Compliance). Representing the Indians were the Indian council and attorney Donald A. Jelinek.[100]

The meeting at Brooks Hall, which the press knew nothing about, was the result of John Trudell's announcement that the islanders wanted title to the disputed island, and they invited the government to comment on its current position. Attorney Browning started the meeting by saying that the government representatives could not make any binding agreements with the Indians, because the government had not authorized them to do so. He mentioned that the federal "government regarded criminal and legislative jurisdiction over the island as a matter separate and apart from title to the island." The lawyer also mentioned that the government's "matter of access to the island was a non-negotiable one" and that "the government [had] been most lenient with the Indians" in allowing their right of access. Browning mentioned the latter because of "several instances of crimes necessitating government access to the island," but, up to this point, the government had looked the other way in regard to the occupation. Relating to title, Browning stated that he hoped the Indians would realize that even Richard Nixon was subject to the law and that title transfer must be conveyed "under the rule of law" and not by any other means not in accordance with the law.[101]

They discussed the subject of navigational aids, and both sides agreed that aids were necessary to prevent possible collisions on the bay. The island group was also willing to make concessions in regards to federal jurisdiction of Alcatraz. The meeting closed with an agreement to meet in a week's time, but the subsequent meeting never took place.[102]

Browning later voiced his impression that the islanders would not settle for anything but title to Alcatraz: "[T]hey will not discontinue their militant stance against government access to the island in the absence of either title to the island or removal therefrom." He also observed that the islanders "neither regard themselves as citizens of the U.S. nor do they regard the island as a part of this country" and that "they see themselves as leaders of a race older than this nation controlling a small, but important, piece of 'land' which they propose to 'run' as their 'own show.'"[103]

The subsequent FBI report of 15 April concerning the meeting mentioned that Browning believed the meeting "accomplished practically nothing" and that "he did not know if any such meetings would actually be held or if it would even be worthwhile to hold any more meetings with the Indians."[104] This last meeting between the government and the Indians was significant, because the islanders had not backed down from their initial demands, but their support had dropped considerably.

After a year-and-a-half, the government's cautious response had worked: The occupation had begun to run its course, and bloodshed had been avoided. Yet acts of violence and the approaching election of 1972 set the stage for the government to seriously consider the removal option. Based on the Indians' lack of public support, the favorable press that the government had obtained, and the unlawful acts that had occurred on Alcatraz, removal would be the government's solution to the occupation. The drama was approaching its final act.

May 1971 brought with it an eerie silence from both the federal government and the Indians who remained on Alcatraz. The executives in the White House knew "they were dealing with public opinion and not just a bunch of Indians." Each decision from the White House was carefully thought out, because the Alcatraz occupiers "were on a world stage." With a limited number of options available, the White House staffers had to take action to end the drama.[105]

On 7 June 1971, unknown to the Indians on Alcatraz Island, a meeting was held in the White House to determine their ultimate fate. The meeting was hosted by Bud Krogh and included Under Secretary Beggs, Admiral Bender of the Department of Transportation, Deputy Attorney General Kleindienst, Harlington Wood of the Department of Justice, Leonard Garment, and Brad Patterson. Krogh subsequently outlined the details of the meeting in a memo to John Ehrlichman.[106]

The group reviewed the current situation and intelligence data from San Francisco. They learned that there were between eleven and fifteen Indians currently on the island, including three children, and reasoned that the adults were armed. The number of people was thought to be at a low point; summer vacation from schools would soon swell the population. It was also reasoned that the group would not vacate the island in the near future.[107]

The officials discussed the collision in January of the two Chevron tankers outside the Golden Gate, which, according to Krogh, "dramatized the importance of proper navigational safeguards in San Francisco Bay." The accident was waiting to happen again, according to the group, because the temporary buoys were "not adequate." These buoys were placed one-quarter of a mile off each end of Alcatraz to replace the twenty-thousand-candle-power lighthouse and the two foghorns, each of which had a range of one mile. The group observed that, "aside from the continuing trespass, the intentional destruction of property, and the general lawlessness of the group on the island, the lack of proper navigational aids [left] the federal government open to a possible negligence action should another maritime disaster occur." The officials learned that, after the tanker accident, the *San Francisco Chronicle* had suggested that environmentalists urge the Indians to vacate Alcatraz. They also concluded that public support, which had been "strong," had "dwindled over time to almost nothing."[108]

The group noted that "although the United States has tolerated the Indian trespass since November 20, 1969, it has moved quickly in all other Indian occupation situations." It observed that "Alcatraz Island has continued to be an open wound—one that has become a symbol of different things to different people." Further, "because of the small population, the lack of present public support, and the long interval of time between now and the next election, *it was the consensus of the group that if the decision is made to forcibly evict the Indians from Alcatraz, now is the most appropriate time to do that.*" Ehrlichman then learned about preparations for the "ultimate decision."[109]

Harlington Wood and Wayne Colburn, chief U.S. marshal, were flying to San Francisco that day to prepare "for the forcible removal of the Alcatraz Indians by a specially trained unit of the U.S. Marshals." Krogh pointed out that GSA would then secure Alcatraz with its Federal Protective Service officers, the Coast Guard would restore all navigational aids, and the

disputed property would become part of the Golden Gate National Recreational Area that President Richard Nixon had recommended on 10 May
1971 after touring the area.[110]

At the conclusion of Krogh's memorandum to Ehrlichman, he wrote and
circled under the "Recommendation" heading that, "in spite of the risk of
violence, I recommend we utilize the above outlined method and procedure
of removing the Alcatraz Indians. The closer we get to the election, the more
troublesome this 'symbol' can become." He believed they "should move now
to preclude a more difficult problem throughout the time span between now
and the election."[111]

On Friday, 11 June 1971, at 1:45 P.M. on the East Coast, Tod Hullin
checked "E" (for Ehrlichman) in the approval section on the memorandum
and wrote, "Bud: E agrees with you. Go! He read Garment's memo also!"[112]
Years later, Leonard Garment said "they knew what President Nixon's feelings were" regarding Alcatraz, and they believed that the removal would be
accomplished "without bloodshed."[113]

The U.S. Marshal Service was mobilized on 11 June 1971. Under direction of the attorney general through the White House, the stage was set,
after nineteen months of lawlessness, for the enforcement of federal law on
Alcatraz Island. The government's invasion force consisted of a disciplined
group of marshals from the San Francisco, Sacramento, and San Diego offices. The United States Coast Guard surrounded Alcatraz, and the perimeter of the island was sealed.[114] The plan was to conduct the removal at low
tide, so the barges could land with barbed wire, which, when erected, would
protect the perimeter of the island from reinvasion.[115] In anticipation of
resistance, the marshals were armed with handguns, M-130 carbos, and
shotguns.[116] In addition, officers of the Federal Protective Service (FPS)
landed on Alcatraz with the U.S. marshals. The FPS, the security arm of
GSA, was formed in April 1971. Three months before the removal, the FPS
was primarily a guard service, but now these former GSA guards were known
as federal protective officers (FPOs). The FPOs sent to Alcatraz Island were
equipped with radio transceivers, .38-caliber revolvers, ammunition, helmets,
batons, and flashlights. Tom Hannon, regional administrator of GSA in
region 9, left his second-story office at 49 Fourth Street and went to the roof
of the Federal Building at 450 Golden Gate Avenue with binoculars to view
the removal. Hannon was in constant contact by radio with his command
center on the eighth floor of 49 Fourth Street and law enforcement personnel
on the scene.[117] Contrary to the FBI's official file, ten FBI agents also participated in the removal.[118]

Three hours after the White House gave authority to remove the Indians from Alcatraz, the islanders, who were enjoying "a beautiful sun baked
afternoon," were surprised by three Coast Guard vessels, a helicopter, and

about twenty to thirty armed U.S. marshals. The federal action met with no resistance and took less than thirty minutes. The fifteen Indians were frisked, and the six men, four women, and five children were put into protective custody. The press was not notified or allowed on Alcatraz during the removal.[119]

The islanders were not at all happy with the removal. Vicki Lee stated, "My little girl said they held a gun to her chest and she asked, 'are they going to kill me?' and my son hid under the bed but came out when they put a gun to his head." The thirty-year-old Shoshone from San Diego, California, said, "I don't think my husband should carry arms for the U.S. [in Vietnam] when his children are at gunpoint at home." She also warned that "we will return to Alcatraz, if not Alcatraz, someplace else. [W]e are prepared to die."[120]

Atha Rider Whitemankiller quipped, "The white man has once again followed the old ways . . . sitting at what he calls the peace table, then ripping us off." The twenty-two-year-old Choctaw from Oklahoma said, "They told us if we cooperated, we would not be handcuffed. They said they wanted to remove us from the island to repair the lighthouse. They were courteous all the way through. They didn't give us any time to collect our belongings."[121]

Whitemankiller stated, "Since when has it been illegal to possess a knife? In every American kitchen, you can find knives."[122] John Trudell later told the press that they had been in secret negotiations since mid-April with the government. The Sioux, who was not on the island when the removal occurred, said that U.S. Attorney James Browning "lied to us. . . . He promised there would be no actions against us while we were still negotiating." Trudell said, "[T]he government talks of honor in Vietnam and lies to its own people."[123]

Attorney Browning said that the theft of $680 worth of copper by Eugene Cox, John D. Halloran, and James Robbins was "the straw that broke the camel's back." The FBI had arrested the trio earlier that morning in San Francisco selling sixteen hundred pounds of copper wire from the prison's electrical system to A and K Metals.[124]

While the copper thieves were being arraigned before U.S. Magistrate Richard Urdan, Browning stated, "[W]e have no desire to prosecute the Indians we took off the island" and "we are not out to fine them and put them in jail."[125] Browning incorrectly told the press that it was his "best belief that it was a decision [to take Alcatraz Island] that was made locally."[126] He said the Justice Department, DOT, and GSA decided to remove the Indians because the Coast Guard wanted to restore the island's navigational aids, the islanders were "harassing passing boats," the Indians were stealing federal property, and the government wanted to include the historic isle in its new Golden Gate National Recreational Area.[127] Actually, John Ehrlichman made the final decision for removal, because the government had finally won its media war and had turned public sentiment against the Indians. The government's actions in denying electricity, water, and telephone service accounted for the small population on the island, which undoubtedly made Ehrlichman's decision easier.[128]

While the fifteen Indians were given lunch and interrogated at nearby Yerba Buena Island, the marshals, with five GSA helmeted guards, swarmed over Alcatraz, carrying high-powered flashlights to search every inch of the island, including its Civil War–era underground tunnels.[129] The Indians were then given overnight accommodations in San Francisco at the Senator Hotel. There, Delbert Lee said that, during the removal, the U.S. marshals "were running around like chickens with their heads cut off."[130]

In securing the island, the government did not allow the press access. One television station landed its helicopter on the island, but the chopper retreated after it was met by angry U.S. marshals aiming weapons at it. A cyclone chain-link fence and highly trained security dogs were then supposedly brought to the island.[131] Years later, Tom Scott said the government never kept dogs on the island.[132] Foxholes were subsequently dug by the FPOs, and law enforcement personnel spent a few nights in them, armed with rifles to repel the Indians.[133] They did, however, paint signs around the perimeter of the island warning boaters of security dogs.[134]

On 13 June 1971, the government allowed the media to visit Alcatraz, and the *San Francisco Chronicle* reported that the tour was "more like an autopsy." They reported that they "found an unrelieved vista of squalor, filth, systematic pilfering and mindless destruction." The initial "romantic theatre" was now closed as the paper published its article entitled "The Dream Is Over: A Sad Visit to Alcatraz." GSA realty officer Thomas Scott told the newspaper that he "had a great deal of respect for Richard Oakes and some of the others who began this." He believed they "were articulate and very intelligent." However, "somehow they began to get a lot of people from the Third and Howard area—wino types—who, when you talked to them, didn't respond, as if they were in a fog. At first, they were so excited, charged up with a real cause. Later, they didn't seem to know what the cause was or why they were here."[135]

On 22 June, Robert Coop, regional director of the Department of Health, Education, and Welfare in San Francisco, wrote to Brad Patterson and commented on the *San Francisco Examiner* editorial on 15 January 1971 entitled "A Dreary Ending on Alcatraz." Coop observed, "As the newspaper [said], the string has run out, and, in my opinion, support for the Indian's position on Alcatraz [had] all but vanished."[136] The editorial mentioned that "the federal government wisely let the Indians play out their string."[137]

Despite the failure of the Indians to gain title to Alcatraz, the occupation remains a significant event in American history. It was the first time that many tribes came together to make a political statement. As a result of the Indians' high visibility on Alcatraz Island, positive policy decisions were made at the highest level in the White House. The historical record shows that the Nixon administration was sympathetic to the plight of American Indians. The White House response was consonant with President Nixon's overall Indian policy, which was positive. The government's early caution stemmed from a fear of bloodshed and negative public reaction and a concern for the occupiers' health and safety.

This essay demonstrates that the government allowed the occupation of Alcatraz to run its course. In the end, it was apparent that the Indians were their own worst enemy. Frustration with the island group grew because of acts of violence and drug abuse and the impending election of 1972. Ultimately, the Nixon administration had to bring the occupation to an end. Even though federal law enforcement personnel evicted the island group, the occupation of Alcatraz, 1969–71, made a difference. It remains a positive symbol for American Indian people today.

NOTES

1. *San Francisco Chronicle*, 10 November 1969, National Archives, San Bruno, California.

2. GSA document date 10 November 1969, Regional Administrator–9A, Latest Indian Possession of Alcatraz to Commissioner, PMDS-D from Tom Hannon, General Services Administration (GSA), Record Group 291, box 5, folder 1, National Archives, San Bruno, California.

3. Richard Oakes, "Alcatraz Is Not an Island: Indian Occupation of Alcatraz," *Ramparts*, December 1972, 38.

4. Ibid.

5. GSA document date 10 November 1969, Regional Administrator–9A, Latest Indian Possession of Alcatraz to Commissioner, PMDS-D from Tom Hannon, GSA RG-291, box 5, folder 1, National Archives, San Bruno, California.

6. Alcatraz Indian Occupation, 1969–71, File 70-51261, Federal Bureau of Investigation case file, Washington, D.C. (hereinafter cited as "FBI case files.")

7. Memo to file by Bradley H. Patterson, Reminiscences on Alcatraz, document date 5 December 1975, White House stationery, Patterson's personal files, Bethesda, Maryland.

8. Ibid.

9. Ibid. (Brad Patterson knew how Tom Hannon felt because he interviewed him in Washington, D.C., in 1975, just three years before his sudden death by heart failure.)

10. Brad Patterson, interview by Garvey, 21 November 1984, The Brookings Institution, Washington, D.C. (Patterson was interviewed on two occasions by Garvey. Patterson knew how Kunzig felt, which is reflected in this paragraph. Sub-

sequent footnotes will be in short title form, with date and location, when they differ from above.)

11. *San Francisco Chronicle*, 21 November 1969, 1.

12. Alcatraz Island Proclamation, National Council on Indian Opportunity, box 4, folder 1, National Archives, Washington, D.C.

13. FBI case files.

14. *San Francisco Examiner*, 22 November 1969, 3, National Archives, San Bruno, California.

15. *San Francisco Chronicle*, 22 November 1969, 1.

16. Subject: Alcatraz Indian Matter, 22 November 1969, National Council on Indian Opportunity Records, National Archives, Washington, D.C.

17. *Los Angeles Times*, 25 November 1969, 24.

18. *Washington Post*, 26 November 1970, N 2.

19. Department of the Interior news release, by Walter J. Hickel, 24 November 1969, National Council on Indian Opportunity, box 4, folder 1, National Archives, Washington, D.C.

20. FBI case files.

21. Alcatraz Island Disposal case files (Hannon for Scott), 1963–71, box 6, Alcatraz news release, region 9, 26 November 1969, GSA RG-291, National Archives, San Bruno, California.

22. FBI case files.

23. Alcatraz timeline, Brad H. Patterson's personal files, Bethesda, Maryland.

24. GSA press release, National Council on Indian Opportunity, box 4, folder 1, National Archives, Washington, D.C.

25. *San Francisco Chronicle*, 27 November 1969, 1.

26. *Oakland Tribune*, 29 November 1969, National Archives, Washington, D.C.

27. Alcatraz Island Disposal case files (Hannon for Scott), 1963–71, box 16, GSA press release, date 1 December 1969, GSA RG-291, National Archives, San Bruno, California.

28. Chronology of San Francisco Regional Council Activities Regarding Indians, National Council on Indian Opportunity, box 4, folder 1, National Archives, Washington, D.C.

29. *San Jose Mercury News*, 2 December 1969, 2.

30. *San Francisco Chronicle*, 3 December 1969, 6.

31. Subject: Off-record conversation with Browning Pipestem regarding Alcatraz, 12 December 1969, National Council on Indian Opportunity, box 4, folder 1, National Archives, Washington, D.C.

32. Memorandum by Leonard Garment, the White House, 23 December 1969, National Council on Indian Opportunity, box 4, folder 1, National Archives, Washington, D.C.

33. Ibid.

34. *Indian Community Action* 5, Arizona-California, December 1969–January 1970, National Council on Indian Opportunity, box 5, folder 4, National Archives, Washington, D.C.

35. Regional Administrator–9A, Alcatraz incident, 6 January 1970, GSA RG-291, container 15, file–Alcatraz 2, second folder, National Archives, San Bruno, California.

36. Ibid.

37. FBI case files.

38. Interagency meeting of 6 January, National Council on Indian Opportunity, box 4, folder 2, National Archives, Washington, D.C.

39. Minutes of San Francisco Regional Council meeting, 7 January 1970, National Council on Indian Opportunity, box 4, folder 2, National Archives, Washington, D.C.

40. Memorandum for the vice president and Leonard Garment; subject: San Francisco federal regional council meeting, 8 January 1970, National Council on Indian Opportunity Records, National Archives, Washington, D.C.

41. *San Francisco Chronicle*, 9 January 1970, National Archives, San Bruno, California.

42. GSA statement, 12 January 1970, National Council on Indian Opportunity, box 4, folder 2, National Archives, Washington, D.C.

43. Ibid.

44. Memorandum for the vice president and Leonard Garment; subject: Alcatraz–visit and meetings of 10, 11, 12 January 1970, National Council on Indian Opportunity, box 4, folder 2, National Archives, Washington, D.C.

45. *San Francisco Examiner*, 17 January 1970, National Archives, San Bruno, California.

46. Note to file: Alcatraz, 20 January 1970, from Tom Hannon, National Council on Indian Opportunity, box 4, folder 2, National Archives, Washington, D.C.

47. U.S. Department of the Interior, Bureau of Indian Affairs, 26 January 1970, letter to Black Beaver II from Louis R. Bruce, BIA commissioner, Indians of All Tribes, Inc., Main Library History Room, San Francisco, California.

48. Points concerning Alcatraz, the White House, 26 January 1970, Nixon Project, file group–IN, box 1, folder title EX IN, 1-1-70 to 4-30-70 (1 or 2), Nixon Project, National Archives, Alexandria, Virginia.

49. Alcatraz–2, January–February 1970, consensus of ad hoc interagency group, National Council on Indian Opportunity, box 4, folder 2, National Archives, Washington, D.C.

50. Ibid.

51. Ibid.

52. Press release, Main Library History Room, box 4, file 7, IOAT, Inc., collection, San Francisco, California.

53. GSA letter to file by Thomas N. Scott, date 2 March 1970; subject: Indian factions–Vern Conway vs. Stella Leach, GSA RG-291, National Archives, San Bruno, California.

54. Memorandum for the vice president and Leonard Garment; subject: Alcatraz, 16 March 1970, National Council on Indian Opportunity, box 4, folder 3, National Archives, Washington, D.C.

55. Memorandum for the vice president and Leonard Garment; subject: Alcatraz, from Robert Robertson, National Council on Indian Opportunity Records, National Archives, Washington, D.C.

56. A proposal for Indians of All Tribes, Incorporated, Alcatraz Island, California, from: Robert Robertson for the USA, 31 March 1970, National Council on Indian Opportunity, box 4, folder 3, National Archives, Washington, D.C.

57. Associated Press release, National Council on Indian Opportunity, box 5, folder 4, National Archives, Washington, D.C.

58. United States government memorandum to Robert Coop, regional director, HEW, San Francisco region, from H. Clyde Mathews, Jr., deputy regional civil rights director, HEW, San Francisco region; subject: Alcatraz–Recent Reaction to Proposal, date 9 April 1970, National Council on Indian Opportunity, National Archives, Washington, D.C.

59. GSA news release, 27 May 1970, statement of the regional administrator, National Council on Indian Opportunity, box 5, folder 3, National Archives, Washington, D.C.

60. *San Francisco Examiner,* 28 May 1970, 1.

61. *Oakland Tribune,* 29 May 1970, E-15.

62. *San Francisco Chronicle,* 1 June 1970, 26.

63. *New York Times,* 3 June 1970, C-33. (Note: Joseph Morris, Blackfoot, an island resident, reported that Indians had set the fires.)

64. *Independent,* Long Beach, California, 4 June 1970, A-4.

65. *San Francisco Chronicle,* 8 June 1970, 1.

66. Letter to file by Thomas N. Scott, Realty Officer, 9 June 1970, GSA, region 9 correspondence copy, GSA RG-291, National Archives, San Bruno, California.

67. *San Francisco Examiner,* 15 June 1970, 33.

68. *New York Times,* 9 July 1970, 1.

69. To Mr. Jerry Warren, the White House, Miss Bobbie Green, the White House, from Robert Robertson; subject: Alcatraz Memorandum, 15 July 1970, National Council on Indian Opportunity, box 4, folder B, National Archives, Washington, D.C.

70. Ibid.

71. Memo to Ken Cole from Tod Hullin, 6 July 1970, and memo from Leonard Garment to John Ehrlichman, 29 July 1970, Nixon Project, File Group–IN, box number 1, folder title, EX IN 1 May 1970–31 July 1970, National Archives, Alexandria, Virginia. (The Kent State incident occurred on 4 May 1970 and resulted in the deaths of four students at the hands of Ohio National Guard troops.)

72. Memo to John Ehrlichman from Don Murdoch, Bobbie Greene; subject: Alcatraz 1970, the White House, Nixon Project, File Group–IN, box 1, folder title, 1 August 1970–30 September, National Archives, Alexandria, Virginia.

73. GSA notes on Operation Parks, GSA, region 9, Alcatraz Records, RG-291, box 10, National Archives, San Bruno, California.

74. Office of the Governor, Ronald Reagan, news release 411, 21 August 1970, GSA, region 9, Alcatraz Records, RG-291, box 15, National Archives, San Bruno, California.

75. *San Francisco Chronicle,* 25 August 1970, 19.

76. Report from Source A and B, document date 31 August 1970, GSA, region 9, Alcatraz Files, RG-291, box 15, folder "Alcatraz Confidential," activities in parks of 28 August 1970, National Archives, San Bruno, California.

77. *San Francisco Chronicle,* 2 September 1970, 31.

78. Press release, GSA Alcatraz Records, RG-291, container 15, folder–Alcatraz confidential, 8th folder, National Archives, San Bruno, California.

79. *Stockton Record,* 3 September 1970, 5.

80. *San Francisco Chronicle,* 3 September 1970, National Archives, San Bruno, California.

81. Memorandum to John Ehrlichman from Leonard Garment; subject: outline of a solution for Alcatraz, date 14 September 1970, and letter dated 15 September 1970, to Coast Guard from Robert L. Kunzig, GSA administrator, Nixon Project, File Group–Krogh, box 10, folder title Alcatraz (1970–71), National Archives, Alexandria, Virginia.

82. Ibid.

83. Ibid.

84. Memorandum to Brad Patterson; subject: Alcatraz paper by John Jolli, 14 October 1970, National Council on Indian Opportunity, box 4, folder 3, National Archives, Washington, D.C.

85. Memorandum to Brad Patterson from Bud Krogh, 9 November 1970, Nixon Project, File Group–Krogh, box 10, folder title Alcatraz (1970–71), National Archives, Alexandria, Virginia.

86. Memo to file, the White House, Washington, D.C., 5 December 1975, Reminiscences on Alcatraz, Brad Patterson personal files, Bethesda, Maryland.

87. *San Francisco Examiner and Chronicle* (Sunday edition), 8 November 1970, A-11.

88. Department of Transportation, United States Coast Guard, 23 November 1970, memo from Commander, 12th Coast Guard District, Mark A. Whalen, to Commandant; subject: Alcatraz Island, GSA, region 9, Alcatraz Records, RG-291, container 15, folder–Alcatraz 4, National Archives, San Bruno, California.

89. *San Jose Mercury News*, 19 November 1970, 49.

90. Memo, recommendation re: Alcatraz with attached revised draft memo, 27 November 1970, the White House, from Geoff Shepard to Bud Krogh, Nixon Project, File Group–Krogh, box 10, folder title, Alcatraz (1970–71) (entire folder), National Archives, Alexandria, Virginia.

91. Ibid.

92. Ibid.

93. Ibid.

94. Ibid.

95. Memorandum to John Ehrlichman from Bud Krogh; subject: Alcatraz, the White House, 11 December 1970, Nixon Project, File Group–Krogh, box 10, folder title, Alcatraz (1970–71), National Archives, Alexandria, Virginia.

96. Letter to IOAT, Inc., BANAC, Aubrey Grossman and Donald Jelnick, from LaNada Means, 21 January 1971, National Council on Indian Opportunity, box 4, folder 2, National Archives, Washington, D.C.

97. FBI case files.

98. Ibid.

99. Ibid.

100. Ibid.

101. Meeting notes, GSA, region 9, Alcatraz Records, RG-291, container 15, folder–correspondence confidential, 6th folder, National Archives, San Bruno, California.

102. Ibid.

103. Ibid.

104. FBI case files.

105. Bradley H. Patterson, Jr., interview, January 1987.

106. Krogh memo to Ehrlichman (JDE), Nixon Presidential Materials Project,

File Group–Krogh, box 10, folder title–Alcatraz (1970–71) (entire folder), 10 June 1971 document date, National Archives, Alexandria, Virginia.

107. Ibid.

108. Ibid.

109. Ibid.

110. Ibid.

111. Ibid.

112. Ibid.

113. Leonard Garment, President Nixon's legal counsel, telephone interview by Garvey, 22 July 1992, San Francisco to Washington, D.C.

114. Dick Billus, chief of U.S. Marshal Service in San Francisco, telephone interview by Garvey, 14 April 1987, San Francisco. (Billus is chief U.S. marshal. In 1971 he was a marshal working in the Sacramento office and arrived on the island three hours after the removal occurred.)

115. Thomas Sarver, former Federal Protective Service officer, General Services Administration, telephone interview by Garvey, 27 September 1989, San Francisco to New Orleans. (Sarver was one of the FPOs who evicted the American Indians.)

116. Dick Billus interview.

117. Carris Radcliff, former Federal Protective Service officer, General Services Administration, interview by Garvey, 24 November 1989, San Francisco. (Radcliff was one of the FPOs who evicted the American Indians from Alcatraz. This is one of two interviews.)

118. Thomas Sarver interview. Lou Lopez, former Federal Protective Service officer, General Services Administration, interview by Garvey, 1 June 1992, San Francisco.

119. *Oakland Tribune*, 12 June 1971, 1.

120. *San Francisco Examiner and Chronicle* (Sunday edition), 13 June 1971, 1.

121. Ibid.

122. *Oakland Tribune*, 12 June 1971, 2.

123. *San Francisco Chronicle*, 12 June 1971, 14.

124. *Oakland Tribune*, 12 June 1971, 2.

125. Ibid.

126. Ibid., 1.

127. *Los Angeles Herald Examiner*, 13 June 1971, 2.

128. Krogh memo to Ehrlichman (JDE), 10 June 1971, Nixon Presidential Materials Project, File Group–Krogh, box 10, folder title–Alcatraz (1970–71) (entire folder), National Archives, Alexandria, Virginia.

129. *Oakland Tribune*, 12 June 1971, 1.

130. *Sacramento Union*, 12 June 1971, 1.

131. *San Francisco Chronicle*, 12 June 1971, 1.

132. Tom Scott interview.

133. Carris Radcliff interview, 14 April 1989.

134. Tom Scott interview.

135. *San Francisco Chronicle*, 14 June 1971, National Archives, San Bruno, California.

136. Coop letter to Patterson, 22 June 1971, Brad Patterson personal files, Bethesda, Maryland.

137. *San Francisco Examiner*, 15 June 1971, E-1.

BOOKS ABOUT ALCATRAZ

Blue Cloud, Peter. 1972. *Alcatraz Is Not an Island*. Berkeley, Calif.: Wingbow Press.

Fortunate Eagle, Adam (Adam Nordwall). 1992. *Alcatraz! Alcatraz! The Indian Occupation of 1969–1971*. Berkeley, Calif.: Heyday Books.

Harvey, Byron. 1970. *Thoughts from Alcatraz*. Phoenix, Ariz.: Arequipa Press.

Johnson, Troy R. 1994. *Alcatraz: Indian Land Forever*. Los Angeles: American Indian Studies Center, University of California.

———. 1995. *You Are on Indian Land! Alcatraz Island, 1969–1971*. Los Angeles: American Indian Studies Center, University of California.

———. 1996. *The Occupation of Alcatraz Island: Indian Self-Determination and the Rise of Indian Activism*. Urbana: University of Illinois Press.

Mankiller, Wilma. 1993. *Mankiller: A Chief and Her People*. New York: St. Martin's Press.

Odier, Pierre. 1982. *The Rock: A History of Alcatraz—The Fort/The Prison*. Eagle Rock, Calif.: L'Image Odier.

13

AMERICAN INDIAN PLACEMAKING

ON ALCATRAZ, 1969–71

Robert A. Rundstrom

We will not ever get anything till we make Alcatraz.[1]

Leslie Marmon Silko wrote that the Hopi deliberately chose an austere physical environment in which to anchor themselves.[2] The high mesas compel the people to come together repeatedly in labor, ceremony, and prayer for the common good. The physical environment, once learned, allowed a Hopi place to evolve across more than seven centuries.

If one were to make a list of other sites in North America as seemingly untenable as the Hopi mesas, Alcatraz Island would have to be written at the top of that list. So difficult is the place that the only long-term attempt to live there was made by those social outcasts deemed too dangerous to live elsewhere and by their overseers. Yet, as foreboding as a site might be, Silko believes that until a viable and balanced relationship to place is found, a people cannot truly be said to have emerged.[3] Place and human identity must be invested in each other for ethnogenesis to occur. In his own effort to identify an Indian sense of place, N. Scott Momaday has named this achievement "reciprocal appropriation," wherein humans invest themselves in place while simultaneously incorporating place into fundamental experience.[4] Moreover, he says, it requires a "moral act of the imagination."

On 9 November 1969, fourteen hardy Indian college students from Bay Area universities and colleges decided to spend the night on Alcatraz—the beginning of what we now recognize as a series of extraordinary acts of imagination. In retrospect, this was the reconnaissance needed for the major landing that took place eleven days later, when eighty-nine men, women, and children began to inhabit the island in more permanent fashion. From my perspective as a geographer, I think that they came to build a new future and to create an Indian place in which a sense of pan-Indian ethnicity could be renewed. In Silko's terms, a people had to emerge. It is appropriate on this anniversary to cast a glance backward and look at some of the ways Alcatraz was made into an Indian place.

With only slight variation, many geographers agree that place consists of four elements: physical site and situation, a tangible created environment, a social milieu, and a set of personal and shared meanings.[5] These are separated for convenience of discussion, but, in reality, they interpenetrate and form an indivisible whole, a context or arena reciprocally shaping and shaped by the social and political will. This geographical view of place, as both agent and creation, is crucial to explaining why Alcatraz was chosen as a protest site, how its features were used and given fresh meaning, and how it was successfully coupled with Indian identity, becoming a lasting symbol of the late twentieth-century political landscape.

Physical Site and Situation

Alcatraz lies astride the treacherous tidal currents of San Francisco Bay, just two and one-half miles inside the Golden Gate (figure 1). A trace of shoals,

Figure 1. View of Alcatraz Island from the south during the 1969 occupation. The buildings on the terrace in the foreground were razed immediately after the occupation was over. Source: Alcatraz Archival Collection, History Room and Special Collections, San Francisco Public Library.

one named for the island, leads to Fort Point at the southern base of the Golden Gate Bridge. Ships and towed barges entering the bay must be piloted carefully north to the Richmond oil terminals or south through a narrow pass set in the one-and-one-quarter-mile gap separating the island from glitzy Fisherman's Wharf in San Francisco. In 1969, the southern route led to the Vietnam War by way of the Alameda Naval Air Station and the Oakland Army Terminal. Foghorns and lights on the two ends of the island warned traffic in these shipping lanes.

Alcatraz is tiny by any measure, a little more than one-quarter mile long and one-eighth of a mile across. Its northern tip actually points to the northwest, so its impressive eastern face is turned away from San Francisco. Its surface rises in two steps to its highest point at the center, approximately 110 feet above the waves. Halfway up at either end, a small terrace breaks the slope, and another relatively flat surface forms the top. All three were carved out in the nineteenth century. The intermittent slopes are rugged and steep, angling up from the water on all sides. With no natural harbor or cove, the island can be safely reached only via a single dock jutting out to the east on artificial pilings. The island's water supply was always piped or shipped in and stored in ground tanks and a water tower.

Alcatraz is no more rugged than the surrounding hills in Marin County and San Francisco, but the eye inevitably falls upon the Rock because of its isolated prominence in the water. Its situation also places it in stark contrast to the continuous cover of grass and flowering plants found in Marin and the gleaming towers and eclectic neighborhoods of the urban area. Patches of low-growing native plants, adapted to the saline and surprisingly arid environment, occur only where a hold among the rocks can be found. The abundant trees and shrubs evident today were all introduced and nurtured. Topsoil always had to be imported for the small gardens tended by the families of the military officers or prison guards who used to live there. In 1969, as always, California seagulls were the most evident form of wildlife. Any outdoor activity seems to attract their attention, and at dawn and dusk they are especially vocal. Pesticides eliminated most of the brown pelicans by the end of the 1960s, but twenty years later they became a common site around the island once again. Seal, otter, and small sharks may be spotted occasionally in the fast water.

In all respects, the natural feel of the place is one of austere beauty, lonely isolation, and inhospitality amid the general hubbub of the shiny, boisterous metropolis surrounding it. Neither the physical nor the created environment ever satisfied the basic biological needs of the island's periodic human residents.

Tangible Created Environment

Little was physically built during the Alcatraz occupation.[6] The overpowering presence of the abandoned buildings from the federal penitentiary era dominated the land then as they do now. Without working plumbing and heating, and with only intermittent electricity, the massive concrete and iron structures could hardly be less appealing as a human home. Yet the built landscape was enormously useful to the occupiers in the early days. The first official document released to the press, the "Proclamation to the Great White Father and All His People," recognized the island for what it was: isolated, run-down, and without transportation, sanitation, employment opportunity, health care, schools, or any of the physical endowment needed to support human occupancy. In short, it was perfectly suitable as an Indian reservation![7] This brand of humor permeated the entire occupation, its ironic inversions functioning as a powerful rhetorical device for incorporating the abandoned prison buildings into personal and shared experience. Its expression in the proclamation was the beginning of the creation of an Indian place.

Graffiti and Other Signs

Beyond the people and their activities, the most visible markers of Indian Alcatraz were the more than two hundred examples of graffiti and signs, many of which were used to subvert and invert names and places.[8] For example, *Bureau of White Affairs* was painted on one window,[9] and *Nixon, Agnew,* and *Alioto* were carefully written in block letters over individual cells in the main cellhouse (figure 2). *Apartment for Rent* hung on the door of another.

The phrase *Indian Land* may have been the most ubiquitous message. The words were part of large-scale signs prominent on the barracks building facing the dock, on the water tower, and on a wall near the old warden's house. Specifically, on the side of the barracks, just above what is now the park rangers' main office, were the words *Indian Land, Indians Welcome,* and *United Indian Property*, the latter transferring the island from federal control as surely as the occupation itself (figure 3). The water tower called out to air and bay traffic, *Welcome, Peace and Freedom*, while declaring the place the *Home of the Free . . . Indian Land. You are on Indian Land* was yet another reminder written in dripping block letters along the walk up to the cellhouse. The shadowy remains of the words written on the barracks building and the water tower persist today as the most tangible expressions of Alcatraz as an Indian place.

Place names are elemental to the panhuman experience, often preceding other aspects of the placemaking process. On Alcatraz, names such as

Figure 2. Photo taken on 7 July 1971. Original caption reads, "Cells in the row Capone was on. Names were lettered overhead by Indian occupiers." Courtesy of California Historical Society, *San Francisco Chronicle* Collection. Clem Albers, photographer.

Figure 3. Large signs on a prominent wall of the old barracks face the dock. Source: Alcatraz Archival Collection, History Room and Special Collections, San Francisco Public Library.

Sioux, *Pomo Room*, and *Paiutes* were painted on interior doors and walls as signifiers of place and perhaps also as markers of tribal "turf," even as a pan-Indian ethnic identity was under construction.[10] Notably, two apartment houses formerly used by prison guards and their families were remade into *Pima House* and *Ira Hayes House No. 1*, the latter gaining a measure of authenticity when the San Francisco Public Health Department issued at least one identification card with that address on it.[11]

The power of signs to invert meaning and incorporate place into experience may have reached greatest complexity in the entrance to the main cellhouse. The stars-and-stripes seal of the U.S. penal system, guarded by that ubiquitous symbol of federal authority, an eagle with outstretched wings, is perched directly over the doorway. At first, a sign reading *This Land Is My Land* was hung around the eagle's neck (figure 4).[12] Later, the seal of the penal system was painted red, white, and blue and the word *FREE* was painted on it with the narrow stripes of the seal serving as the vertical strokes of the letters (figure 5). In two deft moves, the island, the cellhouse, the symbolic power of the eagle and flag, and a popular national anthem all had been appropriated. In addition, the spirit of a prison and a people had been marked for freedom in one stroke of placemaking. In contrast, whites read both signs only as taunts from presumably anti–American Indian radicals. In the remaking of Alcatraz, however, such creations were part of ritual discourses used regularly by Indian occupants.

Any attempt by an outsider to decide the intended audience of these markers inevitably leads to more ambiguity. Many signs must have been aimed at the elements of white society engaged in surveillance during the occupation. Visiting reporters must have been another intended audience. However, I would argue that the most important viewers were the Indian occupants themselves, who were addressing each other using the language of creation to conceive a new place.[13]

In July 1971, a month after the occupation ended, the federal government brought bulldozers and a wrecking ball onto the island, and armed patrols with guard dogs were posted on twenty-four-hour watch. The apartment buildings around the parade ground on the southern terrace were razed, ostensibly because they were crumbling and unsafe (figure 6).[14] Clearly, the more important reason for the destruction was to render the area "placeless." Pima House, Ira Hayes House No. 1, and the other buildings in the area had been used as residences and contained a lot of graffiti. Their destruction was an unambiguous reassertion of federal authority and an unmaking of place no less powerful in its message than the moment in June 1971 when armed federal marshals and FBI officers stepped upon the island.

Figure 4. A subverted sign guarding the entrance to the main cellhouse appropri-
ates the island through an ironic reference. A media photographer self-consciously
adjusts his camera as people cluster near the doorway. Source: Alcatraz Archival
Collection, History Room and Special Collections, San Francisco Public Library.

Figure 5. Further alteration of the shield of the U.S. penal system remakes Alcatraz in several ways. Photo taken on 11 November 1970. Original caption reads, "Eagle, Cornucopias, Shield above entrance to main cell block painted red/white/blue & 'free' written in by Indians." Courtesy of California Historical Society, *San Francisco Chronicle* Collection. Darrel Duncan, photographer.

Proposal for New Construction

For at least some of the occupants, the graffiti and signs were part of an effort to transform the existing landscape, if only temporarily. New construction was intended for the long-term future.[15] Ideas for completely remaking the built environment were aired in a roundtable discussion at the "Gathering of All Indian Tribes," an intertribal conference held in the dining room of the main cellhouse on 23 December 1969. The emerging plan for buildings and grounds aimed to solve the inherent problems of lack of water, limited space, rocky surface, and steep slopes in a way that made use of non-Indian technologies yet also reflected traditional Indian built forms. A passage from the typescript of minutes from the roundtable discussion puts it this way: "Key Idea: It is important to use traditional Indian art ideas as basic to the architectural structures so as to be authentic, and to use contemporary architecture, knowledge and art skills to express these ideas in a way to say that this *must last forever*" (emphasis in original).[16] Ideas for housing included longhouses, tipis, wickiups, hogans, modernized pithouses, and even cliff dwellings cantilevered into the various rock faces of the island.

Figure 6. Photo taken on 7 July 1971. Original caption reads, "Guard John Geagan of American Patrol Service, hired to patrol with sentry dog Whiskey—in background is PIMA house, a former staff dormitory—lighthouse on top." Remains of the warden's house are also shown at the top right. Courtesy of California Historical Society, *San Francisco Chronicle* Collection. Clem Albers, photographer.

Sweat baths, totem poles, sculpture, mosaics, murals, electric cars for on-island use, cable trams for travel to the mainland, helicopters, chemical waste disposal, atomic energy, and a desalinization plant were other ideas raised at the December roundtable.[17]

The result was a planning grant proposal for an All Indian University and Cultural Complex submitted to the National Council on Indian Opportunity at an island meeting on 23 February 1970.[18] The proposed budget of $300,000 was to be spent on razing the old prison infrastructure and creating an initial design for a center for Native American studies, a spiritual center, an ecological center and medicinal herb garden, a marine observatory, and a museum. The community centerpiece was to be a large redwood roundhouse of the type built by the Pomo in northern California. An eagle would grace the roof at the center and serve as a universal symbol of Indian unity. The roundhouse's location on the very top terrace of the island, replacing the main prison cellhouse with the federal eagle over its main entrance, represents yet another inversion of the old Alcatraz.

The government, of course, rejected the proposal, countering with its own idea for a federal tourist park. Indians of All Tribes, Inc., flatly rejected the federal counteroffer.[19] Although none of the Indian ideas for a created environment were ever put into place, they played an important role alongside the graffiti and other signs as aspects of a reciprocal appropriation ongoing between the people and the island.

A Social Milieu

Like others trapped in BIA urban relocation projects across the country in the 1950s and 1960s, Bay Area Indians, in isolation from family and reservation life, needed an environment where they could live and function together, in opposition to federal attempts at detribalization. In some ways, local Indian organizations had been helping out for quite a while. For example, small powwows were held regularly in various parts of the Bay Area. But Alcatraz became the locus for a much larger social experience that quickly spanned the continent, as people from across North America journeyed to the island and stayed for various periods of time.[20] For this to occur, interpersonal experience and feeling had to be given shape and had to be made visible in commonplace and extraordinary ways.[21]

Perhaps the regular powwows were the most common and distinctive means by which a social milieu was created and sustained. The drumming and singing often lasted long into the night, the sound giving shape to island experience while also symbolizing the investment being made. At other times, various specific tribal dances were held on special occasions. People were also compelled to come together regularly to eat the daily meals served in a communal setting inside the main cellhouse.

Ritual gift exchanges were a common feature of island life both during and after Indian visits to the place. Traditionally prepared fish and venison came in on occasion. One person forwarded yellow cedar from the Pacific Northwest for ceremonial purposes.[22] Sometimes, a song, ceremony, poem, or prayer was brought as a gift.

Educating the Children

A major purpose of education is to articulate experience. In our schools, children are taught to love and honor the state as a matter of course.[23] Children's books and atlases repeatedly emphasize the centrality of an Anglo-American nationality. While making abstract places more "real," this also marginalizes those who do not fit the dominant social pattern. In an effort to combat this, an island school was organized to articulate Indian political and cultural experience to the children. One of the goals was to interconnect aspects of the island with the children's emerging identities, a process fundamental to place-making. Figure 7, a classroom photograph taken by a newspaper photogra-

Figure 7. Photo taken on 2 January 1970. Original caption reads, "Alcatraz classroom (third floor, old security officer's quarters)." Courtesy of California Historical Society, *San Francisco Chronicle* Collection. Vincent Maggiora, photographer.

pher, presents an unusually clear example. I assume the room was set up for an early class meeting, perhaps the first one, in which various kinds of introductions were being made. The assignment on the lower-right portion of the blackboard indicates that each student was asked to write his or her name, age, home address, school, and grade level on one side of a sheet of paper. More important, on the reverse students were to draw a "picture of something about *Alcatraz*" along with an "Indian design." Apparently, teachers were striving to introduce the children formally to their instructors, to each other, and to the place. The latter may be seen as the beginning of an Alcatraz child's first formal effort at reciprocal appropriation.

Another glimpse into the role of education in placemaking is provided by an apparent fragment of a lesson written on 5 May 1970 that I found in the archives.[24] Unlike the one on the blackboard, the strategy here was to get the children to consider the differences between Indian and white ways of thinking about land, nature, and religion, and the historical links between these three. An Indian tradition of living in balance with nature, developing a religious tie to the land, and giving thanks for life was set in opposition to an emphasis by whites on disrespect, the Bible, and taking land from others. Clearly, as happens everywhere, Alcatraz children were being given various models for thinking about place and its cultural and historical significance.

Political Organization

Politics creates place when people make both the place and the political ideals and goals with which it is being invested demonstrably visible to outsiders. This can be an especially powerful form of social cohesion, because the boundaries of a place periodically need defending against intrusion from outside forces.[25] On Alcatraz, the threat of intrusion was not periodic but incessant. A council was quickly put in place soon after the initial arrival, and assignments were given to individuals for the purpose of overseeing various social functions: education, finance, security, health, food and supplies, transportation, housing, and so on. A formal organizational chart and regular council meetings in the prison chapel gave the proposed system visibility as an ideal. Alcatraz Council was given authority over the various functions, but the people, or the "membership," as they were later called, actually empowered the council. The council served to implement the decisions of its membership; it had no authority to negotiate with the public or federal government without membership approval. Those serving on the council were to receive no compensation, and they could be recalled by two-thirds of the membership. Under the proposed bylaws for Indians of All Tribes, Inc., membership was determined largely on the basis of commitment to place: "Every Indian on Alcatraz Island in San Francisco Bay is a member of the corporation if he or she (a) is registered with the coordinator's office as a resident, and (b) has lived continuously on Alcatraz for at least seven days."[26] Also, membership would be lost if an individual Indian left Alcatraz for more than seventy-two hours in a calendar week without permission from the council.

From the beginning, the distribution of political authority was organized so that no single person was in charge as a leader, president, or director of either the initial occupation effort or later island operations, an aspect of the Indian social network that was difficult for outsiders to grasp. Print and television media, in particular, were anxious to single out a spokesperson, preferably someone photogenic and charismatic, a process not unlike the creation of individual "chiefs" for separate "tribes" during initial colonization. On the eve of the first occupation, during the gathering at Fisherman's Wharf for the trip out to the island, it was clear that no single individual was in charge of the whole operation.[27] Responding to an article in the *Los Angeles Herald Examiner*, Lou Trudell made the same point in a letter to the editor written on 12 August 1970: "There is definitely no one leader or president here . . . , nor has there ever been. We have a seven man council but none are so-called leaders or chiefs. The leaders are the whole body, the whole population on Alcatraz for without them there would be no Alcatraz and there would be no hope."[28]

Outreach

While the political and educational apparatus was emerging on the island, a broader network of external social relations was sought with Indians on reservations across the country. The need to sustain good relations with the reservations is a recurrent theme in minutes of council meetings and other formal discussions on the island for which there is an archival record. Some saw it as a key to the success of the occupation. At the December 1969 intertribal conference, the Overall Aims and Goals Committee submitted its recommendations, including adopting an advisory committee consisting of members drawn from various tribes; keeping all tribal councils informed of activities and problems on Alcatraz; and sending island literature and documents to all tribal councils and Indian organizations.[29]

The main idea was to funnel information and assistance around Indian Country using Alcatraz as a central node or point of distribution.[30] For example, financial savings derived largely from donations went to support political actions elsewhere: one thousand dollars to the March 1970 dispute at Fort Lawton, Washington; and fifty dollars to the Pit River Indians for their land claim project. "Runners" were also sent out to the reservations to gather information, interpret the Alcatraz occupation, and assist with local concerns.[31]

Alcatraz also had an Indian voice reaching out to sustain the urban social network in Indian Country. "Radio Free Alcatraz" first broadcast on 22
December 1969 and was picked up by the Pacifica network and relayed to
stations in the Bay Area (KPFA), Los Angeles (KPFK), and New York
(WBAI). For fifteen minutes on weekday evenings, John Trudell played
music, reported on Indian affairs, and presented information on Indian history and culture. In a letter asking for support from a potential financier,
Trudell argued for an "uncensored voice" in the mass media, "allowing urban and reservation Indians to communicate directly and regularly with one
another. . . . Here is an opportunity for Indian identity and a common purpose to emerge on the national scene."[32]

Personal and Shared Meanings

The meaning of place was monitored and conveyed in myriad ways on Alcatraz. Some of these have already become evident, indicating the interpen-
etration of meaning with social behavior, created environment, and natural
physical environment. Place makes human feelings concrete, so they can be
dealt with in ritual and narrative; these, in turn, reassure individual and group
identity. Place also anchors identity so "the terror of facing the world alone
is extinguished."[33]

But the meaning of place must be protected and insulated from outside
attack, especially those assaults that may be masked by outward displays of
good intentions.[34] Protection is necessary because of the moral meaning a
place has for its residents and the moral code that applies first to locals.
Outsiders cannot be expected to behave correctly and, as a result, do not
enjoy full courtesies.[35] For example, the Public Relations Department repeatedly had to fend off attempts by non-Indians to become part of the place.
Non-Indians were permitted to visit, but only by special permission, and they
could never become island residents. Grace Thorpe wrote many cordial and
carefully worded letters in reply to requests by non-Indians for access to the
island. While thanking one of the numerous sympathizers for her support,
Thorpe was firm in declaring Alcatraz a decidedly Indian place. She added,
"I am certain that you understand; this is our first 'free' land since the white
man came."[36] In another thank-you letter, she wrote: "Our seizure of Alcatraz is the awakening of Indian self-determinism and Indian unity. It is the
beginning of the Indian's rightful claim, not only to his land, but also his own
destiny and power."[37]

Aside from well-meaning sympathizers, other non-Indians wanted Indians of All Tribes to finance their visit and support them while they wrote
a story, a play, or poetry, produced a film, or, in one case, conducted a pup-

pet show.[38] White self-aggrandizement at the expense of reservation Indians is well known, and Alcatraz must have seemed like a similar opportunity once donations began to stream in. If a few requests had been granted, more would have flooded in, expenditures would have accumulated rapidly, and the still-emerging island culture would have been severely compromised.

The written and spoken word are powerful symbols of meaning, but so, too, is song.[39] The importance of sustaining crucial social interaction through drumming and singing has already been noted. Rhythm, volume, and performance time are all important factors, but the shared meaning of the words and vocables and the joy found in sharing memory of them are just as essential. Richard Oakes wrote: "We did a lot of singing in those days. I remember the fires at night-time, the cold of the night, the singing around the campfire of the songs that aren't shared by the white people . . . the songs of friendship, the songs of understanding. We did a lot of singing. We sang into the early hours of the morning. It was beautiful to behold and beautiful to listen to."[40]

Identity and unity also were symbolized in both personal and shared artwork, the invocation of Plains Indian symbols, and a sense of island history that seems to have been widely shared. Individual works of art poured out during and immediately after the occupation, after the unfortunate accident that took thirteen-year-old Yvonne Oakes's life, and after federal marshals removed the last residents in June 1971. Most extant works include a physical representation of the island and various symbols of political and cultural meaning. A pencil sketch appearing at the end of an editorial entitled "Alcatraz: The Idea" in the second newsletter is representative (figure 8). Benevolent and reverent faces carved Rushmore-like in the island walls surround the stern declaration "Indian Land." Yet it seems strange to see various prison buildings and the lighthouse in the same drawing. The symbolic clash of the two aspects may be resolved by the closing phrase of the editorial: "Alcatraz the Idea and Alcatraz the Island Must Always Be in Harmony."

The use of Plains Indian symbols in graphics officially produced by Indians of All Tribes encouraged unification around another kind of shared meaning. For example, the letterhead used in late 1970 and 1971 featured a gray, full-length silhouette of a stereotypical Plains war chief with feathered headdress and aquiline nose. The island pass issued to residents and visitors was imprinted with three classic Plains images: a tipi, a bison, and the feathered chief.[41] The invocation of the 1868 Treaty of Fort Laramie between Sioux bands and the federal government as justification for permanent transfer of the island was yet another reminder of the implicit value of Plains Indian symbolism.[42]

Many of the occupants of Alcatraz were well aware of the Indian history

Figure 8. Drawing from *Alcatraz Indians of All Tribes Newsletter* 1:2 (February 1970), 3. Courtesy of San Francisco National Maritime Historical Park Library, Fort Mason Center, San Francisco, California, Harry Dring Papers.

on the island, starting with the Civil War, when some of the Indians who fought on the side of the Confederacy were incarcerated here as POWs. In the 1870s, a Pyramid Lake Paiute and several Modoc people were sent to the island for crimes against the government, and uncooperative Hopi and Apache were labeled *hostiles* and put on the Rock for awhile just before 1900. The famous 1946 escape attempt and riot featured another noted Indian resident, Clarence Karnes, whose alias was "The Choctaw Kid." In 1964, five Sioux briefly occupied the island. The people who knew this history felt the connections, which formed another thread in the fabric of Alcatraz. Richard Oakes wrote: "Alcatraz was a place where thousands of people had been imprisoned, some of them Indians. We sensed the spirits of the prisoners. At times it was spooky, but mostly the spirit of mercy was in the air. The spirits were free. They mingled with the spirits of the Indians that came on the island and hoped for a better future."[43]

Conclusion

A complete and complex society evolved on Alcatraz, with all the positive and negative connotations that implies. Place is so complex that no study can claim to be comprehensive, and this one is limited in a specific way. As a geographer interested in how seemingly stark and inhospitable places can be transformed and humanized, I have interpreted Alcatraz as an Indian place composed of four indivisible elements: physical site and situation, a tangible created environment, a social milieu, and a set of personal and shared meanings. My interpretation suggests that a balance between humans and others was struck there. Place became incorporated into the people, just as they invested themselves into its past, present, and future. In Silko's and Momaday's terms, Alcatraz became a place of cultural emergence through the process of reciprocal appropriation.

Alcatraz has an unusually austere physical environment mantled with grim reminders of past human use. Yet, compared to other Vietnam-era political sites, it was occupied in protest for a very long period of time. The grim past was successfully inverted using humor and symbolism to, in effect, rearrange the tangible, created environment. A distinctive social context evolved through many commonplace and extraordinary events, especially those involving education, politics, and the efforts to establish an intertribal nationwide network, with the island at its center. Personal and shared meanings developed through the use of everyday written and spoken language and song. Finally, outpourings of artwork and a shared sense of island history further wrapped people and place together.

The web of symbolic meaning may be of greatest and most lasting importance. The unique twinning of place and human identity that occurred on Alcatraz for so many assured the island lasting significance as the emergence-place of modern pan-Indian identity and collective protest. As such, Alcatraz persists symbolically today in the mind of each person who was there or who followed its story.[44] Its present use as a federal park showcasing a gaudy prison history and interpretations of white criminality in no way diminishes this fact.

Construction of Alcatraz, and the power with which it was invested, makes its continuing resurrection as a symbolic reference point inevitable. Between 1970 and 1978 alone, thirty-four other protest occupations occurred in Indian Country, all of which refer to Alcatraz for their symbolic power in one way or another. For those who were there, a mere listing of some of the place names invokes Alcatraz as progenitor, a parent in a line of descent: BIA headquarters, Ellis Island, Fort Lawton, Gresham, Mount Rushmore, Moss Lake, Pit River, Pyramid Lake, Rattlesnake Island, Red Lake, Shiprock, Wounded Knee, and any of the Long Walks.

Alcatraz continues today to serve as both a mythic and empirical point of reference. In February 1994, the American Indian Movement began the latest in a series of Long Walks with a sunrise ceremony on the island. These ceremonies, invoking the ritual significance of place, begin with drumming and singing at Fisherman's Wharf. Passage across the narrow channel is marked by continued singing on board ship. On the island, ritual rhetoric, pipe-smoking, prayers, and more singing are featured. They mark the beginnings of individual events, symbolic journeys for justice, just as the occupation itself began a larger series of events. Such personal and shared invocations testify to the continuing power of Alcatraz as an Indian place.

NOTES

Completion of this essay was assisted by a grant from the University of Oklahoma Faculty Research Fund.

1. Statement made by a participant in the Staff and Physical Operations roundtable discussion at the Indians of All Tribes National Conference on Alcatraz Island, 23 December 1969, file 32, box 1, Alcatraz Archival Collection, History Room and Special Collections, San Francisco Public Library (hereinafter referred to as SFPL).

2. Leslie Marmon Silko, "Landscape, History, and the Pueblo Imagination," in *On Nature: Nature, Landscape, and Natural History*, ed. D. Halpern (San Francisco: North Point Press, 1987), 94.

3. Ibid., 92.

4. N. Scott Momaday, "Native American Attitudes to the Environment," in *Seeing with a Native Eye: Essays on Native American Religion*, ed. W. H. Capps (New York: Harper and Row, 1976), 80.

5. See John Agnew and James Duncan, *The Power of Place: Bringing Together Geographical and Sociological Imagination* (Boston: Unwin Hyman, 1989); R. J. Johnston, *A Question of Place: Exploring the Practice of Human Geography* (Oxford, England: Blackwell, 1991), 97; Edward Relph, "Modernity and the Reclamation of Place," in *Dwelling, Seeing, and Designing: Toward a Phenomenological Ecology*, ed. D. Seamon (New York: State University of New York Press, 1993), 34–36; idem, *Place and Placelessness* (London: Pion, 1976); Yi-Fu Tuan, "Language and the Making of Place: A Narrative-Descriptive Approach," *Annals of the Association of American Geographers* 81:4 (1991): 684–96; idem, "Place: An Experiential Perspective," *Geographical Review* 65:2 (1975): 151–65; and idem, *Space and Place: The Perspective of Experience* (Minneapolis: University of Minnesota Press, 1977).

6. I omit from consideration the controversial fire that gutted several buildings and temporarily put the lighthouse out of service on the evening of 1 June 1970. A fire is typically considered destructive, but it also might be understood as a tool for intentionally reconfiguring the created environment of a place. It would be worthy of discussion here if one could clearly establish intent. However, Indian responsibility for the Alcatraz fire has never been established. Indeed, a number of possible explanations for the fire's origin have been offered and debated over the years.

7. Adam Nordwall wrote the proclamation (source: Don Patterson, interview, 28 March 1994), which may have been the first place this observation was recorded. The proclamation is reproduced in Indians of All Tribes's *Alcatraz Is Not an Island*, ed. P. Blue Cloud (Berkeley, Calif.: Wingbow Press, 1972), 40–42; and in the *Journal of American Indian Education* 9 (January 1970): 16–18. The metaphor of the island as a reservation was widely used. See, especially, Richard Oakes, "Alcatraz Is Not an Island," *Ramparts* 11:6 (December 1972): 38, 40.

8. See John Noxon, *Inventory of Occupation Graffiti, 1969–1971* (San Francisco: Division of Cultural Resources Management, Western Region, National Park Service, 1971).

9. The General Services Administration's (GSA) caretaker on the island, John Hart, saw the humor in the creation of the Bureau of Caucasian Affairs and willingly cooperated with the occupation when he was offered a post as its head. See Oakes, "Alcatraz Is Not an Island," 39.

10. The names are mentioned in Blue Cloud, *Alcatraz Is Not an Island,* 25.

11. Ira Hayes (Pima) was one of the soldiers who helped raise the U.S. flag on Iwo Jima during World War II and who later became a symbol of the plight of urban Indians. The identification card addressed to "Ira Hayes House No. 1, Alcatraz" is in file 14, box 1, SFPL.

12. The sign was made and hung around the eagle's neck by Don Patterson, former chair of the board of directors, San Francisco Indian Center (source: Patterson interview).

13. For an illuminating discussion of how Red Power rhetoric was used in ritual self-address, see Randall A. Lake, "Enacting Red Power: The Consummatory Function in Native American Protest Rhetoric," *Quarterly Journal of Speech* 69 (1983): 127–42.

14. At several points during the occupation, the GSA characterized the buildings as very dangerous, notably on 12 January 1970, four days after thirteen-year-old Yvonne Oakes had died from a fall, and in a news release on 27 May 1970. Both statements are in file 27, box 2, SFPL.

15. An idea for razing all the existing buildings on Alcatraz and replacing them with a massive new university-culture-ecology complex originated with Adam Nordwall. The proposal was initially used mainly as a publicity strategy to raise money to build a new Indian center in San Francisco after an October 1969 fire destroyed the old one (source: Patterson interview).

16. The quoted passage is item 2, page 1 of "Gathering of All Indian Tribes, Round Table Discussion: Design and Lay-Out," 23 December 1969, file 32, box 1, SFPL.

17. These features are listed in "Indians of All Tribes Conference, Design and Lay-Out," *Alcatraz Indians of All Tribes Newsletter* 1:2 (February 1970): 8–9, which is found in folder 268, box 18, HDC 648, Harry Dring Papers, San Francisco National Maritime Historical Park Library, Fort Mason Center, San Francisco, California (hereinafter referred to as FTMASON); and in "Gathering of All Tribes, Round Table Discussion: Design and Lay-Out," file 32, box 1, SFPL.

18. See "Meeting with Federal Officials on the Island of Alcatraz, February 23, 1970," file 36, box 1, SFPL.

19. See Robert Robertson, "A Proposal," and "Indians of All Tribes, Inc., Reply to Counter-Proposal of Robert Robertson for the U.S.A., April 3, 1970," both of which are in file 16, box 3, SFPL.

20. For insight into the variety of opinions about the social need for Alcatraz, see Adam Fortunate Eagle [a.k.a. Adam Nordwall], *Alcatraz! Alcatraz!: The Indian Occupation of 1969–1971* (Berkeley, Calif.: Heyday Books, 1992); Blue Cloud, *Alcatraz Is Not an Island;* Oakes, "Alcatraz Is Not an Island"; and Wilma Mankiller and Michael Wallis, *Mankiller: A Chief and Her People* (New York: St. Martin's Press, 1993), 186–95. Also see the brief essays by LaDonna Harris (172–73) and Lenada

James (229–31) in *Indian Self-Rule: First-Hand Accounts of Indian-White Relations from Roosevelt to Reagan*, ed. K. R. Philp (Salt Lake City, Utah: Howe Bros., 1986).

21. Tuan, "Place: An Experiential Perspective," 161.

22. For example, the yellow cedar and game meat were indicated in a letter from the Baileys [Tacoma, Washington] to Richard Tyler and Charley Williams, 22 December 1970, in file 14, box 1, SFPL.

23. Tuan, "Place: An Experiential Perspective," 162.

24. The handwritten lesson plan is in file 4, box 2, SFPL. The actual notes written by the anonymous instructor read as follows:

   1. Living in balance with nature?

   2. Worship is thru thanks for living and for the betterment or respect of his fellow men.

   3. White man's entrance into country was in same line of respect as for his Indian brothers and sisters. Indian showed respect for white man when he landed.

   4. White man's religion is in same line of one book! The Bible!

   5. Land, basis of religion for the Indian, was taken away from him.

25. Tuan, "Place: An Experiential Perspective," 163.

26. In item 1, section 3, "Criteria," of "Proposed By-Laws," folder 085, box 2, HDC 440, Alcatraz Field Collection Documents, Golden Gate National Recreation Area, FTMASON.

27. Patterson interview. Yet, as Patterson also suggests, Richard Oakes was a leader of the student segment of the island population during his brief time there by virtue of his position as president of the Native American Student Association at San Francisco State University.

28. From the typescript titled "Copy of letter dated August 12, 1970 to 'Mr. Schultz' of the *L.A. Herald Examiner*," found in file 24, box 1, SFPL.

29. These are items numbered 5, 11, and 12 in "Overall Aims and Goals, Committee Recommendations for Adoption," file 32, box 1, SFPL.

30. There was resistance to this idea among some reservation Indians, who viewed Alcatraz as distant and secondary compared to local issues of justice and land rights. Although the occupiers' intent may have been to function as a clearinghouse more than a central authority, reservation resistance to making Alcatraz the center of Indian Country reinforces my earlier point regarding the distribution of authority.

31. The financial contributions are described in the minutes from general meetings. The decision to send $1,000 to Fort Lawton was approved on 20 March 1970 (file 37, box 1, SFPL), and the Pit River decision was made on 7 May 1970 (file 38, box 1, SFPL). The information on runners comes from the *Alcatraz Indians of All Tribes Newsletter*, 16. This idea was formalized in a proposal to create a traveling Indian university. At one point, a bus trip was made to help the Pyramid Lake Paiute people in a local dispute over use of the lake.

32. Letter from John Trudell and Al Silbowitz [the latter worked for KPFA] to David Fuller, The San Francisco Cambium Fund, 2 January 1970, in file 9, box 4, SFPL.

33. Silko, "Landscape, History, and the Pueblo Imagination," 93.

34. For example, the power of language in creating place is reflected in efforts by a state to suppress its use. In the early days of the occupation, the federal government was already asking the news media to suppress information and news releases

coming from Alcatraz. Except for those in the Bay Area, most newspapers carried only limited stories about Alcatraz. The suppression was understood by those on the island, adding to the cohesion and shared sense of mission. See "Staff and Physical Operations" [one of the 23 December 1969 roundtable discussions at the intertribal conference], file 32, box 1, SFPL.

35. The power of language also was controlled and made to serve Indian purposes in interesting ways. For example, the cost of subscribing to the *Alcatraz Indians of All Tribes Newsletter*—thus, the cost of gaining access to Indian words and art, much of which was about Alcatraz itself—was set on a racial basis: Indians paid three dollars, while non-Indians were charged six dollars.

36. Letter from Grace Thorpe to Gladys Kaye, 17 March 1970, in file 22, box 1, SFPL.

37. Letter from Grace Thorpe to Tom Quinn, 23 March 1970, in file 22, box 1, SFPL.

38. See files labeled "Inward Correspondence," box 1, SFPL.

39. Naming is a symbol of placemaking, as mentioned in note 10. Suggestions for name changes at the intertribal conference included "Indian Island," "Turtle Island," "Pelican Island," and "American Indian Island."

40. Oakes, "Alcatraz Is Not an Island," 39.

41. An example of the letterhead is in file 25, box 1, SFPL. A representative island pass with Plains Indian symbols is in folder 076, box 2, HDC 440, Alcatraz Field Collection Documents, Golden Gate National Recreation Area, FTMASON.

42. For a detailed discussion of how Plains Indian symbols came to represent a pan-Indian ethnicity, see John C. Ewers, "The Emergence of the Plains Indian as the Symbol of the North American Indian," *Annual Report of the Smithsonian Institution* (1964): 531–44.

43. Oakes, "Alcatraz Is Not an Island," 40.

44. Wilma Mankiller, principal chief of the Cherokee Nation, emphasizes this in Mankiller and Wallis, *Mankiller: A Chief and Her People*. Another example of Alcatraz's continuing symbolism at quite personal levels occurred during my research for this paper. The background is as follows: In September 1993, Ponca City, Oklahoma, celebrated the centennial of its birth in the historic Cherokee Strip land rush. The city commemorated the event with a grand unveiling of a controversial life-size bronze statue on a broad plaza in front of city hall. The statue depicts a young man leaping off his horse to drive a stake into the land. The title, since removed, was "This Land Is Mine!" During my interview with Don Patterson, he asked me if I had seen it, immediately pointed out the connection to the sign he had made on Alcatraz (see note 12), and spoke of the continuity in geographical and social terms, the give-and-take, between Indians and non-Indians in particular places over the past twenty-five years.

14

THE EAGLES I FED

WHO DID NOT LOVE ME

Woody Kipp

The two F4-B Phantom jets came in low, very low, at about two hundred feet, probably traveling at somewhere around five hundred miles per hour. Five hundred was just cruising speed for these birds. I had seen them go faster in Vietnam. I had seen them twist and turn and hurl fiery death toward the ground in the form of 250-, 500-, and 1,000-pound bombs. They were, as we say in the Blackfeet, *stoonatopsi*, dangerous. For the twenty months I had spent as a support combat engineer with the First Marine Air Wing on the outskirts of the Vietnamese city of DaNang, the sleek killing machines had been on my side. Now they were not on my side; now they were hunting me.

In 1969, native militants took over the abandoned prison island of Alcatraz to call attention to the destitute conditions of the natives of America. After a year and a half on the island, living in primitive conditions, the natives were forced to leave their watery fortress. A fire had been lighted, however; the protests were just beginning. On 27 February 1973, the American Indian Movement (AIM), in concert with a grassroots political activist group called the Oglala Sioux Civil Rights Organization (OSCRO), took armed control of the village of Wounded Knee, South Dakota.

Alcatraz was the call to arms. There were other marches, protests, walks across the country to keep the native movement visible, but Wounded Knee was the crucible that formed many of today's native leaders, whether or not they were at the siege. At Wounded Knee, those who chose to come told white America, "We might not be able to live like our ancestors, but when push comes to shove, we can still die like our ancestors, die in the Indian way, defending our homeland and our people."

In 1973, in the village of Wounded Knee, there was a white Catholic church next to the mass grave that contained the bodies of the nearly four hundred Sioux men, women, and children who were massacred in 1890 by the 7th Cavalry, Custer's old unit. The church is no longer there. Sometime in the 1970s, after the occupation, it burned to the ground. I have never heard why or how it burned. I can only guess.

The 1973 takeover of Wounded Knee village was the first armed resistance by natives since the Wounded Knee massacre in 1890. The takeover was a response to a century of maniacal oppression by white society, an oppression that goes on today—subtler, smilingly, but it continues. Young whites today have a favorite refrain about this historical oppression: "Why should I have to pay for something my grandfather did?" I tell them that, although the overt acts of military warfare may have ended, the policies and principles espoused by their grandfathers are still in place in Indian Country. I ask them, "Why else would it be that I, on paper, own 648 acres of trust land on the Blackfeet Reservation but cannot use any of it because of Bureau of Indian Affairs rules and regulations?" Surely, I tell them, if a white man owned 648 acres of land, he would be able to pressure his legislators into enacting a law that allowed him the use of the land he owned. It is in the interest of white colonialism that the Indian cannot use the land he supposedly owns on his own reservation. Instead, white farmers and ranchers depend on Bureau of Indian Affairs (BIA) bureaucrats to block the land up for them and offer it to the highest bidder; moreover, the bidders drink cocktails with the bankers in the towns surrounding the reservations—bankers whose institutions do not loan money to Indians, especially Indians like me with waist-length braids.

That, in part, was what Wounded Knee was about, at least for me. Others who were there had their own reasons. But one issue was clear: It was a rebellion by those who had been on this land for millennia, eighteen to sixty thousand years, according to the latest archaeological estimates. And we say this: You may be in physical control of the land, white man, but spiritually we are still the landlords; until you come into union with the land, you are always going to be an outsider, someone who has disregarded all the tenets of the holy Christ you claim as a guide. Remember, white brothers and sisters, we read today—scientific tracts, literature, philosophy, books on business management. And sometimes we read the Christian Bible and it makes us wonder if you are truly aware that this earth plane is but a lesson to prepare us to come into conjunction with the song of the universe, with all those exalted ideas you promote but cannot seem to practice: truth, beauty, and justice.

Alcatraz, Fort Lawton, Wounded Knee will be viewed by future generations as a birthing time, a painful agony that had to be endured in the search for survival. My daughter Dameon, now twenty-one, was born the evening AIM and OSCRO took over the village of Wounded Knee, at approximately the same time that the Indians were entering Clive Guildersleeve's corrupt trading post. She signaled a beginning. My other daughter, Avalon, was born in the redneck town of Conrad, Montana, on New Year's Eve, the first baby born in Pondera County that year. Normally, like many other towns, Conrad provides gifts to the first baby born in a new year and to the mother. The town officials were going to give the gifts to Avalon, but when they found out she was from the Blackfeet Reservation, they decided to wait until the first white baby was born. Small thing, that. But the people in Indian Country can recite a litany of small things over the past century. And, in time, small things, like New Year's babies, grow. I picture, in my mind, my daughter Dameon being born while Indians were overrunning the village of Wounded Knee.

In Vietnam, *overrun* was a scary word. It was a term I became familiar with while reading the U.S. military newspaper *Stars and Stripes* during my stint there. To hear that a village or an outpost had been overrun by the Viet Cong was bad news. Ultimately, though, that is what Wounded Knee was about—native people being overrun by white people, smothered by the technological superiority of gunpowder diplomacy, backed up by papal bulls that, in effect, gave the go-ahead to the ethnic cleansing of the North American continent.

We—a Blackfeet named Bradley LaPlant; Rudy Thunder Hawk, an Oglala from Pine Ridge; and I—were manning a bunker when the Phantoms came over the first time. The afternoon was gray and cloudy and chilly. LaPlant and I had walked into Wounded Knee under cover of darkness some ten days before, along with thirty-seven other people, guided from Douglas Horse's place in Porcupine by young Oglala boys who knew the terrain.

When I worked at the DaNang airfield, I became accustomed to the illumination flares that lit up the surrounding countryside as U.S. Marines searched the night for Viet Cong. After I left Vietnam, I was sure I had seen my last illumination flare.

On the way to Wounded Knee, with snow covering the ground, my companions and I were confronted with the roar of an engine; a large vehicle was nearby. Then came a spotlight sweeping across the mostly flat landscape. Luckily, we happened to be walking along a ravine; as the spotlight moved in our direction, we slid into the ravine and held our breaths, the light going over us and moving eerily across the white ground. The clank and rumble of the machine, an armored personnel carrier, brought the reality of the situation home to me. This was a bona fide military operation, not like a street battle with cops wielding batons and mace. Armored personnel carriers packed .30-caliber machine guns whose rapid fire made the Gatling guns that cut down the Wounded Knee victims of 1890 look like pistols. A few minutes later, the armored personnel carrier, not more than a half-mile away, launched an illumination flare. It was not close enough to illuminate us, but it was certainly close enough to make me realize that here, in my own country, I was the "gook" they were looking for.

And now the Phantoms were looking for me. I guess I felt like the dog owner who feeds and coddles his Doberman Pinscher only to wake one day to find the dog at his throat. I had fed these machines so they could do their killing work in both North and South Vietnam. Now I could appreciate the terror felt by the Viet Cong and the North Vietnamese who were on the receiving end of these sleek, dangerous planes whose nose cone radar costs several million dollars.

I was nineteen when I sailed for Vietnam on the USS *General John Mitchell*. I was told I was going to fight communist aggression. Nineteen year olds can be fed a lot of hype and they believe it. I attended school through high school in Cut Bank, Montana. In Cut Bank, we were taught that the communists were trying to take over the world and enslave us all. "Dangerous bastards, them communists," it was parroted in the oil-cowtown backwater eddies of Cut Bank. It did not occur to me as an Indian youth that my people had already undergone enslavement. Actually, for us, the communists might have been a welcome relief; at least they believed in doing things communally the way we did in the old days.

The communists had replaced the local Blackfeet as the bogeyman. Cut Bank Creek, flowing by on the western edge of Cut Bank, separates the Indians from the whites. Robbie Quist, a well-known folk and country singer in Montana with whom I played basketball in high school, talks about Cut Bank Creek as the "river of fear"; at least, that's the way it is perceived by the whites.

I am enrolled as Blackfeet. My great-great-grandfather, Three Suns, was the last of the Blackfeet headmen to give in to the missionaries; his Grease Melters Clan ultimately was starved into submission by the Indian agent.

I am not a Kipp by blood. The full-blood who is my adopted father, Joe Kipp (Eagle Moccasin), also was not a Kipp by blood; his father, the first to live permanently on Cut Bank Creek after the allotment of aboriginal land-holdings, was known as Cut Bank John Kipp. He, too, was not a Kipp by blood. He was a survivor of Baker's massacre on the Marias, which was very similar to the Wounded Knee massacre in that 173 Blackfeet—men, women, and children—of Heavy Runner's camp, afflicted with deadly smallpox, were shot to death while sleeping. The army troops were guided to the camp by half-Mandan, half-English Indian trader Joe Kipp. Actually, they were looking for the camp of Mountain Chief. Kipp apparently felt some guilt over having guided the army to the wrong camp, because he adopted some of the children who survived the massacre. Eagle Moccasin's wife was my great-aunt, and that is how I came to be a Kipp. My maternal grandmother was the daughter of Wolverine. The allotted land I own on the Blackfeet Reservation is Wolverine land.

Like all border towns, Cut Bank had some ideas about Indian people that influenced what I would come to think about American society. Cut Bank's wealth was derived from land that had been wrested from the Blackfoot Confederacy, land that contained wealth the Blackfeet knew nothing about: Under it were oil and gas; on the surface, left flat by receding glaciers, it was rich and arable. For the whites, it grew bumper crops of wheat and barley. This land that once had felt the great thundering weight of the buffalo herds now supported the domesticated breeds of European cattle. Cut Bank is not cordial toward its Blackfeet neighbors; the feeling is mutual.

My nephew, Clayton Hirst, was electrocuted in a cell in the county jail in Cut Bank in March 1975; then he was hung up to simulate a suicide. We exhumed the body under court order and sent it to California for a new autopsy. The California pathologist, not tied to the politics of Cut Bank's Glacier County, affirmed what a spirit-calling medicine man had already told us, that Clayton had died at the hands of three men with, as the spirits called it, "shiny pins on their chests": badges, law and order badges. Since then, even though I grew up in Cut Bank, I no longer list it as my hometown. We employed a young, energetic lawyer, Kent Russel, from the firm of renowned criminal lawyer Melvin Belli. When the all-white jury exonerated the accused lawmen of murder, our lawyer said it would be some time before Indians could expect justice in the state of Montana. These kinds of killings are what Wounded Knee was about.

The Vietnamese, like the buffalo-culture Blackfeet, lived a life devoid of high technology, farming their plots of ground with water buffalo. Bucolic they were; and because they lived simply, close to the land, close to their Buddhist beliefs and their heritage, the white invaders in Vietnam hated them. It took me a while to realize that the arrogant attitude of the American soldiers and marines and airmen toward the Vietnamese people—the drunken arrogance that knocked over a Buddhist shrine in a Vietnamese home without the least bit of remorse—was the same arrogance that had come riding and shooting across the plains of America into Blackfeet country. At some point during my stint in Vietnam, I began to realize that the hatred and contempt the Americans felt toward the nontechnological Vietnamese peasants was the same hatred and contempt that had moved without conscience throughout the American West in the last century.

A specific instance of this hatred occurred during the sixty days I spent in the 3d Marine Amphibious Force brig a short distance outside the Da-Nang air base. I was thrown into the brig for what the Uniform Code of Military Justice called "fraternizing with Vietnamese nationals." We did fraternize. She was about twenty-five, with more-than-waist-length, shiny black hair and the extraordinary dark and pale beauty of the half-breed French-Vietnamese who were the results of France's invasion of Vietnam. We fraternized regularly. I had come to know how to get off the base and into her village of Hoa Phat—marines called the village "Dog Patch" after the cartoon town of Li'l Abner fame. One night, fraternizing heavily, anticipating sex and drunk on Johnny Walker Red that had come from U.S. airmen who would trade us nearly anything to get a U.S. Marine Corps k-bar combat knife, we stumbled on some particularly well-hidden military police as we zigzagged down the lone street of Hoa Phat village. Thus, the brig.

While in the 3d MAF brig, we prisoners were sent to load cement chunks from an old French bunker that the Americans had demolished for no other reason than to give us something to do under the rubric of *hard labor*, which sentence had been pronounced upon us. We loaded the cement chunks slowly, in the searing red-dirt sun, onto the bed of a military truck. The pieces were irregular in shape and weight, with some weighing well over one hundred pounds. With the truck loaded, we climbed aboard, and somebody rolled a joint of Vietnamese pot. Pot was sold by the ubiquitous Vietnamese children or, in this instance, traded for somebody's military field jacket.

The guards varied, some not giving a damn whether we smoked a joint while we were away from the brig area proper. The guards were marines, too, usually of low rank, their liberal or conservative attitudes depending on how much they loved authority. There were some who would let us drink from our canteens of water only when they told us to drink. They had authority in the form of .45-caliber pistols and shotguns. Our guards this day were liberal; they told us that we had better smoke all of the pot by the time we were done working. The guards in the brig area were hard core: They would check inside your mouth, your armpits, between your ass cheeks, in your ears, to make sure you hadn't put some pot in a gum wrapper and hidden it on your body for later.

En route to the unloading place, we found places to sit on the concrete chunks and passed the joints around. The day was brilliant sunshine, so hot the body sweated in repose. Where the road crossed a rice paddy, it had been built up and reinforced to handle the heavy military traffic that swarmed daily, hauling military goods that made the war go. From the roadway to the rice paddy was a drop of some fifteen feet. A burly, redheaded marine was sitting in the front of the load with his arms resting on the cab of the truck. Suddenly, he reached down and grabbed a chunk of concrete that must have weighed at least fifty pounds. He lifted the concrete chunk to arm's length overhead and then threw it over the side of the truck. I was sitting on that side, and, as we passed, I looked back to see where he had thrown the concrete. An old Vietnamese man and his bicycle were tumbling down the bank toward the rice paddy; the heavy weight would have hit him from above, in the head or shoulders, and he probably was badly hurt or dead. Some of the marines guffawed. Some, like me, when they realized what had happened, sat silent, knowing that this had nothing to do with saving the free world from communism; this was an act of infamy, of racial hatred. To this day, I feel ashamed for not having at least said something to the redheaded marine about his act of gratuitous violence—violence that he could get away with simply because he was an American, a superior technological being.

The attitude of the redhead was not new to me. That attitude was in Cut Bank—maybe in a bit more subdued form in the years I lived there, but it was there. Which is not to say that there aren't Indians consumed with that same kind of racial hatred. It is not, however, a hatred that jibes with our traditional teachings of the four sacred colors—red, white, black, and yellow—the skin colors of the four colors of human beings who walk the earth. Those colors are used in all native ceremonies and are to be respected. Hatred based on color and race was what had made me ashamed of my parents because they were materially poor, living in a white town; that attitude did not take into account the fact that my white boyhood friend was brutally beaten with a belt by his mother, while I received no corporal punishment from my parents. With welts on his legs and back, he would take refuge in our home; he called my adopted father Pop, the same as I did.

I was employed by the U.S. government to fight what it called "communist aggression," but the aggressive racial hatred of the Americans toward the pastoral Vietnamese would have much to do with why I went to Wounded Knee a few years later. In Vietnam, we loaded bombs twenty-four hours a day, three eight-hour shifts, fulfilling our role as a combat engineer support unit to the Marine Air Wing who, in addition to supporting the ground troops in South Vietnam, were daily bombing the infrastructure of North Vietnam. At least, that was the official policy, that American planes were bombing bridges, weapons plants, and other crucial targets. How many innocent civilians got caught in that saturation bombing may never be known. We plied our deadly trade with rough terrain, six-thousand-pound forklifts, M-60 hydraulic cranes, and bent backs, the handling of bombs as ceaseless as the monsoon rains. I was lucky. I did not have to take part in the search-and-destroy missions that would later come back to haunt those who did as war-induced delayed stress syndrome.

In the Native American cosmology, hate can certainly cause suffering for those who feel its brunt and those who practice it. For those who practice it, the only way it can be dealt with is psychically, morally, spiritually. Many American veterans who tried to deal with the delayed stress in the physical plane in which American society operates self-destructed after bringing pain and suffering to their own families.

Although we did not participate in the ground war of the grunts, the place where we worked—the bomb revetments—was not safe. Bombs were off-loaded from the semi-trucks bringing them from the ships in DaNang harbor and were piled high in the revetments; next door was another revetment, surrounded by dirt pushed twenty feet high by bulldozers. This revetment held tens of thousands of gallons of JP5 jet fuel, more volatile than gasoline. We knew, from our intelligence sources who had interrogated Viet Cong prisoners of war, that the Viet Cong considered the fuel dump a prime target for mortars and rockets. Once, Lance Corporal Seeley made the wry observation that, if the Viet Cong were ever to zero in on the fuel dump with mortars or rockets, it would be *sayonara* fuel dump, *sayonara* bomb dump, sayonara jarheads. Nobody on shift that night refuted his observation, but the looks he received were enough for him not to mention it again.

Later, when my friend John Pinkerton arrived in Camp Pendleton, California, from DaNang, he told me that, during the Tet offensive, our collective bomb dump–fuel dump fears had been realized with a stupendous explosion, fire, and concussion that knocked down the building in which we had worked on our engineer equipment. Our building was about a mile and a half away from the explosion, but it shattered like a frigid pane of glass. I was happy to be in California and not DaNang when that happened.

And now, here, on the plains of the great Sioux Nation, in the current state of South Dakota, the fighter bombers, the F4-B Phantoms that I, for twenty long months, had identified with, were looking for me. I knew these birds of prey: They never make social calls; they're always business, always serious as a heart attack. They belong to my uncle. Sam. Hey, Uncle! Uncle Sam, look, it's me, your nephew, Woody; it's me who fed your birds while you were negotiating or doing whatever it is you big shots do during a war. Remember, I didn't spend all of my time over there with Vietnamese women, drinking air force whiskey, standing in line for clap shots. Hell, no! I prosecuted the war to its full extent even if I didn't know what we were fighting for. Actually, Uncle, I thought we were fighting for all those good things I learned about in high school civics and government classes—you know, freedom, democracy, justice, one-man-one-vote, death to the oppressors, freedom from hunger, equality, love of fellow man no matter what he looks like or how bad his breath is. You remember. You should; you taught me these things, made me eager to join the battalions primed to knock on heaven's gate in your defense.

Actually, Uncle, I feel much closer to those ideals when I am fighting for my own people here in my home country, where I'm more sure about what the war is trying to accomplish. We Indians lack freedom. We know freedom because, before you came here, we lived freedom. It was a way of life, not just a buzzword to be used to decimate peoples because of their color or their beliefs. Granted, even before you sallied onto the scene we had wars. But, in those wars, there was still an element of honor, of the sanctity of life created by the Great Mystery. In Vietnam, in your war zone, there was no honor.

My Blackfeet companion, LaPlant, had been in Vietnam, so the warplanes were not a new sight to him. My friend Thunder Hawk, however, had spent most of his life on the Pine Ridge Reservation; for him, the sight of fighter bombers being sent against us took the war to a new and unimagined level. His incredulous stare followed the planes across the sky until they were nearly out of sight. "Looks like they're going to bomb us," he said. I explained to him that Phantoms carried their weaponry under their wings, and these planes had been empty. "Yeah," said LaPlant, "they're just trying to psyche us out."

In Vietnam, we used psychological warfare. After finding out that the Vietnamese have a superstitious dread of playing cards bearing the ace of spades, we dropped thousands of ace of spades cards from airplanes in suspected Viet Cong strongholds; grunts tacked the cards to trees in the jungle. The Phantoms did not drop ace of spades cards on us in Wounded Knee. Nor, as in the movie *Apocalypse Now*, did they play classical music for us. We would have appreciated both.

The psychological warfare of sending the Phantoms over Wounded Knee did not have much of an effect. With the U.S. Air Force involved in this caper, it was we who felt we had achieved a psychological/symbolic victory. We wanted attention on a massive scale focused on the federal government's failure to honor our treaty rights. The Phantoms signaled that the upper echelon of the American government was involved—Congress, the Pentagon, the presidency. Whoever had sent the Phantoms was playing by the rules that had been in effect since Columbus landed. America has always believed in using force to solve problems, especially in relation to nontechnological cultures. The great majority of native people who involved themselves in the Wounded Knee struggle expected the U.S. government to use force against them. Force does not work very well, however, with people who have made the commitment to die, if necessary, to bring attention to their cause. We knew that, militarily, we didn't stand a snowball's chance in hell. We knew the government could wipe us out before Bob Dylan could finish singing "The Times They Are A-Changin'." When a people are ready to die for their beliefs, it is futile to threaten them with loss of life. We craved attention. The Phantoms were attention, big time.

The Phantoms made another pass, higher this time. Apparently, the pilots had calculated that the militants below would not be frozen in shock the second time around and might turn their ancient deer-hunting rifles to the sky. The word had been out since the previous evening that, by five o'clock this day—the day the Phantoms came—if we had not surrendered, laid down our weapons, and given up our outmoded beliefs in decency and freedom, the federal troops would come in. At about two o'clock in the afternoon, a messenger from the leaders of the protest came to our bunker and told us to go one at a time to Crow Dog's tipi. Crow Dog's tipi, with a sweatlodge directly in front of it, stood just forty yards below the mass gravesite of 1890, out in the open below the church that is no longer there. The spirits who communicate with Crow Dog had told him during the occupation that a white man's bullet had been turned around by the spirit forces and sent back to him because he was shooting at this sweatlodge. Indians believe these things can happen. Most white men scoff at the idea. During the Wounded Knee trials following the occupation, the government would not release the ballistics information on the kind of bullet that had struck the federal marshal, paralyzing him.

Crow Dog was raised in the traditional way, without benefit of—or, possibly, without the curse of—the English language. He was central to all that the American Indian Movement accomplished in its heyday. Crow Dog used to remind me of a story that was written by Norman Mailer à la Ernest Hemingway concerning the Spanish bullfight. Mailer's story dealt with a bullfighter who, when he was at peak performance, could handle the bulls with magnificence, enthralling the aficionados of the bullfight with his ease and grace. Then, on other days, he was bad, and the crowd would not forgive him, throwing cups of piss at him and snarling his name in contempt. It was Lame Deer who probably summed up the credo of many contemporary spiritual leaders in Indian Country. He said people respected him not because he was good, meaning morally upright, but because he had the power. Power in the Indian way means you can make contact with the beings of the spiritual world and receive guidance from them on the proper way to live, even if, like Lame Deer and later Crow Dog, you do not always follow their advice. Crow Dog gave direction to the movement, but sometimes he weakened and went on a wild Indian drinking spree.

I started from the bunker to Crow Dog's tipi and sweatlodge. At that time, I had not been exposed to the intricacies of native spiritual belief, because my adopted parents had been Catholicized. My father used to go into the sweatlodge on the ranch at Cut Bank Creek, but he went alone, his children going instead to catechism school. He did not speak the Blackfeet language to us; his generation had received severe, sometimes corporal, punishment for speaking Indian languages. Like many contemporary natives, I sensed the power of the Indian spiritual belief. One of my older adopted sisters, Katherine, the murdered Clayton Hirst's mother, was psychic, always seeing and hearing beings and noises and sights that none of the rest of us could fathom. Her husband, a half-breed who leaned heavily toward white beliefs, would tell her she was imagining things. I knew better. I knew there was something, disembodied and frightening, out there.

We had hung around Douglas Horse's place in Porcupine for several days before walking into Wounded Knee. During that time a Lakota woman,

Cordelia Attack Him, came and asked if we wanted to go to a spiritual ceremony. LaPlant declined, even though he is a bona fide spiritual teacher and practitioner today. He was afraid of it then. I went, and it turned out to be a seminal event in my life. Cordelia's husband, Johnny Attack Him, led us to the ceremony, which was performed by Cordelia's brother, Alphonse Good Shield. Cordelia and Johnny are both dead today, but I thank them for inviting me to that ceremony. For me, it was as startling as any revelation in the Bible. Before Wounded Knee, I was attending the School of Journalism at the University of Montana on the G. I. Bill. Afterward, I no longer had any interest in white academia; the ceremony had opened another world to me.

During the course of the ceremony, Alphonse, who died not long after the Wounded Knee occupation, said he was going into Wounded Knee to see what was happening there. It was my introduction to the concept and practice of spirit travel—a person being able to leave his physical body, go somewhere in the spirit, and return. Soon, with Cordelia translating from the Lakota into English—quite often medicine men are not allowed to speak English in their ceremonies—Alphonse said Crow Dog, at that moment, was holding a yuwipi ceremony in Wounded Knee. He also said that he had passed three men who were walking out of Wounded Knee toward Porcupine and that shortly they would be in Porcupine. I was highly skeptical of what Alphonse had said, and I let it go as a flight of the imagination.

The ceremony ended after midnight, and we retired to Johnny Attack Him's home in Porcupine. Alphonse came to his sister's home after the ceremony. We were visiting over coffee when Cordelia called from the kitchen that someone was yelling outside. Immediately Johnny had the lights in the house turned off. FBI agents were known to be in the neighborhood attempting to apprehend people getting ready to walk into Wounded Knee. Supporters of the occupation, such as the Attack Him family, were under surveillance. We all stepped outside the darkened house and listened. Soon there was a shout from a willow-covered hill a short distance away. The shout was in the Lakota language, but many Lakota had been recruited by the Dickie Wilson regime and had turned against the occupation supporters. Alphonse quieted our fears; he said it was the three men he had seen walking out of Wounded Knee while he was traveling in the spirit world. Soon three figures emerged from the darkness at the base of the hill. Again they said something in Lakota, and Johnny answered them. In a minute, they were at the house. It was Ron Poteet, Ted Means, and Herb Powless. Later, I would remember something another Blackfeet had said about how, as a young man, he had become intrigued by what he called the "mysteries of the medicines." There, standing outside Cordelia and Johnny Attack Him's house, I felt that intrigue. I began going into sweatlodges in the spring of

1974 with Blackfeet holy man Sam Spotted Eagle (Big Road). Twenty years later, I am not so naïve, but I am still intrigued.

As I walked to Crow Dog's tipi, I knew that the federal marshals, who were scrunched into their armored personnel carriers only half a mile away, were watching me. Day and night—with the military starlight scopes that make nighttime vision possible—they watched us. Every now and then, shots were exchanged between the Indians and the marshals. The night before, an Indian had been shot in the hand and treated for the wound by Crow Dog. Indian women of the movement became battlefield nurses, with their own improvised operating room.

Crow Dog was in the sweatlodge with several leaders of the occupation force: Dennis Banks, Russell Means, Clyde and Vernon Bellecourt, Carter Camp, Stan Holder. Traditionally, men sweat together. Holy women ran sweats for women. Standing outside the sweatlodge, I could hear them praying and singing the sweatlodge songs, purifying themselves against the contamination of the modern world, calling on the spirit world to help deliver us from the white devils with their machine guns and arrogance, beseeching the Great Mystery to intervene on our behalf because it was apparent that the white brother had forgotten his original instructions. That is one thing that is hard about the road of prayer. Even though, in the physical world, we perceive whites as embodiments of material evil and greed, still must we pray for them, for their understanding that there is a spiritual world toward which they, like us, are inexorably moving; and that, truly, there is payment and reward for how one conducts oneself on this earth.

I grew up around white people in Cut Bank, and nearly all my childhood friends were white. In a high school with a population of some four hundred students, only half a dozen were natives. Nevertheless, for a certain period of my involvement with the movement, I truly believed the white race was the devil incarnate. White people have a hard time fathoming the chagrin and utter disappointment experienced by natives when they become aware of the true history of red-white relations since the arrival of Europeans in this hemisphere. In school, the history teachers did not tell us that Columbus cut off the hands of Indians who failed to bring him gold; they did not mention the deceit and chicanery used by the Europeans to gain control of Indian homelands; they omitted the fact that, during the Reformation in Europe—the period when science took over the minds of the whites, making them more physical than spiritual beings—the natives clung to their spiritual teachings even though whites regarded them as primitive and savage, with no reasoning power. A Western writer of the nineteenth century characterized natives as not having the power to think in the abstract, when, in fact, native belief systems are based on symbolism and abstractions.

The Wounded Knee occupation was more than a week old by the time I stood outside Crow Dog's sweatlodge, waiting for him to emerge. Another AIM soldier had informed me that, when Crow Dog came out, he was going to paint our faces with the sacred red paint. It was symbolic: Plains warriors never went to their deaths without the sacred paint on their faces, if they could help it. It was a sign to the Creator that, even in death, they were holding to the original instructions.

In the time since the insurrection had started, the federal government had barred media teams from further entry into the Wounded Knee area. From the scanty journalism training I had received at the University of Montana in the year I had been there prior to the occupation, I knew that this was a news blackout. The government was trying to keep the occupation out of the evening news, trying to create the impression that we were just a bunch of loudmouthed radicals whose aberrant behavior did not reflect the attitudes of the true natives of America toward the good white folks who had brought them death, destruction, disease, and the joy of riding with the Lone Ranger.

In spite of the news blackout, some of the more daring journalists had managed, with help, to sneak into Wounded Knee village under cover of darkness. They wrote their stories and either carried them out themselves or trusted those who were ferrying goods in and out of the village to get the stories delivered and into print. After the occupation was over, media analysts would intone that the radicals had manipulated the media for their own ends. So it appears that those Indians were capable of reasoning, after all! Yes, the media comprised the primary weapon, much more effective than the deer-hunting rifles or even the lone AK-47 that was photographed and shown on national television to prove that these really were communists. The AK-47 had been captured in Vietnam by a native veteran. In Wounded Knee, it was strictly a psychological weapon. There were no bullets for it.

Many of the foreign journalists knew nothing about natives at all. I overheard a British journalist, pointing to the sacred sweatlodge, asking an American journalist, "What the hell is all this hocus-pocus about?" Many of the foreign journalists had been flown halfway around the world to capture the essence of this strange and highly incongruous uprising, red Indians challenging Uncle Sam to a duel on the high plains.

A communiqué had been received from the government forces directing the journalists to evacuate the area by five o'clock that evening; the government would assume no responsibility for the safety of those who were in Wounded Knee after that hour. Some journalists made plans to leave, while others sought places to hide where they might possibly capture the action and win a Pulitzer Prize for reporting. We scorned those who wanted out, gave thumbs up to those with the tenacity to stay. Stay with us, journalist friend. If you die, maybe we can get you into heaven, even if your face isn't painted with the sacred red. Stay with us and get the story of a lifetime, or die trying. In Missoula, Montana, just before we left for the occupation, we had held a rally in support of those at Wounded Knee. A young Lakota girl, Anita Iron Cloud, carried a sign with an old warrior motto: "Better to die on your feet than live on your knees." In Missoula, it had been merely a militant, revolutionary slogan; here it had meaning.

A crush of journalists swarmed around the sweatlodge as we waited for Crow Dog to emerge. A young French female photojournalist was near the door of the lodge when it was opened after the fourth and final round. Inside, we could hear Crow Dog's voice giving instructions to the men seated inside. The journalists pushed closer, their pens at the ready, trying to get a good quote from the medicine man inside, something to titillate the readers in Bonn, London, Paris, Tokyo. The young Frenchwoman, dressed in a fashionable skirt of nearly immodest length, was squatting in the doorway of the lodge, peering into the darkness, probably unaware that the men were naked or maybe not caring, in the interest of a possible front-page story. The push became a shove, and the woman lost her balance, falling headfirst into the lodge, her professionalism exerting itself as she tried to protect the lens of the expensive camera dangling from her neck. However, there was sacrifice: Although she saved her camera, she certainly lost her composure. She managed to squirm back out the doorway of the lodge through the gaggle of journalists; more than one gave her a knowing smile of camaraderie, signaling their knowledge of how hard it was to be a war correspondent. She stood off at a distance by herself, looking stern and a bit perplexed by her initiation into the native sweatlodge.

Inside Crow Dog's tipi, a buffalo skull altar had been set up. As he painted my face, he prayed in the Lakota tongue. When he finished, he looked me in the eye and gave a nod of his head, and I went out. On the way back to the bunker, I wondered if the federal marshals, with their telescopic sights, could see the paint on my face. In keeping the traditions of my own people, I have had my face painted many times since Wounded Knee, in the Blackfeet Medicine Pipe Dance. It is not a dance of warfare; men, women, and children are all painted as a sign that they are following the ways of the Creator.

The weapons carried by the Indians during the occupation were the kind found in most American homes where hunters live: .22s, .30.30s, .30.06s, .270s, and at least one .300 H&H Magnum that had somehow come into the control of LaPlant, who had entered Wounded Knee weaponless. My weapon, bought for forty dollars at Paul's Second Hand Store in Missoula just before we left for the occupation, was a snub-nosed .38. A gun like that is accurate only for a few yards. It would be close-up fighting before I could effectively retaliate against the barbarians. I longed for a good piece of military equipment such as we had in Vietnam—armor-piercing bullets that could penetrate the armored personnel carriers if aimed at the right place, grenades, bazookas, something big and dangerous and powerful. I longed for something potent enough to answer the Blackfeet Crazy Dog prayer: "Give me the power to make the enemy cry."

With my face painted for war, I accepted the possibility that we would die that afternoon when the federal forces moved in at five o'clock. I thought of the refrain voiced by the natives, the refrain supposedly uttered by the mystic and warrior Crazy Horse: "It's a good day to die." I tried to work my mind into a state that made that phrase as glamorous and glorious as it sounded when we were drunk or stoned, but it didn't come. Instead, I kept thinking of my tiny daughter just a few days old.

Thoughts of the wild killing frenzy that took place on this very ground where we now waited came back to me hauntingly that long afternoon: the Lakota fleeing the hot belch of the Hotchkiss guns fired by Custer's 7th Cavalry—running, screaming, falling, dying, wondering why the Great Mystery was allowing this to happen. What had they done wrong? In later years, when I read the teachings of the white psychic Edgar Cayce—one of the few white religious leaders that Indians understand—only then did it seem possible to me that these massacres were part of a larger plan. Cayce maintains that, long ago, the Christian faith, under the rule of the Roman emperors, at the councils of Trent, Constantinople, and Nicaea, threw out the concept of karma from Christian teachings, the belief that human beings return many times to the earth for lessons until they come into compliance with universal law.

Thinking about Bigfoot's slaughtered band was both frightening and reassuring that afternoon. The attitude of white people toward the killing of Indians, Vietnamese, Japanese, Koreans, blacks, anyone who was not white, was the reason we waited on that proven plain of death that afternoon. I had not yet considered the power of nonviolence, which would later become a dominant theme in my life; I was willing to make war that afternoon, if only with a snub-nosed .38.

The power of white European technology boggles my mind even today. It is as Sitting Bull said: "The white man can make anything. He just doesn't know how to share it." The white technological power is so great that our only defense against it is to declare ourselves ready to die and hope this declaration will fall upon the ears of the white leadership in such a way as to make them consider their own mortality.

There was no way out of it now as the clock ticked relentlessly toward the five o'clock deadline. Crow Dog the medicine man had painted us to die. Crow Dog, who had grown up differently from us, vision questing when we were chasing girls and drinking beer, said this is how it must be. There had been no talk of surrender, no talk of wiping the paint from our faces and lying compliantly upon the ground, weaponless as the marshals handcuffed us. No, truly, better to die on our feet, with honor. As my brother Curly Bear was wont to say, "If we can't get along, then we'll just have to get it on."

Again, a Blackfeet refrain came back to me from the days when we controlled most of what is now Montana plus parts of Alberta and Saskatchewan in Canada: "Better to die when the hair is long and black in defense of your people than to wither away into old age." We held no illusions of winning militarily; the only possible victory we could imagine as five o'clock approached was that, if we were killed, the world would know about it. Maybe world opinion about the atrocities committed against Indians would bring change into Indian Country. *Hoka hey!*

The scenarios we imagined that afternoon in our bunker were bleak. If the armored personnel carriers moved in, they would touch off the Indian rifles, and the carriers would respond with their .30-caliber machine guns, spewing death at a terrible rate. If there is anything the American soldier loves it is his rapid firepower. He does not understand that there is more to a war than firepower. That's what defeated him in Vietnam.

Perhaps the Pentagon generals had decided to arm the Phantom jets with twenty-millimeter cannons instead of risking a ground assault that could kill some of their ground troops; such casualties would work against them in the next elections. Although I was afraid for my life that day, in retrospect it gives me satisfaction to know that I had analysts in the Nixon administration fearing for their political lives. Although Richard Nixon would fall from grace later due to Watergate, at this time he was the only president who had given land back to the Indians: He had returned the sacred Blue Lake to Taos Pueblo. This was an indication that at least he, unlike many other Americans, was aware that there were still living, breathing natives in the United States; John Wayne had not killed the last of the wagon-burning hostiles. We knew that, with worldwide media attention focused on the occupation, the decision would come from high up in the administration as to how to handle the deadline.

In the final hour, the fear turned to adrenalin: "Fuck you, white guys! We may not know how to live in your screwed-up technological society, but we still remember how to die as Indians. Come on in. The gates are open." Five o'clock came, and the armored personnel carriers remained squat and silent. Our eyes and ears were peeled for the slightest movement, the tiniest sound that would signal the beginning of the assault. We expected the roar of the Phantoms. They would be high this time, coming at us at an angle so they could fire. Silence. Then it was six o'clock. The messenger came to the bunker and said the deadline had been extended for twenty-four hours. We would live for at least one more day.

That day turned into a lot of days; the occupation eventually lasted for seventy-one days, during which a baby was born in Wounded Knee village and some men were killed, others wounded. The roadblocks around Wounded Knee were removed shortly after the deadline day. We went to Rushville, Nebraska, to do some business and were arrested upon returning to Wounded Knee. The roadblocks had been put up again during the few hours of our absence. We were taken to the tribal jail in Pine Ridge and later transferred to the jail in Rapid City, where we were detained for a couple of weeks. When we were released, we were monitored out of South Dakota and told not to come back until it was time to go to trial for obstructing justice and taking part in a civil disorder. We went home and continued working to raise money and awareness about the occupation. I was happy to see my baby girl.

After Wounded Knee, I went home to the Blackfeet Reservation. I had realized during Good Shield's ceremony how little I knew about my own people, their language, their mythology, their history. My people had watched Wounded Knee on the evening news. They were divided about its effectiveness, its purpose. Some who had been friends before Wounded Knee stopped talking to me and looked the other way when I passed them on the street. There is nothing so lonely as a pariah among his own people. Jobs were scarce. We were not in the good graces of the tribe's political leaders, who depend on the federal dollar to continue their colonial existence. Still, that is all they know today; they cannot be blamed for their method of survival. I was naïve to think I could go home and study my people's traditional ways for a year or two—learn all about them—and then return to the University of Montana for my journalism degree. I ended up staying home for fourteen years before I returned to the university. You need more than a year or two to learn about a people who have been on this land for somewhere between eighteen and sixty thousand years.

In 1991 I received a journalism degree from the university. Now I run a sweatlodge in the Bitterroot Valley, traditional home of the Flathead people until they were forced at gunpoint to move further north to make way for the white settlers. My sweatlodge is built at the country home of Joseph Epes Brown, who lived with Oglala holy man Black Elk in the 1940s. Joseph is old and suffers from Alzheimer's disease.

The young students I counsel today are hardly aware of the Wounded Knee siege. They have never heard of the Alcatraz occupation. To them, it is history. To us who were there, it is also history—a history, we hope, that created a consciousness that will reach into the lives of young Indians and perhaps white Americans. Many native people said they supported the goals of the movement but could not condone the violent approach. I agree. However, after a surgeon analyzes and interprets, he sometimes must pick up the knife and cut. Alcatraz. Fort Lawton. The Trail of Broken Treaties. Wounded Knee. Better to die on your feet . . .

15

REFLECTIONS OF AN AIM ACTIVIST:

HAS IT ALL BEEN WORTH IT?

Karren Baird-Olson

Several times when I have served on a panel discussing gen-
der or racial role expectations, the moderator has introduced me by asking the
audience to guess which one of the panel members is a member of the American Indian Movement (AIM). If no one knows me, no one chooses me. I am
the small strawberry blonde, blue-eyed, middle-aged woman wearing a black
dressed-for-success suit accessorized with (fake) pearl earrings and choker. Appearances can also be deceptive where social groups are involved. For example, the view that some people hold of AIM as a violent organization and the
belief that its actions are nonproductive or even counterproductive serve as
more examples of faulty perception based on stereotypes.

The argument I will make in the next pages is based on personal experience and is not meant to be a comprehensive sociological treatise, albeit
sociology is my professional area and certainly has shaped my personal view
of the world. In addition, I grew up in Montana and, as a twenty-one-year-
old bride, moved to the Fort Peck Assiniboine and Sioux Reservation in
1958. My home is still there. My son and my ex-husband still live there.
Thus, both my professional training and my almost forty years of firsthand
experience of reservation life have shaped my personal analysis of the impact of AIM. Based on this grounded perspective, I will argue that AIM was
a primary facilitator in bringing rapid change as well as empowerment to
many native people and communities. Until AIM was established, change
in many areas of Indian Country[1] had moved at such a slow pace that improvements in social conditions and alleviation of human suffering were, for
all intents and purposes, nonexistent to both its residents and to the general public's eye. AIM created a broad-based public awareness that helped to
open long-closed doors and enabled major personal and institutional change.

My first purpose for writing this essay is to correct at least a few of the
myths surrounding AIM. Specifically, I will catalog five contributions AIM

has made to the well-being of the First Peoples as well as to those who share this land with us. My second purpose is to tell the story of an illustrative incident of U.S. government misconduct that occurred in Washington, D.C., in July 1976—an incident that has not been discussed in the social science literature. By recounting this incident, I hope to achieve two goals: (1) to identify some of the unsung heroines and heroes of the 1970s native activist period of American history that followed the occupation of Alcatraz Island, and (2) to point out the personal, social, and economic price that has been paid by many AIM activists, both women and men; sometimes the price has been a bitter one, especially in light of the denunciations and misrepresentations of some about their goals and tactics. I will begin this analysis and testimony by turning back the pages of my own life, and the life of AIM, first to the late 1960s and early 1970s and then to late June 1976.

My Introduction to AIM

Shortly after my children and I moved from Montana to Chicago in November 1969, we met Phyllis Fast Wolf and her family. We were both Plains Indian families from northwestern reservations with similar cultures, ties that helped strengthen the rapport our families immediately felt for each other. Phyllis, her husband, Frank, her daughter, Pat, and her sons not only helped us adapt to the urban world but also introduced us to the activities of a newly formed grassroots group of people who called themselves AIM (American Indian Movement). Honoring their invitations, I joined them at one of the first sit-ins at an archaeological dig and later at the sit-in at Belmont Harbor.

In the early fall of 1972, I returned to Missoula, Montana, where Myrna Boyd, a dear friend who had moved to Missoula from the Fort Peck Assiniboine and Sioux Reservation, found me. She told me that she had had a dream that I would be coming back to Montana. She told me about the most recent activities of AIM. This time I was invited to join an activity called the Trail of Broken Treaties. Because of my respect for her, because I had already learned that freedom does not come without some danger, and because of other, more personal reasons, I accepted the invitation.

Since my children were in school, they remained with my parents in Lewistown, Montana. Myrna's nine children were going to make the cross-country trek; as their "auntie," I would help tutor them. On a lovely fall day, several carloads of AIM supporters (I also took my car) headed southeast to the Northern Cheyenne Reservation, where we would meet the main group. Collecting more people as we traveled, we would then head through the Dakotas, go on to Minnesota, and finally reach Washington, D.C., in October. This trip would change the complete direction of my life.

Although there needs to be much more written from the perspectives of the participants in the Trail of Broken Treaties, the objective of this essay is not to describe that historically significant event. My focus is on a telling event that occurred four years later during the 1976 reunion, an incident I will use as a pedagogical device to illustrate my continuing commitment to the American Indian Movement.

The 1976 Incident: Harassing and Arresting the Innocent

I do not remember when it was decided that as many as possible of the 1972 Trail of Broken Treaties participants would return to Washington, D.C., during America's Bicentennial activities. As I sit here at my computer in Kansas, I find it hard to believe that it has been more than two decades since the Trail and nearly twenty years since the harassment and arrest of the innocent in 1976.åI have promised that I would write about both times, but I always thought I would do it when I became an elder, because I thought my life would slow up a bit as I grew older. That has not happened. However, the time has come for us who were actually there to tell our own stories. I have asked some friends and family members to help me remember some of the things that went on that summer in D.C. Thus, the following account of the 1976 incident is based not only on my own remembrance but also on the recollections of others—my children, Shawn, John, and Nolee; Caleb Shield; Theresa McKey; Laurie Whitright; and Ruby Whitright Fowler.[2]

I do remember that, as soon as my children heard about the plans for the 1976 gathering, they said they were going; they refused to be left behind in Montana again, as they had been when I traveled with the Trail of Broken Treaties caravan to Washington, D.C., in 1972. In 1976, because of my job, my three children and I could not leave with the Montana contingent, so I told the Fort Peck group that we would meet them at the American University campsite no later than July 4.

Our preparations for the trip began during the spring of 1976. We planned to drive to Washington, D.C., camping and sightseeing along the way, and after the work was done, we would travel until we had just enough money to return home. The trip would provide three lessons for my children: (1) active participation in the creation of governmental policies; (2) visits to important historical sites; and (3) an appreciation of the diversity of this land and its peoples. Another reason for the trip, and certainly not the least important, was that it would be one of our last family activities before my older daughter left for college.

The unaware have often expressed amazement that a single woman would travel with three children across the country, as well as take an active part in protesting against the abuses of the U.S. government. In the first place, I was used to driving across the country by myself, but during this trip I was not alone. Three responsible young people—two teenagers (one seventeen and one sixteen) and a preteenager of twelve—were with me. More important, I wanted my children to know that they did not have to be passive victims, that they could make positive changes not only in their own lives but also in the lives of others if they had the courage to take action, to do something.

So one day in late June, we headed east. Our 1967 four-door Chevy Impala sedan was filled with camping gear, clothes, food, a U.S. map, a AAA trip plan, a journal, a camera, books, a short mother, and three long-legged children. The tent poles were tied to the side of the car, and John Mike's GI Joe, dressed like Custer, was strapped to the hood ornament. We arrived in Washington, D.C., in time for the Fourth of July activities, joining the 320 American Indians from all over the country who camped on the sports field of American University in the summer of 1976.

During one of our camp meetings, it was decided that we should take the children and young people to visit the Bureau of Indian Affairs (BIA) building where we had been surrounded and put under siege in 1972. Considering that the government had overreacted to our presence in 1972, we were not sure how officials would respond to our attempts to visit our "embassy" this time around. We were a peaceful group, but in case the government tried to surround us again, we decided to take mostly older children and young people—forty youngsters in all—for the first trip. Ten adults were chosen to go as chaperons and tour guides for the first tour. Among that group were eleven of us from Fort Peck: Myrna Boyd and three of her children, Laurie, Chauncey, and Donald; Caleb Shields; David Campbell; the two McKey girls; and my two daughters, Shawn and Nolee, and me. My son, John Mike, would be among those who would remain at camp as a security guard. He was to go on the next tour.

The morning of our first tour was sunny and warm. In anticipation of a typical, sultry Washington, D.C., summer day, we did not take jackets. We wore Levis, summer tops, and sandals or cowboy boots. A few of us had cameras and small purses. Someone had loaned us a big yellow school bus. After telling John Mike that we would see him that afternoon, I climbed into the bus. I joked with Myrna about how I always seemed to end up chaperoning a bunch of kids on bumpy rides in buses that made me carsick. I had no idea that being carsick would be the least of my concerns.

As we drove from the American University to the BIA building, those of us who had been to D.C. before pointed out various historical sites to the kids. We laughed, we sang, and we veterans of 1972 told the others stories about how we were surrounded in the BIA building and how the government overreacted to a group of people who had come to stay in their embassy. Someone wondered if it would happen again. We agreed that this was the Bicentennial; this was obviously a tour group of youngsters and a few adults; ergo, we would be given the opportunity to have a peaceful visit. Everyone relaxed. It was a nice day.

We arrived at the BIA building in the late morning. The bus driver let us off on the sidewalk leading to the front entrance with the large, double metal doors. As the group walked toward the doors, we old-timers pointed out remembered landmarks. We came up the steps and found that the doors had been locked. We were denied access to our own embassy! For a few minutes we stood dazed. Then we regrouped. We decided to sit down, sing, and pray until the doors were opened.

Shortly thereafter, several expensively dressed white men came out to tell us that they were afraid we were carrying weapons and were going to take over the BIA building. We were told that if we agreed to be searched and to go in groups of ten or fewer at a time, we would be admitted. This was a flimsy excuse, since our summer clothing would have made it very difficult, if not impossible, for any of us to conceal the types of weapons necessary to take over the building. Also, it would have been extremely difficult to supervise so many children and young people during such an action.

The sun began to reach high noon; those of us from the semiarid plains of northeastern Montana began to notice the humidity. Someone found a water faucet on one side of the U-shaped building. Our stomachs began to tell us that we had not eaten since early that morning. Still we sat, and still we prayed and sang.

Then they came: dozens of black-helmeted men wearing black clothing and riding dark motorcycles, coming in lines down the avenue. I remember feeling sick to my stomach. Déjà vu. But this time my two daughters and other young people were with me. I told Nolee and Shawn that I wanted them to leave. I knew they could find their way back to the university campsite. But they would not leave without me, nor would they leave with me. So I stayed with them.

The group agreed that we would continue our peaceful protest; that we would not initiate nor respond with violence. We told the children that, whatever happened to us adults, they were not to fight back. I kept my daughters close to me. Shawn understood that if something happened to me, she was responsible for her twelve-year-old sister, Nolee. All of us who had long hair braided it.[3]

The goon squad began to move in file across the lawn. We moved around the building into the inner rectangular-shaped courtyard of the building. Beyond the sidewalk, a grassy knoll rose slightly above us. We sat in a close circle, praying and singing. People had begun to gather on the knoll to watch the event. Others were watching from the windows of the BIA building. Television crews arrived. Someone came out of the building and turned off the water faucet. We were sweating so heavily we had no need for bathrooms.

I realized it must be close to mid-afternoon. The storm troopers had moved in so closely that their boots touched our bottoms where we sat on the cement. Nolee looked up at a black man, younger and even taller than the other troopers, who was standing behind her. She asked him why he was doing this. She wondered why, since his people had been so mistreated, he was not joining us. I was impressed by her insights. I looked up at the man and was heartened by the painful expression on his face. He had heard her.

Minutes after this encounter between a Native American child and a young black man, someone in our group cried out. She had been struck with a trooper's club. I pushed my daughters into the center of the circle and reminded them to remain flat on their stomachs. I felt my back being hit. I lowered my head. And then I felt myself being lifted into the air. I knew that two men had hold of me. I was lifted above their heads and then dashed to the cement. The seconds in air were like flying.

There must have been pain when the flying ended. Part of the metal figurines on my Western belt buckle were ripped off. I have snapshots of bruises on my arms and torso and face, but I don't remember feeling pain from the impact. Nor do I remember pain when my face was ground into the cement after I lifted my head to call out reassurances to Nolee. I had heard her cry out when I was manhandled, and I did not want her to try to come to my rescue.

I figured out how to move my head ever so slightly so I could watch what was happening to the children. I saw Nolee being held against the wall. I could not see Shawn. Later we were told that the children were roughly grabbed out of the middle of the circle and slammed up against the wall of the building. A young black trooper had broken out of the line and would not participate in the violence. I like to believe he was the man Nolee questioned.

At least three paddy wagons arrived. We were handcuffed with plastic cuffs and thrown into the vehicles. I was in one with the other adult women. The cuffs cut into our wrists. But I quickly discovered that, if I pulled against the plastic straps, they tightened. I realized that if I could keep from straining against them, and if I continued to sweat in the oppressive heat, I probably could slide at least one hand out of the handcuffs once I was out of official scrutiny. The doors of the wagon were barely closed and it had hardly begun to move before I was out of my handcuffs and removing the cuffs from the other women. We prayed.

My daughters later told me that one of our Fort Peck girls was cut badly by her cuffs. The children were separated from the adults. We were all taken to a Washington, D.C., jail, where we were questioned and booked. We women were in a holding pen where we could hear our men. We asked about the children. The officials would not tell us anything. I prayed silently. A peace came to me. I was later to come to understand that it was an experience similar to what Christians call "a peace beyond all understanding." Once again, as a group but in separate cells, we women and men sang and prayed until we were ordered to stop.

One by one we were taken out to be booked. While I was being photographed, I joked with Myrna that this experience was a bit like being in beauty queen line-ups for contestant photo sessions. My humor was not appreciated by the jail officers.

Each of us women was questioned separately by plainclothes police who looked and sounded suspiciously like FBI agents. My interrogator asked me, "Why are you involved in all of this?" He then asked me why did not I help them (law enforcement agents) fight for higher wages? My response to the first question was that they knew so much about me that it was obvious the query was purely rhetorical. The agent had enough grace to look somewhat embarrassed. My initial response to his second question was amazement. I replied that he probably made more in one year than several hard-working Fort Peck people could make together in the same time.

Later we compared notes and found that we had been asked basically the same questions. The questioners seemed to think that three of us—Myrna, a woman from the state of Washington, and I—were "ringleaders." They would not tell us where our children were.

The women's section of the jail was full. Recently, the city's prostitutes had been rounded up to keep them out of sight during the Bicentennial. We were taken to the jail library. Bare mattresses were thrown on the floor. I don't remember if we were given blankets. I do remember that I was glad my clothes had dried out while we were in the holding tank and during the questioning and booking, because the room was very cold from the air conditioning. A kindly black woman brought us baloney and "boughten" white bread sandwiches. I was so hungry they almost tasted good. Still wearing my sweaty clothes, I sank onto the bare mattress and looked over at Myrna. The last things I remember before falling asleep were her smile and her quiet chuckle when I whispered, "I have been in some real fixes with you. But this takes the cake!"

We were awakened before dawn. I cannot remember if we were given showers. I think not. We were taken to a cafeteria warmed by the comforting smells of bacon, sausage, eggs, grits, biscuits, and coffee. Black women behind the counters encouraged us to eat heartily and praised us for our courage. "Right on, sisters!" they said. The other female inmates told us this was a highly unusual breakfast. They were pleased because they, too, had benefited from our activism.

However, as I talked later in the holding pen with several young women who were being detained for prostitution, they did not understand how we could risk so much for no immediate payback. Incarceration was part of the package that came with working on the streets. Our incarceration was not part of an immediate economic package. One young woman was supporting a child and taking classes part time to be a dentist. I talked with her about the various forms of oppression that both women and racial minorities experience. I like to think that she heard me.

The lawyers for the street women came to see them. We AIM women waited, sitting against the wall. I had just leaned my head against the wall and closed my eyes when I heard my name called. Another expensively dressed white male was at the bars of the cage, asking if there was a Karren Baird-Olson in there. Startled, I replied, "Yes, I am Karren." He beckoned me over to the bars. He was obviously upset. Talking in a low voice, he told me that taking a message to an inmate in this manner was highly unusual. But he had been instructed "from higher up" to tell me that my girls were OK, that they and the other youngsters were being well taken care of. And word had come from my mother in Montana that if the girls and I were not released by noon, my sister, who lived in New York City, would fly down to get the girls out.

Later, I found out what had happened. When we were surrounded and taken off to jail, observers contacted the other campers at the American University. The camp leaders called our families. By the next morning, my mother had reached at least one of Montana's congressional representatives, who found out where we were. She never would tell me just how she had managed to do so much in such a short time. But then she always was a woman of action. She did say that if I wanted to stay in jail that was my business, but her granddaughters were not going to remain in such a place. (How I miss her!)

It was after eleven A.M. when we were taken from the tank to appear before a judge. Dozens of onlookers, including media people, were milling around outside of the courtroom. I caught a glimpse of the children. I could see the back of Shawn's head, and I knew that Nolee had to be close by. Several women and men approached us while we were waiting to enter the court chambers. They were lawyers who had come to assist us for no charge. One woman who had graduated from an Ivy League college told me that she had been talking with my daughters. She reported that Myrna's daughter Laurie, a boy named Sugar Frank, and Shawn had taken charge of the other young people. They had protected, reassured, and comforted them. The lawyer was so impressed with Shawn that she encouraged me to have Shawn apply to her alma mater, Bryn Mawr College.

We were taken into the courtroom, where we waited again until a white judge and lawyers entered. We women were called to stand before the judge, sitting behind his desk on the elevated platform. He looked down and told us that if we would sign an agreement stating we would never return again to Washington, D.C., he would let us all go immediately. I remember being amazed at his nerve. I knew that we had done nothing wrong, and his "solution" was unconstitutional. I remember saying something terse such as "no way" and moving back to the court benches. The other women followed. I remember the anger on his and the other men's faces. All of the lawyers—the prosecutors as well as our newly found defense counsel—disappeared behind closed doors.

We waited again. A short time later, we were told that all charges had been dropped. We were escorted outside into the bright sunlight, where we found the rest of our group and where I tried to duck away from the photographers and reporters. I do not remember how we were returned to the campsite. I think someone paid for taxis. Much to my joy, I finally could hold my girls. They told me that a black matron had washed their clothes, allowed them to shower, fed them very well, and kept praising them for their courage. "Right on!" she said over and over.

I remember the pain and outrage on my son's face when he saw the bruises on my face and arms. He held me and his sisters and then helped me to find a shower and clean clothes.

As I write this, I realize that I am weeping over this incident for the first time. I cry not for myself but for the children who must be subjected to such experiences in order to be able to grow up in a world where all human beings are treated with respect.

AIM's Contributions

There are those, both American Indians and non-Indians, who criticize AIM, who say AIM created more problems than solutions. I cannot speak for every position that has been taken against AIM, but it has been my experience that there are four types of people who take such a stance. The first are the ignorant, those who do not know what AIM was all about. They heard about or saw only the reactive, short-term violence and/or the hangers-on who claimed to be AIM and used the movement as an excuse for doing their own violent things. The second type are the people who have been so colonized that they passively accept their own subjugation. The third group are those who are fearful. They fear change unless it is very slow, and/or they fear the danger that comes with freedom. The fourth group are those who have something to gain from the continued oppression of American Indians and/ or the misrepresentation of AIM.

It is not the purpose of this essay to discuss internal conflicts in AIM nor to address the strengths and shortcomings of AIM's organizational structure. However, I will note that all organizations have internal disagreements. No group has perfect harmony. Since American Indian groups are like all other human organizations, there are disagreements from time to time, but AIM's internal problems are no worse than those of other groups.

Overall, I believe that the social structure of the movement has been one of its greatest strengths. Why? The lack of a formal structure has been an extremely valuable strategic force. Members come to whatever activities they can participate in, not because someone has coerced them, but because of individual, internalized motivation and commitment. Just as traditional warriors went in and out of battle as they were able, so have traditional AIM people given of themselves to the goal of sovereignty. Bureaucrats, such as BIA officials, and paramilitary professionals, such as law enforcement agents—including the FBI—like to see lists of members and officers and organizational charts. Such information makes their job easier when they are trying to determine accountability. Also, these data make the task of neutralizing members' effectiveness much easier. It is difficult to accomplish such an ignoble objective when there are no lists and when every member is respected and honored. If leaders are killed or silenced, there are always others to replace them. The movement does not die.

In addition to providing an alternative organizational model, the American Indian Movement has made at least six primary contributions, not only to native individuals, but also to urban and reservation communities. AIM provided courageous role models; refuted racist myths and stereotypes about Indian people; created a national network of visible activists; initiated major institutional changes; enforced personal and institutional respect; and renewed hope for the future.

Role Models

I have been around long enough to remember when there were signs that read, "No Indians nor dogs allowed." I remember people saying, "A good Indian is a dead Indian." I remember my paternal grandfather wanting to talk about being part-Indian and my grandmother hushing him. I remember my oldest daughter being given an "F" in first grade for coloring children brown. I remember my husband being afraid that, if I protested the grade, she would be hurt more.

The American Indian Movement brought an unprecedented number of the courageous, the wise, the honest, the generous, and the spiritual together. We came from all parts of Indian Country, urban and rural. United, we said, we no longer have to be silent. We can ask for respect. In a spiritual and sophisticated manner, we learned how to beat the white man at his own game; how to challenge the "apples"; and how to renew the traditional roles of strong women. AIM members gave of themselves and provided role models for their communities.

Refutation of Racist Myths and Stereotypes

Although some efforts had been made in the past to challenge prejudice and discrimination against American Indians, for the most part this had been neither on a national scale nor on a widespread basis. AIM destroyed and/ or seriously undermined dangerous prejudices about the First Peoples and provided new choices and alternate paths for Indians all across the country. American Indians were given an alternative to the pervasive image of the silent, apathetic, helpless, dumb, pagan Indian to emulate.

Major Institutional Changes

I have seen more broad, sweeping changes in the last two decades since the late 1970s than I have seen or heard about since the formation of the Plains reservations in the late 1800s. There had always been caring individuals in education, in the criminal justice system, in the churches, in welfare programs, and in other social institutions. But they were not united and they had little power. After AIM came into the public eye, fearful bureaucrats began to make much-needed changes. For example, I have seen major reforms in education. I have taught in reservation schools and in urban schools with American Indian students. My own children have gone to both types of schools. I have seen the damage of undisguised racism as well as the effects of culturally insensitive policies; both results have driven children and teenagers out of the schools. To give only one specific example of the changes brought by AIM: When a Fort Peck Reservation math teacher made a derogatory remark about my younger daughter Nolee's American Indian heritage and then said that "C" was a good grade in math for an Indian student, the school, fearful of my AIM connections, took my promise of a civil suit seriously. Nolee received a public apology. She was given the "A's" and "B's" she had earned.

Network of Grassroots Activists: Rural and Urban

Many of the original AIM members had lived both on and off their reservations. Their urban experiences had taught them how to deal with all types of white people. In addition, in the urban settings people from the various tribes and nations were able to compare stories. Out of this shared knowledge came what is sometimes called the concept of pan-Indianness. AIM provided an organized mode of expression, a constructive outlet for frustration and anger, a social network or community of doers, people who walked their talk.

Personal and Institutional Respect

The American Indian Movement also brought a new sense of respect, not only for oneself but from others as well. For example, during the 1972 Caravan and during the 1976 trek, I saw so-called winos and alkies become sober, responsible members of our mobile communities. If they had withdrawal symptoms, I never heard any complaints. They had something to work for. They had been given hope for the future.

One of my favorite examples of changed views of native people in the non-Indian community occurred about a year after we had returned to Montana after the Trail of Broken Treaties. Because it was winter, my AIM friends had left me at the door of the college hangout so I would not have to walk with them in the thirty-below-zero weather from the parking lot.

I walked up the stairs and into the lounge. Much to my disgust, I recognized three "rednecks" sitting at a table to my right. I tried to ignore their raucous laughter and lewd remarks. "Hey, baby, where are all your bucks?" "Let me show you how a real man screws!"

Just as I turned to go find my companions, they came up the stairs into full view of the ignorant men. My friends carried themselves proudly. Two of them braided their hair in the traditional manner. Like me, they wore beaded jewelry and ribbon shirts. There was no doubt that the men were also AIM. My three brothers looked at me. They looked at the white men behind me. They understood what had been happening. They began moving toward them. For the first time in my life, I saw Montana racists shut their filthy mouths. They literally slumped down into their seats and then quickly sneaked out the back door.

Hope

As seen earlier, AIM brought hope: For some, it was the first time; for others, it was a renewed vision for the future; for still others, a new definition.

And, most important, the accomplishments of those often turbulent years ensure that there is hope for future generations. This is not to say that all the doors have been opened. They have not. But the ceilings of opportunity are a little higher.

My children tell me that my activism as well as theirs has taught them that they do not have to keep silent about injustice, as so many of our ancestors were forced to do. They have learned that individuals can make a difference, and a united people can make an even bigger difference in ensuring a world where equity is given more than lip service.

The Sacrifices of Activists

What has happened to the role models—those early activists who broke the trails? Because I am familiar mostly with the lives of the activists from my home, I will look only at the Fort Peck group. We have all made at least one major sacrifice for our activism, for our courage, and we have often paid with blood.

Murder

Two of the young Fort Peck men who were with us in 1976 have been murdered. When my three-year-old granddaughter Shelena Sky, Shawn's younger daughter, was beaten and kidnapped in 1985, the FBI did not help with our search for her. Within days after her death, a young agent told me that they would have intervened earlier if I had not been involved with AIM and ERA "stuff."

Unresolved Grief, Post-traumatic Stress Syndrome, and Alcohol Abuse

All of us have been victims of violent crime. We have been traumatized by rape or attempted rape and/or verbal and physical attacks designed to "put us in our place." The spirits of three of our Fort Peck women have been broken not only from the overreaction of whites to their peaceful activism but also from the "apples" and the fearful members of our own tribes. The three women have turned to alcohol to numb themselves or to commit slow suicide. For many of the same reasons, two of the young men also misuse alcohol.

Unemployment or Underemployment

Because we are regarded as troublemakers, we have been denied certain employment opportunities. To give just one example: During the late 1970s,

I occasionally worked part-time for *The Herald News*, a reservation area weekly newspaper owned by a non-Indian family, and I became friendly with a young editor who was a newcomer to the area and was not tied into the local power structure. He told me that, during meetings of local leaders that he covered for his news beat, the "good ol' boys" openly talked about preventing me from working in order to force me to leave the reservation.

Denial of Personal/Professional Opportunities

All of us have experienced this type of backlash. Some of the most dramatic examples have occurred when conservative people have penalized our children because of our activism. For example, the judges in the 1982 Northeastern Montana Miss America Pageant, held in Wolf Point on the Fort Peck Reservation, conspired not to give my younger daughter the title because they feared her views would reflect mine. Again, a newcomer to the area who was not tied into the non-Indian power structure provided us with the documentation. Although several lawyers who were friends of mine volunteered to handle the case pro bono, Nolee eventually decided not to go to court because of the notoriety it would bring her.

Personal Loneliness

Today, in general, older heterosexual women experience difficulty in finding supportive male partners. Considering the experiences of the AIM women I know, I believe we have suffered even greater loneliness than the average older woman.

Until recently, if asked what type of woman I am, I would have said I am an average, college-educated woman who grew up in the 1940s and 1950s and, like countless other aware women, became an activist in the 1960s and 1970s. I have come to realize, however, that I, like all of the other early AIM women, am not average. We are exceptional women; we are trailblazers. But nearly all of us have paid dearly for that, not only in terms of general social acceptance but also in terms of finding supportive and lasting personal companionship. Based on my own experience and the experiences of other AIM women over the years, I have noticed four types of men who come "sniffing around" AIM women.[4] These categories are not mutually exclusive.

First, there have been the proper, established men who find us exotic but not proper enough for long-term commitment or marriage. At first these men appear very sincere. Then, as the novelty wears off, we find that they want to keep us on a shelf like sports trophies, out of sight and out of mind, until they want a little vicarious excitement in their lives.

Second are the weak and dependent men who want to be taken care of rather than to be help-mates. A number of these men are chemically dependent. The majority of the men in this category are over forty years of age and want to be center stage in their women's lives. They are not secure enough to be able to wait; they want immediate attention. These men want young "poodles" who unquestioningly serve their masters, or they want sexual companions who will also take emotional and financial care of them.

A third category are the younger men, sometimes young enough to be our sons, who respect what we have accomplished. They want to be with us, but they have little to offer us. If we accept young men into our lives, we find that we are spending a good amount of time and energy attempting to educate them so we can communicate more easily. Often they are willing to learn, but the only men we want to rear are our sons and grandsons.

Rarely are there men in the fourth category. They are the ones whose strength and courage match ours. One of the strong men who came into my life during the 1970s died a mysterious death while he was organizing against environmental pollution in the Southwest. Often, however, even the most courageous feel threatened by our strength. And, on the other hand, when we weep, when we are fearful, when we show our vulnerability, they disappear, literally or figuratively. Most of all, although they expect us to understand their commitment to human rights, they are jealous of our dedication to others and our love affair with the search for justice.

So most of us older AIM women have resigned ourselves to unsatisfying relationships with men; those who are not resigned are alone. And being alone is not easy. If we are separated from our indigenous communities, it is even harder. At least we know that most of our daughters have strong men beside them. At least most of our sons stand beside their women. But this is only partial comfort, for we do not live just for our children and grandchildren. We try not to give up hope for finding companionship. In the meantime, we keep so busy that we are too exhausted when night comes to notice how empty and lonely our beds are.

Conclusion

Would I do it all over again? Yes. The only other choices were silent resignation, bitterness, and/or self-destruction, all of which would have doomed not only me but also my children and grandchildren. Thorough housecleaning is always messy for a time, but the ultimate result is worth the temporary upheaval.

The results of our housecleaning—the reorganization of reservation social institutions and our personal lives that began in the late 1960s—were most apparent during the 1970s. Contrary to the claims of its detractors and enemies, AIM did not die during the 1980s. Individuals as well as the movement have been busy integrating all that was accomplished. The bright young butterflies of hope of the 1960s and 1970s who turned to the elders and medicine people for guidance are now elders themselves—including me. In addition to being traditional, we are lawyers, writers, professors, movie stars, musicians, and politicians. And some of us are medicine people.

Our youthful activism brought us a respect that many of us never expected. We were fighting for respect for our children and grandchildren and never imagined that we would also receive respectful recognition. In my own life today, hardly a month goes by without at least one person calling or writing to say "thank you" for doing what I did or for being a role model.

Leonard Peltier has honored me by allowing me to speak officially on his behalf. Almost every semester, Leonard and I speak for a few minutes when I take my Kansas State University (KSU) corrections class students to Leavenworth Penitentiary. Despite the wary watch of the guards and tour guides, he sometimes gives me a brief hug. Few words are needed. We are still alive. There are so many of us who now walk in the spirit world.

Russell Means has honored the KSU Indian students twice in the last five years by serving as our keynote speaker during our annual Native American Heritage Month. Two years ago, when he came for the second time, we gave each other a spontaneous, long hug. There were tears in our eyes. What could words say?

So much has happened since Leonard, Russell, and I first met that fall of 1972. Who would have guessed that Leonard would become internationally known for his ongoing sacrifice; that Russell would become a movie star, making socially significant movies; and that I would become a university professor?

We are more than old war horses reliving our days of glory. We have been given the gift of a second rebirth. During the first rebirth, we emerged out of a cocoon of darkness, oppression, and hopelessness: the prison of colonization. We were shiny, fragile, gloriously beautiful silver creatures reaching for Father Sky, the stars, the moon, and the sun. Today, in our second incarnation, we are benefiting from the world we helped create during the early days of our activism. We helped build the ideological shelters whereby the doors to education and employment could be opened more easily and the old spiritual ways could be followed more openly. This time, our wings are sturdy gold, and we move more easily between Father Sky and Mother Earth.

Once again we are redefining *community*. We have learned how to use Euro-American technology to help us communicate through media such as this. We are not abandoning the richness of oral tradition; we have only added to it. We do this because we know that we all—white, red, black, and yellow peoples—share this earth. We are all related. We know that we are all in danger. If other peoples are unable or unwilling to learn how to communicate with and respect all life forms, then we will have to help lead the way to healing, or we will all go down together. Mother Earth can do without us; we cannot do without her.

Mitakuye Oyasin

NOTES

1. Joanna Grey gives a clear definition of Indian Country: "Indian country once was the term used for a specific geographical area, the place where Indians lived. It had clear and definite jurisdictional overtones. Indian country today has a much more ambiguous definition (except where federal criminal jurisdiction applies) much the same as the fictional 'Marlboro Country.' It is an image, a sociological phenomenon." See Joanna Grey, "White Law in Indian Country" (ms., University of New Mexico, Department of Sociology), 5.

2. We were part of the group of twenty-six people who came from the Fort Peck Assiniboine and Sioux Reservation, located in the northeast corner of Montana. In addition to me and my children, Shawn, John Mike, and Nolee, there were Myrna Boyd; Myrna's nine children—Theresa, Anita, Jackie, Chauncey, Laurie, Donald, Boyd, Ruby, and Myrna (Porky); Myrna's two grandchildren—one-and-one-half-year-old Tanya and six-month-old Althea; Theresa McKey and her two daughters, Iris and Patti; David Campbell; George (Fish) Redstone; Lyn Birthmark; and Pearl Nation and three of her children who made, at our expense, the long trek across the country.

3. We knew that there was a very real danger of being attacked by the Swat Squad. If that happened, long flowing hair makes a handy thing to grab and to pull. Braids are more difficult to grab. Also, braids are cooler on a hot, humid day.

4. The first time I heard the term *sniffing around* was in 1958 when my husband and I had gone home to the reservation during Montana State University's spring break. He and his friends were talking about the attention some of the reservation men were giving me. One of my husband's friends used the term, thereby comparing the men to dogs. The use is an example of Indian humor.

16

THE BLOODY WAKE OF ALCATRAZ:

POLITICAL REPRESSION OF THE

AMERICAN INDIAN MOVEMENT

DURING THE 1970S

Ward Churchill

The reality is a continuum which connects Indian flesh sizzling over Puritan fires and Vietnamese flesh roasting under American napalm. The reality is the compulsion of a sick society to rid itself of men like Nat Turner and Crazy Horse, George Jackson and Richard Oakes, whose defiance uncovers the hypocrisy of a declaration affirming everyone's right to liberty and life. The reality is an overwhelming greed which began with the theft of a continent and continues with the merciless looting of every country on the face of the earth which lacks the strength to defend itself.

—Richard Lundstrom

In combination with the fishing rights struggles of the Puyallup, Nisqually, Muckleshoot, and other nations in the Pacific Northwest from 1965 to 1970, the 1969–71 occupation of Alcatraz Island by the San Francisco area's Indians of All Tribes coalition ushered in a decade-long period of uncompromising and intensely confrontational American Indian political activism.[1] Unprecedented in modern U.S. history, the phenomenon represented by Alcatraz also marked the inception of a process of official repression of indigenous activists without contemporary North American parallel in its virulence and lethal effects.[2]

The nature of the post-Alcatraz federal response to organized agitation for native rights was such that by 1979 researchers were describing it as a manifestation of the U.S. government's "continuing Indian Wars."[3] For its part (in internal documents intended to be secret), the Federal Bureau of

Investigation (FBI)—the primary instrument by which the government's policy of anti-Indian repression was implemented—concurred with such assessments, abandoning its customary counterintelligence vernacular in favor of the terminology of outright counterinsurgency warfare.[4] The result, as the U.S. Commission on Civil Rights officially conceded at the time, was the imposition of a condition of official terrorism upon certain of the less compliant sectors of indigenous society in the United States.[5]

In retrospect, it is apparent that the locus of both activism and repression in Indian Country throughout the 1970s centered squarely on one group, the American Indian Movement (AIM). Moreover, the crux of AIM activism during the 1970s, and thus of the FBI's campaign to "neutralize" it,[6] can be found in a single locality: the Pine Ridge (Oglala Lakota) Reservation, in South Dakota. The purpose of this essay, then, is to provide an overview of the federal counterinsurgency program against AIM on and around Pine Ridge, using it as a lens through which to explore the broader motives and outcomes attending it. Finally, conclusions will be drawn as to the program's implications, not only with respect to American Indians, but concerning non-indigenous Americans as well.

Background

AIM was founded in 1968 in Minneapolis by a group of urban Anishinabe (Chippewa), including Dennis Banks, Mary Jane Wilson, Pat Ballanger, Clyde Bellecourt, Eddie Benton Benai, and George Mitchell. Modeled loosely after the Black Panther Party for Self-Defense established by Huey P. Newton and Bobby Seale in Oakland, California, two years previously, the group took as its first tasks the protection of the city's sizable native community from a pattern of rampant police abuse and the creation of programs for jobs, housing, and education.[7] Within three years, the organization had grown to include chapters in several other cities and had begun to shift its focus from civil rights issues to an agenda more specifically attuned to the conditions afflicting native North America.

What AIM discerned as the basis of these conditions was not so much a matter of socioeconomic discrimination against Indians as it was their internal colonization by the United States.[8] This perception accrued from the fact that, by 1871 when federal treaty-making with native peoples was permanently suspended, the rights of indigenous nations to distinct, self-governing territories had been recognized by the United States more than 370 times through treaties duly ratified by its Senate.[9] Yet, during the intervening century, more than 90 percent of treaty-reserved native land had been expropriated by the federal government, in defiance of both its own constitution and international custom and convention.[10] One consequence of this was creation of the urban diaspora from which AIM itself had emerged; by 1970, about half of all Indians in the United States had been pushed off their land altogether.[11]

Within the residual archipelago of reservations—an aggregation of about fifty million acres, or roughly 2.5 percent of the forty-eight contiguous states—indigenous forms of governance had been thoroughly usurped through the imposition of U.S. jurisdiction under the federal government's self-assigned prerogative of exercising "plenary [full and absolute] power over Indian affairs."[12] Correspondingly, Indian control over what had turned out to be rather vast mineral resources within reservation boundaries—an estimated two-thirds of all U.S. "domestic" uranium deposits, one-quarter of the low sulfur coal, 20 percent of the oil and natural gas, and so on—was essentially nonexistent.[13]

It followed that royalty rates set by the U.S. Bureau of Indian Affairs (BIA), in its exercise of federal "trust" prerogatives vis-à-vis corporate extraction of Indian mineral assets, amounted to only a fraction of what the same corporations would have paid had they undertaken the same mining operations in nonreservation localities.[14] The same principle of underpayment to Indians, with resulting "super-profit" accrual to non-Indian business entities, prevailed with regard to other areas of economic activity handled by the Indian bureau, from the leasing of reservation grazing land to various ranching interests, to the harvesting of reservation timber by corporations such as Weyerhauser and Boise-Cascade.[15] Small wonder that, by the late 1960s, Indian radicals such as Robert K. Thomas had begun to refer to the BIA as "the Colonial Office of the United States."[16]

In human terms, the consequence was that, overall, American Indians—who, on the basis of known resources, comprised what should have been the single wealthiest population group in North America—constituted by far the most impoverished sector of U.S. society. According to the federal government's own data, Indians suffered, by a decisive margin, the highest rate of unemployment in the country, a matter correlated to their receiving by far the lowest annual and lifetime incomes of any group in the nation.[17] It also corresponded well with virtually every other statistical indicator of extreme poverty: a truly catastrophic rate of infant mortality and the highest rates of death from malnutrition, exposure, plague disease, teen suicide, and accidents related to alcohol abuse. The average life expectancy of a reservation-based Indian male in 1970 was less than forty-five years; reservation-based Indian females could expect to live less than three years longer than their male counterparts; urban Indians of either gender were living only about five years longer, on average, than their relatives on the reservations.[18]

AIM's response to its growing apprehension of this squalid panorama was to initiate a campaign consciously intended to bring about the decolonization of native North America: "Only by reestablishing our rights as sovereign nations, including our right to control our own territories and resources, and our right to genuine self-governance," as Dennis Banks put it in 1971, "can we hope to successfully address the conditions currently experienced by our people."[19]

Extrapolating largely from the example of Alcatraz, the movement undertook a multifaceted political strategy combining a variety of tactics. On the one hand, it engaged in activities designed primarily to focus media attention, and thus the attention of the general public, on Indian rights issues, especially those pertaining to treaty rights. On the other hand, it pursued the sort of direct confrontation meant to affirm those rights in practice. It also began systematically to reassert native cultural/spiritual traditions.[20] Eventually, it added a component wherein the full range of indigenous rights to decolonization/self-determination were pursued through the United Nations venue of international law, custom, and convention.[21]

In mounting this comprehensive effort, AIM made of itself a bona fide national liberation movement, at least for a while.[22] Its members consisted of "the shock troops of Indian sovereignty," to quote non-AIM Oglala Lakota activist Birgil Kills Straight.[23] They essentially reframed the paradigm by which U.S.-Indian relations are understood in the late twentieth century.[24] They also suffered the worst physical repression at the hands of the United States of any "domestic" group since the 1890 massacre of Big Foot's Minneconjou by the 7th Cavalry at Wounded Knee.[25]

Prelude

AIM's seizure of the public consciousness may in many ways be said to have begun in 1969 when Dennis Banks recruited a young Oglala named Russell Means to join the movement. Instinctively imbued with what one critic described as a "bizarre knack for staging demonstrations that attracted the sort of press coverage Indians had been looking for,"[26] Means was instrumental in AIM's achieving several of its earliest and most important media coups: painting Plymouth Rock red before capturing the Mayflower replica on Thanksgiving Day 1970, for example, and staging a "4th of July Countercelebration" by occupying the Mount Rushmore National Monument in 1971.[27]

Perhaps more important, Means proved to be the bridge that allowed the movement to establish its credibility on a reservation for the first time. In part, this was because when he joined AIM he brought along virtually an entire generation of his family—brothers Ted, Bill, and Dale, cousin Madonna Gilbert, and others—each of whom possessed a web of friends and acquaintances on the Pine Ridge Reservation. It was therefore natural that AIM was called upon to "set things right" concerning the torture-murder of a middle-aged Oglala in the off-reservation town of Gordon, Nebraska, in late February 1972.[28] As Bill Means would later recall, "When Raymond Yellow Thunder was killed, his relatives went first to the BIA, then to the FBI, and to the local police, but they got no response. Severt Young Bear [Yellow Thunder's nephew and a friend of Ted Means] then . . . asked AIM to come help clear up the case."[29] Shortly, Russell Means led a caravan of some thirteen hundred Indians into the small town, announcing from the steps of the courthouse, "We've come here today to put Gordon on the map . . . and if justice is not immediately forthcoming, we're going to take Gordon off the map." The killers, brothers named Melvin and Leslie Hare, were quickly arrested, and a police officer who had covered up for them was suspended. The Hares soon became the first whites in Nebraska history sent to prison for killing an Indian, and "AIM's reputation soared among reservation Indians. What tribal leaders had dared not do to protect their people, AIM had done."[30]

By fall, things had progressed to the point that AIM could collaborate with several other native rights organizations to stage the Trail of Broken Treaties caravan, bringing more than two thousand Indians from reservations and urban areas across the country to Washington, D.C., on the eve of the 1972 presidential election. The idea was to present the incumbent chief executive, Richard M. Nixon, with a twenty-point program redefining the nature of U.S.-Indian relations. The publicity attending the critical timing and location of the action, as well as the large number of Indians involved, were calculated to force serious responses from the administration to each point.[31]

Interior Department officials who had earlier pledged logistical support to caravan participants once they arrived in the capitol reneged on their promises, apparently in the belief that this would cause the group to meekly disperse. Instead, angry Indians promptly took over the BIA headquarters building on 2 November, evicted its staff, and held it for several days. Russell Means, in fine form, captured the front page of the nation's newspapers and the six o'clock news by conducting a press conference in front of the building, while adorned with a makeshift "war club" and a "shield" fashioned from a portrait of Nixon himself.[32]

Desperate to end what had become a major media embarrassment, the Nixon administration agreed to reply formally to the twenty-point program within a month and to provide $66,000 in transportation money immediately, in exchange for a peaceful end to the occupation.[33] The AIM members honored their part of the bargain, leaving the BIA building on 9 November. But, explaining that "Indians have every right to know the details of what's being done to us and to our property," they took with them a vast number of "confidential" files concerning BIA leasing practices, operation of the Indian Health Service (IHS), and so forth. The originals were returned as rapidly as they could be photocopied, a process that required nearly two years to complete.[34]

Technically speaking, the government also honored its end of the deal, providing official—and exclusively negative—responses to the twenty points within the specified timeframe.[35] At the same time, however, it initiated a campaign utilizing federally subsidized Indian "leaders" in an effort to discredit AIM members as "irresponsible . . . renegades, terrorists and self-styled revolutionaries."[36] There is also a strong indication that it was at this point that the Federal Bureau of Investigation was instructed to launch a secret program of its own, one in which AIM's capacity to engage in further political activities of the kind and effectiveness displayed in Washington was to be, in the vernacular of FBI counterintelligence specialists, "neutralized."[37]

Even as this was going on, AIM's focus had shifted back to the Pine Ridge area. At issue was the 23 January 1973 murder of a young Oglala named Wesley Bad Heart Bull by a white man, Darold Schmitz, in the off-reservation village of Buffalo Gap, South Dakota. As in the Yellow Thunder case, local authorities had made no move to press appropriate charges against the killer.[38] At the request of the victim's mother, Sarah, Russell Means called for a demonstration at the Custer County Courthouse, in whose jurisdiction the crime lay. Terming western South Dakota "the Mississippi of the North,"[39] Dennis Banks simultaneously announced a longer-term effort to force abandonment "of the anti-Indian attitudes which result in Indian-killing being treated as a sort of local sport."[40]

The Custer demonstration on 6 February followed a very different course from that of the protest in Gordon a year earlier. An anonymous call had been placed to the main regional newspaper, the *Rapid City Journal*, on the evening of 5 February. The caller, saying he was "with AIM," asked that a notice canceling the action "because of bad weather" be prominently displayed in the paper the following morning. Consequently, relatively few Indians turned out for the protest.[41] Those who did were met by an amalgamated force of police, sheriff's deputies, state troopers, and FBI personnel when they arrived in Custer.[42]

For awhile, there was a tense standoff. Then, a sheriff's deputy manhandled Sarah Bad Heart Bull when she attempted to enter the courthouse. In the mêlée that followed, the courthouse was set ablaze—reportedly, by a police tear gas canister—and the local Chamber of Commerce building was burned to the ground. Banks, Means, and other AIM members, along with Mrs. Bad Heart Bull, were arrested and charged with riot. Banks was eventually convicted and sentenced to three years imprisonment and became a fugitive; Sarah Bad Heart Bull served five months of a one-to-five-year sentence. Her son's killer never spent one day in jail.[43]

Wounded Knee

Meanwhile, on Pine Ridge, tensions were running extraordinarily high. The point of contention was an escalating conflict between the tribal administration headed by Richard "Dickie" Wilson, installed on the reservation with federal support in 1972, and a large body of reservation traditionals who objected to Wilson's nepotism and other abuses of his position.[44] Initially, Wilson's opponents had sought redress of their grievances through the BIA. The BIA responded by providing a $62,000 grant to Wilson for purposes of establishing a Tribal Ranger Group—a paramilitary entity reporting exclusively to Wilson, which soon began calling itself Guardians of the Oglala Nation (GOONs)—with which to physically intimidate the opposition.[45] The reason underlying this federal largess appears to have been the government's desire that Wilson sign an instrument transferring title of a portion of the reservation known as the Sheep Mountain Gunnery Range—secretly known to be rich in uranium and molybdenum—to the U.S. Forest Service.[46]

In any event, forming the Oglala Sioux Civil Rights Organization (OSCRO), the traditionals next attempted to obtain relief through the Justice Department and the FBI. When this, too, failed to bring results, they set out to impeach Wilson, obtaining signatures of more eligible voters on their petitions than had cast ballots for him in the first place. The BIA countered by naming Wilson himself to chair the impeachment proceedings, and the Justice Department dispatched a sixty-five-member Special Operations Group (SOG, a large SWAT unit) of U.S. marshals to ensure that "order" was maintained during the travesty. Then, on the eve of the hearing, Wilson ordered the arrest and jailing of several members of the tribal council he felt might vote for his removal. Predictably, when the impeachment tally was taken on 23 February 1973, the incumbent was retained in office. Immediately thereafter, he announced a reservationwide ban on political meetings.[47]

Defying the ban, the traditionals convened a round-the-clock emergency meeting at the Calico Hall, near the village of Oglala, in an effort to determine their next move. On 26 February, the Oglala elders sent a messenger to the newly established AIM headquarters in nearby Rapid City to request that Russell Means meet with them. One of the elders, Ellen Moves Camp, later said, "We decided we needed the American Indian Movement in here. . . . All of our older people from the reservation helped make that decision. . . . This is what we needed, a little more push. Most of the reservation believes in AIM, and we're proud to have them with us."[48] Means arrived on the morning of the 27 February, then drove on to the village of Pine Ridge, seat of the reservation government, to try to negotiate some sort of resolution with Wilson. For his trouble, he was physically assaulted by GOONs in the parking lot of the tribal administration building.[49] By then, Dennis Banks and a number of other AIM members had arrived at the Calico Hall. During subsequent meetings, it was decided by the elders that they needed to draw public attention to the situation on the reservation. For this purpose, a two-hundred-person AIM contingent was sent to the symbolic site of Wounded Knee to prepare for an early morning press conference; a much smaller group was sent back to Rapid City to notify the media and to guide reporters to Wounded Knee at the appropriate time.[50]

The intended press conference never occurred because, by dawn, Wilson's GOONs had established roadblock on all four routes leading into (or out of) the tiny hamlet. During the morning, these positions were reinforced by uniformed BIA police, then by elements of the marshals' SOG unit, and then by FBI "observers." As this was going on, the AIM members in Wounded Knee began the process of arming themselves from the local Gildersleeve Trading Post and building defensive positions.[51] By afternoon, Gen. Alexander Haig, military liaison to the Nixon White House, had dispatched two special warfare experts—Col. Volney Warner of the 82d Airborne Division, and Col. Jack Potter of the 6th Army—to the scene.[52]

Documents later subpoenaed from the Pentagon revealed Colonel Potter directed the employment of 17 APCs [tanklike armored personnel carriers], 130,000 rounds of M-16 ammunition, 41,000 rounds of M-40 high explosive [for the M-79 grenade launchers he also provided], as well as helicopters, Phantom jets, and personnel. Military officers, supply sergeants, maintenance technicians, chemical officers, and medical teams [were provided on site]. Three hundred miles to the south, at Fort Carson, Colorado, the Army had billeted a fully uniformed assault unit on twenty-four hour alert.[53]

Over the next seventy-one days, the AIM perimeter at Wounded Knee was placed under siege. The ground cover was burned away for roughly a quarter-mile around the AIM position as part of the federal attempt to staunch the flow of supplies—food, medicine, and ammunition—backpacked in to the Wounded Knee defenders at night; at one point, such material was airdropped by a group of supporting pilots.[54] More than 500,000 rounds of military ammunition were fired into AIM's jerry-rigged "bunkers" by federal forces, killing two Indians—an Apache named Frank Clearwater and Buddy Lamont, an Oglala—and wounding several others.[55] As many as thirteen more people may have been killed by roving GOON patrols, their bodies secretly buried in remote locations around the reservation, while they were trying to carry supplies through federal lines.[56]

At first, the authorities sought to justify what was happening by claiming that AIM had "occupied" Wounded Knee and that the movement had taken several hostages in the process.[57] When the latter allegation was proven to be false, a press ban was imposed, and official spokespersons argued that the use of massive force was needed to "quell insurrection." Much was made of two federal casualties who were supposed to have been seriously injured by AIM gunfire.[58] In the end, it was Dickie Wilson who perhaps summarized the situation most candidly when he informed reporters that the purpose of the entire exercise was to see to it that "AIM dies at Wounded Knee."[59]

Despite Wilson's sentiments—and those of FBI senior counterintelligence specialist Richard G. Held, expressed in a secret report prepared at the request of his superiors early in the siege[60]—an end to the standoff was finally negotiated for 7 May 1973. AIM's major condition, entered in behalf of the Pine Ridge traditionals and agreed to by government representatives, was that a federal commission would meet with the chiefs to review U.S. compliance with the terms of the 1868 Fort Laramie Treaty with the Lakota, Cheyenne, and Arapaho nations.[61] The idea was to generate policy recommendations as to how the United States might bring itself into line with its treaty obligations. A White House delegation did, in fact, meet with the elders at the home of Chief Frank Fools Crow, near the reservation town of Manderson, on 17 May. The delegates' mission, however, was to stonewall all efforts at meaningful discussion.[62] They promised a follow-up meeting on 30 May but never returned.[63]

On other fronts, the authorities were demonstrating a similar vigor. Before the first meeting at Fools Crow's house, the FBI had made 562 arrests of those who had been involved in defending Wounded Knee.[64] Russell Means was in jail awaiting release on $150,000 bond; OSCRO leader Pedro Bissonette was held against $152,000; AIM leaders Stan Holder and Leonard Crow Dog were held against $32,000 and $35,000, respectively. Scores of others were being held pending the posting of lesser sums.[65] By the fall of 1973, agents had amassed some 316,000 separate investigative file classifications on those who had been inside Wounded Knee.[66]

This allowed federal prosecutors to obtain 185 indictments over the next several months (Means alone was charged with thirty-seven felonies and three misdemeanors).[67] In 1974, AIM and the traditionals used the 1868 treaty as a basis on which to challenge in federal court the U.S. government's jurisdiction over Pine Ridge; however, the trials of the "Wounded Knee leadership" went forward.[68] Even after the FBI's and the prosecution's willingness to subvert the judicial process became so blatantly obvious that U.S. District Judge Fred Nichol was compelled to dismiss all charges against Banks and Means, cases were still pressed against Crow Dog, Holder, Carter Camp, Madonna Gilbert, Lorelei DeCora, and Phyllis Young.[69]

The whole charade resulted in a meager fifteen convictions, all of them on such paltry offenses as trespass and "interference with postal inspectors in performance of their lawful duties."[70] Still, in the interim, the virtual entirety of AIM's leadership was tied up in a seemingly endless series of arrests, incarcerations, hearings, and trials. Similarly, the great bulk of the movement's fundraising and organizing capacity was diverted into posting bonds and mounting legal defenses for those indicted.[71]

On balance, the record suggests a distinct probability that the post–Wounded Knee prosecutions were never seriously intended to result in convictions at all. Instead, they were designed mainly to serve the time-honored—and utterly illegal—expedient of "disrupting, misdirecting, destabilizing or otherwise neutralizing" a politically objectionable group.[72] There is official concurrence with this view: As army counterinsurgency specialist Volney Warner framed matters at the time, "AIM's best leaders and most militant members are under indictment, in jail or warrants are out for their arrest. . . . [Under these conditions] the government can win, even if nobody goes to [prison]."[73]

The Reign of Terror

While AIM's "notables" were being forced to slog their way through the courts, a very different form of repression was being visited upon the movement's rank-and-file membership and the grassroots traditionals of Pine Ridge. During the three-year period beginning with the siege of Wounded Knee, at least sixty-nine members and supporters of AIM died violently on the reservation.[74] During the same period, nearly 350 others suffered serious physical assault. Overall, the situation on Pine Ridge was such that, by 1976, the U.S. Commission on Civil Rights was led to describe it as a "reign of terror."[75]

Even if only documented political deaths are counted, the yearly murder rate on the Pine Ridge Reservation between 1 March 1973 and 1 March 1976 was 170 per 100,000. By comparison, Detroit, the reputed "murder capital of the United States," had a rate of 20.2 per 100,000 in 1974. The U.S. average was 9.7 per 100,000. In a nation of two hundred million persons, the national murder rate comparable with that on Pine Ridge between 1973 and 1976 would have left 340,000 persons dead for political reasons alone in one year, 1.32 million in three years. The political murder rate at

Pine Ridge was almost equivalent to that in Chile during the three years after a military coup supported by the United States killed President Salvador Allende.[76]

Despite the fact that eyewitnesses identified the assailants in twenty-one of these homicides, the FBI—which maintains preeminent jurisdiction over major crimes on all American Indian reservations—did not manage to get even one of the killers convicted.[77] In many cases, the bureau undertook no active investigation of the murder of an AIM member or supporter.[78] In others, people associated with the victims were falsely arrested as the perpetrators.[79]

When queried by reporters in 1975 as to the reason for his office's abysmal record in investigating murders on Pine Ridge, George O'Clock, agent in charge of the FBI's Rapid City resident agency—under whose operational authority the reservation falls most immediately—replied that he was "too short of manpower" to assign agents to such tasks.[80] O'Clock neglected to mention that, at the time, he had at his disposal the highest sustained ratio of agents to citizens enjoyed by any FBI office in the history of the bureau.[81] He also omitted the fact that the same agents who were too busy to look into the murders of AIM people appear to have had unlimited time to undertake the previously mentioned investigations of the AIM activists. Plainly, O'Clock's pat explanation was and remains implausible.

A far more likely scenario begins to take shape when it is considered that, in each instance where there were eyewitness identifications of the individuals who had killed an AIM member or supporter, those identified were known GOONs.[82] The FBI's conspicuous inability to apprehend murderers on Pine Ridge may thus be explained not by the incompetence of its personnel but by the nature of its relationship to the killers. In effect, the GOONs seem to have functioned under a more-or-less blanket immunity from prosecution provided by the FBI so long as they focused their lethal attentions on targets selected by the bureau. Put another way, it appears that the FBI used the GOONs as a surrogate force against AIM on Pine Ridge in precisely the same manner that Latin American death squads have been utilized by the CIA to destroy the opposition in countries like Guatemala, El Salvador, and Chile.[83]

The roots of the FBI/GOON connection can be traced back at least as far as 23 April 1973, when U.S. Marshals Service Director Wayne Colburn, driving from Pine Ridge village to Wounded Knee, was stopped at what the Wilsonites referred to as "the Residents' Roadblock." One of the GOONs manning the position, vocally disgruntled with what he called the "soft line" taken by the Justice Department in dealing with AIM, leveled a shotgun at the head of Colburn's passenger, Solicitor General Kent Frizzell. Colburn was forced to draw his own weapon before the man would desist. Angered, Colburn drove back to Pine Ridge and dispatched a group of his men to arrest everyone at the roadblock. When the marshals arrived at the Pennington County Jail in Rapid City with those arrested, however, they found an FBI man waiting with instructions to release the GOONs immediately.[84]

By this time, Dickie Wilson himself had reestablished the roadblock, using a fresh crew of GOONs. Thoroughly enraged at this defiance, Colburn assembled another group of marshals and prepared to make arrests. Things had progressed to the point of a "High Noon" style showdown when a helicopter appeared, quickly landing on the blacktop road near the would-be combatants. In it was FBI counterintelligence ace Richard G. Held, who informed Colburn that he had received instructions "from the highest level" to ensure that no arrests would be made and that "the roadblock stays where it is."[85]

Humiliated and increasingly concerned for the safety of his own personnel in a situation where the FBI was openly siding with a group hostile to them, Colburn ordered his men to disarm GOONs whenever possible.[86] Strikingly, though, when the marshals impounded the sort of weaponry the Wilsonites had up until then been using—conventional deer rifles, World War II surplus M-1s, shotguns, and other firearms normally found in a rural locality—the same GOONs began to reappear sporting fully automatic military-issue M-16s and well stocked with ammunition.[87]

The Brewer Revelations

It has always been the supposition of those aligned with AIM that the FBI provided such hardware to Wilson's GOONs. The bureau and its apologists, of course, have pointed to the absence of concrete evidence with which to confirm the allegation and have consistently denied any such connection, charging those referring to it with journalistic or scholarly "irresponsibility."[88]

Not until the early 1990s, with publication of extracts from an interview with former GOON commander Duane Brewer, was AIM's premise borne out.[89] The one-time death squad leader makes it clear that the FBI provided him and his men not only with weaponry but with ample supplies of armor-piercing ammunition, hand grenades, "det cord" and other explosives, communications gear, and additional paraphernalia.[90] Agents would drop by his house, Brewer maintains, to provide key bits of field intelligence that allowed the GOONs to function in a more efficient manner than might otherwise have been the case. And, perhaps most important, agents conveyed the plain message that members of the death squad would enjoy virtual immunity from federal prosecution for anything they did, so long as it fell within the realm of repressing dissidents on the reservation.[91]

Among other murders which Brewer clarifies in his interview is that of Jeanette Bissonette, a young woman shot to death in her car as she sat at a stop sign in Pine Ridge village at about one o'clock on the morning of 27 March 1975. The FBI has insisted all along, for reasons that remain mysterious, that it is "probable" Bissonette was assassinated by AIM members.[92] Brewer, on the other hand, explains, on the basis of firsthand knowledge, that the killing was "a mistake" on the part of his execution team, which mistook Bissonette's vehicle for that of area resistance leader Ellen Moves Camp.[93]

It is important to note that, at the same time that he functioned as a GOON leader, Duane Brewer also was second-in-command of the BIA police on Pine Ridge. His police boss, Delmar Eastman—primary liaison between the police and the FBI—was simultaneously in charge of all GOON operations on the reservation.[94] In total, it is reliably estimated that somewhere between one-third and one-half of all BIA police personnel on Pine Ridge between 1972 and 1976 moonlighted as GOONs. Those who did not become directly involved covered for their colleagues who did, or at least kept their mouths shut about the situation.[95]

Obviously, whatever small hope AIM and the Oglala traditionals might have held for help from local law enforcement quickly disappeared under such circumstances.[96] In effect, the police were the killers, their crimes not only condoned but, for all practical intents and purposes, commanded and controlled by the FBI. Other federal agencies did no more than issue largely uncirculated reports confirming that the bloodbath was, in fact, occurring.[97] "Due process" on Pine Ridge during the crucial period was effectively nonexistent.

The Oglala Firefight

By the spring of 1975, with more than forty of their number already dead, it had become apparent to the Pine Ridge resisters that they had been handed a choice of either acquiescing to the federal agenda or being annihilated. All other alternatives, including a 1974 electoral effort to replace Dickie Wilson with AIM leader Russell Means, had been met by fraud, force, and unremitting violence.[98] Those who wished to continue the struggle and survive were therefore compelled to adopt a posture of armed self-defense. Given that many of the traditionals were elderly and thus could not reasonably hope to defend themselves alone, they asked AIM to provide physical security for them. Defensive encampments were quickly established at several key locations around the reservation.[99]

For its part, the FBI seems to have become increasingly frustrated at the capacity of the dissidents to absorb punishment and at the consequent failure of its own counterinsurgency campaign to force submission. Internal FBI documents suggest that the coordinators of the Pine Ridge operation had come to desire some sensational event that might serve to justify, in the public mind, a sudden introduction of the kind of overwhelming force that would break the back of the resistance once and for all.[100]

Apparently selected for this purpose was a security camp set up by the Northwest AIM group at the request of traditional elders Harry and Cecilia Jumping Bull on their property along Highway 18, a few miles south of the village of Oglala. During the early evening of 25 June 1975, two agents, Ron Williams and Jack Coler, escorted by a BIA policeman (and known GOON) named Robert Eccoffey, entered the Jumping Bull compound. They claimed to be attempting to serve an arrest warrant on a seventeen-year-old Lakota AIM supporter named Jimmy Eagle on spurious charges of kidnapping and aggravated assault.[101]

Told by residents that Eagle was not there and had not been seen for weeks, the agents and their escort left. On Highway 18, however, the agents accosted three young AIM members—Mike Anderson, Norman Charles, and Wilfred "Wish" Draper—who were walking back to camp after taking showers in Oglala. The agents drove the young men to the police headquarters in Pine Ridge village and interrogated them for more than two hours. As the men reported when they finally returned to the Jumping Bulls' house, no questions had been asked about Jimmy Eagle. Instead, the agents had wanted to know how many men of fighting age were in the camp, what sort of weapons they possessed, and so on. Thus alerted that something bad was about to happen, the Northwest AIM contingent put out an urgent call for support from the local AIM community.[102]

At about eleven o'clock the following morning, 26 June, Williams and Coler returned to the Jumping Bull property. Driving past the compound of residences, they moved down into a shallow valley, stopped, exited their cars in an open area, and began to fire in the general direction of the AIM encampment in a treeline along White Clay Creek.[103] Shortly, they began to take a steadily growing return fire, not only from the treeline, but from the houses above. At about this point, agent J. Gary Adams and BIA police officer/GOON Glenn Two Birds attempted to come to Williams's and Coler's aid. Unexpectedly taking fire from the direction of the houses, they retreated to the ditch beside Highway 18.[104]

Some 150 SWAT-trained BIA police and FBI personnel were prepositioned in the immediate area when the firefight began. This, especially when taken in combination with the fact that more than two hundred additional FBI SWAT personnel were on alert awaiting word to proceed post haste to Pine Ridge from Minneapolis, Milwaukee, and Quantico, Virginia, raises the probability that Williams and Coler were actually assigned to provoke an exchange of gunfire with the AIM members on the Jumping Bull land.[105] The plan seems to have been that they would then be immediately supported by the introduction of overwhelming force, the Northwest AIM group would be destroyed, and the FBI would be afforded the pretext necessary to launch an outright invasion of Pine Ridge.[106]

A number of local AIM members had rallied to the call to come to the Jumping Bulls' home. Hence, instead of encountering the eight AIM shooters they anticipated, the two agents encountered about thirty, and they were cut off from their erstwhile supporters.[107] While the BIA police, reinforced by GOONs, put up roadblocks to seal off the area, and the FBI agents on hand were deployed as snipers, no one made a serious effort to get to Williams and Coler until 5:50 P.M. By then, they had been dead for some time, along with a young Coeur D'Alene AIM member, Joe Stuntz Killsright, killed by FBI sniper Gerard Waring as he attempted to depart the compound.[108] Except for Killsright, all the AIM participations had escaped across country.

By nightfall, hundreds of agents equipped with everything from APCs to Vietnam-style Huey helicopters had begun arriving on the reservation.[109] The next morning, Tom Coll, an FBI "public information specialist" imported for the purpose, convened a press conference in Oglala—the media was barred from the firefight site itself—in which he reported that the dead agents had been "lured into an ambush" by AIM, attacked with automatic weapons from a "sophisticated bunker complex," dragged wounded from their cars, stripped of their clothing, and then executed in cold blood while one of them pleaded with his killer(s) to spare him because he had a wife and children. Each agent, Coll asserted, had been "riddled with 15–20 bullets."[110]

Every word of this was false, as Coll well knew—the FBI had been in possession of both the agents' bodies and the ground on which they were killed for nearly eighteen hours before he made his statements—and the report was retracted in full by FBI Director Clarence Kelley at a press conference conducted in Los Angeles a week later.[111] By then, however, a barrage of sensational media coverage had "sensitized" the public to the need for a virtually unrestricted application of force against the "mad dogs of AIM." Correspondingly, the bureau was free to run air assaults and massive sweeping operations on Pine Ridge—complete with the wholesale use of no-knock searches and John Doe warrants—for the next three months.[112] By the end of that period, its mission had largely been accomplished.[113] In the interim, on 27 July 1975, given the preoccupation of all concerned parties with the FBI's literal invasion of Pine Ridge, it was finally determined that the time was right for Dickie Wilson to sign a memorandum transferring the Gunnery Range to the federal government. On 2 January 1976, a more formal instrument was signed, and in the spring Congress passed a public law assuming U.S. title over this portion of Oglala territory.[114]

The Case of Leonard Peltier

It is unlikely that the FBI intended that its two agents be killed during the Oglala firefight. Once Coler and Williams were dead, however, the bureau capitalized on their fate, not only as the medium through which to pursue its anti-AIM campaign with full ferocity, but as a mechanism with which to block an incipient congressional probe into what the FBI had been doing on Pine Ridge. The latter took the form of a sympathy play: Bureau officials pleaded that the "natural" emotional volatility engendered among their agents by the deaths made it "inopportune" to proceed with the investigation at the present time. Congress responded on 3 July 1975 by postponing the scheduling of preliminary interviews, a delay that has become permanent.[115]

Still, with two agents dead, it was crucial for the bureau's image that someone be brought directly to account. To fill this bill, four names were selected from the list of thirty shooters that field investigators had concluded were participants in the exchange. Targeted were a pair of Anishinabe/Lakota cousins, Leonard Peltier and Bob Robideau, and Darrelle "Dino" Butler, a Tuni, all heads of Northwest AIM. Also included was Jimmy Eagle, whose name seems to have appeared out of expediency, since the bureau claimed Williams and Coler were looking for him in the first place (all charges against him were later simply dropped, without investiture of discernible prosecutorial effort).[116]

Butler and Robideau, captured early on, were tried first as codefendants, separate from Peltier.[117] The latter, having managed to avoid a trap set for him in Oregon, had found sanctuary in the remote encampment of Cree leader Robert Smallboy, in northern Alberta.[118] By the time he was apprehended, extradited via a fraudulent proceeding involving the presentation to a Canadian court of an "eyewitness" affidavit from a psychotic Lakota woman named Myrtle Poor Bear, and docketed in the United States, the prosecution of his cohorts was ready to begin.[119] Peltier was thus scheduled to be tried later and alone.

During the Butler/Robideau trial, conducted in Cedar Rapids, Iowa, in the summer of 1976, the government's plan to turn the defendants—and AIM itself—into examples of the price of resistance began to unravel. Despite the calculated ostentation with which the FBI prepared to secure the judge and jurors from "AIM's potential for violence" and another media blitz designed to convince the public that Butler and Robideau were part of a vast "terrorist conspiracy," the carefully selected all-white midwestern panel of jurors was unconvinced.[120] After William Muldrow of the U.S. Commission on Civil Rights testified for the defense regarding the FBI-fostered reign of terror on Pine Ridge and Director Kelley himself admitted under oath that he knew of nothing that might support many of the bureau's harsher characterizations of AIM, the jury voted to acquit on 16 July 1976.[121]

The "not guilty" verdict was based on the jury's assessment that although both defendants acknowledged firing at the agents and Robideau admitted that he had, in fact, hit them both,[122] they had acted in self-defense. Jury foreman Robert Bolin later recounted that, under the conditions described by credible witnesses, "we felt that any reasonable person would have reacted the same way when the agents came in there shooting." Besides, Bolin continued, their personal observations of the behavior of governmental representatives during the trial had convinced most jury members that "it was the government, not the defendants or their movement, which was dangerous."[123]

Although the Cedar Rapids jury had essentially determined that Coler and Williams had not been murdered, the FBI and federal prosecutors opted to proceed against Peltier. In a pretrial conference, they analyzed what had "gone wrong" in the Butler/Robideau case and, in a report dated 20 July 1976, concluded that among the problems encountered was the fact that the defendants had been allowed to present a self-defense argument and their lawyers had been permitted "to call and question witnesses" and subpoena government documents.[124] They then removed the Peltier trial from the docket of Cedar Rapids Judge Edward McManus and reassigned it to another, Paul Benson, whom they felt would be more amenable to their view.[125]

When Peltier was brought to trial in Fargo, North Dakota, on 21 March 1977, Benson ruled inadmissible virtually everything presented by the defense at Cedar Rapids, including the Butler/Robideau trial transcript itself.[126] Prosecutors then presented a case against Peltier that was precisely the opposite of what they—and their FBI witnesses—had presented in the earlier trial.[127] A chain of circumstantial evidence was constructed, often through fabricated physical evidence,[128] perjury,[129] and demonstrably suborned testimony,[130] to create a plausible impression among jurors—again white midwesterners—that the defendant was guilty.

Following a highly emotional closing presentation by assistant prosecutor Lynn Crooks, in which he waved color photos of the agents' bloody bodies and graphically described the "cold-bloodedness" with which "Leonard Peltier executed these two wounded and helpless human beings," the jury voted on 18 April, after only six hours of deliberation, to convict on both counts of first-degree murder.[131] Bensen then sentenced Peltier to serve two consecutive life terms in prison, and the prisoner was transported straightaway to the federal "super-maximum" facility at Marion, Illinois.[132]

Almost immediately, an appeal was filed on the basis of FBI misconduct and multiple judicial errors on Bensen's part. The matter was considered by a three-member panel of the 8th Circuit Court—composed of Judges William Webster, Donald Ross, and Gerald Heaney—during the spring of 1978. Judge Webster wrote the opinion on behalf of his colleagues, finding that, although the record revealed numerous reversible errors on the part of the trial judge and many "unfortunate misjudgments" by the FBI, the conviction would be allowed to stand.[133] By the time the document was released, Webster was no longer there to answer for it. He had moved on to a new position as director of the FBI. On 12 February 1979, the U.S. Supreme Court declined, without stating a reason, to review the lower court's decision.[134]

Undeterred, Peltier's attorneys had already filed a suit under the Freedom of Information Act (FOIA) to force disclosure of FBI documents withheld from the defense at trial. When the paperwork, more than twelve thousand pages of investigative material, was finally produced in 1981, they began the tedious process of indexing and reviewing it.[135] Finding that the bureau had suppressed ballistics reports that directly contradicted what had been presented at trial, they filed a second appeal in 1982.[136] This led to an evidentiary hearing and oral arguments in 1984, during which the FBI's chief ballistics expert, Evan Hodge, was caught in the act of perjuring himself,[137] and Lynn Crooks was forced to admit that the government "really has no idea who shot those agents."[138]

Crooks then attempted to argue that it did not matter anyway, because Peltier had been convicted of "aiding and abetting in the murders rather than of the murders themselves."[139] This time, the circuit court panel—now composed of Judges Heaney and Ross, as well as John Gibson—took nearly a year to deliberate. On 11 October 1986, they finally delivered an opinion holding that the content of Crooks's own closing argument to the jury, among many other factors, precluded the notion that Peltier had been tried for aiding and abetting. They also concluded that the circumstantial ballistics case presented by the prosecution at trial was hopelessly undermined by evidence even then available to the FBI.[140] Still, they refused to reverse Peltier's conviction, because "[w]e recognize that there is evidence in this record of improper conduct on the part of some FBI agents, but we are reluctant to impute even further improprieties to them" by remanding the matter to trial.[141] On 5 October 1987, the Supreme Court once again refused to review the lower court's decision.[142] Most recently, a third appeal, argued on the basis of habeas corpus (If Peltier was never tried for aiding and abetting, and if the original case against him no longer really exists, then why is he in prison?) was filed. In November 1992, the 8th Circuit, without ever really answering these questions, allowed his "conviction" to stand. The matter remains pending before the Supreme Court, but that august body is expected to decline once again to review the matter.

Aftermath

The government repression of AIM during the mid-1970s had the intended effect of blunting the movement's cutting edge. After 1977, events occurred in fits and starts rather than within a sustained drive. AIM's core membership, those who were not dead or in prison, scattered to the winds; many, like Wounded Knee security head Stan Holder, sought other avenues into which to channel their activism.[143] Others, exhausted and intimidated by the massive violence directed against them, "retired" altogether from active politics.[144] Among the remainder, personal, political, and intertribal antagonisms—often exacerbated by the rumors spread by federal provocateurs—instilled a deep and lasting factional fragmentation.[145]

In 1978, Dennis Banks, occupying the unique status in California of having been officially granted sanctuary by one state of the union against the extradition demands of another, sought to renew Indian activism by organizing what he called the "Longest Walk."[146] To some extent replicating, on foot, the Trail of Broken Treaties caravan of 1972, the Walk succeeded in its immediate objective: The walkers made it from Alcatraz Island—selected as a point of departure because of the importance of the 1969–71 occupation in the formation of AIM—to Washington, D.C., presenting a powerful manifesto to the Carter administration in July.[147] But there was no follow-up, and the momentum was quickly lost.

Much hope was placed in the formation of the Leonard Peltier Defense Committee (LPDC) the same year, and, for a time, it seemed as though it might serve as a kind of sparkplug re-energizing the movement as a whole.[148] However, with the 12 February 1979 murder of AIM chair John Trudell's entire family on the Duck Valley Reservation in Nevada, apparently as a deterrent to the effectiveness of Trudell's fiery oratory, events took an opposite tack.[149] The result was the abolition of all national officer positions in AIM: "These titles do nothing but provide a ready-made list of priority targets for the feds," as Trudell put it at the time.[150] The gesture completed a trend against centralization which had begun with the dissolution of AIM's national office at the time Banks went underground in 1975, a fugitive from sentencing after his conviction on charges stemming from the Custer Courthouse confrontation.[151]

In 1979 and 1980, large-scale "survival gatherings" were held outside Rapid City in an attempt to bring together Indian and non-Indian activists in collaborative opposition to uranium mining and other corporate "development" of the Black Hills.[152] An ensuing organization, the Black Hills Alliance (BHA), achieved momentary national prominence but petered out after the demise of domestic uranium production in the early 1980s dissolved several of the more pressing issues it confronted.[153]

Meanwhile, Russell Means, fresh out of prison, launched a related effort in 1981, occupying an 880-acre site in the Black Hills to establish a "sustainable, alternative, demonstration community" and "to initiate the physical reoccupation of Paha Sapa by the Lakota people and our allies." The occupation of Wincanyan Zi Tiyospaye (Yellow Thunder Camp), named in memory of Raymond Yellow Thunder, lasted until 1985.[154] By that time, its organizers had obtained what on its face was a landmark judicial opinion from a federal district judge: Not only did the Yellow Thunder occupiers have every right to do what they were doing, the judge decreed, but the Lakota—and other Indians as well—are entitled to view entire geographic areas such as the Black Hills, rather than merely specific sites within them, to be of sacred significance.[155] The emergent victory was gutted, however, by the Supreme Court's controversial "G-O Road decision" in 1988.[156]

Elsewhere, an AIM security camp was established on Navajo land near Big Mountain, Arizona, during the mid-1980s to support the traditional Diné elders of that area in their resistance to forced relocation.[157] It is still being maintained today. Similarly, AIM contingents became involved in the early 1990s in providing physical security to Western Shoshone resisters to forced removal from their land in Nevada.[158] Comparable scenarios have been played out in places as diverse as northern Minnesota and Wisconsin, Oregon, California, Oklahoma, Illinois, Florida, Georgia, Nebraska, Alaska, and upstate New York. The issues involved have been as wide ranging as the localities in which they have been confronted.

Another potential bright spot that ultimately was eclipsed was the International Indian Treaty Council (IITC). Formed at the request of the Lakota elders in 1974 to "carry the message of indigenous people into the community of nations" and to serve more generally as "AIM's international arm," it had, by August 1977, gotten off to a brilliant start, playing a key role in bringing representatives of ninety-eight native groups throughout the Americas together in an unprecedented convocation before the United Nations Commission on Human Rights. This led directly to the establishment of a formal Working Group on Indigenous Populations—mandated to draft a Universal Declaration of the Rights of Indigenous Peoples for incorporation into international law by 1992—under the U.N. Economic and Social Council.[159]

Despite this remarkable early success, the 1981 departure of its original director, Cherokee activist Jimmie Durham, caused the IITC to begin to unravel.[160] By 1986, his successors were widely perceived as using the organization's reputation as a vehicle for personal profit and prestige, aligning themselves for a fee with various nation-state governments against indigenous interests. Allegations also abounded that they were using their de facto diplomatic status as a medium through which to engage in drug trafficking. Regardless of whether such suspicions were well founded, IITC today has been reduced to the stature of a small sectarian corporation, completely divorced from AIM and the traditional milieu that legitimated it, subsisting mainly on donations from the very entities it was created to oppose.[161]

With the imminence of the Columbian Quincentenary celebration, the early 1990s presented opportunities for the revitalization of AIM. Indeed, the period witnessed a more-or-less spontaneous regeneration of autonomous AIM chapters in at least sixteen localities around the country.[162] In Colorado, an escalating series of confrontations with Columbus Day celebrants beginning in 1989 and organized by the state AIM chapter led to the galvanizing of a coalition of some fifty progressive organizations, Indian and non-Indian alike, by 1992.[163] In Denver, the city where Columbus Day was first proclaimed an official holiday, quincentenary activities were stopped in their tracks. Much the same process was evident in San Francisco and, to a lesser extent, in other locations.

Perhaps ironically, the most vicious reaction to the prospect of a resurgent movement came not from the government per se but from a small group in Minneapolis professing itself to be AIM's "legitimate leadership." How exactly it imagined it had attained this exalted position was a bit murky, there having been no AIM general membership conference to sanction the exercise of such authority since 1975. Nonetheless, in July 1993 the clique constituted itself under the laws of the state of Minnesota as National-AIM, Inc., announced the formation of a national board and a central committee, and provided the address of what it described as the AIM National Office.[164] Among the very first acts of this interesting amalgam—which proudly reported it was receiving $4 million per year in federal funding and more than $3 million annually from corporations such as Honeywell—was the issuance of letters "expelling" most of the rest of the movement from itself.[165]

A Legacy

It may be, as John Trudell has said, that "AIM died years ago. It's just that some people don't know it yet."[166] Certainly, the evidence indicates that it is no longer a viable organization. And yet there is another level to this reality, one that has more to do with the spirit of resistance than with tangible form. Whatever else may be said about what AIM was (or is), it must be acknowledged that, as Russell Means contends:

> Before AIM, Indians were dispirited, defeated and culturally dissolving. People were ashamed to be Indian. You didn't see the young people wearing braids or chokers or ribbon shirts in those days. Hell, I didn't wear 'em.

People didn't Sun Dance, they didn't Sweat, they were losing their languages. Then there was that spark at Alcatraz, and we took off. Man, we took a ride across this country. We put Indians and Indian rights smack dab in the middle of the public consciousness for the first time since the so-called Indian Wars. And, of course, we paid a heavy price for that. Some of us are still paying it. But now you see braids on our young people. There are dozens of Sun Dances every summer. You hear our languages spoken again in places they had almost died out. Most important, you find young Indians all over the place who understand that they don't have to accept whatever sort of bullshit the dominant society wants to hand them, that they have the right to fight, to struggle for their rights, that in fact they have an obligation to stand up on their hind legs and fight for their future generations, the way our ancestors did. Now, I don't know about you, but I call that pride in being Indian. And I think that's a very positive change. And I think—no, I know—AIM had a lot to do with bringing that change about. We laid the groundwork for the next stage in regaining our sovereignty and self-determination as nations, and I'm proud to have been a part of that.[167]

To the degree that this is true—and much of it seems very accurate—AIM may be said to have succeeded in fulfilling its original agenda.[168] The impulse of Alcatraz was carried forward into dimensions its participants could not yet envision. That legacy even now is being refashioned and extended by a new generation, as it will be by the next, and the next. The continuity of native North America's traditional resistance to domination was reasserted by AIM in no uncertain terms.

There are other aspects of the AIM legacy, to be sure. Perhaps the most crucial should be placed under the heading of "Lessons Learned." The experience of the American Indian Movement, especially in the mid-1970s, provides what amounts to a textbook exposition of the nature of the society we now inhabit, the lengths to which its government will go to maintain the kinds of domination AIM fought to cast off, and the techniques it uses in doing so. These lessons teach what to expect, and, if properly understood, how to overcome many of the methodologies of repression. The lessons are applicable not simply to American Indians but to anyone whose lot in life is to be oppressed within the American conception of business as usual.[169]

Ultimately, the gift bestowed by AIM is, in part, an apprehension of the fact that the Third World is not something "out there." It is everywhere, including behind the façade of liberal democracy that masks the substance of the United States.[170] It exists on every reservation in the nation, in the teeming ghettos of Brownsville, Detroit, and Compton, in the barrios and migrant fields and sharecropping farms of the Deep South.[171] It persists in the desolation of the Appalachian coal regions. It is there in the burgeoning prison industry of America, warehousing by far the largest incarcerated population on the planet.[172]

The Third World exists in the nation's ever-proliferating, militarized police apparatus. And it is there in the piles of corpses of those—not just AIM members, but Black Panthers, Brown Berets, Puerto Rican independentistas, labor organizers, civil rights workers, and many others—who tried to say "no" and make it stick.[173] It is there in the fate of Malcolm X and Fred Hampton, Mark Clark and Ché Payne, Geronimo ji Jaga Pratt and Alejandina Torres, Susan Rosenberg and Martin Luther King, George Jackson and Ray Luc Lavasseur, Tim Blunk and Reyes Tijerina, Mutulu Shakur and Marilyn Buck, and many others.[174]

To win, it is said, one must know one's enemy. Winning the sorts of struggles these people engaged in is unequivocally necessary if we are to effect a constructive change in the conditions they faced and we continue to face. In this, there are still many lessons to be drawn from the crucible of AIM experience. These must be learned by all of us. They must be learned well. And soon.

NOTES

1. On the fishing rights struggles, see American Friends Service Committee, *Uncommon Controversy: Fishing Rights of the Muckleshoot, Puyallup and Nisqually Indians* (Seattle: University of Washington Press, 1970). On the Alcatraz occupation, see Peter Blue Cloud, ed., *Alcatraz Is Not an Island* (Berkeley, Calif.: Wingbow Press, 1972). Also see Adam Fortunate Eagle (Nordwall), *Alcatraz! Alcatraz! The Indian Occupation of 1969–1971* (Berkeley, Calif.: Heyday Books, 1992).

2. This is not to say that others—notably, members of the Black Panther party—have not suffered severely and often fatally at the hands of official specialists in the techniques of domestic political repression in the United States. The distinction drawn with regard to American Indian activists in this respect is purely proportional. For comprehensive background on the experiences of non-Indians, see Robert Justin Goldstein, *Political Repression in Modern America, 1870 to the Present* (New York: Schenkman Publishing/Two Continents Publishing Group, 1978).

3. Bruce Johansen and Roberto Maestas, *Wasi'chu: The Continuing Indian Wars* (New York: Monthly Review Press, 1979).

4. Counterinsurgency is not a part of law enforcement or intelligence-gathering missions. Rather, it is an integral subpart of low-intensity warfare doctrine and methodology, taught at the U.S. Army's Special Warfare School at Fort Bragg, North Carolina; see Maj. John S. Pustay, *Counterinsurgency Warfare* (New York: The Free Press, 1965); also see Michael T. Klare and Peter Kornbluh, eds., *Low Intensity Warfare: Counterinsurgency, Proinsurgency, and Antiterrorism in the Eighties* (New York: Pantheon Books, 1988). For an illustration of the FBI's use of explicit counterinsurgency terminology to define its anti-Indian operations in 1976, see Ward Churchill and Jim Vander Wall, *The COINTELPRO Papers: Documents from the FBI's Secret Wars against Dissent in the United States* (Boston: South End Press, 1990), 264.

5. U.S. Department of Justice, Commission on Civil Rights, *Events Surround-*

ing Recent Murders on the Pine Ridge Reservation in South Dakota (Denver: Rocky Mountain Regional Office, 31 March 1976).

6. In his then-definitive study of the bureau, Sanford J. Ungar quotes a senior counterintelligence specialist to the effect that "success in this area is not measured in terms of arrests and prosecutions, but in our ability to neutralize our targets' ability to do what they're doing"; *FBI: An Uncensored Look behind the Walls* (Boston: Little, Brown, 1975), 311.

7. On the early days of the Black Panther party, see Gene Marine, *The Black Panthers* (New York: New American Library, 1969). On the beginnings of AIM and its obvious reliance on the Panther model, see Peter Matthiessen, *In the Spirit of Crazy Horse*, 2d ed. (New York: Viking Press, 1991), 34–37.

8. Although AIM was probably the first to attempt to put together a coherent program to challenge the internal colonization of American Indians, it was by no means the first to perceive the native situation in this light. That distinction probably belonged to the Cherokee anthropologist Robert K. Thomas, with his brief but influential essay "Colonialism: Internal and Classic," first published in the 1966–67 issue of *New University Thought*.

9. The United States is constitutionally prohibited, under Article 1, from entering into treaty relations with any entity other than another fully sovereign nation. Senate ratification of a treaty therefore confirms formal U.S. recognition of the unequivocal sovereignty of the other party or parties to the instrument. The texts of 371 ratified treaties between the United States and various indigenous nations appear in Charles J. Kappler, *Indian Treaties, 1778–1883* (New York: Interland Publishing, 1972). The United States suspended such treaty-making by law in 1871 (ch. 120, 16 Stat. 544, 566, now codified at 25 U.S.C. 71), with the provision that "nothing herein contained shall be construed to invalidate or impair the obligation of any treaty heretofore lawfully made with any Indian nation or tribe."

10. Following the findings of the Indian Claims Commission in its 1979 Final Report, an independent researcher has summarized that "about half the land area of the [United States] was purchased by treaty or agreement . . . ; another third of a [billion] acres, mainly in the West, were confiscated without compensation; another two-thirds of a [billion] acres were claimed by the United States without pretense of a unilateral action extinguishing native title"; see Russel Barsh, "Indian Land Claims Policy in the United States," *North Dakota Law Review* 58 (1982): 1–82. The last category mentioned, to which native title is still plainly applicable, amounts to about 35 percent of the forty-eight contiguous states; it should be contrasted to the approximately 2.5 percent of the "lower forty-eight" currently retaining reservation trust status.

11. U.S. Bureau of the Census, *1970 Census of the Population, Subject Report: American Indians* (Washington, D.C.: U.S. Government Printing Office, 1972).

12. U.S. Plenary Power Doctrine is perhaps best articulated in the Supreme Court's 1903 *Lonewolf v. Hitchcock* opinion (187 U.S. 553). The most relevant statutes are the 1885 Major Crimes Act (ch. 341, 24 Stat. 362, 385, now codified at U.S.C. 1153), the 1887 General Allotment Act (ch. 119, 24 Stat. 388, now codified as amended at 25 U.S.C. 331 et seq.), and the Indian Reorganization Act (ch. 576, 48 Stat. 948, now codified at 25 U.S.C. 461-279).

13. On resource distribution, see Michael Garrity, "The U.S. Colonial Empire Is as Close as the Nearest Indian Reservation," in *Trilateralism: The Trilateral Com-*

mission and Elite Planning for World Government, ed. Holly Sklar (Boston: South End Press, 1980), 238–68.

14. See, generally, Joseph G. Jorgensen, ed., *Native Americans and Energy Development* 2 (Cambridge, Mass.: Anthropology Resource Center/Seventh Generation Fund, 1984).

15. See, generally, Roxanne Dunbar Ortiz, ed., *Economic Development in American Indian Reservations* (Albuquerque: Native American Studies Center, University of New Mexico, 1979).

16. Robert K. Thomas, "Colonialism: Classic and Internal," *New University Thought* 4:4 (Winter 1966–67).

17. U.S. Department of Health, Education, and Welfare (DHEW), *A Study of Selected Socio-Economic Characteristics of Ethnic Minorities Based on the 1970 Census, Vol. 3: American Indians* (Washington, D.C.: U.S. Government Printing Office, 1974). It should be noted that the economic and health data pertaining to certain sectors of other U.S. minority populations—inner city blacks, for example, or Latino migrant workers—are very similar to those bearing on American Indians. Unlike these other examples, however, the data on American Indians encompass the condition of the population as a whole.

18. U.S. Bureau of the Census, Population Division, Racial Statistics Branch, *A Statistical Profile of the American Indian Population* (Washington, D.C.: U.S. Government Printing Office, 1974).

19. Dennis J. Banks, speech before the United Lutheran Board, Minneapolis, Minnesota, March 1971.

20. Notable in this respect was the resuscitation of the Lakota Sun Dance, forbidden by the BIA since 1881. In August 1972, AIM members showed up en masse to participate in the ceremony at Crow Dog's Paradise, on the Rosebud Reservation. As the revered Oglala spiritual leader Frank Fools Crow put it in 1980: "Before that, there were only one, two Sun Dances each year. Just a few came, the real traditionals. And we had to hold 'em in secret. After the AIM boys showed up, now there are [Sun Dances] everywhere, right out in the open, too. Nobody hides anymore. Now, they're all proud to be Indian." The same principle pertains to the resurgence of numerous other ceremonies among a variety of peoples.

21. The U.N. component was developed pursuant to the creation of the International Indian Treaty Council (IITC), "AIM's international diplomatic arm," in 1974. Under the directorship of Cherokee activist Jimmie Durham, IITC was responsible for convening the first Assembly of Indigenous Nations of the Western Hemisphere at the U.N. Palace of Nations in Geneva, Switzerland, during the summer of 1977. IITC then became the world's first nongoverning organization (NGO; type-II, consultative) in the U.N. and played a major role in bringing about the establishment of the Working Group on Indigenous Populations—charged with annual review of native grievances and drafting a Universal Declaration of the Rights of Indigenous Peoples—under auspices of the U.N. Economic and Social Council (ECOSOC) in 1981. With Durham's departure from IITC the same year, the organization went into decline. The progressive dynamic it inaugurated, however, is ongoing. See, generally, Glenn T. Morris, "International Law and Politics: Toward a Right to Self-Determination for Indigenous Peoples," in *The State of Native America: Genocide, Colonization and Resistance*, ed. M. Annette Jaimes (Boston: South End Press, 1992), 55–86.

22. The term *National Liberation Movement* is not rhetorical. Rather, it bears a precise meaning under Article 1, Paragraph 4 of Additional Protocol I of the 1949 Geneva Convention. Also see United Nations Resolution 3103 (XXVIII), 12 December 1973.

23. Birgil Kills Straight, mimeographed statement circulated by the Oglala Sioux Civil Rights Organization (Manderson, S.Dak.) during the 1973 siege of Wounded Knee.

24. By the mid-1970s, even elements of the federal government had begun to adopt AIM's emphasis on colonialism to explain the relationship between the United States and American Indians. See, for example, U.S. Commission on Civil Rights, *The Navajo Nation: An American Colony* (Washington, D.C.: U.S. Government Printing Office, September 1975).

25. This remained true until the government's 1993 slaughter of eighty-six Branch Davidians in a single hour near Waco, Texas. The standard text on the 1890 massacre is, of course, Dee Brown's *Bury My Heart at Wounded Knee: An Indian History of the American West* (New York: Holt, Rinehart & Winston, 1970).

26. Robert Burnette with John Koster, *The Road to Wounded Knee* (New York: Bantam Books, 1974), 196.

27. Peter Matthiessen, *In the Spirit of Crazy Horse*, 2d ed. (New York: Viking Press, 1991), 38, 110.

28. Yellow Thunder, burned with cigarettes, was forced to dance nude from the waist down for the entertainment of a crowd assembled in the Gordon American Legion Hall. He was then severely beaten and stuffed, unconscious, into the trunk of a car, where he froze to death. See Rex Weyler, *Blood of the Land: The U.S. Government and Corporate War against the American Indian Movement* (New York: Everest House, 1982), 48. Also see Matthiessen, *In the Spirit of Crazy Horse*, 59–60.

29. Quoted in Weyler, *Blood of the Land*, 49.

30. Alvin M. Josephy, Jr., *Now That the Buffalo's Gone: A Study of Today's American Indian* (New York: Alfred A. Knopf, 1982), 237.

31. The best overall handling of these events, including the complete text of the Twenty Point Program, is Vine Deloria, Jr.'s *Behind the Trail of Broken Treaties: An Indian Declaration of Independence* (New York: Delta Books, 1974).

32. See editors, BIA, *I'm Not Your Indian Anymore* (Rooseveltown, N.Y.: Akwesasne Notes, 1973).

33. The money, in unmarked twenty-, fifty- and hundred-dollar bills, came from a slush fund administered by Nixon's notorious Committee to Reelect the President (CREEP) and was delivered in brown paper bags. The bagmen were administration aids Leonard Garment and Frank Carlucci (later National Security Council chief and CIA director, respectively, under Ronald Reagan).

34. It was from these files that, among other things, the existence of a secret IHS program to perform involuntary sterilizations on American Indian women was first revealed. See Brint Dillingham, "Indian Women and IHS Sterilization Practices," *American Indian Journal* 3:1 (January 1977).

35. The full text of administration response is included in BIA, *I'm Not Your Indian Anymore*.

36. The language is that of Webster Two Hawk, then president of the Rosebud Sioux tribe and the federally funded National Tribal Chairmen's Association. Two Hawk was shortly voted out of both positions by his constituents, replaced as Rose-

bud president by Robert Burnette, an organizer of the Trail of Broken Treaties. See Ward Churchill, "Renegades, Terrorists and Revolutionaries: The Government's Propaganda War against the American Indian Movement," *Propaganda Review* 4 (April 1989).

37. One firm indication of this was the arrest by the FBI of Assiniboine/Lakota activist Hank Adams and Les Whitten, an associate of columnist Jack Anderson, shortly after the occupation. They were briefly charged with illegally possessing government property. The men, neither of whom was an AIM member, were merely acting as go-betweens in returning BIA documents to the federal authorities. The point seems to have been to isolate AIM from its more moderate associations. See Deloria, *Behind the Trail of Broken Treaties*, 59.

38. Although he had stabbed Bad Heart Bull repeatedly in the chest with a hunting knife, Schmitz was charged only with second-degree manslaughter and released on his own recognizance.

39. Don and Jan Stevens, *South Dakota: The Mississippi of the North; or, Stories Jack Anderson Never Told You* (Custer, S.Dak.: self-published pamphlet, 1977).

40. More broadly, AIM's posture was a response to what it perceived as a nationwide wave of murders of Indians by whites. These included not only the murders of Yellow Thunder and Bad Heart Bull but those of a nineteen-year-old Papago named Phillip Celay by a sheriff's deputy in Arizona, an Onondaga Special Forces veteran (and member of the honor guard during the funeral of John F. Kennedy) named Leroy Shenandoah in Philadelphia, and, on 20 September 1972, of Alcatraz leader Richard Oakes near San Francisco. See Ward Churchill and Jim Vander Wall, *Agents of Repression: The FBI's Secret Wars against the Black Panther Party and the American Indian Movement* (Boston: South End Press, 1988), 123.

41. The individual receiving the call was reporter Lynn Gladstone. Such calls are a standard FBI counterintelligence tactic used to disrupt the political organization of targeted groups. See Brian Glick, *War at Home: Covert Action against U.S. Activists and What We Can Do about It* (Boston: South End Press, 1989).

42. A 31 January 1973 FBI teletype delineates the fact that the bureau was already involved in planning the police response to the Custer demonstration. It is reproduced in Churchill and Vander Wall, *The COINTELPRO Papers*, 241.

43. Weyler, *Blood of the Land*, 68–69.

44. The average annual income on Pine Ridge at this time was about $1,000; Cheryl McCall, "Life on Pine Ridge Bleak," *Colorado Daily*, 16 May 1975. Wilson hired his brother Jim to head the tribal planning office at an annual salary of $25,000 plus $15,000 in "consulting fees"; *New York Times*, 22 April 1975. Another brother, George, was hired at a salary of $20,000 to help the Oglala "manage their affairs"; Wilson's wife was named director of the reservation Head Start program at a salary of $18,000; his son "Manny" (Richard Jr.) was placed on the GOON payroll, along with several cousins and nephews; Wilson also upped his own salary from $5,500 per year to $15,500 per year, plus lucrative consulting fees, within his first six months in office; Matthiessen, *In the Spirit of Crazy Horse*, 62. When queried about the propriety of all this, Wilson replied, "There's no law against nepotism"; editors, *Voices from Wounded Knee, 1973* (Rooseveltown, N.Y.: Akwesasne Notes, 1974), 34.

45. In addition to this BIA "seed money," Wilson is suspected of having misappropriated some $347,000 in federal highway improvement funds to meet GOON

payrolls between 1972 and 1975. A 1975 General Accounting Office report indicates that the funds had been expended without any appreciable road repair having been done and that the Wilsonites had kept no books with which to account for this mysterious situation. Nonetheless, the FBI declined to undertake a further investigation of the matter.

46. The Gunnery Range, comprising the northwestern eighth of Pine Ridge, was an area "borrowed" from the Oglala by the War Department in 1942 as a place to train aerial gunners. It was to be returned at the end of World War II, but it never was. By the early 1970s, the Oglala traditionals had begun to agitate heavily for its recovery. The deposits had been secretly discovered in 1971, however, through a technologically elaborate survey and mapping project undertaken jointly by the National Aeronautics and Space Administration (NASA) and a little-known entity called the National Uranium Resource Evaluation Institute (NURE). At that point, the government set out to obtain permanent title over the property; its quid pro quo with Wilson seems to have been his willingness to provide it. See J. P. Gries, *Status of Mineral Resource Information on the Pine Ridge Indian Reservation, S.D.* (Washington, D.C.: BIA Bulletin No. 12, U.S. Department of Interior, 1976). Also see Jacqueline Huber et al., *The Gunnery Range Report* (Pine Ridge, S.Dak.: Office of the Oglala Sioux Tribal President, 1981).

47. *Voices from Wounded Knee*, 17–26.

48. Quoted in Matthiessen, *In the Spirit of Crazy Horse*, 66.

49. Burnette and Koster, *The Road to Wounded Knee*, 74.

50. The action was proposed by OSCRO leader Pedro Bissonette and endorsed by traditional Oglala chiefs Frank Fools Crow, Pete Catches, Ellis Chips, Edgar Red Cloud, Jake Kills Enemy, Morris Wounded, Severt Young Bear, and Everette Catches. See *Voices from Wounded Knee*, 36.

51. Weyler, *Blood of the Land*, 76–78.

52. One of their first actions was to meet with Colonel Vic Jackson, a subordinate of future FEMA head Louis Giuffrida, brought in from California to "consult." Through an entity called the California Civil Disorder Management School, Jackson and Giuffrida had devised a pair of "multi-agency domestic counterinsurgency scenarios," code-named "Garden Plot" and "Cable Splicer," in which the government was interested. Thus there is more than passing indication that what followed at Wounded Knee was, at least in part, a field test of these plans. See Weyler, *Blood of the Land*, 80–81. Also see Ken Lawrence, *The New State Repression* (Chicago: International Network against the New State Repression, 1985).

53. Weyler, *Blood of the Land*, 83. The quantity of M-16 ammunition should actually read 1.3 million rounds. The military also provided state-of-the art communications gear, M-14 sniper rifles and ammunition, "Starlight" night vision scopes and other optical technology, tear gas rounds and flares for M-79 grenade launchers, and field provisions to feed the assembled federal forces. All of this was in flat violation of the Posse Comitatus Act (18 USCS § 1385), which makes it illegal for the government to deploy its military against "civil disturbances." For this reason, Colonels Warner and Potter and the other military personnel they brought in wore civilian clothes at Wounded Knee in an effort to hide their involvement.

54. Bill Zimmerman, *Airlift to Wounded Knee* (Chicago: Swallow Press, 1976).

55. Clearwater was mortally wounded on 17 April 1973 and died on 25 April;

Voices from Wounded Knee, 179. Lamont was hit on 27 April, after being driven from his bunker by tear gas. Federal gunfire then prevented others from reaching him until he died from loss of blood; ibid., 220.

56. Robert Burnette later recounted how, once the siege had ended, Justice Department Solicitor General Kent Frizzell asked his assistance in searching for such graves; Burnette and Koster, *The Road to Wounded Knee*, 248. Also see *Voices from Wounded Knee*, 193.

57. The "hostages" were mostly elderly residents of Wounded Knee: Wilbert A. Reigert (age 86), Girlie Clark (75), Clive Gildersleeve (73), Agnes Gildersleeve (68), Bill Cole (82), Mary Pike (72), and Annie Hunts Horse (78). Others included Guy Fritz (age 49), Jeane Fritz (47), Adrienne Fritz (12), and Father Paul Manhart (46). When South Dakota Senators George McGovern and James Abourezk went to Wounded Knee on 2 March to "bring the hostages out," the supposed captives announced they had no intention of leaving. Instead, they stated that they wished to stay to "protect [their] property from federal forces" and that they considered the AIM people to be the "real hostages in this situation." See Burnette and Koster, *The Road to Wounded Knee*, 227–28.

58. The first federal casualty was an FBI agent named Curtis Fitzpatrick, hit in the wrist by a spent round on 11 March 1973. Interestingly, with his head swathed in bandages, he was evacuated by helicopter before a crowd of reporters assembled to witness the event; Burnette and Koster, *The Road to Wounded Knee*, 237–38. The second, U.S. Marshal Lloyd Grimm, was struck in the back and permanently paralyzed on 23 March. Grimm was, however, facing the AIM perimeter when he was hit. The probability, then, is that he was shot—perhaps unintentionally—by one of Wilson's GOONs, who, at the time, were firing from positions behind those of the marshals; *Voices from Wounded Knee*, 128.

59. Quoted in *Voices from Wounded Knee*, 47.

60. Held was simultaneously serving as head of the FBI's Internal Security Section and as Special Agent in Charge (SAC) of the bureau's Chicago office. He had been assigned the latter position, in addition to his other duties, in order that he might orchestrate a cover-up of the FBI's involvement in the 1969 murders of Illinois Black Panther leaders Fred Hampton and Mark Clark. At the outset of the Wounded Knee siege, he was detached from his SAC position—a very atypical circumstance—and sent to Pine Ridge in order to prepare a study of how the bureau should deal with AIM "insurgents." The result, entitled "FBI Paramilitary Operations in Indian Country"—in which the author argued, among other things, that "shoot to kill" orders should be made standard—is extremely significant in light of subsequent bureau activities on the reservation and Held's own role in them.

61. The terms of the stand-down agreement are covered in ibid., 231. The full text of the treaty may be found in Kappler, *Indian Treaties, 1778–1883*, 594–96.

62. Federal representatives purposely evaded the issue, arguing that they were precluded from responding to questions of treaty compliance because of Congress's 1871 suspension of treaty-making with Indians (Title 25 USC § 71). As Lakota elder Matthew King rejoined, however, the Indians were not asking that a new treaty be negotiated. Rather, they were demanding that U.S. commitments under an existing treaty be honored, a matter that was not only possible under the 1871 act but required by it. See *Voices from Wounded Knee*, 252–54.

63. Instead, a single marshal was dispatched to Fools Crow's home on the ap-

pointed date to deliver to those assembled there a note signed by White House counsel Leonard Garment. The missive stated that "the days of treaty-making with Indians ended in 1871, 102 years ago"; quoted in *Voices from Wounded Knee*, 257–58.

64. U.S. House of Representatives, Committee on the Judiciary, Subcommittee on Civil and Constitutional Rights, *1st Session on FBI Authorization, March 19, 24, 25; April 2 and 8, 1981* (Washington, D.C.: 97th Cong., 2d sess., U.S. Government Printing Office, 1981).

65. Weyler, *Blood of the Land*, 95; Burnette and Koster, *The Road to Wounded Knee*, 253.

66. *1st Session on FBI Authorization.*

67. Ibid. Means was convicted on none of the forty federal charges. Instead, he was finally found guilty in 1977 under South Dakota state law of "criminal syndicalism" and served a year in the maximum security prison at Sioux Falls. Means was, and will remain, the only individual ever convicted under this statute; the South Dakota legislature repealed the law while he was imprisoned. Amnesty International was preparing to adopt him as a "prisoner of conscience" when he was released in 1979; Amnesty International, *Proposal for a Commission of Inquiry into the Effect of Domestic Intelligence Activities on Criminal Trials in the United States of America* (New York: Amnesty International, 1980).

68. For excerpts from the transcripts of the "Sioux sovereignty hearing" conducted in Lincoln, Nebraska, during the fall of 1974, see Roxanne Dunbar Ortiz, ed., *The Great Sioux Nation: Sitting in Judgment on America* (New York/San Francisco: International Indian Treaty Council/Moon Books, 1977).

69. Tried together in the second "leadership trial," Crow Dog, Holder, and Camp were convicted of minor offenses during the spring of 1975. Holder and Camp went underground to avoid sentencing. Crow Dog was granted probation (as were his codefendants when they surfaced) and then placed on charges unrelated to Wounded Knee the following November. Convicted and sentenced to five years, he was imprisoned first in the federal maximum security facility at Lewisburg, Pennsylvania, and then at Leavenworth, Kansas. The National Council of Churches and Amnesty International were preparing to adopt him as a prisoner of conscience when he was released on parole in 1977. See Weyler, *Blood of the Land*, 189; Amnesty International, *Proposal for a Commission of Inquiry* .

70. As a congressional study concluded, this was "a very low rate considering the usual rate of conviction in Federal Courts and a great input of resources in these cases"; *1st Session on FBI Authorization.*

71. This is a classic among the counterintelligence methodologies utilized by the FBI. For example, according to a bureau report declassified by a Senate select committee in 1975, agents in Philadelphia, Pennsylvania, offered as an "example of a successful counterintelligence technique" their use of "any excuse for arrest" as a means of "neutralizing" members of a targeted organization, the Revolutionary Action Movement (RAM), during the summer of 1967. "RAM people," the document went on, "were arrested and released on bail, but they were re-arrested several times until they could no longer make bail." The tactic was recommended for use by other FBI offices to "curtail the activities" of objectionable political groups in their areas. The complete text of this document can be found in Churchill and Vander Wall, *Agents of Repression*, 45–47. More broadly, see U.S. Senate, Select Committee to Study Government Operations with Respect to Intelligence Activities, *Final Re-*

port: *Supplementary Detailed Staff Reports on Intelligence Activities and the Rights of Americans, Book 3* (Washington, D.C.: 94th Cong., 2d sess., U.S. Government Printing Office, 1976).

72. This is the standard delineation of objectives attending the FBI's domestic counterintelligence programs (COINTELPROs); see the document reproduced in Churchill and Vander Wall, The *COINTELPRO Papers*, 92–93.

73. Quoted in Martin Garbus, "General Haig of Wounded Knee," *The Nation*, 9 November 1974.

74. A complete list of those killed and their dates of death is contained in Churchill and Vander Wall, *The COINTELPRO Papers*, 393–94.

75. U.S. Department of Justice, *Events Surrounding Recent Murders on the Pine Ridge Reservation in South Dakota*.

76. Johansen and Maestas, *Wasi'chu*, 83–84.

77. FBI jurisdiction on reservations accrues under the 1885 Major Crimes Act (ch. 341, 24 Stat. 362, 385, now codified at 18 USC 1153).

78. For example, Delphine Crow Dog, sister of AIM's spiritual leader, was beaten unconscious and left to freeze to death in a field on 9 November 1974; AIM member Joseph Stuntz Killsright was killed by a bullet to the head and apparently shot repeatedly in the torso after death on 26 June 1975.

79. Consider the case of brothers Vernal and Clarence Cross, both AIM members, who had car trouble and stopped along the road outside Pine Ridge village on 19 June 1973. Individuals firing from a nearby field hit both men, killing Clarence and severely wounding Vernal. Another bullet struck nine-year-old Mary Ann Little Bear, who was riding in a car driven by her father, traveling in the opposite direction. The bullet hit her in the face, blinding her in one eye. Her father identified three individuals to police and FBI agents as the shooters. None of the three was interrogated. Instead, authorities arrested Vernal Cross in the hospital, charging him with murdering Clarence (the charges were later dropped). No charges were ever filed in the shooting of Mary Ann Little Bear. See Weyler, *Blood of the Land*, 106.

80. Quoted in Johansen and Maestas, *Wasi'chu*, 88. Actually, O'Clock's position fits into a broader bureau policy. "When Indians complain about the lack of investigation and prosecution on reservation crime, they are usually told the Federal government does not have the resources to handle the work"; U.S. Department of Justice, *Report of the Task Force on Indian Matters* (Washington, D.C.: U.S. Government Printing Office, 1975), 42–43.

81. In 1972, the Rapid City Resident Agency was staffed by three agents. This was expanded to eleven in March 1973 and augmented by a ten-member SWAT team shortly thereafter. By the spring of 1975, more than thirty agents were assigned to Rapid City on a long-term basis, and as many as two dozen others were steadily coming and going while performing "special tasks." See Johansen and Maestas, *Wasi'chu*, 93; U.S. Department of Justice, *Report of the Task Force on Indian Matters*, 42–43.

82. In the Clarence Cross murder, for example, the killers were identified as John Hussman, Woody Richards, and Francis Randall, all prominent members of the GOONs. Or again, in the 30 January 1976 murder of AIM supporter Byron DeSersa near the reservation hamlet of Wamblee, at least a dozen people identified GOONs Billy Wilson (Dickie Wilson's younger son), Charles David Winters, Dale Janis, and Chuck Richards among the killers. Indeed, the guilty parties were still on the scene

when two FBI agents arrived. Yet the only person arrested was a witness, an elderly Cheyenne named Guy Dull Knife, because of the vociferousness with which he complained about the agents' inaction. The BIA police, for their part, simply ordered the GOONs to leave town. See U.S. Commission on Civil Rights, *American Indian Issues in South Dakota: Hearing Held in Rapid City, South Dakota, July 27–28, 1978* (Washington, D.C.: U.S. Government Printing Office, 1978), 33.

83. On the CIA's relationship to Latin American death squads, see Penny Lernoux, *Cry of the People: United States Involvement in the Rise of Fascism, Torture, and Murder, and the Persecution of the Catholic Church in Latin America* (New York: Doubleday, 1980).

84. *Voices from Wounded Knee*, 189. Frizzell himself has confirmed the account.

85. Ibid., 190.

86. The directive was issued on 24 April 1973.

87. *Voices from Wounded Knee*, 213; Weyler, *Blood of the Land*, 92–93.

88. See, for example, Athan Theoharis, "Building a Case against the FBI," *Washington Post*, 30 October 1988.

89. Churchill, "Death Squads in America: Confessions of a Government Terrorist," *Yale Journal of Law and Liberation* 3 (1992). The interview was conducted by independent filmmakers Kevin Barry McKiernan and Michelle DuBois several years earlier but not released in transcript form until 1991.

90. *Det cord* is detonation cord, a rope-like explosive often used by the U.S. military to fashion booby traps. Brewer also makes mention of bureau personnel introducing him and other GOONs to civilian right-wingers who provided additional ordnance.

91. Another example of this sort of thing came in the wake of the 27 February 1975 beating and slashing of AIM defense attorney Roger Finzel, his client, Bernard Escamilla, and several associates at the Pine Ridge Airport by a group of GOONs headed by Duane Brewer and Dickie Wilson himself. The event being too visible to be simply ignored, Wilson was allowed to plead guilty to a petty offense carrying a ten-dollar penalty in his own tribal court. Federal charges were then dropped on advice from the FBI—which had spent its investigative time polygraphing the victims rather than their assailants—because pressing them might constitute "double jeopardy"; Churchill and Vander Wall, *Agents of Repression*, 186, 428.

92. At one point, the bureau attempted to implicate Northwest AIM leader Leonard Peltier in the killing. This ploy was abandoned only when it was conclusively demonstrated that Peltier was in another state when the murder occurred; interview with Peltier defense attorney Bruce Ellison, October 1987 (tape on file).

93. Both Moves Camp and Bissonette drove white over dark blue Chevrolet sedans. It appears the killers simply mistook one for the other in the dark. The victim, who was not herself active in supporting AIM, was the sister of OSCRO leader Pedro Bissonette, shot to death under highly suspicious circumstance by BIA police officer cum GOON Joe Clifford on the night of 17 October 1973; Churchill and Vander Wall, *Agents of Repression*, 200–203.

94. Eastman, although a Crow, is directly related to the Dakota family of the same name, made famous by the writer Charles Eastman earlier in the century. Ironically, two of his relatives, sisters Carole Standing Elk and Fern Matthias, purport to be AIM members in California.

95. Churchill, "Death Squads in America," 96.

96. Structurally, the appropriation of the formal apparatus of deploying force possessed by client states for purposes of composing death squads—long a hallmark of CIA covert operations in the Third World—corresponds quite well with the FBI's use of the BIA police on Pine Ridge; see A. J. Languuth, *Hidden Terrors: The Truth about U.S. Police Operations in Latin America* (New York: Pantheon Press, 1978); also see Edward S. Herman, *The Real Terror Network: Terrorism in Fact and Propaganda* (Boston: South End Press, 1982).

97. See, for example, U.S. Department of Justice, *Events Surrounding Recent Murders on the Pine Ridge Reservation in South Dakota.*

98. In late 1973, Means took a majority of all votes cast in the tribal primaries. In the 1974 runoff, however, Wilson retained his presidency by a two-hundred-vote margin. A subsequent investigation by the U.S. Commission on Civil Rights revealed that 154 cases of voter fraud—non-Oglala people being allowed to vote—had occurred. A further undetermined number of invalid votes had been cast by Oglala who did not meet tribal residency requirements. No record had been kept of the number of ballots printed or how and in what numbers they had been distributed. No poll watchers were present in many locations, and those who were present at the others had been appointed by Wilson rather than an impartial third party. There was also significant evidence that pro-Means voters had been systematically intimidated and, in some cases, roughed up by Wilsonites stationed at each polling place; U.S. Commission on Civil Rights, *Report of Investigation: Oglala Sioux Tribe, General Election, 1974* (Denver: Rocky Mountain Regional Office, October 1974). Despite these official findings, the FBI performed no substantive investigation, and the BIA allowed the results of the election to stand; Churchill and Vander Wall, *Agents of Repression*, 190–92.

99. As the Jumping Bulls' daughter Roselyn later put it, "We asked those AIM boys to come help us . . . [defend ourselves against] Dickie Wilson and his goons"; quoted in an unpublished manuscript by researcher Candy Hamilton (copy on file), 3.

100. See, for example, a memorandum from SAC Minneapolis (Joseph Trimbach) to the FBI director, dated 3 June 1975 and captioned "Law Enforcement on the Pine Ridge Indian Reservation," in which Trimbach recommends that armored personnel carriers be used to assault AIM defensive positions.

101. No such warrant existed. When an arrest order was finally issued for Eagle on 9 July 1975, it was for the petty theft of a pair of used cowboy boots from a white ranch hand. Eagle was acquitted even of this when the case was taken to trial in 1976. Meanwhile, George O'Clock's assignment of two agents to pursue an Indian teenager over so trivial an offense at a time when he professed to be too short-handed to investigate the murders of AIM members speaks for itself; Matthiessen, *In the Spirit of Crazy Horse*, 173.

102. Ibid., 156.

103. The agents followed a red pickup truck onto the property. Unbeknownst to them, it was full of dynamite. In the valley, the truck stopped and its occupants got out. Williams and Coler also stopped and got out of their cars. They then began firing toward the pickup, a direction that carried their rounds into the AIM camp, where a number of noncombatant women and children were situated. AIM security then began to fire back. It is a certainty that AIM did not initiate the firefight because, as Bob Robideau later put it, "Nobody in their right mind would start a

gunfight using a truckload of dynamite for cover." Once the agents were preoccupied, the pickup made its escape. Northwest AIM was toying with the idea of using the explosives to remove George Washington's face from the nearby Mount Rushmore National Monument; interview with Bob Robideau, May 1990 (notes on file).

104. Matthiessen, *In the Spirit of Crazy Horse*, 158.

105. An additional indicator is that the inimitable William Janklow also seems to have been on alert, awaiting a call telling him things were underway. In any event, when called, Janklow was able to assemble a white vigilante force in Hot Springs, S.Dak., and drive about fifty miles to the Jumping Bull property, arriving there at about 1:30 P.M., an elapsed time of approximately two hours.

106. A further indication of preplanning by the bureau is found in a 27 June 1975 memorandum from R. E. Gebhart to Mr. O'Donnell at FBIHQ. It states that Chicago SAC/internal security chief Richard G. Held was contacted by headquarters about the firefight at 12:30 P.M. on 26 June at the Minneapolis field office. It turns out that Held had already been detached from his position in Chicago and was in Minneapolis—under whose authority the Rapid City resident agency, and hence Pine Ridge, falls—awaiting word to temporarily take over from Minneapolis SAC Joseph Trimbach. The only ready explanation for this highly unorthodox circumstance, unprecedented in bureau history, is that it was expected that Held's peculiar expertise in political repression would be needed for a major operation on Pine Ridge in the immediate future; Johansen and Maestes, *Wasi'chu*, 95.

107. Matthiessen, *In the Spirit of Crazy Horse*, 483–85.

108. The FBI sought to "credit" BIA police officer Gerald Hill with the lethal long-range shot to the head fired at Killsright at about 3 P.M., despite the fact that he was plainly running away and therefore presented no threat to law enforcement personnel (it was also not yet known that Coler and Williams were dead). However, Waring, who was with Hill at the time, was the trained sniper of the pair and was equipped accordingly. In any event, several witnesses who viewed Killsright's corpse in situ—including Assistant South Dakota Attorney General William Delaney and reporter Kevin Barry McKiernan—subsequently stated that it appeared to them that someone had fired a burst from an automatic into the torso at close range and then had tried to hide the fact by putting an FBI jacket over the postmortem wounds; ibid., 183.

109. The agents' standard attire was Vietnam-issue "boonie hats," jungle fatigues, and boots. Their weapons were standard army M-16s. The whole affair was deliberately staged to resemble a military operation in Southeast Asia; see the selection of photographs in Churchill and Vander Wall, *Agents of Repression*.

110. Williams and Coler had each been shot three times. The FBI knew, from the sound of the rifles during the firefight, if nothing else, that AIM had used no automatic weapons. Neither agent was stripped. There were no bunkers but rather only a couple of old root cellars and tumbledown corrals, common enough in rural areas and not used as firing positions, in any event. (The bureau would have known this because of the absence of spent cartridge casings in such locations.) Far from being "lured" to the Jumping Bull property, they had returned after being expressly told to leave (and they were supposed to be serving a warrant). Instructively, no one in the nation's press corps thought to ask how, exactly, Coll might happen to know either agent's last words, since nobody from the FBI was present when they were killed; Joel D. Weisman, "About That 'Ambush' at Wounded Knee," *Columbia Jour-*

nalism Review (September–October 1975); also see Churchill, "Renegades, Terrorists and Revolutionaries."

111. This was the director's admission, during a press conference conducted at the Century Plaza Hotel on 1 July 1975, in conjunction with Coler's and Williams's funerals. It was accorded inside coverage by the press, unlike the page one treatment given Coll's original disinformation; Tom Bates, "The Government's Secret War on the Indian," *Oregon Times*, February–March 1976.

112. Examples of the air assault technique include a thirty-five-man raid on the property of AIM spiritual leader Selo Black Crow near the village of Wamblee, on 8 July 1975. Crow Dog's Paradise, on the Rosebud Reservation, just across the line from Pine Ridge, was hit by a hundred heliborne agents on 5 September. Meanwhile, an elderly Oglala named James Brings Yellow had suffered a heart attack and died when agent J. Gary Adams suddenly kicked in his door during a no-knock search on 12 July. By August, such abuse by the FBI was so pervasive that even some of Wilson's GOONs were demanding that the agents withdraw from the reservation; see Churchill and Vander Wall, *The COINTELPRO Papers*, 268–70.

113. By September, it had become obvious to everyone that AIM lacked the military capacity to protect the traditionals from the level of violence being imposed by the FBI by that point. Hence, AIM began a pointed disengagement in order to alleviate pressure on the traditionals. On 16 October 1975, Richard G. Held sent a memo to FBIHQ advising that his work in South Dakota was complete and that he anticipated returning to his position in Chicago by 18 October; a portion of this document is reproduced in ibid., 273.

114. "Memorandum of Agreement between the Oglala Sioux Tribe of South Dakota and the National Park Service of the Department of Interior to Facilitate Establishment, Development, Administration and Public Use of the Oglala Sioux Tribal Lands, Badlands National Monument" (Washington, D.C.: U.S. Department of Interior, 2 January 1976). The act assuming title is P.L. 90-468 (1976). If there is any doubt as to whether the transfer was about uranium, consider the law as amended in 1978—in the face of considerable protest by the traditionals—to allow the Oglala to recover surface use rights any time they decided by referendum to do so. Subsurface (mineral) rights, however, were permanently retained by the government. Actually, the whole charade was illegal insofar as the still-binding 1868 Fort Laramie Treaty requires three-fourths express consent of all adult male Lakota to validate land transfers, not land recoveries. Such consent, obviously, was never obtained with respect to the Gunnery Range transfer; see Huber et al., The *Gunnery Range Report*.

115. The congressional missive read, "Attached is a letter from the Senate Select Committee (SSC), dated 6-23-75, addressed to [U.S. Attorney General] Edward S. Levi. This letter announces the SSC's intent to conduct interviews relating . . . to our investigation at 'Wounded Knee' and our investigation of the American Indian Movement. . . . On 6-27-75, Patrick Shae, staff member of the SSC, requested we hold in abeyance any action . . . in view of the killing of the Agents at Pine Ridge, South Dakota."

116. The selection of those charged seems to have served a dual purpose: (1) to "decapitate" one of AIM's best and most cohesive security groups, and (2), in not charging participants from Pine Ridge, to divide the locals from their sources of outside support. The window dressing charges against Jimmy Eagle were explicitly dropped in order to "place the full prosecutorial weight of the government on Le-

onard Peltier"; quoted in Jim Messerschmidt, *The Trial of Leonard Peltier* (Boston: South End Press, 1984), 47.

117. Butler was apprehended at Crow Dog's Paradise during the FBI's massive air assault there on 5 September 1975. Robideau was arrested in a hospital, where he was being treated for injuries sustained when his car exploded on the Kansas Turnpike on 10 September; Churchill and Vander Wall, *Agents of Repression*, 448–49.

118. Acting on an informant's tip, the Oregon state police stopped a car and a motor home belonging to actor Marlon Brando near the town of Ontario on the night of 14 November 1975. Arrested in the motor home were Kamook Banks and Anna Mae Pictou Aquash, a fugitive on minor charges in South Dakota; arrested in the automobile were AIM members Russell Redner and Kenneth Loudhawk. Two men—Dennis Banks, a fugitive from sentencing after being convicted of inciting the 1972 Custer Courthouse "riot" in South Dakota, and Leonard Peltier, a fugitive on several warrants, including one for murder in the deaths of Williams and Coler—escaped from the motor home. Peltier was wounded in the process. On 6 February 1976, acting on another informant's tip, the Royal Canadian Mounted Police arrested Peltier, Frank Black Horse (a.k.a. Frank DeLuca), and Ronald Blackman (a.k.a. Ron Janvier) at Smallboy's Camp, about 160 miles east of Edmonton, Alberta; Matthiessen, *In the Spirit of Crazy Horse*, 249–51, 272–78. On the outcome for Dennis Banks and the others, see Ward Churchill, "Due Process Be Damned: The Case of the Portland Four," *Zeta* (January 1988).

119. Poor Bear, a clinically unbalanced Oglala, was picked up for "routine questioning" by agents David Price and Ron Wood in February 1976 and then held incommunicado for nearly two months in the Hacienda Motel in Gordon, Nebraska. During this time, she was repeatedly threatened with dire consequences by the agents unless she "cooperated" with their "investigation" into the deaths of Coler and Williams. At some point, Price began to type up for her signature affidavits that incriminated Leonard Peltier. Ultimately, she signed three mutually exclusive "accounts"; one of them—in which Peltier is said to have been her boyfriend and to have confessed to her one night in a Nebraska bar that he had killed the agents—was submitted in Canadian court to obtain Peltier's extradition on 18 June 1976. Meanwhile, on 29 March Price caused Poor Bear to be on the stand against Richard Marshall in Rapid City, during the OSCRO/AIM member's state trial for killing Martin Montileaux. She testified that she was Marshall's girlfriend and that he had confessed the murder to her one night in a Nebraska bar. Marshall was then convicted. Federal prosecutors declined to introduce Poor Bear as a witness at either the Butler/Robideau or Peltier trials, observing that her testimony was "worthless" due to her mental condition. She has publicly and repeatedly recanted her testimony against both Peltier and Marshall, saying she never met either of them in her life. For years, members of the Canadian Parliament have been demanding Peltier's return to their jurisdiction due to the deliberate perpetration of fraud by U.S. authorities in his extradition proceeding; in addition, they have threatened to block renewal of the U.S.-Canadian Extradition Treaty in the event the United States fails to comply. The Poor Bear affidavits are reproduced in Churchill and Vander Wall, *The COINTELPRO Papers*, 288–91. On Poor Bear's testimony against Marshall and her recantations, see Churchill and Vander Wall, *Agents of Repression*, 339–42. On the position of the Canadian Parliament, see, for example, "External Affairs: Canada-U.S. Ex-

tradition Treaty—Case of Leonard Peltier, Statement of Mr. James Fulton," in *House of Commons Debate, Canada* 128:129 (Ottawa: 1st sess., 33d Par. Official Report, Thurs., 17 April 1986).

120. The disinformation campaign centered in the bureau's "leaks" of the so-called Dog Soldier Teletypes on 21 and 22 June 1976—in the midst of the Butler/Robideau trial—to "friendly media representatives." The documents, which were never in any way substantiated but were nonetheless sensationally reported across the country, asserted that two thousand AIM "dog soldiers," acting in concert with SDS (a long-defunct white radical group) and the Crusade for Justice (a militant Chicano organization), had equipped themselves with illegal weapons and explosives and were preparing to embark on a campaign of terrorism that included "killing a cop a day . . . sniping at tourists . . . burning out farmers . . . assassinating the Governor of South Dakota . . . blowing up the Fort Randall Dam," and breaking people out of the maximum security prison at Sioux Falls. The second teletype is reproduced in Churchill and Vander Wall, *The COINTELPRO Papers,* 277–82.

121. Defense attorney William Kunstler queried Kelley as to whether there was "one shred, one scintilla of evidence" to support the allegations made by the FBI in the Dog Soldier Teletypes. Kelley replied, "I know of none." Nonetheless, the FBI continued to feature AIM prominently in its *Domestic Terrorist Digest,* distributed free of charge to state and local police departments nationally; Churchill and Vander Wall, *The COINTELPRO Papers,* 276.

122. The initial round striking both Coler and Williams was a .44 magnum. Bob Robideau testified that he was the only AIM member using a .44 magnum during the firefight; Robideau interview, November 1993 (tape on file).

123. Videotaped NBC interview with Robert Bolin, 1990 (raw tape on file).

124. FBI personnel in attendance at this confab were director Kelley and Richard G. Held, by then promoted to the rank of assistant director, James B. Adams, Richard J. Gallagher, John C. Gordon, and Herbert H. Hawkins, Jr. Representing the Justice Department were prosecutor Evan Hultman and his boss, William B. Grey; memo from B. H. Cooke to Richard J. Gallagher, 10 August 1976.

125. McManus professes to have been "astonished" when he was removed from the Peltier case; Matthiessen, *In the Spirit of Crazy Horse,* 566.

126. *United States v. Leonard Peltier,* CR-75-5106-1, U.S. District Court for the district of North Dakota, 1977 (hereinafter referred to as Peltier Trial Transcript).

127. Butler and Robideau were tried on the premise that they were part of a conspiracy that led to a group slaying of Williams and Coler. Peltier was tried as the "lone gunman" who had caused their deaths. Similarly, at Cedar Rapids, agent J. Gary Adams had testified that the dead agents followed a red pickup onto the Jumping Bull property; during the Fargo trial, he testified that they had followed a "red and white van" belonging to Peltier. The defense was prevented by the judge's evidentiary ruling at the outset from impeaching such testimony on the basis of its contradiction of sworn testimony already entered against Butler and Robideau; see Peltier Trial Transcript and *United States v. Darrelle E. Butler and Robert E. Robideau,* CR76-11, U.S. District Court for the district of Iowa, 1976, for purposes of comparison; the matter is well analyzed in Messerschmidt, *The Trial of Leonard Peltier* .

128. No slugs were recovered from Williams's and Coler's bodies, and two separate autopsies were inconclusive in determining the exact type of weapon from which the fatal shots were fired. The key piece of evidence in this respect was a .223-cali-

ber shell casing that the FBI said was ejected from the killer's AR-15 rifle into the open trunk of Coler's car at the moment he fired one of the lethal rounds. The bureau also claimed that its ballistics investigation proved only one such weapon was used by AIM during the firefight. Ipso facto, whichever AIM member could be shown to have used an AR-15 on 26 June 1975 would be the guilty party. The problem is that the cartridge casing was not found in Coler's trunk when agents initially went over the car with fine-tooth combs. Instead, it was supposedly found later, on one of two different days, by one of two different agents, and turned over to someone whose identity neither could quite recall, somewhere on the reservation. How the casing got from whoever and wherever that was to the FBI crime lab in Washington, D.C., is, of course, equally mysterious. This is what was used to establish the "murder weapon"; Peltier Trial Transcript, 2114, 3012–13, 3137–38, 3235, 3342, 3388.

129. Agent Frank Coward, who did not testify to this effect against Butler and Robideau, claimed at the Fargo trial that, shortly after the estimated time of Coler's and Williams's deaths, he observed Leonard Peltier, whom he conceded he had never seen before, running away from their cars and carrying an AR-15 rifle. This sighting was supposedly made through a 7x rifle scope at a distance of eight hundred meters (one-half mile) through severe atmospheric heat shimmers, while Peltier was moving at an oblique angle to the observer. Defense tests demonstrated that any such identification was impossible, even among friends standing full-face and under perfect weather conditions. In any event, this is what was used to tie Peltier to the "murder weapon"; ibid., 1305.

130. Seventeen-year-old Wish Draper, for example, was strapped to a chair at the police station at Window Rock, Arizona, while being "interrogated" by FBI agents Charles Stapleton and James Doyle; he thereupon agreed to "cooperate" by testifying against Peltier; ibid., 1087–98. Seventeen-year-old Norman Brown was told by agents J. Gary Adams and O. Victor Harvey during their interrogation of him that he would "never walk this earth again" unless he testified in the manner they desired; ibid., 4799–4804, 4842–43). Fifteen-year-old Mike Anderson was also interrogated by Adams and Harvey. In this case, they offered both the carrot and the stick: to get pending charges dismissed against him if he testified as instructed and to "beat the living shit" out of him if he did not; ibid., 840–42. All three young men acknowledged under defense cross-examination that they had lied under oath at the request of the FBI and federal prosecutors.

131. Crooks's speech is worth quoting in part: "Apparently, Special Agent Williams was killed first. He was shot in the face and hand by a bullet . . . probably begging for his life, and he was shot. The back of his head was blown off by a high powered rifle. . . . Leonard Peltier then turned, as the evidence indicates, to Jack Coler lying on the ground helpless. He shoots him in the top of the head. Apparently feeling he hadn't done a good enough job, he shoots him again through the jaw, and his face explodes. No shell comes out, just explodes. The whole bottom of his chin is blown out by the force of the concussion. Blood splattered against the side of the car"; ibid., 5011.

132. Peltier's being sent directly contravenes federal Bureau of Prisons regulations restricting placement in that facility to "incorrigibles" who have "a record of unmanageability in more normal penal settings." Leonard Peltier had no prior convictions and therefore no record, unmanageable or otherwise, of behavior in penal settings.

133. *United States v. Peltier*, 858 F.2d 314, 335 (8th Cir. 1978).

134. *United States v. Peltier*, 440 U.S. 945, cert. denied (1979).

135. Another six thousand-odd pages of FBI file material on Peltier are still being withheld on the basis of "national security."

136. At trial, FBI ballistics expert Evan Hodge testified that the actual AR-15 had been recovered from Bob Robideau's burned-out car along the Wichita Turnpike in September 1975. The weapon was so badly damaged by the fire, Hodge said, that it had been impossible to perform a match-comparison of firing pin tool marks by which to link it to the cartridge casing supposedly found in the trunk of Coler's car. However, by removing the bolt mechanism from the damaged weapon and putting it in an undamaged rifle, he claimed, he had been able to perform a rather less conclusive match-comparison of extractor tool marks with which to tie the Wichita AR-15 to the Coler car casing. Among the documents released under provision of the FOIA in 1981 was a 2 October 1975 teletype written by Hodge stating that he had, in fact, performed a firing pin test using the Wichita AR-15 and that it had failed to produce a match to the crucial casing; *United States v. Peltier*, Motion to Vacate Judgment and for a New Trial, Crim. No. CR-3003, U.S. District Court for the district of North Dakota (filed 15 December 1982). The 8th Circuit Court's decision to allow the appeal to proceed, despite Judge Bensen's rejection of the preceding motion, is listed as *United States v. Peltier*, 731 F.2d 550, 555 (8th Cir. 1984).

137. During the evidentiary hearing on Peltier's second appeal, conducted in Bismarck, North Dakota, during late October 1984, it became apparent that AIM members had used—and the FBI had known they had used—not one but several AR-15s during the Oglala firefight. This stood to destroy the "single AR-15" theory used to convict Peltier at trial. Moreover, the evidentiary chain concerning the Coler car casing was brought into question. In an effort to salvage the situation, bureau ballistics chief Evan Hodge took the stand to testify that he, and he alone, had handled ballistics materials related to the Peltier case. Appeal attorney William Kunstler then queried him concerning margin notes on the ballistics reports that were not his own. At that point, he retracted, admitting that a lab assistant, Joseph Twardowski, had also handled the evidence and worked on the reports. Kunstler asked whether Hodge was sure that only he and Twardowski had had access to the materials and conclusions adduced from them. Hodge responded emphatically in the affirmative. Kunstler then pointed to yet another handwriting in the report margins and demanded a formal inquiry by the court. Two hours later, a deflated Hodge was allowed by Judge Bensen to return to the stand and admit he had "misspoken" once again; he really had no idea who had handled the evidence, adding or subtracting pieces at will.

138. *United States v. Peltier*, CR-3003, Transcript of Oral Arguments Before the U.S. Eighth Circuit Court of Appeals, St. Louis, Mo., 15 October 1985, 19.

139. Ibid., 18.

140. U.S. 8th Circuit Court of Appeals, "Appeal from the United States District of North Dakota in the Matter of *United States v. Leonard Peltier*," Crim. No. 85-5192, St. Louis, Mo., 11 October 1986.

141. Ibid., 16.

142. The high court declined review despite the fact that the 8th Circuit decision had created a question—deriving from a Supreme Court opinion rendered in *U.S. v. Bagley* (U.S. 105 S. Ct. 3375 [1985])—of what standard of doubt must be met before an appeals court is bound to remand a case to trial. The 8th Circuit had formally con-

cluded that, while the Peltier jury might "possibly" have reached a different verdict had the appeals evidence been presented to it, it was necessary under Bagley guidelines that the jury would "probably" have rendered a different verdict before remand was appropriate. Even this ludicrously labored reasoning collapses upon itself when it is considered that, in a slightly earlier case, the 9th Circuit had remanded on the basis that the verdict might possibly have been different. It is in large part to resolve just such questions of equal treatment before the law that the Supreme Court theoretically exists. Yet it flatly refused to do its job when it came to the Peltier case; Ward Churchill, "Leonard Peltier: The Ordeal Continues," *Zeta* (March 1988).

143. Holder moved into secondary education and now works for Indian control of their schools in Kansas and Oklahoma. Others, such as Wilma Mankiller, Ted Means, and Twila Martin, have moved into more mainstream venues of tribal politics. Still others, such as Phyllis Young and Madonna (Gilbert) Thunderhawk, have gone in the direction of environmentalism.

144. Examples include Jimmie Durham and John Arbuckle, both of whom now pursue—in dramatically different ways—careers in the arts.

145. Actually, this began very early on: AIM national president Carter Camp shot founder Clyde Bellecourt in the stomach in 1974 over a factional dispute instigated by Bellecourt's brother Vernon. In the ensuing turmoil, Russell Means openly resigned from AIM but was quickly reinstated; see Matthiessen, *In the Spirit of Crazy Horse*, 85–86.

146. Banks was granted sanctuary by California Governor Jerry Brown in 1977 because of campaign statements by South Dakota Attorney General William Janklow such as, "[T]he way to deal with AIM leaders is a bullet in the head"; he also said that, if elected, he would "put AIM leaders either in our jails or under them." Enraged by Brown's move, Janklow responded by threatening to arrange early parole for a number of South Dakota's worst felons on condition that they accept immediate deportation to California. During his time of "refugee status," Banks served as chancellor of the AIM-initiated D-Q University, near Sacramento; *Rapid City Journal*, 7 April 1981.

147. Rebecca L. Robbins, "American Indian Self-Determination: Comparative Analysis and Rhetorical Criticism," *Issues in Radical Therapy/New Studies on the Left* 13:3–4 (Summer–Fall 1988).

148. An intended offshoot of the Peltier Defense Committee designed to expose the identity of whoever had murdered AIM activist Anna Mae Pictou Aquash in execution style on Pine Ridge sometime in February 1976 (at the onset, it was expected that this would be members of Wilson's GOONs) quickly collapsed when it became apparent that AIM itself might be involved. It turned out that self-proclaimed AIM national officer Vernon Bellecourt had directed security personnel during the 1975 AIM general membership meeting to interrogate Aquash as a possible FBI informant. They were, he said, to "bury her where she stands," if unsatisfied with her answers. The security team, composed of Northwest AIM members, did not act on this instruction, instead incorporating Aquash into their own group. The Northwest AIM group was rapidly decimated after the Oglala firefight, however, and Aquash was left unprotected. It is instructive that, once her body had turned up near Wamblee, Bellecourt was the prime mover in quashing an internal investigation of her death. For general background, see Johanna Brand, *The Life and Death of Anna Mae Aquash* (Toronto: James Lorimer Publishers, 1978).

149. Killed were Trudell's wife, Tina Manning, their three children—Ricarda Star (age five), Sunshine Karma (age three), and Eli Changing Sun (age one)—and Tina's mother, Leah Hicks Manning. They were burned to death as they slept in the Trudells's trailer home; the blaze occurred less than twelve hours after Trudell delivered a speech in front of FBI headquarters during which he burned an American flag. Although there was ample reason to suspect arson, no police or FBI investigation ensued; Churchill and Vander Wall, *Agents of Repression*, 361–64.

150. Personal conversation with the author, 1979.

151. None of this is to say that the LPDC did not continue. It did, even while failing to fulfill many of the wider objectives set forth by its founders. In terms of service to Peltier himself, aside from maintaining an ongoing legal appeals effort, the LPDC is largely responsible for the generation of more than fourteen million petition signatures worldwide, all of them calling for his retrial. It has also been instrumental in bringing about several television documentaries, official inquiries into his situation by several foreign governments, an investigation by Amnesty International, and Peltier's receipt of a 1986 human rights award from the government of Spain. At present, the LPDC is engaged in a campaign to convince President Bill Clinton to bestow clemency.

152. *Keystone to Survival* (Rapid City, S.Dak.: Black Hills Alliance, 1981).

153. On the U.S. uranium industry and its impact on reservation and reservation-adjacent lands, see Ward Churchill and Winona LaDuke, "Native North America: The Political Economy of Radioactive Colonization," in *The State of Native America: Genocide, Colonization, and Resistance*, ed. M. Annette Jaimes (Boston: South End Press, 1992), 241–66.

154. On the occupation, see Ward Churchill, "Yellow Thunder Tiospaye: Misadventure or Watershed Action?" *Policy Perspectives* 2:2 (Spring 1982).

155. *United States v. Means et al.*, Civ. No. 81-5131, U.S. District Court for the district of South Dakota (9 December 1985).

156. *Lyng v. Northwest Indian Cemetery Protection Association*, 485 U.S. 439 (1988).

157. Anita Parlow, *Cry, Sacred Ground: Big Mountain, USA* (Washington, D.C.: Christic Institute, 1988).

158. Ward Churchill, "The Struggle for Newe Segobia: The Western Shoshone Battle for Their Homeland," in Churchill, *Struggle for the Land: Indigenous Resistance to Genocide, Ecocide and Expropriation in Contemporary North America* (Monroe, Maine: Common Courage Press, 1993), 197–216.

159. On the early days of IITC, see chapter 7, "The Fourth World," in Weyler, *Blood of the Land*, 212–50.

160. On Durham's recent activities, see "Nobody's Pet Poodle: Jimmie Durham, an Artist for Native North America," in Ward Churchill, *Indians Are Us? Culture and Genocide in Native North America* (Monroe, Maine: Common Courage Press, 1993), 89–113).

161. See, generally, Rebecca L. Robbins, "Self-Determination and Subordination: The Past, Present and Future of American Indian Governance," in Jaimes, *The State of Native America*, 87–121, esp. 106–7. For further contextualization, see Glenn T. Morris and Ward Churchill, "Between a Rock and a Hard Place: Left-Wing Revolution, Right-Wing Reaction, and the Destruction of Indigenous Peoples," *Cultural Survival Quarterly* 11:3 (Fall 1988).

162. Colorado, Dakota, Eastern Oklahoma, Florida, Illinois, Maryland, Mid-Atlantic (LISN), Northern California, New Mexico (Albuquerque), Northwest, Ohio, Southeast (Atlanta), Southern California, Texas, Western Oklahoma, Wraps His Tail (Crow). These organized themselves as the Confederation of Autonomous AIM Chapters at a national conference in Edgewood, New Mexico, on 17 December 1993.

163. M. Annette Jaimes, "Racism and Sexism in the Media: The Trial of the Columbus Day Four," *Lies of Our Times* (September 1992).

164. Incorporation documents and attachments on file. The documents of incorporation are signed by Vernon Bellecourt, who is listed as a central committee member; the address listed for annual membership meetings is Bellecourt's residence. Other officers listed in the documents are Clyde Bellecourt, Dennis Banks, Herb Powless, John Trudell, Bill Means, Carole Standing Elk, and Sam Dry Water. Trudell and Banks maintain that they were not informed of the incorporation and did not agree to be officers.

165. Expulsion letter and associated documents on file. Bill Means states that he was asked but refused to sign the letter.

166. Statement during a talk at the annual Medicine Ways Conference, University of California at Riverside, May 1991.

167. Statement during a talk at the University of Colorado at Denver, February 1988 (tape on file).

168. This assessment, of course, runs entirely counter to those of pro-Wilson publicists such as syndicated columnist Tim Giago—supported as he is by a variety of powerful non-Indian interests—who has made it a mission in life to discredit and degrade the legacy of AIM through repeated doses of disinformation. Consider, as one example, his eulogy to Dickie Wilson—in which he denounced careful chroniclers of the Pine Ridge terror such as Onondaga faithkeeper Oren Lyons and Peter Matthiessen, described the victims of Wilson's GOONs as "violent" and "criminal," and embraced Wilson himself as a "friend"—in the 13 February 1990 edition of *Lakota Times*. In a more recent editorial, Giago announced that his research indicates that "only 10" people were actually killed by Wilson's gun thugs on Pine Ridge during the mid-1970s, although the FBI itself concedes more than forty such fatalities. Then, rather than professing horror that his "friend" might have been responsible for even ten murders, Giago uses this faulty revelation to suggest that the Wilson regime really was not so bad after all, especially when compared to AIM's "violence" and irreverence for "law and order."

169. A good effort to render several of these lessons can be found in Brian Glick, *War at Home: Covert Action against U.S. Activists and What We Can Do about It* (Boston: South End Press, 1989).

170. For superb analysis of this point, see Isaac Balbus, *The Dialectic of Legal Repression* (New York: Russell Sage Foundation, 1973).

171. A fine survey of the conditions prevailing in each of these sectors can be found in Teresa L. Amott and Julie A. Matthaei, *Race, Gender and Work: A Multicultural Economic History of the United States* (Boston: South End Press, 1991).

172. For details and analysis, see Ward Churchill and J. J. Vander Wall, eds., *Cages of Steel: The Politics of Imprisonment in the United States* (Washington, D.C.: Maisonneuve Press, 1992).

173. For a survey of the repression visited on most of these groups, see Churchill and Vander Wall, *The COINTELPRO Papers*.

174. For biographical information concerning those mentioned who are currently imprisoned by the United States, see *Can't Jail the Spirit: Political Prisoners in the United States* (Chicago: Committee to End the Marion Lockdown, 1989).

CONTRIBUTORS

KARREN BAIRD-OLSON earned a Ph.D. in 1994 from the University of New Mexico. She is an assistant professor of sociology at Kansas State University, Manhattan.

LaNADA BOYER lives on the Fort Hall Indian Reservation in Idaho and is pursuing an interdisciplinary doctorate of arts in political science, economics, and sociology at Idaho State University.

EDWARD D. CASTILLO is the director of the Native American Studies Program at Sonoma State University, Rohnert Park, California. His most recent book, co-authored with Robert H. Jackson, is *Indians, Franciscans, and Spanish Colonization: The Impact of the Mission System on California Indians.*

DUANE CHAMPAGNE is an associate professor of sociology and director of the American Indian Studies Center at the University of California, Los Angeles. He is the author or editor of numerous books, including *The Native North American Almanac; Native America; Portrait of the Peoples;* and *The Chronology of Native North American History.*

WARD CHURCHILL is an associate professor of American Indian studies and communication at the University of Colorado at Boulder. His many publications include *Agents of Repression: The FBI's Secret Wars against the Black Panther Party and the American Indian Movement.*

VINE DELORIA, JR., is a professor in the Department of History at the University of Colorado at Boulder. His numerous publication include *God Is Red; Custer Died for Your Sins;* and *Red Earth, White Lies.*

TIM FINDLEY was a writer for the *San Francisco Chronicle* at the time of the Alcatraz occupation. He is now a consultant on media affairs to the Truckee-Carson Irrigation District in Fallon, Nevada.

JACK D. FORBES is professor emeritus and long-time chair of the Department of Native American Studies at the University of California, Davis. He has authored numerous books, including *Columbus and Other Cannibals.*

ADAM (NORDWALL) FORTUNATE EAGLE served as chairman of the United Bay Area Council of American Indian Affairs in Oakland from 1961 to 1976. He now lives on the Shoshone-Paiute Reservation near Fallon, Nevada, and is the author of *Alcatraz! Alcatraz! The Indian Occupation of 1969-71*. FBI reports refer to him as the principle organizer of the occupation of Alcatraz Island.

LENNY FOSTER is the director of the Navajo Nation Corrections Project and the spiritual advisor for fifteen hundred Indian inmates in state and federal prisons in the western United States. He has been with the American Indian Movement since 1969.

JOHN GARVEY received a master's degree in public history from San Diego State University in 1993. He now works for the Government Services Administration in San Francisco.

GEORGE P. HORSE CAPTURE is deputy assistant director for cultural resources at the National Museum of the American Indian, Smithsonian Institution. His writings include "An American Indian Perspective," in *Seeds of Change: A Quincentennial Commemoration*, ed. Herman J. Viola and Carolyn Margolis.

TROY JOHNSON is an associate professor of history and American Indian studies at California State University, Long Beach. His publications include *Alcatraz: Indian Land Forever; You Are on Indian Land! Alcatraz Island, 1969-1971*; and *The Occupation of Alcatraz Island: Indian Self-Determination and the Rise of Indian Activism*.

LUIS S. KEMNITZER is a professor emeritus of anthropology at San Francisco State University and an occasional lecturer at Dull Knife Memorial College, Lame Deer, Montana. He organized the first Native American studies course at San Francisco State in 1969; among his students was Richard Oakes, a leader of the 1969 Alcatraz occupation.

WOODY KIPP, a journalist and Vietnam War veteran, is minority affairs advisor in the School of Journalism, University of Montana, Missoula. He writes widely on Native American and Western issues, including "Phantoms at Wounded Knee," published in the literary magazine *Cutbank*.

JOANE NAGEL is a professor of sociology at the University of Kansas, Lawrence. She is the author of *American Indian Ethnic Renewal: Red Power and the Resurgence of Identity and Culture*.

ROBERT A. RUNDSTROM, an associate professor of geography at the University of Oklahoma, Norman, is the author of "A Cultural Interpretation of Inuit Map Accuracy," published in the *Geographical Review*. His research focuses on the geography of ethnicity and the social construction of places.

STEVE TALBOT is a professor of sociology and anthropology at San Joaquin Delta College, Stockton, California, and is also teaching Native American studies at the University of California, Davis. He is the author of *Roots of Oppression: The American Indian Question*.

INDEX

A'Ani language, 144, 149
Academic Support Committee, 109, 110
Adams, Hank, 18
Adams, J. Gary, 255
African Americans, 16, 120
Agnew, Spiro, 60
Akwesasne Counselor Organization, 16
Akwesasne Mohawk, 132
Akwesasne Notes, 16, 106
Alaska Native Claims Settlement Act, 18
Alaska Natives, 18
Alaska Native villages, 18
Alcatraz! Alcatraz!, 2
Alcatraz Council, 161, 162, 163, 197, 198
Alcatraz Island: as battlefield, 25; chosen as
    protest site, 187; citizenship, 197, 198;
    compared to Kent State, 168; compared
    to reservation, 62, 81, 93, 121, 122, 143,
    189; description, 188; fire on, 86, 166;
    governing body established, 125; govern-
    ment counterproposal, 163, 164, 165;
    graffiti on, 189; Indian-controlled "free"
    real estate, 129; as Indian-managed urban
    sanctuary and national historic site, 161;
    as Indian territory, 155; liberated, 108;
    lighthouse, 29, 162, 166; loss of, 128;
    meaning of seizure to Indians, 134; not an
    island, 4, 128, 239; occupied, 1, 2, 4, 25–
    31, 90, 113, 114, 133, 143, 153, 201; oc-
    cupiers of, on a world stage, 174; occupi-
    ers strip and sell scrap metal from, 173;
    omnibus Indian culture center on, 163;
    planning occupation of, 57, 59, 60, 61, 68,
    107, 117, 137; plans for development, 26,
    27, 28, 29, 193, 195; proclamation, 61, 62,
    105; security force, 84, 125; showcase for
    Indian heritage and culture, 164; surplus
    property, 56; Trail of Tears starts on, 260;
    unique importance, 129; uses to be made

of, 60, 63; utilities on, 92, 162, 166, 157;
    warden's house, 123
—occupation of: beginning of awareness
    and involvement, 151, 152; birthing
    time, 208; bloody wake, 6; call for self-
    determination, 50; call to arms, 207; as
    catalyst, 32, 41, 128, 202, 203; and con-
    frontation politics, 168; demands, 166;
    dissension, 85; as dramatic demonstra-
    tion, 75, 77, 78; end of, 29, 177, 178,
    179; factionalism, 126, 127; government
    position, 1, 92, 96; as great culture clash,
    129, 130; Indian invasion, 66–70; leader-
    ship, 198; legacy, 1, 4, 134, 263; as mas-
    terstroke of Indian activism, 30; as pivot-
    al experience, 30, 128, 130; as political
    theater, 127; and Poor People's March,
    46; and psyche of Indian people, 146;
    Public Relations Department, 199; rea-
    son for, 91; and reawakened Indian na-
    tion, 138, 151, 152; as reminder of ongo-
    ing relationship, 100; removal, 99, 138,
    170, 172, 173, 175, 176, 177, 178; as sig-
    nificant event in American history, 136,
    143, 144, 179; as success or failure, 32; as
    symbol, 45, 57, 94, 157, 158, 162, 179,
    187, 202; as target of interest to stu-
    dents, 90; as testing ground, 112; under-
    lying goals of, 32; as victory, 31
Alcatraz Island school, 196, 197
Alcatraz–Red Power Movement, 2, 9, 10,
    11, 13, 14, 19, 33, 35, 36, 37, 38, 39
Alexian Brothers Novitiate, 36
Allegheny Seneca Reservation, 130
Allende, Salvador, 252
All Indian University and Culture Com-
    plex, 195
American Friends Service Committee, 13,
    54

UNIVERSITY OF ILLINOIS PRESS
1325 SOUTH OAK STREET
CHAMPAIGN, ILLINOIS 61820-6903
WWW.PRESS.UILLINOIS.EDU